JUNIOR LEAGUE
of memphis

The Junior League of Memphis is an organization of women committed to promoting voluntarism, developing the potential of women, and improving communities through the effective action and leadership of trained volunteers. Its purpose is exclusively educational and charitable.

1922–2002

30th Anniversary of *Party Potpourri*, celebrating the
JLM's 80 years of service to our community

1st Edition	January, 1971	10,000
2nd Edition	August, 1971	10,000
3rd Edition	June, 1972	20,000
4th Edition	January, 1975	20,000
5th Edition	June, 1977	30,000
6th Edition	June, 1980	30,000
7th Edition	January, 1988	10,000
8th Edition*	November, 1993	20,000
9th Edition*	February, 1994	36,000
10th Edition	November, 2001	15,000

(*Southern Living® Hall of Fame edition)

Suggested Retail price $14.95

Manufactured by
Favorite Recipes® Press
an imprint of

FRP

P.O. Box 305142
Nashville, Tennessee 37230
800-358-0560

Contents

Editors

Mrs. Milton Lyman Knowlton, Jr.   Mrs. William Metcalf Prest

Committee

Mrs. John Apperson, Jr.
Mrs. John R. Bondurant
Mrs. Snowden Boyle, Jr.
Mrs. Ronald Byrnes
Mrs. William A. Coolidge, Jr.
Mrs. Floyd Humphreys Duncan
Mrs. Thomas Farnsworth, Jr.
Mrs. E. James House
Mrs. Allen Holt Hughes
Mrs. Kenneth O. King
Mrs. Charles McGee
Mrs. William Neely Mallory
Mrs. William G. Phillips, III
Mrs. Richard Ranson
Mrs. James Guy Robbins
Mrs. Loyd C. Templeton
Mrs. Randolph Turner
Mrs. Spencer Wooten, III

Typists

Mrs. Frank A. Cianciolo
Mrs. Richard D'Alonzo
Miss Flora Maury
Mrs. Ralph Monger, Jr.
Mrs. John H. Shute, Jr.
Mrs. Edwin P. Voss

Foreword

Party Potpourri represents three years of tremendous thought and effort on the part of the membership of the Junior League of Memphis. In order to make our book as foolproof as possible, the recipes, suggestions, and ideas have been carefully evaluated and tested. We have striven to put together a complete guide for entertaining...from the planning of the menus to the planning of the party itself. Most of our recipes will serve between 6 and 12, with the exception of the tidbit variety of food. It was our thought that the hostess would be able to work up or down from this basic premise. Most of all, we have tried to convey our feeling that successful entertaining is truly a potpourri of many ingredients...careful planning, delicious food, fascinating company, with a pinch of fantasy, whimsy, flair, good humor, and a large dollop of imagination.

Our menus and parties were planned to be intentionally elaborate. This is so that the hostess may take from them those things which best suit her way of living. We hope that every reader will bring her own special touches to our parties.

Boundless bouquets go to the membership of our League and to our friends who, first of all, gave us their cherished party recipes and ideas and then helped us try them out. The proceeds from this publication go to further community improvements in our city. The Junior League greatly appreciates your interest and hopes that you will enjoy using your **Party Potpourri** often and treasure it as a friend.

Idea Contributors

These are the people who shared some of their ideas which are incorporated in the parties. Their suggestions were the springboard from which our parties evolved. Those who have contributed recipes are listed alongside their respective recipes.

Mrs. Robert Armistead
Mrs. William T. Arthur, Jr.
Mrs. Earl Beasley
Mrs. Albert W. Biggs
Mrs. Alice Condon Bingham
Mrs. Susan Hyde Boone
Mrs. Denby Brandon, Jr.
Mrs. Grace Lake Brown
Mrs. John P. W. Brown
Mrs. Bland W. Cannon
Mrs. Nancy Barber Cook
Mrs. Giles Coors, Jr.
Mrs. Dan Copp, Jr.
Mrs. John T. Crews
Mrs. Robert M. Crump, Jr.
Mrs. Alexander W. Dann, Jr.
Mrs. Frank T. Donelson, Jr.
Mrs. Charles B. Dudley, Jr.
Mrs. Daisy Fisher
Mrs. Joseph N. Fisher
Mrs. C. Niles Grosvenor, III
Mrs. George Guckenberger
Mrs. Samuel Gully
Mrs. Robert Haralson
Mrs. Douglas Hartley
Mrs. James F. Hughes
Mrs. J. B. Igleheart
Mrs. E. William James
Mrs. William Carrington Jones
Mrs. C. L. Kennedy
Mrs. Franklin Kimbrough

Mrs. Mary Jo Kimbrough
Mrs. R. Henry Lake
Mrs. Richard Leatherman, Jr.
Mrs. Ted I. Lewis
Mrs. Nils Liebendorfer
Mrs. Charles Lowrance, III
Mrs. Lon McFarland
Mrs. B. Percy Magness, Jr.
Mrs. Judy Miller
Mrs. Howard S. Misner
Mrs. Ralph Monger, Jr.
Mrs. James W. Moore
Mrs. George Nickey
Mrs. Richard Owenby
Mrs. Clyde L. Patton
Mrs. Eugene J. Pidgeon
Mrs. Dorothy Smith Pidgeon
Mrs. Robert M. Ruch
Mrs. John L. Salmon
Mrs. M. Ames Saunders, Jr.
Miss Helen Skor
Mrs. Jesse Rogers Snyder
Mrs. Fred Tarkington, Jr.
Mrs. R. B. Thomas
Mrs. Thomas H. Todd, Jr.
Mrs. John Tully
Mrs. Edwin P. Voss
Mrs. Barbara Walters
Mrs. Edward W. Walthal, Jr.
Mrs. Alexander Wellford, Sr.

Good Morning

"Good Morning"

Breakfasts, Brunches, and Coffees

What better time than the "top of the morning" to entertain friends? At a breakfast or brunch the hostess has several distinct advantages. First of all, mid or late morning is a rather delightful and unique time of day for entertaining; secondly, guests are usually ravenous and anxious to be fed; and thirdly, they are so grateful for having someone else prepare their first meal of the day, that they will hardly notice if the toast burns!

Very special company breakfasts usually occur before 10:00 A.M., and fall into two categories . . . breakfast in bed and breakfast out of bed. Breakfast in bed to some guests is the epitome of luxury, but to others, it is as distasteful as sleeping with crumbs in the sheets. Ascertain how it will be received before you go to the trouble. If you do decide to bestow this favor upon your houseguests, make the meal simple and conventional for ease in preparing and eating.

Breakfast out of bed also falls into two categories . . . the sleep-as-late-as-you-like breakfast and the seated-at-the-dining-table breakfast. As for the first situation, let your guests, as they arise, serve themselves from an array of foods which will stand out without ruination. Set out packaged cereals, fresh fruits, chilled fruit juices in vacuum containers, and coffee cake in the breakfast room. For those who must have something hot, provide an electric toaster and electric skillet and let them cook their own toast and eggs. Breakfast in the dining room isn't as simple and easy for the hostess, but oh, what a treat for guests. Set the table with your best organdy or linen place mats and napkins, bring out some gay china, set a bowl of fresh flowers in the middle, draw back the draperies, and let the sun shine in!

Did your houseguests bring their four children and two dogs with them? Send all of their children and yours out-of-doors for a picnic breakfast!

The proper time for a brunch is in the neighborhood of noon, between 10:30 A.M. and 1:00 P.M. Everything about a brunch can be simplified. Gay, informal everyday china, bright table linens, unusual flower arrangements are all appropriate for most morning get-togethers. Many dishes are easily served buffet style, utilizing chafing dishes and electrical hot trays to keep foods at the proper temperature.

The food at a morning gathering often becomes a sumptuous repast incorporating many delicious foods not usually considered for that first meal of the day. An "eye-opener" or steaming cup of coffee is a welcome sight to guests on arrival. Most brunch drinks contain some nourishment, such as fruit juice, egg, etc., and should be mild in flavor and alcoholic content. The Bloody Mary is one of the most widely served brunch drinks. Other drinks often served at this time of day are Screwdrivers, Bull Shots, Milk Punch, or Salty Dogs. Though usually reserved for very special occasions, champagne is always acceptable, but it is certainly an elegant way to start the day. However, one gastronome has been known to say that champagne is the most delectable fruit that could be set before a breakfast guest. It complements the flavor of most breakfast dishes and can be served from the beginning of the meal to the end.

In the South the morning coffee has become as popular as the afternoon tea party as a means of entertaining the ladies. The coffee should begin around 10:30 or 11:00 and last through the noon hour. Coffee, like tea, should be poured by a friend of the hostess. As an extra touch, whip heavy cream to serve with the coffee, rather than serving it in its usual liquid form.

There is an air of camaraderie among guests at a morning gathering, a feeling of intimacy not achieved at parties given at any other time of day. Often an event of mutual interest is the reason for the get-together, as in the case of a pre-football game party, hunt breakfast, wedding or christening brunch. But even without a raison d'être, a breakfast shared with good friends is a festive occasion.

Most of the following menus would be suitable for a midnight after-the-theatre supper as well as a morning affair, and all of them are guaranteed to create mouth-watering memories for your most honored guests.

Christening Brunch

A traditional party given by proud parents or godparents celebrating the christening of "le petit bébé".

INVITATIONS: Invite your guests when you telephone to ask them to come to the church ceremony.

MENU:

Champagne
Poached Eggs Florentine
or
Chicken Liver and Mushroom Casserole
Curried Fruit
French Bread or Hot Rolls
Christening Cake

DECORATIONS AND SERVING SUGGESTIONS: Seat your guests at individual tables. If the baby is a girl, use white place cards bordered with pink. Punch a small hole in an upper corner of the place card and insert a small pink butterfly. Center each table with a pot of pink azaleas, or any pink flower you desire. If the baby is a boy, use place cards bordered with blue and insert a small bumblebee. Use bachelor's-buttons, Dutch iris, or any blue flower for your centerpieces. Black-eyed Susans or daisies are other good choices; they continue the black and yellow color scheme of the bumblebees. If the christening party is held later in the day and no meal is planned, place your christening cake on a cake stand, surround the base of the stand with baby's-breath or small bouquets of tiny flowers, and use it as your centerpiece. This is a round cake with edges decorated with swags and the top decorated with sprays of tiny flowers. The writing on the cake reads "Le Petit Bébé" (therein lies its charm). To make your christening cake choose any cake flavor (chocolate, white, yellow, etc.), and ice with a smooth frosting, preferably one made with a cream cheese base. Color combinations for the cake decorations depend on the sex of the child and the color scheme of the party. Several suggestions are: pink frosting with blue decorations; yellow frosting with blue decorations; white frosting with blue decorations.

Kentucky Derby Day Brunch

They're off! That famous "Run for the Roses" makes for a fun and exciting day. For golf devotees, change this to a party centered around the Masters' Golf Tournament.

INVITATIONS: For the Derby — Have a replica of a betting ticket printed or use a postcard. The card should have apropos words written around all four edges, such as Jockeys, Horses, Roses, Nags, Juleps, Win, Place, Show, Silks, Horseshoes. In the center write: "You may not win at the _____'s Place, But we hope you Show!" For the golf tournament — Send a card around which you have written the words: "Bogey, Eagle, Hole-in-One, Birdie, Double Bogey, Fore, Caddy, Slice, etc." In the center write: "Come to the _____'s and see the Green Giants at the Masters'."

MENU: *Bluegrass Mint Juleps
Fried Chicken   *Baked Country Ham, sliced
Scrambled Eggs   *Garlic Cheese Grits
*Biscuits
*Mrs. McGee's Derby Pie   Coffee

DECORATIONS AND SERVING SUGGESTIONS: Derby Day — Have ready as guests arrive mint juleps in frosted cups. When filled with sized ice an antique dry sink with copper liner makes an interesting container for the julep cups. For non-drinkers, serve a pretty fruit punch with a sprig of mint. Have popcorn and peanuts for snacks. The buffet table can be decorated with red roses, statues of horses, and lengths of colorful silks. Set up betting booths or tables and have tickets printed on colored paper. Because of the complication with odds, sell (for 25¢, 50¢, $1.00) win tickets only. Use a blackboard to list horses and provide newspapers and tout sheets.

Golf Tournament — Serve Bloody Marys instead of mint juleps. Decorate the buffet table with green felt to resemble a golfing green complete with flag and ball. Use several small containers of azalea or dogwood around the "green". A blackboard lists the players and their standing in the tournament. A Calcutta is held with bidding for the players.

Bachelor Brunch

When "one of the boys" leaves the ranks of bachelorhood, this party is a perfect send-off! With a slight change in decorations, it can also be a fun way to honor someone who is retiring or transferring to another city.

INVITATIONS: Purchase invitations at a party or import shop or, if you dare, send black-bordered cards intimating the sad demise of the honored guest's bachelorhood.

MENU:

Bull Shot
Cheddar Cheese Scrambled Eggs
Chism Marinated Steak   Spoon Bread
Mush Muffins or Monkey Bread
Fruit Thaïs
or
Peach Fritters with Orange Sauce
Rosé

DECORATIONS AND SERVING SUGGESTIONS: A ball and chain centerpiece can be made from a child's ball sprayed with black paint. The paper chain is made by linking strips of black construction paper, as in kindergarten. Red carnations in two small black wicker baskets flank the ball and chain. Use a black and white print or checked cloth and red napkins; or, instead of red carnations, use bachelor's-buttons and co-ordinating napkins. For a retirement party centerpiece, use miniature golf, fishing, hunting or gardening equipment stuck on wires in baskets of flowers. Travel folders could also be featured on the table.

Ride to the hounds, then return to the "tack room" (decorated with the bold look of plaid plus bright, glowing color) for hearty food, substantial enough to satisfy appetites sharpened by a successful hunt.

INVITATIONS: Send two-toned folded informals geared to the basic colors in your plaid tablecloths (see below). For example, if your tablecloths have a mustard background and a red plaid, use mustard colored paper and line it with red, leaving a border of mustard around the red. Write party information in bold black.

MENU: **Mulled Citrus Punch   Irish Coffee**
             Dove au Vin or Doves for Brunch
                     Scrambled Eggs
         Cheese Grits   Lemon Apples
     Irish Scones   Blueberry Breakfast Roll

DECORATIONS AND SERVING SUGGESTIONS: Cover the buffet and individual tables with plaid cloths that overlay a longer under-skirt which matches the predominant color of your chosen plaid. The vibrant colors of the plaid cloths should be repeated in the invitations, the name cards, and the flowers. Though the tablecloths all match, give each table an individual personality by having a different colored centerpiece on each one. Match napkins to the centerpiece and tuck a single matching flower (same as centerpiece) into each napkin. For example, if your centerpiece features yellow flowers, use yellow napkins with a yellow flower. Use fold-over place cards and tuck a flower in one open end. Handsome flower containers can be made by setting a Revere-type container (enamel-ware, lacquer, etc.) on a footed Oriental stand (which doesn't **have** to be black . . . spray them gay colors to match your linens); then fill with fringy flowers, such as dahlias, spider mums, or Shasta daisies.
Note: This brunch also would be perfect for Christmas morning or for "kicking-off" an afternoon of football.

New Orleans Brunch

Moss-draped trees, bougainvillaea that clings to intricate lacework grilles, intimate courtyards of mossy brick closing out a twentieth century world, all convey the essence of New Orleans. This brunch, inspired by the cuisine of the Vieux Carré, is perfect for your patio or terrace or for your own Mardi Gras celebration.

INVITATIONS: Fold a piece of white paper into thirds. Write party information inside and draw pots of geraniums at random for decoration. Fold the invitation shut and draw wrought iron gates on the two sides with black India ink.

MENU I: Planters Punch
Eggs Hussarde
Bananas au Rhum   Coffee with Chicory

MENU II: Milk Punch
Grillades, with Grits   Hot Fruit Compote
French Bread
Creamy Pralines

DECORATIONS AND SERVING SUGGESTIONS: Use a white tablecloth, with geranium-colored napkins. **Centerpiece:** Geranium pyramid. Group three or four small pots of geraniums in a very large clay saucer. To form the top of the pyramid place a fifth pot of geraniums in the center so that its bottom rests on the rims of the other pots. Tie each pot just below the rim with velvet ribbon. The pots for the flowers may be left natural or spray-painted black. For other occasions, the following may be effectively substituted for geraniums: African violets, tiny trailing ivy, fuschia or lacy fern.

Good Morning World

An early coffee with this dreamy menu is a most pleasant way for the gracious hostess to say, "Get up with the birds and have coffee with me."

INVITATIONS: Use pretty stationery printed with birds nesting, or nests with eggs. Write inside . . . "Good Morning, World", and the party information.

MENU: Real French Chocolate or Coffee Punch
Miss Ruth's Pastry   Butter Sticks
Bacon Wraps (with prunes)
or
Avocado Fingers
Pumpkin Bread, spread with cream cheese
Muffin Cakes with Citrus Glaze   Cheese Straws
Chicken Livers Stroganoff
Fruits with Molded Confectioners' Sugar
Coffee

DECORATIONS AND SERVING SUGGESTIONS: Purchase an artificial bird's nest (available at a florist's). Use one large nest and several small ones. Line the nest with plastic wrap and plant nest with wild strawberry plants or some other small trailing greenery. Add to the nest one or two alabaster eggs (available at an import store). Set the large nest on a raised candle pedestal or use three pedestals of different heights for smaller nests. A china "feathered friend" may be placed on the edge of the nest.

Menu Ideas

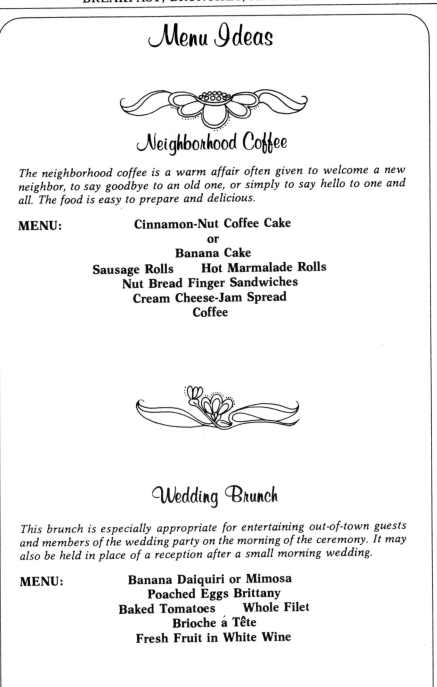

Neighborhood Coffee

The neighborhood coffee is a warm affair often given to welcome a new neighbor, to say goodbye to an old one, or simply to say hello to one and all. The food is easy to prepare and delicious.

MENU:

Cinnamon-Nut Coffee Cake
or
Banana Cake
Sausage Rolls   Hot Marmalade Rolls
Nut Bread Finger Sandwiches
Cream Cheese-Jam Spread
Coffee

Wedding Brunch

This brunch is especially appropriate for entertaining out-of-town guests and members of the wedding party on the morning of the ceremony. It may also be held in place of a reception after a small morning wedding.

MENU:

Banana Daiquiri or Mimosa
Poached Eggs Brittany
Baked Tomatoes   Whole Filet
Brioche á Tête
Fresh Fruit in White Wine

Mushroom Morning

Fill a long, low basket with fat, fresh mushrooms staked on florist picks, and tuck parsley here and there. If the wood of your table is particularly beautiful, use no cloth or place mats. The feeling is "down-to-earth", fresh, natural.

MENU: **Bloody Mary**
Eggs Baked in Mushroom Sauce or Mushroom Soufflé
Platter of Bacon and Ham   Brioche á Tête
Baked Pears
or
Blueberry Tarts au Cointreau

Sunday Brunch

Sunday morning, Sunday morning . . . all the world seems in a lazy-daze on Sunday morning. A perfect time for this leisurely, elegant brunch. Serve it on your terrace, dappled in morning sunshine. An easy centerpiece: Spray-paint a ring mold hot pink, dark green, white or black and bunch with fresh flowers. Spray a round, taller container with same color and place in center of mold. Fill with flowers.

MENU: **Iced Coffee Punch**
Chicken Livers in Wine or Chicken Livers in Madeira
Thin Slices of Fresh Tomato
Scrambled Eggs   Sausage
Mrs. M. A. Richardson's Prune Cake or Banana Muffins

At Noon

"At Noon"

Luncheons

Luncheon may be light or lavish, depending upon your mood, time, or budget. High noon or "noonish" is generally accepted as the time and guests will vary from few to many.

It is always nice to serve sherry or some light drink while waiting for stragglers to arrive or while last minute goodies are cooking in the kitchen. Here's your chance for the "long drink" such as a frozen daiquiri, if you prefer the alcoholic variety. As hostess, keep a firm grip on the libation period, remembering that there is much of the day left to navigate! On the other side of the coin, you might wish to serve iced tea, iced coffee, a tomato juice cocktail or fruit based punch. Do avoid serving soft drinks before lunch, as they tend to put a damper on even the most delicious fare, and **never** serve such with your meal. Sidestep the repetition of a tomato juice cocktail preceding some tomato-based food. In all things, complement, don't clash! Tea or wine complement almost any luncheon. Coffee with dessert is generally offered. Another nice touch is to offer your guests hot tea at the end of the luncheon.

Luncheon may be served buffet or the hostess may have plates already served. However one does serve, it is a good idea to have extra servings of everything for those with healthy appetites. Do remember that luncheon fare is usually light. You may serve a vegetable or a salad or a starch, but seldom all three. Enjoy your guests and don't spend most of your time in the kitchen, appearing occasionally with beaded brow and furrowed frown. This invariably leads to the "Let me help."—"Oh, no, relax (even if I do look as if I'll drop)" syndrome. By thoughtful planning and organization, you will prevent any Jack-in-the-box tendencies on your part and lend an air of ease and elegance to your hospitality.

With all things running smoothly (don't forget the rolls warming in the oven or the soufflé rising), throw your calorie counter to the wind and enjoy your friends and food.

The Merry Month of May

Raise your own Maypole to celebrate the coming of spring and invite your friends to this sunny day luncheon.

INVITATIONS: Write party message on inside of an informal. Select informals which sport bouquets of spring flowers, nesting birds, or chapeaus.

MENU: **May Wine**
Lobster Mousse
Grapefruit and Avocado Salad with Piquant French Dressing
(see Piquant French Dressing)
Cheese Wafers
Butter Crunch Crust

DECORATIONS AND SERVING SUGGESTIONS: (1) Use your best organdy place mats or cloth. Festoon the back of each chair with a generous bouquet of pastel grosgrain ribbons. **Centerpiece—** Create a Maypole surrounded by a moat of fresh flowers. Use a block of green Styrofoam covered with moss for the base of Maypole. Place a gift wrap tube in the base and wrap the tube in pastel ribbon. Place spring flowers in crescent shaped salad plates or in a spray-painted ring mold and arrange around base of Maypole. Run strips of pastel ribbon from top of Maypole to miniature baskets put at each place setting. Crown pole with same bouquet of ribbons as used on backs of chairs. Staple each person's name to a basket for place cards. Fill baskets with pastel mints or tiny spring flowers; or plant baskets with petite wild strawberry plants. Serve May Wine putting fat strawberries in bottom of each wine glass. (2) Make this luncheon your patio-christening party for the girls. Let the seafood mousse set the mood for the table decorations . . . live goldfish in a crystal bowl, a basket of lovingly collected sea shells, or an arrangement of different sized conch shells filled with flowers or coral. Serve the salad in individual baking shells. The cavities of conch shells also make dandy cigarette bins. Salmon and sea green has to be your color scheme!

Lazy Daze

Cooling breezes rustle the trees, birds chirp and the flowers add a dash of vivid color when you choose the outdoors as a backdrop for lunch. Set the table in gay colors to complement Mother Nature and offer friends a retreat from the usual. The menu is elegant, cold and easy to prepare.

INVITATIONS: Choose one featuring buzzing bees, birds, or flowers.

MENU:

Ivory Coast Curry Soup

or

Chilled Green Soup

Eggs in Aspic

Delicious Summer Salad   Sesame Seed Crackers

Toffee Ice Cream Pie

or

Cantaloupe with Lime Sherbet

DECORATIONS AND SERVING SUGGESTIONS: To prepare cantaloupe dessert: Cut ripe melons in half, remove seeds, and fill cavity with a scoop of sherbet. Garnish with sprig of mint.

FUN AND GAMES: If you are really taken with the idea of eating out-of-doors, here is an additional party idea for mixed company . . . an afternoon of La Dolce Vita, a Fête Champêtre, an idyll For Lovers Only. The mood should be dreamy, the food elegant and cold. No hot dogs and paper plates for this rustic feast. What **is** needed is a lush, green lawn, enormous shade trees, a gentle breeze, fine china, silver, and crystal . . . recommended food, a cold poached salmon, cold sliced veal, pâtés, brioche, pickled shrimp, a wheel of cheese, fresh fruit and an endless flow of fine wine. This is a gala picnic with a set beginning but with no set end. Guests may choose to stay till the sun settles and the night birds sing.

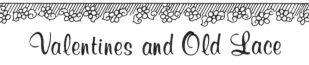

Valentines and Old Lace

This Valentine luncheon is especially suited to express your fondness and appreciation for those ladies who hold a special place in your heart. Every woman from grandmother to granddaughter will be delighted to receive this Valentine remembrance.

INVITATIONS: Have your florist deliver one long-stemmed red rose (with note attached) to each guest. Note reads, "Will you be my Valentine on (date) (time) (place)". You can also make a nosegay of fake violets and deliver them with a note yourself. Wrap the stems of the violets with florist tape; cut a hole in the center of a small paper doily and pull the stems through.

MENU: *****Madeira**
*****Curried Eggs**
*****Mandarin Oranges in Avocado**
*****Sesame Seed Crackers, heated**
*****Cream Cheese Tarts, with Strawberries**

DECORATIONS AND SERVING SUGGESTIONS: Set your table with your best white lace cloth or mats, or make runners of white eyelet to serve as place mats. Fill demitasse cups, or any special collection of small containers, with fresh or fake violets and tie cup with a velvet bow to hold a place card. Center your table with a white or gold bird cage filled with live or artificial white lovebirds. Bunch red or violet-hued nosegays in feeding cups and put a paper lace doily in bottom of cage. Crown the bird cage with a plump velvet bow or a cluster of plumes. To serve dessert: Center plates with a paper lace doily and place tarts on doilies.

FUN AND GAMES: Give each guest a chance to reminisce about her favorite beaus of yesteryear . . . especially fun for grandmothers and great-aunt Susies.

Christmas Shoppers' Luncheon
Marguerite Piazza

One of Memphis' most glamorous citizens, one of the nation's renowned entertainers, Marguerite Piazza entertains friends with this traditional Christmas luncheon. The spirit of Christmas fills the house, as good friends gather amid the hustle and bustle of last minute gift buying.

INVITATIONS: Noted on Christmas cards or by telephone.

MENU:
Sherry   Dubonnet
Hearty Vegetable Soup, with Parmesan Cheese
Sandwiches: Chicken Salad   Ham   Turkey
Carrot Sticks and Celery Curls
Miniature Doughnuts   Coffee

DECORATIONS AND SERVING SUGGESTIONS: Garlands of greenery are draped on the mantle, and the handsome home is ablaze with red Christmas candles. A snowman stands on the piano surrounded by greenery. A diamond-shaped piece of white felt covers the dining room table, resembling snow, and snowmen "ski" on the felt. The serving of sherry and dubonnet takes place in the living room. Sandwiches are served from large silver platters with a place card designating the kind of sandwich on each tray. Carrots and celery are tossed in a large silver bowl for a mixed bouquet. Soup spoons stand in another silver container, and the soup is ladled from a silver tureen kept hot on a warming tray. China mugs are used for the soup and guests sprinkle Parmesan cheese atop. China salad plates accompany the mugs. Glowing silver candelabra are on the table and sideboard. The sideboard holds the silver coffee urn, china cups, and doughnuts.

Christmas Holiday Luncheon

The Christmas holiday luncheon is a cheerful occasion that could be given early in the season to launch shoppers on their way or later to provide a relaxing retreat from the bustle of last minute shopping.

INVITATION: (1) Write the following in white ink on red or green invitation:

"The stockings are hung
And the baking is done
Now is the time to have some fun
Time
Place
Date."

(2) Or, cut candy cane shapes from red construction paper to fit lengthwise into a standard envelope. Write information in white ink diagonally across cane to represent stripes.

MENU:
Chablis
Creamed Salmon and Ripe Olives
or
Crab Meat Casserole
Ned's Eggplant Sticks
Crisp Cucumber Aspic
Plum Pudding Tarts or Eggnog Frosted Cake

DECORATIONS AND SERVING SUGGESTIONS: For a sleigh centerpiece, spray-paint a shoe box black or cover it with foil. Fill with pine boughs (sprayed white), lollipops, and bright glass ornaments. Glue a large candy cane to each side of box, both facing the same way, for sleigh runners. Hang small candy canes over front and rear of box. This may be placed on either a red or green runner stretching the length of the table, or on a wide roll of cotton sprinkled with glitter and edged with pine or holly. For your place cards, as well as take home favors: (1) Put a lovely glass Christmas tree ornament at each place; tie a red or green bow and a gift tag with the person's name through the loop at the top of the ornament. (2) Use wooden ornaments, painting each person's name on an ornament. (3) Bake small loaves of bread, seal in plastic wrap and tie with ribbon. Attach each guest's name to a loaf and set at every place.

Everyone watches the football games on New Year's Day. Enthusiastic fans make this a great party and one that is a tradition in many homes. The menu below is one that will "sit out" well for a long morning and afternoon of sports. Guests may eat when they choose.

INVITATIONS: Cut a football out of folded brown paper (have it "hinge" at the top). Decorate it with black felt pen to resemble a football. On the inside, write around the edges: SUGAR—ROSE—ORANGE—COTTON. Party information is in center.

MENU:
> *Bloody Marys   Bull Shots
> *Wheel of Cheese with Crackers
> Corned Beef in Foil, with Hot Mustard
> Barbecued Chicken (legs only)   Sliced Swiss Cheese
> *Roast Beef Baked in Salt (served cold)
> *with Sour Cream-Horseradish Sauce
> *Chafing Dish of Black-Eyed Peas Cooked with Ham Hock
> Thin Slices of Pumpernickle, Rye, and Salt-Rising Bread
> Hot Rolls
> Country Cole Slaw   Relish Tray
> *Pecan Tassies   Fudge Cakes
> Coffee

DECORATIONS AND SERVING SUGGESTIONS: The buffet table can be covered with a green felt cloth on which is drawn white lines to represent a football field. **Centerpieces:** (1) An oiled and polished football surrounded by standing pennants of the teams playing. Giant mums in florists vials are set between the pennants. (2) A flower football, made by studding oasis shaped like a football with orange flowers, using black shoestring for laces.

FUN AND GAMES: Each person writes his choice of the final score for each game and these are put in separate baskets, one basket per bowl game. The "kitty" for each game is put in that game's basket. When events are over, those who come closest to guessing the final scores win the wagers.

Tailgate Picnic

Here's a chance to let nature set the scene. Gather your group, pack up the back of a station wagon, or a nice clean truck, and go to any lovely spot where you'll be welcomed from beach to wooded glen. A good way to play on a crisp fall day before THE BIG football game . . . or escape with friends to fly a kite when spring fever becomes contagious.

INVITATIONS: Draw or cut out cars from a magazine. Buy sheets of construction paper in bright assorted colors; fold each sheet in half. Paste a picture of a car on the construction paper making sure the top of the car is even with the fold of the paper. Cut out along the outline of the car; write party message inside.

MENU: **Tomato Bouillon**
            Freeze-Ahead Poor Boy Sandwiches
                        Stuffed Eggs
                             Beer
            Viennese Brownies   Coffee

DECORATIONS AND SERVING SUGGESTIONS: Provide each guest with his own box lunch tied with ribbons in the school colors of your favorite team. Decorate boxes with amusing cartoons or pictures pertaining to the event being celebrated. A second idea is to wrap the poor boy sandwiches in foil, and then slip each into a long, thin, colored paper bag. Provide one bag per guest; twist top of each bag and tie with "school colors". Place all sandwich bags in one large container. Provide one tablecloth for each four guests. Roll cloths napkin-fashion, tie with colored ribbons, and tag each with the names of four guests who will use the cloth. This idea might be a good mixer or ice breaker in case you have some guests who do not know one another well. When rolling the cloths, include four napkins inside. Fly triangular pennants in school colors from the aerial of the car or from each side of the rear of the car. This will help your guests locate the fun. To freeze your poor boy sandwiches: Slit the buns lengthwise, spread with butter and fill with any combination of meat and cheese, making certain you omit dressings, fresh vegetables, and cooked eggs. Seal sandwiches in foil and freeze. When thawing the sandwiches, leave them in the foil so that they will be ready to put into individual bags without further preparation. Take along condiments, pickles, and dressings. After stuffing eggs your favorite way, press the halves back together and wrap each "whole egg" in plastic wrap. Fill egg cartons with the stuffed eggs so that they will arrive at the picnic in perfect condition. Serve dessert and coffee at your car after the game.

"Soupçon"

Though this porridge is hot, 'tis not nine days old as the old adage suggests. Nothing seems to warm the soul like steaming bowls of soup . . . lovingly homemade and served in quantity.

INVITATION: By telephone.

MENU: **Hearty Vegetable Soup**
                            or
           Bean Soup or Soup Virginia McKinney
           Spinach and Mandarin Orange Salad
           French Bread   Crocks of Butter
         Apple Pie en Papillote or Black Bottom Pie

DECORATIONS AND SERVING SUGGESTIONS: This is an informal gathering of close friends. Use pottery mugs and plates and nubby place mats. **Centerpiece:** (1) fresh parsley bunched in a copper mold, tin mold or pottery casserole. In the spring this same centerpiece may be used with a butterfly or bumblebee on a long wire stuck into the parsley. (2) Or, fill old brown snuff jars with small mums and march them down the length of your table. Tuck your napkins into the water glasses. If you have large enough mugs, the silverware can be wrapped in each napkin, the napkin tied with yarn and stood upright in each mug . . . then let mugs take the place of soup bowls. Make certain there is an ample supply of butter for each guest. If you can find very small crocks, fill them with butter and set at each place. When homemade soup is being served, it deserves to be brought to the table "in toto"! Ladle the soup at the table from a pottery tureen or a copper kettle. If your choice of soup is the vegetable or the bean, you may wish to serve hot-from-the-oven Whole Kernel Corn Bread (see Index) rather than French bread.

Grand Slam

"Come for lunch and bridge" . . . *Few invitations come that are more pleasant than this one. An ideal way to introduce someone new in town or an out-of-town visitor. A comfortable way to spend a leisurely afternoon with old cronies.*

INVITATIONS: Cut out the shape of a heart and diamond from red paper; cut out the shape of a club and spade from black paper. Write a bit of party information on each one of the four suit symbols and enclose the four in an envelope for each guest.

MENU I (Summer):

Edith's Stacked Salad Sandwich
Quick Peppermint Ice Cream
with
Dot Jones' Chocolate Sauce
Icebox Cookies or Sand Tarts

MENU II (Winter):

*****Cheese Fondue**
*****Fresh Fruit Salad with Poppy Seed Dressing**
(see Poppy Seed Dressing)
*****Layer Cookies**

DECORATIONS AND SERVING SUGGESTIONS: Key your flowers and bridge cloth to a deck of floral contemporary playing cards. For place cards, pull napkins through round, clip-type metal curtain rings and clamp tally in pincers of ring. Write each guest's name on a tally.

To make this party very special, award clever, inexpensive prizes to the high and low scorers (a small potted plant, seed packets, gardening gloves, any useful cooking gadget, etc.).

Luncheon for the Sew and Sews

Your sewing club chums will gladly drop their darning needles and embroidery threads to be entertained with this luncheon built around their favorite pastime.

INVITATIONS: Cut out a miniature tissue dress pattern (skirt, bodice, sleeves). On each piece write a part of the message.

MENU I (Summer):

Sherry Sour
Chicken Chaudfroid
Anchovy-Stuffed Eggs
or
Creamed Chicken Salad
Asparagus Vinaigrette
Hot Rolls
Mandarin Mousse
White Rhine

MENU II (Winter):

Shrimp, Mushroom and Artichoke Casserole
Molded Broccoli Salad
Lemon Muffins
Filled Chocolate Cups or Mocha Dessert
Chablis

DECORATIONS AND SERVING SUGGESTIONS: Use a bright tablecloth to harmonize with the flowers. In a Revere bowl, make a floral "pincushion" by bunching flowers such as zinnias, cornflowers or small mums. Stick knitting needles among the flowers. For place cards and favors, use dime store pincushions at each place. Attach name cards to pincushions by spearing each with a hatpin. Use a variety of pinked piece goods for napkins (a lovely way to empty your scrap bag). If you are fortunate enough to possess a patchwork quilt in good condition, use it as your tablecloth!

Bridal Luncheon

The bridal luncheon or bridesmaids' luncheon is a traditional occasion filled with gaiety and the thrilling anticipation of the wedding.

INVITATIONS: Ask the bride for as many of her soon-to-be-useless calling cards as there will be guests. Write "Honoring" above her name and tie this with a tiny blue satin ribbon to your own calling cards on which you have written the date, hour and address.

MENU I (Summer):

Mrs. Dudley's Salmon Mousse or Crab Meat Mousse
Gourmet Ice-Pickle Sticks
Tomato Sandwiches or Asparagus Foldovers
Angel Food Cake with Sour Cream
Champagne

MENU II (Winter):

Cold Orange-Tomato Soup
Oysters Florentine
Yellow Squash Salad
Vachébé
Chablis

DECORATIONS AND SERVING SUGGESTIONS: A blue and white color scheme would be most apropos since blue is a color often associated with romance. A flocked sheer cloth over a blue glazed chintz cloth sets the mood for this party. Fill your most beautiful silver bowl with a pastel palette of delicate white and blue flowers, with butterflies and tiny birds (doves or bluebirds) tucked in the arrangement. If the luncheon is for the bride herself, remember her with a gift of something old, something new, something borrowed, and something blue. If it is given by the bride for her bridesmaids, wrap the gifts to them with silver paper and tie with blue velvet ribbon. Place gifts on the table as place cards. For an after-luncheon treat serve divinity kisses, with charms baked in each one. The guest who gets the wedding ring is the next one to be married!

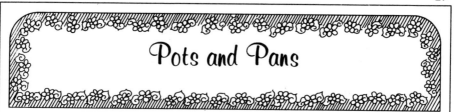

Pots and Pans

If the kitchen is foreign territory for the bride-to-be, help provide a few basic essentials with this kitchen shower.

INVITATIONS: Make a skillet from black construction paper and cut a slit in center. Make a large daisy and slip petals through slit in the skillet. Write party message on petals of flower.

MENU:

Watercress Soup
*Crêpes, filled with Chicken or Crab Meat
*Tomato Aspic,
with Stuffed Artichoke Hearts
Minted Pineapple Soufflé
White Burgundy

DECORATIONS AND SERVING SUGGESTIONS: Hang a "chore-girl" on your front door. Use a grater for her body; draw a face and paste onto the grater; use measuring spoons and/or can openers for the arms and long handled spoons for the legs. If you know the color scheme of the bride's kitchen, try to build decorations and table setting around these same colors. Buy a set of canisters for the bride, fill them with flowers, and arrange on your table as the centerpiece. At the party's end, present them to the honoree, flowers and all. Suspend a mobile of kitchen utensils from the chandelier. Put a potholder with a name attached (or embroidered) on each guest's chair to serve as a place card and as a favor. **Millie Mop Top**—Place the handle of a mop in a brand new trash can; the mop top will serve as hair. Make the face on a dustpan using scouring pads for eyes and a small scrub brush for the mouth; secure dustpan to mop. Straighten a coat hanger and attach for the arms. Wrap arms in dish towels and add rubber gloves for hands. Drape an apron around the trash can for the body. "Millie" could serve as a group gift from the bridal attendants as well as a conversation piece.

FUN AND GAMES: Place presents in a new, large, plastic wastebasket which has been tied with colorful ribbon or yarn.
Two bridal shower themes that solve the problem of what-to-give are: "A few of my favorite things" shower or an "I couldn't live without" shower.

Great Expectations

"Mum" is the word for this event. The element of surprise for the soon-to-be mother adds to the fun. A shower of this sort suits first babies best, but good friends might want to shower a mother of many with silly or humorous gifts or even replenish her well-used baby stock.

INVITATIONS: Use your white informals bordered in yellow and attach a small bow of the same color. Word your invitation like a birth announcement.

MENU I: **Chicken Mold Fitzmaurice**
Grapefruit-Orange Salad with Piquant French Dressing
(see Piquant French Dressing)
Hot Rolls
Chocolate Icebox Cake

MENU II: **Shrimp in Cheese Sauce**
or
Easy Creamed Shrimp
Avocado Mousse with Citrus Fruit
Hot Rolls
Assorted Cookies

DECORATIONS AND SERVING SUGGESTIONS: If you possess a cupid or other endearing figurine-like container, let this statuette dictate your floral centerpiece. Place an oasis in the flower container; use one tall rose in the center as the high point (this rose should be ¾ the height of the statue). Arrange more roses around the central one to form a pyramid effect. Fill in with acacia, baby's-breath, or any yellow or white flower. Cover your table with a white cutwork or organdy cloth and use an undercloth of yellow polished cotton. Tie your napkins with silk ribbon in soft colors and tuck your place card under the bow.

FUN AND GAMES: Here are several ideas for decorative as well as useful gift containers which the mother-to-be may take home with her. (1) Spray-paint a wicker laundry basket lemon yellow and festoon with flowers and ribbons. (2) Use a baby's buggy, a baby's plastic bath tub, or a diaper pail to hold the gifts.

Menu Ideas

Viva les Champignons

Here are two luncheon menus featuring mushrooms . . . a lovely change from all those casseroles-for-lunch. Both menus are as suitable for supper as they are for lunch.

MENU:

Mushroom Soufflé with Shrimp and Almond Sauce
Asparagus with Lemon Butter
Endive-Avocado Salad   Hot Rolls
Peach Whiskey Mold
Chablis or Moselle

Hail and Farewell

This menu would serve well as a welcoming luncheon for a new neighbor or as a good-by luncheon for a close friend. Dress your table in red and white checks and feature blue cornflowers. Red, white, and blue—a fitting tribute to compliment France's beloved mushroom!

MENU:

Creamed Mushrooms
Green Beans with Water Chestnuts
and Almonds
Tomato with Frozen Cucumber Salad
Hot Rolls
Meringue Tart
Chablis or Moselle

On a Clear Day

This easy, light luncheon allows the busy hostess to see her way clear to entertain her bridge group or sewing circle. This can also be a quick pick-me-up after tennis or shopping.

INVITATIONS: This is the time to use your telephone.

MENU: Avocado Sandwiches   Congealed Gazpacho
Pecan Apple Tartlets

DECORATIONS AND SERVING SUGGESTIONS: In lieu of place mats, put out bright lacquer or wicker trays ahead of time. Egg cups or rice bowls can serve as individual containers for nosegays of flowers to be placed on each tray. Orange juice cans, opened at both ends, and lacquered in a contrasting color make napkin rings. Arrange food on plates in kitchen and set on the individual trays. This individual "tray-service" is also a convenient way to serve a large crowd when you cannot seat everyone at tables.

Luncheon if You're Lucky

The new bride relies on luck and a sense of humor when she gives her first luncheon. For that special occasion when she wants wonderful results with minimal requirements of skill, this party will fill the bill.

INVITATIONS: The bride uses her new informals.

MENU: Chicken Divan
Orange Salad Mold   Hot Rolls
Caramel Ice Cream Pie
or
Pots de Crème
Rhine or Red Bordeaux

DECORATIONS AND SERVING SUGGESTIONS: A tin coffee can can be wrapped with multicolored fat yarn and filled with a bouquet of the season for a centerpiece. Tie napkins with same yarn. Place mats are easily made by covering cardboard with gaily patterned adhesive paper.

Grandmother Has Sunday Lunch

Grandmother's rocking chair may be replaced by the rocket but we hope that Sunday lunch at her house will remain a lasting family custom. For those who get to enjoy, rather than prepare, this scrumptious family tradition, remember . . . your time is coming!

MENU: **Chicken in Foil**
Patrician Potatoes or Squash Casserole
Vegetables with Mustard Sauce
Stuffed Pear Salad
Hot Rolls
Strawberry Jam Cake or Fannie Jones' Lemon Cake Pudding

Rites of Spring

A meatless luncheon suitable for Lent, fast days, or just for celebrating the appearance of crocus and buttercups . . . bird songs and warming earth.

MENU I: **Cheese Entrée**
or
Make-Ahead Cheese Soufflé, with Shrimp Sauce
Fresh Mushrooms in Garlic Butter, on Toast Points
Strawberry Shortcake
Mint Iced Tea

MENU II: **Shrimp Remoulade in Tomato Aspic Ring**
Hot Asparagus Sandwich
Frozen Lime Pie
Mint Iced Tea

DECORATIONS AND SERVING SUGGESTIONS: Cross your table with 2 to 3-inch wide ribbons, placed 14 inches apart, and secure underneath with double sided tape. Run another ribbon lengthwise down the table so that squares are formed by ribbons. Place settings go inside squares. Purchase trays of bedding plants at a flower mart. Line several handled wicker baskets with colored tissue so that tissue extends 2 or 3 inches above edge of baskets. Then line tissue-filled basket with foil (do **not** extend above basket edge). Tie a narrow ribbon around rim of basket. Plant bedding plants inside wicker baskets to form living centerpieces. March baskets up length of table. Perch large butterflies on basket handles.

Simple as Pie Luncheon

Simple Simon says use the telephone to call guests; then serve them this easy-does-it luncheon. Rewarding results with very little effort.

MENU: **Spinach Quiche or Quiche Lorraine**
Tomato Aspic
Kirsch on Pound Cake or Marinated Melon Balls

Ladybug Luncheon

Even the dessert gets into the act when you charm your garden club with this clever salute to the gardener's friend.

INVITATION: "Ladybug, ladybug, fly to my home" reads the message written on red and white stationery or over-sized postcards.

MENU: **Cream of Peanut Soup**
Curried Chicken Salad
or
Exotic Chicken Salad
Cold Italian Tomatoes
Hot Rolls
Lemon Flower Pots
White Burgundy or Rhine

DECORATIONS AND SERVING SUGGESTIONS: Ladybug-trimmed clothespins clip together the place cards and napkins, which are rolled in a tubular shape, and placed on top of each plate. Use seed packets for place cards! **Centerpieces:** (1) Group several perfect heads of green crinkly cabbage in middle of table. In center of each head cut a hole to hold a small container of red flowers. At the last minute, tuck heads of additional flowers in the leaves and perch tiny ladybugs on the leaves. (2) Use a basket (you may spray it to match your color scheme) filled with fresh or dried flowers among which several ladybugs are interspersed on wires. Trim basket handle with a fat butterfly. If you choose, the table decorations may be expanded to include other garden familiars . . . butterflies, bumblebees, ceramic snails, toads, or song birds. The obvious color of your table linens . . . bright green or sky blue.

Teatime

"Teatime"

Afternoon Parties

An afternoon party often follows a traditional pattern which may be expanded by drawing on your own individuality and by using your personal touches. In this chapter, basic patterns for teas are presented with the idea that new twists may be added! Changing a familiar theme is the special forte of every hostess with a true talent for entertaining. The afternoon party or tea is usually given in honor of a visiting celebrity, a new bride, a debutante, or house guests.

The formal invitation is either engraved on a three by five ecru or white card or written by hand on your best personal notepaper. An invitation that asks for "the pleasure of your company" tells the invited guests that this will be a party to remember.

The formal tea requires a table large enough to hold a service for tea and a service for coffee. When candlelight is used in the room in which the formal tea is served, the curtains are always drawn, as if for an evening entertainment. Tall ivory, white, or palest pink candles are most formal and effective.

For exceptionally large teas or receptions, it is sensible to have a caterer take care of at least part of the menu, which leaves you free to concentrate on those things which need your personal touch. Ask your close friends to "pour" for you during the afternoon. Tea is always poured; it is never passed.

Now add a stately, breath-taking centerpiece to your table and the room will be filled with a charming atmosphere, reflecting the care and thought given to the party. Have a nosegay made for the honored guest instead of the usual corsage. It is especially appropriate for the young honoree.

The tea table should be beautiful, above all. Careful attention has been given the menus in this section . . . our uppermost thoughts have been on food that is beautiful to behold, as well as delicious to consume.

For the hostess planning refreshments for an afternoon party, it is helpful to know that she can figure 10 "bites" per person, 2 to 3 cups of coffee or tea and 3 to 4 cups of punch per guest. See "Purchasing Food" for instructions for making coffee and tea in quantity, and for quantities of filling for tea sandwiches.

English Holiday Tea

Honor a friend or celebrate the Christmas season with this traditional afternoon English tea.

INVITATIONS: Use white cards, bordered with green or red, which are embossed with a small Christmas tree or wreath.

MENU: **Eggnog**
or
Mrs. Phillip's Christmas Punch
Shrimp Sandwiches   Asparagus Rolls
Scotch Shortbread   Cheese Turnovers   Jam Tea Dainties
Peppermint Meringues
Rum Cake
Tea

DECORATIONS AND SERVING SUGGESTIONS: Use traditional Christmas decorations throughout the party area. Place a white cutwork tablecloth over an underlying cloth of red. For your centerpiece, fill an elaborate silver bowl with red and pink carnations and freshly cut holly. This arrangement is flanked by two three-branched candelabra. In the center candle holder of each candelabrum, place a smaller arrangement of carnations; fill the other holders with red candles. Clarence Moody's Holiday Odor Punch (not for consumption), see Index, could be simmered on the range for a heady Christmasy smell. Of course, play favorite carols softly in the background.

Pinwheel sandwiches can be versatile and colorful. Have bakery trim crusts from 1 loaf of unsliced bread. Cut loaf lengthwise in slices ¼-inch thick. Spread with tinted cream cheese spreads or with seasoned pimiento cheese. Roll up, jelly-roll fashion, wrap in foil and refrigerate overnight. Cut into ⅜-inch slices. Before serving, cover with a damp cloth, while cheese spread comes to room temperature.

To prolong the life of candles — Put them in the freezer for a few hours before lighting. They'll drip less.

Formal Afternoon Reception

The formal afternoon reception is a stately occasion honoring a bride, a debutante or a celebrated guest.

INVITATIONS: Use heavy white or ecru 3 x 5 or 4 x 6-inch cards engraved in black ink. The time is stated from a certain hour until another hour, as 3 o'clock until 5 o'clock.

MENU:
Champagne Punch
or
Citrus Punch with Frozen Flowers or Fruit
Parsley-Bacon Sandwiches   Ground Chicken Sandwiches
Open Faced Cucumber Rounds or Cucumber Tea Sandwiches
Glazed Fruit Tartlets   Petit Choux, with French Cream
Fresh Strawberries, with Mock Devonshire Cream
(see Ruby Fruit)
Fudge Cakes   Cheese Wafers
Tea

DECORATIONS AND SERVING SUGGESTIONS: Use your prettiest tablecloth, one of cutwork, organdy or lace. The centerpiece is a very large Victorian arrangement of pastel flowers (blue Dutch iris, several varieties of yellow and white narcissi, Peace roses, Pink Radiance roses). Flank the centerpiece with elaborate candelabra holding ivory rope candles. Have the silver water pitcher and silver goblets on one side table or server, and the punch bowl and cups on another side table.

When preparing tea sandwiches for freezing, spread first with butter (never margarine or salad dressing), then spread with filling. Remember hard-boiled eggs and fresh vegetables do not freeze well.

A new way with sugar lumps for tea—Drop tiny bits of lemon juice on the sugar cubes to be used for tea (careful you don't dissolve sugar). You can also try this with orange juice, lime juice, or brandy.

Reception for the Bride or Debutante

An elegant afternoon introducing the new bride or debutante.

INVITATION: (1) A 3 x 5 or 4 x 6-inch pastel card with message printed or written in white ink. (2) Or use a white card with pastel border, using matching ink for invitations.

MENU:
May Wine or Orange Punch
Butterfudge Fingers   Vernon's Spiced Nuts
Melting Moments
Tiny Charlottes   Cheese Straws
Lily Sandwiches   Watercress Sandwiches
Egg and Anchovy Sandwiches
Jam Hearts

DECORATIONS AND SERVING SUGGESTIONS: Use pale pink re-embroidered organdy or white organdy tablecloth with underlying pastel cloth—pink would be most effective. The flowers should be fragile as the entire feeling of this party is feminine. Arrange a magnificent display of pale to deep pink and white roses, baby's breath and stock. Use palest pink candles in 3 branch candelabra. In center holder of candelabrum, place a smaller arrangement of flowers matching the centerpiece. Present a nosegay of delicate flowers to the honoree.

Make sandwiches using one slice dark bread and other white. Make a checkerboard pattern on your serving tray. Cover sandwiches with a damp cloth, then with plastic wrap to prevent drying.

The Oriental Occidental

This party presents the golden opportunity to enjoy Oriental décor with tea served in the familiar American manner.

INVITATIONS: Copy Chinese letters down the left side of pastel colored rice paper. Write your party message in heavy black ink.

MENU:
Cocoons
Stuffed Cocktail Tomatoes (with seafood)
Oriental Chews
Lemon Squares or Apricot Almond Cakes
Ginger-Chicken Sandwiches
Bacon-Wrapped Water Chestnuts or Chutney and Hot Bacon
Smoked Salmon Ball
Green Tea

DECORATIONS AND SERVING SUGGESTIONS: With this type of tea, you may leave your table bare, decorating it with a runner made from an obi or from silk brocade. Use lacquer bowls or old Imari for serving pieces. Place a large Oriental bowl on a teakwood base for your centerpiece. Fill the bowl with an Oriental flower arrangement using Fuji chrysanthemums, iris, gladiolus or wisteria blossoms. Oriental music is very exotic . . . if you're so inclined, play some softly in the background. Records may be rented from a public library's record department.

When working with cream cheese or butter, always allow it to come to room temperature before mixing in other ingredients.

Freeze bread before cutting into fancy shapes with cookie cutters. Spread with filling while bread is still stiff. No more mashed or torn bread.

A soft cream cheese filling can easily be piped through a cake decorator. Thus, your sandwiches will be exceptionally beautiful, as well as delicious.

Menu Ideas

Sherry Party

A friendly warm invitation when the weather turns cold.

INVITATIONS: A more informal invitation may be used here. Use a warm green note paper or small notes with pictures of grapes or fruit on them.

MENU:

Dill Shrimp Dip
with Raw Vegetables
Crab Meat Dip
Stuffed Date Drops or Cheese Puffs with Dates
Ham Filled Party Biscuit or Asparagus Foldovers
Cheese Pineapple   Chocolate Cookie Brittle   Eggnog Cakes
Tea   Sherry

DECORATIONS AND SERVING SUGGESTIONS: As an effective background for the centerpiece, stitch a pretty avocado green runner for your table and center it with a tall compote of purple, green and black grapes. Use candelabra entwined with ivy. Continue the ivy on down to the ends of the runner. Use avocado green candles. Offer your guests both a heavy cream sherry and a dry sherry.

Dessert Spectaculars

Ice Cream Cake
Marshmallow Pudding   Tipsy Pudding
Frozen Soufflé with Hot Strawberry Sauce
Coconut Charlotte Russe
Mazie's Miracle

Whatever the occasion, welcoming a new neighbor, a committee meeting at your home, or an earth shaking occasion like "meeting in-laws", bedazzle guests with a single dessert spectacular. Set your table as the stage to present an unforgettable treat. Lace, organdy, and bouquets of fresh flowers would lend the perfect atmosphere; then add a tea service for hot tea or coffee and your finest china. These desserts require thought and time to prepare, as they are works of art!

Small Fry

"Small Fry"

Children's Parties

Today is my Birthday
and I will be three
My friends are coming to play
with me.

There is an unforgettable light in a child's eyes on His Birthday. This chapter was composed to keep the shine in Mother's eyes also. In it you will find planned parties that only need be put into action. The primary age group is from 3 to 12. Hobo Haven was written for teenagers and it was felt "Haints and Hags and Halloween" could be adapted for them also. However, it is suggested that you refer to informal entertaining and picnics for this age group.

For a teenagers' party involving dancing, an idea worth mentioning is to have your husband announce that the boy who dances with the most girls wins $5.00. After the girl has been twirled, turned, and twisted about the floor, she signs the boy's card which is turned in after the party. Remember when the boys were signing the girls' cards?

Back to the little ones. Before the age of 3 most mothers choose to remain with their children throughout the party. Therefore, some sort of refreshment should be provided for their enjoyment. It could be soft drinks, coffee, tea and sherry. A plate of cookies also relieves the hostess from serving birthday cake to the mothers.

In plantation days a child's birthday party was very much of a tea or sherry party for mothers, while the children romped in the yard in their best organdy dresses, French bonnets, and velvet pants. If your accommodations make this feasible, this type party is delightful and charming for all ages; but a more modern day version is a luncheon for both age groups. Serve the adults a cold salad plate while the toddlers feast on hot dogs.

The following are a few party rules to keep in mind when entertaining preschoolers:
(1) A large number of children is in itself upsetting to most young children. Six will seem like a large and gay group and even four will be a party.
(2) For every 6 children over the age of 4 there should be 2 adults at the party. However, too many adults interfere by chatting with one another, or correcting their little ones too often.

(3) Do not use a child's party to discharge your social obligations. Flip to the various other sections of **Party Potpourri** for that.

(4) Do not let your party last too long, for children tire easily. An hour and a half is sufficient.

(5) Never try to surprise a child with a party. Anticipation is half the fun.

(6) Have plenty of bright decorations, particularly balloons.

(7) Make the food festive and easy to eat. Always include a pitcher of water in the menu.

And now read through "Children's Parties" and find just the right party for your little one. You may find yourself weaving yarn through the trees, making tepees out of birthday cake or snowmen from popcorn balls. Whichever you choose, HAVE FUN. Whether entertaining 18 eight-year olds or 8 eighty-year olds, this is the most important rule of all.

Children are fascinated with food served in unusual shapes. A peanut butter and jelly sandwich cut with a rabbit cookie cutter is certain to bring a delightful smile.

A delightful party for little girls, ages 7-9, is a cupcake bake. Let them make their own cupcakes, using a cake mix, then bake and decorate them.

Have a puzzle or game party for the teenagers. Write out the invitations, then cut into pieces, place in an envelope and mail. Those invited must piece invitation together to get the message. Make puzzle cookies: Roll out your favorite cookie recipe and cut in puzzle shapes (use a cardboard pattern). When baked, ice with bright frosting. Fun for the party: Have games and puzzles set up all around the party area.

Rub-a-Dub-Dub

Take a summer birthday cruise for 2 to 4 year olds and enjoy swimming, sunning and sailing!

INVITATIONS: Make party invitations using blue, green and white construction paper in shape of a sand pail with shovel. On pail write:

> Sail a boat fast;
> Sail a boat slow!
> Swim a little,
> Swing a little,
> And a fishing we will go!
> Time
> Place
> Attire: Bathing suit

MENU: **Boat Cake   Ice Cream**
                   Hawaiian Punch

DECORATIONS AND SERVING SUGGESTIONS: In back yard, set up 2 card tables and cover with blue crepe paper or a sheet. Make portholes from white construction paper, outline with black ink, and fasten around tablecloth sides. Tie balloons to ends of sticks and place sticks in large sand bucket which has been filled with sand. Use this as a centerpiece. Put ice cream in individual paper cups. Top with triangular boat sail made from blue or green construction paper and attached to a toothpick. The children may eat refreshments "picnic style" on beach towels around the yard.

FUN AND GAMES: Borrow enough plastic wading pools so that there is one pool for every 3 children. Fill pools with plastic boats and toys and place one pool under a slide for added fun. Fill an extra pool with goldfish and have children fish for their take-home goldfish with paper cups. Small packages of goldfish food may also be given as favors.

A Tyme to Rhyme with Mother Goose

Storybook enchantment for ages 2 to 5. Nursery school or birthday friends will enjoy an afternoon with familiar and well-loved characters.

INVITATIONS: Folded construction paper makes the shoe in which the old woman lived.

The invitation opens to read:
"There was an old woman
Who lived in a shoe.
She's having a party
And especially wants you.
Come to my Mother Goose Party!"

MENU: Lamb Cake   Humpty Dumpty Delight
                Sherbet Punch

DECORATIONS AND SERVING SUGGESTIONS: Mistress Mary's Garden—Place a row of pinwheels on each side of front walk. **Inside**—Bunches of balloons with Humpty Dumpty's face drawn on them with magic markers and Mother Goose posters on the walls. **Table**—10 x 16-inch crepe paper place mats made with grain running lengthwise. Ruffle each end of mat by stretching paper. For place cards, tie crayons with colored yarn and attach a name card. These are also favors. **Jack Horner's Pie Centerpiece**—Cover two 12-inch paper pie plates with crepe paper. Tape 3-inch paper ruffle to bottom of pie plate edge. Tie streamers to lollipop bundles and place lollipops in "pie", running a streamer to each child's place. Cover lollipops with top plate. Have Mother Goose (an eager grandmother) recite "Little Jack Horner" as each child pulls his streamer. **Cake**—Lamb Cake is made in a metal lamb cake mold, iced with white frosting, and sprinkled with coconut. **Punch**—Served from Jack and Jill's plastic pail. (Do not use metal!) **Humpty Dumpty Delight**—Decorate oval sugar cookies to resemble Humpty Dumpty. Slice small cartons of Neapolitan ice cream across all 3 colors and set upright. Place a Humpty Dumpty atop each ice cream "wall". See Index for Sherbet Punch.

FUN AND GAMES: Brick a doorway halfway up with brick-designed paper. Through cup hook in top center of door frame, hang a well rope with bucket attached. Each child lowers bucket into well for a prize. Mother Goose leads in acting out familiar rhymes and telling stories. She and guests may play "Ring Around Rosie", "London Bridge", "Here We Go 'Round the Mulberry Bush".

A Tisket, a Tasket,
Fill Your Easter Basket

Thoughts of Peter Rabbit, Easter baskets, and hunting for brightly colored eggs especially appeal to children 3 to 5. A colorful way for a little one to become a year older or just to enjoy Easter.

INVITATIONS: Make a folded invitation of pastel construction paper cut in the shape of an egg. Decorate front with stripes, stars, dots, etc. Inflate balloons and, with magic marker, write party information on them. Deflate and place inside egg. Written inside egg is the following:

> "A birthday party there will be
> Blow up the balloon and you will see."

MENU: **Flowerpot Ice Cream   Easter Nest Cakes**
Lemonade

DECORATIONS AND SERVING SUGGESTIONS: Easter Nest Cakes—Ice store-bought shortcake cups with 7-minute frosting. Tint grated coconut green by shaking in a jar with a few drops of green food coloring. Sprinkle tinted coconut generously on the iced cakes and fill the center of the nests with pastel colored jelly beans. Little chicken, duck or bunny figures may be placed on the individual cakes. **Place Mats**—Large construction paper eggs, gaily decorated with each child's name. **Easter Egg Tree**—Paint tree branch gold and secure with florist's clay in a decorated flowerpot. Attach blown and decorated eggs to branch. Punch hole in each end of an egg with ice pick, blow out inside, rinse well and boil; dye pastel colors and tie to branch with pastel ribbon. Ribbon may also be glued to one end of egg, then tied to branch. Miniature baskets filled with Easter candy may be substituted for eggs; then give the baskets as favors. See Index for Flowerpot Ice Cream.

FUN AND GAMES: Give each child a pail filled with Easter "grass". Have a hunt for wrapped candy eggs, two of which are gold. Give prizes to those who find the gold eggs, the most eggs, and the least eggs.

Mothers and Daughters

"Ladies", ages 3 to 6, bring their doll babies to this all-pink birthday tea party. Make this party a special one for the real mommies by inviting them to stay for lunch, if you're so inclined.

INVITATIONS: Fold in thirds lengthwise a 17 x 6-inch piece of stiff pink paper. Draw a doll figure and cut out, leaving the dolls' hands joined. Unfold and write a part of the birthday message on each doll's dress.
"August twenty-first is my birthday.
What fun we'll have if you'll come to play!
Get all dressed up like a big lady,
And bring along your favorite baby!"

MENU: Birthday Cake (all pink) Pink Puff Sherbet
Instant Spiced Tea
or
Pink Lemonade

DECORATIONS AND SERVING SUGGESTIONS: Think pink! Rent or borrow a long, low child-sized table and chairs. Cover with pink oilcloth. Set a place for each "lady" and her baby, using grown-up-sized plates and teacups for the little girls and child-sized china for the dolls. Simulated lace paper napkins add a sophisticated note. Set several small nosegays of pink flowers, real or paper, down length of table for centerpieces. For favors, give child's make-up (lipstick, powder puff, nail polish, etc.) and a plastic hand mirror (on which you have written her name with magic marker) to each guest. Glue tiny flower cut-outs on dolls' plastic baby bottles and "present" one to each baby. **Pink Puff Sherbet**—In a blender put ¾ c. sugar, 1 c. water and 1 banana. Blend. Then add juice of 1 lemon and juice of 1 orange; blend. Add 1 box frozen strawberries; blend. Add 1 egg; blend. Put in refrigerator trays and freeze. When half frozen, take out and stir. Return to freezer. One hour before serving take out, stir, and return to freezer. Can garnish with whipped cream. Serves 6-8. See Index for Instant Spiced Tea recipe.

FUN AND GAMES: Give each child a large piece of paper, instructing her to draw a portrait of her mother. These may be taken home. Have a contest for best-dressed mother and best-dressed doll.

Come to the Big Top!

The big top comes to your home with brightly colored balloons and a rollicking, frolicking clown. A "dream-come-true" day for 4 to 6 year olds.

INVITATIONS: Fold paper in half to fit any sized envelope. On front of invitation, glue an animal picture (cut from magazine, cereal box, etc.). Overlay animal with black bars and border edge with black. Front should resemble a cage. Inside invitation write party particulars and enclose a balloon, piece of gum or confetti. What excitement if you ask the children to dress in costume!

MENU: Popcorn   Cotton Candy
         Big Top Birthday Cake   Peanuts
              Lemonade   Bozo Balls

DECORATIONS AND SERVING SUGGESTIONS: Decorate door with balloons and a smiling clown's face. Inside, place stuffed animals in orange crates, large clown cut-outs on the walls, and cone-shaped clown hats around the room (one for each child). Serve cotton candy from a child's cotton candy machine, popcorn and peanuts in individual bags, and balloons! balloons! balloons!
Table — String twisted crepe paper streamers from the light fixture to the ends of the serving table. Center the table with Big Top Birthday Cake and make two rows of boxes of animal crackers down the table center. Set a hand puppet at each place and tie to every chair back a helium-filled balloon inscribed with a child's name. Balloons, puppets, and animal crackers may be take-home favors. See Index for recipes for Big Top Birthday Cake and Bozo Balls.

FUN AND GAMES: Circus Clown — Have a teenage helper dress as a clown, with an ear-to-ear mouth and great floppy feet! After a tumbling performance, he presents each child with a clown hat. **Kiddie Band** — Pass out children's musical instruments and let the children form a circus band led by the clown. **Peanut Hunt** — Hide unshelled peanuts. Give each child a sack and award a prize to the one who finds the most.

For children ages 6 to 10, it is that special time of year when snow may fall any day, Santa will come without fail, or a birthday may be just around the corner.

INVITATIONS: Let the guest of honor make wintry or Christmas invitations from shirt cardboard, colored construction paper or felt. Example: Make felt Christmas tree, write message on paper Christmas balls and attach to tree.

MENU: Snowman Sandwiches
                 Christmas Wreath Salad
        Gingerbread Men   Popcorn Balls
             Peppermint Eggnog Punch

DECORATIONS AND SERVING SUGGESTIONS: Centerpiece Ideas—Use any of the following ideas: Decorate child's red galosh as Santa Claus Boot and fill with candy canes; decorate a live tree with favors; make a Della Robbia tree by spray-painting a small branch and hanging on it jellied fruit slices; make a snowman from three graduated popcorn balls. **Salad Platter**—Make red gelatin fruit salad in large ring mold. Unmold on bed of lettuce and place a Christmas candle in center. **Snowman Sandwiches**—Using a cookie cutter, cut out snowmen, or other Christmas related shapes, from white bread. Spread with favorite filling and top with another identical cut-out. See Index for other recipes.

FUN AND GAMES: Who Put The Carrot In The Snowman's Nose? —Draw snowman's head on poster board; cut hole for nose. Prop board on an easel, or in front of a large box. Blindfold each child and give him a carrot to drop through the snowman's nose. **Santa's Surprise Package**—Giftwrap a prize in a small box. Place the wrapped box inside a slightly larger box and wrap it. Repeat 6 or 7 times until you have a nest of boxes. Place children in a circle. As Christmas music plays, have them pass the large gift-wrapped box around the circle. Stop the music, and the child holding the box must unwrap it, after putting on rubber gloves. This is repeated until the smallest box is left, and the child who opens it wins the prize.

A Fairy Walk

When gardens or wooded glens are once more filled with elfin creatures, and spring, April Fool's Day, May Day or Midsummer Night weaves its mysterious spell, then gather all the young misses ages 6 to 9 and take them on a Fairy Walk.

INVITATIONS: Pattern butterfly wings from gift wrap or nylon net. Write message on a small rectangle of paper, roll scroll-fashioned, and attach roll as body. Use pipe cleaners for antennae.

MENU: **Peanut Butter and Honey Sandwiches**
or
Tinted Cream Cheese Sandwiches
Fresh Strawberries (stems on)   Unshelled Nuts
Rock Candy
Dixie Cups   Cupcakes
Hard-boiled Eggs (shells dyed blue)
Dewdrop Lemonade

DECORATIONS AND SERVING SUGGESTIONS: Fairy's Well—Bury tub in ground to brim and fill with lemonade. Bank with ferns and flowers. Sip lemonade through "magic wands" (straws). **Bear Claws**—Make giant hand cookies or other large decorated cookies and hang in trees. **Leprechaun's Lunch Box**—Line individual quart-sized berry boxes with colored napkin; or use two plastic ones nested and tied with bright ribbon; or use plastic sand buckets which may be taken home as favors. Write guests' names on buckets with magic marker. Fill boxes with a picnic lunch for each child. Cut sandwiches in shape of butterflies. Ice cupcakes in party colors; sprinkle with edible metallic decorations.

FUN AND GAMES: Fairy Bells—Tell everyone, "If you believe, you will see the fairies." Give each a straw. "This is your magic wand. Use it wisely, and it will bring you magic. Whenever you hear a bell, say 'Hark! Hark!', and put your ear to the ground to hear the fairy bells." Dress a child in elfin garb; let him run through the woods ringing bells occasionally. Proceed until you come to "Fairy's Well". Everyone lies down and drinks through her "magic wand". Serve "Leprechaun's Lunch". **Nature Hunt**—Hunt for fairy lore: colored leaves, moss, bird feathers, mimosa beans, sweetgum balls, tree bark, forked twig, small stone, mushrooms, fern. **Hunt**

for Pot of Gold—Fill a small black iron pot with "gold" objects: gold foil-wrapped chocolates, yellow hair ribbons, crayons, oranges, etc. **Spider's Web**—Wind yarn of different colors around trees, bushes, etc. to weave web. Give each child her end of a color to wind up. At end of each yarn is a present, wrapped and hidden.

A-B-C Block (made of ice cream)—*Cut two-inch square block of ice cream. Etch around edges and write letters with whipped cream forced through a pastry tube or cake decorator. Instant cake decorator in assorted colors may also be used in place of whipped cream. Freeze immediately.*

Fancy cookies from a mix—*Use the rolled refrigerated dough that comes in the dairy case. Let stand at room temperature about an hour; then roll out, cut, decorate, and bake.*

In candy hunts, use individually wrapped candies to avoid melting and stickiness.

A Blast-off

Junior astronauts perform final tests prior to a space shot at this red-white-and-blue birthday party for 5 to 10 year olds. 10-9-8-7-6-5-4-3-2-1 Blastoff!

INVITATIONS: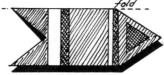

MENU: Astronaut Cake   Ice Cream Balls
Astro Fuel (Tang)
Rock Candy   Milky Way Candy Bars

DECORATIONS AND SERVING SUGGESTIONS: Display American flag at entrance to "launch pad". For centerpiece, build a rocket from 2 oatmeal boxes, one on top of the other, covered with foil. Make nose cone from half circle of foil to top rocket. Surround spaceship with foil cups filled with "moon-rock" candy, "lunar" lollipops, Milky Way candy bars. For place cards, write name of each boy on a fist-sized rock with magic marker. Use midnight blue tablecloth. Lead red crepe paper streamers from rocket tail to each child's seat. Serve food on aluminum pie pans. Put "Astro Fuel" in plastic cups with red and white straws. Plant a tiny American flag in each ice cream ball. See Index for Ice Cream Balls recipe. **Astronaut Cake**—Bake a rectangular sheet cake; cut triangular pieces from one end of cake and place at other end for nose cone. Decorate to resemble a spaceship.

FUN AND GAMES: Shoot-the-Moon—Place moon map on wall. Equip each boy with space gun and suction cup darts. Let him aim for "Sea of Tranquillity". Closest shot wins. **Astronaut Senses Test**—To test sight and memory, place many household items such as spoon, soap, crayon, etc. on a table. After a few minutes remove articles and have contestants list on paper as many items as they remember. Blindfold children for the rest of tests. Let child taste chocolate, grape drink, licorice, etc.; smell perfume, coffee, vinegar, etc.; hear clock ticking, paper tearing, keys rattling, etc.; feel key, spoon, cup, etc. Astronaut who correctly identifies the most items wins.

Powwow Party

Cowboys and Indians whoop it up with Wild West games and a hearty cookout. A "heap of fun" party for after school, Saturday lunch, ceremonial banquet or birthday party for a boy, age 5 to 10.

INVITATIONS: Construction paper teepee inscribed "Come to Powwow! At _____'s Teepee, Address, Date, Time, R.S.V.P." Request cowboy or Indian costumes.

MENU: **Lassoed Hot Dogs and Slaw**
Campfire Beans
Corn Chips
Teepee Cake   Ice Cream
Apple Cider (in tin cups)

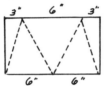

DECORATIONS AND SERVING SUGGESTIONS: See Index for Campfire Beans and Teepee Cake recipes. **Teepee Centerpiece**—Tie tops of 8 to 10 rolled kites together to resemble a teepee. Surround the teepee with cowboys and Indians. **Broomstick Cowboy**— "Dress" a broomstick with cowboy clothes which have been stuffed with rags or newspaper. Make a face on broom straws, top with cowboy hat, and put lasso in hand.

FUN AND GAMES: Give each guest an Indian headdress to color. To make headdress, cut bottom off a grocery sack, then cut at seams to make a flat piece of paper. Fold paper into accordian pleats. With scissors, cut each pleat in the shape of a feather, leaving a 1-inch band. As guests finish coloring, staple band of headdress to fit. **Shoot the Apache**—Draw Indian face on balloons, tape feathers on and put balloons in trees. Guests shoot with dart gun or bows and suction cup arrows. **Pony Ride**—Always appropriate for cowboys and Indians. Pitch **Horseshoes. Peace Pipe**— Guests sit in circle and hear tales of Indian lore and smoke "peace pipe" favors. Other favors are headdresses, bandana scarves cut out with pinking shears, and kites from teepee centerpiece.

Haints and Hags and Halloween

On this eerie eve bewitch 7 to 12 year old ghosts and goblins with revelry that promises to counteract all evil spells.

INVITATIONS: (1) Use burnt-edged paper with message on it, place in a bottle and deliver. (2) Using construction paper, cut out pumpkin, ghost, bat, or skull and crossbones and write party information in disappearing ink. Invitation must be ironed to "get the message".

MENU: *Barbecued Frankfurters
Deviled Eggs   *Potato Chips
*Witches Brew
Ice Cream Pumpkin or *Jack O'Lantern Cake

DECORATIONS AND SERVING SUGGESTIONS: Night Fright— Have guests enter house through a maze of large boxes, tires, chairs, a mattress to walk on, and a spider's web made of yarn. Cut a huge black cat from cardboard and hang from a tree. Make him wink with a blinking orange Christmas bulb in one of his eyes. Have Styrofoam surfboards as tombstones, smoky writing on mirrors, doctor's satchel filled with dead flowers. **Table—**Cover a glass-topped table with a sheet or colored paper cloth and light from beneath. Secure a tree branch in a flowerpot. Tie on lollipops which have been covered with white facial tissue to resemble ghosts. Draw ghost faces with black ink. For place cards use cake icing tube to put each guest's name on an apple. **Jack O'Lantern Cake—**Bake devil's food cake in two well-greased flame-proof 1½-quart bowls. Cool and remove. Place the two flat sides together, making a ball. Ice with orange frosting. Make grooves with spatula in icing to give a pumpkin-like appearance. Set a candle in top for stem. See Index for recipes for Barbecued Frankfurters, Witches Brew, and Ice Cream Pumpkin.

FUN AND GAMES: Deadman's Game—Blindfold each child and have him identify "body parts". Use peeled grapes for eyeballs, spaghetti for intestines, liver for heart, dough for brains, turkey carcass for rib cage, rubber gloves filled with water for hands, warm ketchup for blood and wig for hair. **Apple Dodge—**Tie strings to apples and hang them from a tree branch or doorjamb. Tie each child's hands behind him. The first one to bite his apple wins.

Hobo Haven

For the teenage crowd this party spells informal fun with favorite food and a carefree air. Perfect for saying goodbye to a young friend who's going traveling.

INVITATIONS: Paint small sticks black (to resemble "hobo sticks"). Cut red bandana squares and put construction paper "clothes" in bandanas giving party information. Tie bandana onto stick and deliver, or, omitting stick, put bandanas into envelopes and mail.

MENU:
        Steak Sandwiches or Spicy Beef
        French Fries or Potato Chips
        Campfire Beans
        Tossed Green Salad
    Ad Lib Sundaes   **Fudge Cakes**

DECORATIONS AND SERVING SUGGESTIONS: Ad Lib Sundaes —Provide guests with a variety of ice creams (at least three different kinds), and "crowning glories", such as whipped cream, nuts, cherries and bananas. Scoop ice cream beforehand and return scoops to freezer to harden. Allow 3 to 4 scoops per person. Let each make his own sundae. This idea can be modified and guests can make their own milk shakes in blenders. **Steak Sandwiches** —Cook sirloin steaks on the grill, allowing ¼ pound meat per sandwich. Slice steak and place on bun with a slice of onion and a slice of hot pepper cheese. Wrap in foil and heat in 350° oven for 10 to 15 minutes. **Table** —Red and white checked tablecloths on card tables. Red bandana napkins, tin or paper plates and cups. Large tin cans in center of table hold candles. Write guests' names on bright paper and pin to old clothing (blue jeans, T-shirts, denim jackets) and place over chair backs for place cards. See Index for recipes for beans, salad and Fudge Cakes.

FUN AND GAMES: Hobo Hunt —Divide guests into groups of 4 to 6. Give each group a list of things to collect and set a time limit. Items to collect should be synonymous with hobos . . . an old boot, toy train, railroad track, cigar butts, etc. The group returning with most correct items wins the prize. **Music** —Phonograph with plenty of danceable records is a must.

Potpourri

"Potpourri"

Potpourri

The determining factors for successful party giving are difficult to prescribe. Perhaps one of the most important factors is an imaginative hostess who really **wants** her guests. She isn't merely paying back obligations with the same old tired modes of entertaining. The parties under this heading are basically fun and need a fun-loving host and hostess who are ready to try their hands at something new. This chapter offers a mixture of many casual parties which do not stand on ceremonies. Instead, "Potpourri" owes its charm to whimsy, warmth, and inventiveness.

For successful party giving, planning ahead is imperative. A time schedule for preparing your party may seem like folly, but whether the party be for six or sixty, it is a necessity. A schedule will afford the hostess time to dress her party as painstakingly as she does herself, with ease and assurance. No matter what the occasion, write down the complete menu far in advance, jotting down which foods can be made ahead and frozen or stored in plastic wrap in the refrigerator. List the serving dishes you plan to use, so that they can be polished several days ahead. Make certain you have a serving piece for everything you plan to serve. One hostess we know sets the table several days in advance, and then covers it with a sheet to protect it from dust. If special decorations are involved, make them a month ahead. Eventually, if you entertain enough, you'll amass a stockpile of party giving goods. You'll even be able to mix and match them, and decorating for a party will become easier and easier.

Your children and pets, no matter how much you love them, may not be so loved by your guests. Neither should be seen nor heard from, unless you are sure of your guests' feelings toward the two. Even if your guests do not object, the appearance should be brief!

You don't smoke? But others do. If you want to preserve those fine china plates (which you have scattered about because they match your décor), you had best put some good old identifiable ashtrays around. Place gaily colored match packets near the ashtrays.

The Buffet

A buffet is the modern woman's answer to serving a complete meal to more guests than she can seat at her dining room table. To help the hostess in the execution of the service, there are four principles that should be followed:

(1) Orderly arrangement of the food: Remember, once your guest has picked up his plate, he has only one workable hand. If any dish requires two serving utensils (and a meat course often does), put it first, followed by the plates, then the remainder of the dinner. Place flatware at the end to cure the buffet balancing act. Wrap a complete place setting of flatware in a napkin and secure with one or two colored pipe cleaners or ribbon. Also keep in mind how difficult your main course is to eat. Rock Cornish game hens are delicious, but to attack the bird while balancing a plate in your lap might mean a bird on the plate being worth two on the floor!

If it is possible to have a maid help you, place small tags on the buffet table marking the exact spots where you wish each dish to be placed. That way, the maid does not have to rely on the hostess's telling her and no mistakes are made. Additional time is saved by a note in each serving piece telling what goes in it!

(2) A steady surface from which to eat: One's lap is not steady and the hostess is liable to wind up with a food-drenched guest or a mess on the carpet. Ideally, the food should be served from a sideboard or kitchen table with guests seated at a dining table. When you must use the table to serve from, a supply of card tables, lap trays, or TV tables will be needed.

(3) The passed food: Have the host or a maid circulate with a tray of poured iced tea, water, wine, or whatever the drink. Then pass the bread. Set up a special table on which you place the coffee and the dessert and let guests help themselves from this.

(4) Extra touches: Be certain there are plenty of salt and pepper shakers available for guests. Many a buffet dinner has suffered due to lack of salt and pepper. Place small trays containing cream and sugar and salt and pepper around the eating areas, so that guests may help themselves at will.

The Cocktail Party

A cocktail party consists mainly of lots of people. To some it is an anathema, to others it's nirvana . . . a chance to eat and drink and visit . . . but always a whole evening's fun crammed into one or two hours. No matter how those you invite feel about cocktail parties, endeavor to make yours different . . . super to those who like cocktail parties anyway, and surprisingly enjoyable to those who don't. Here are some tips on producing one of these affairs:

(1) Spark the crowd with a sprinkling of new faces: Everyone gets tired of the same old group and the same conversations. One hostess we know says she always invites at least one gorgeous creature, preferably unattached, to start the conversation buzzing. Invite a couple who are newcomers to town. You'll do them, and yourself, a favor. Ask a famous somebody (though perhaps only locally well-known) because, secretly, everyone likes to brush shoulders with celebrities.

(2) Keep the number you invite within reason: Consider the size of your entertainment areas, the amount of help you will have in preparing the party, and your budget. (If the size of the crowd is straining your funds, it's too large.) Too often, the cocktail party is given as an "easy way out", or as the "big pay-off" for mounting social obligations. However, if you find you must give a large party, why not give two smaller ones instead of one large bash? This is easier to do than it might first appear. In fact, they can be given on consecutive nights or weekends. At the smaller party, guests will feel more warmly received and you'll be less harried.

(3) The cocktail supper: When your party takes on the proportions of cocktails and supper, be kind to the guests and provide them with small plates and napkins. This will allow them to help themselves and return to the rest of the party. It also disperses the traffic at the food.

(4) The bar: It changes with the seasons, just as it does with the guests. Therefore, arrange the bar accordingly (plenty of gin and rum in the warmer months and heavy on the bourbon and Scotch during the winter). Always include soft drinks, coffee, or tomato juice for those non-drinkers. A variety of mixes, such as tonic, soda, soft drinks, plus some of the new instant mixes in packets, should

be on your shopping list. The fixings should include cherries, small onions, olives, sliced oranges and, of course, lemons and limes. Misery is a lukewarm drink, so have plenty of ice on hand.

Mix up several jars of standard cocktails before the party. Martinis, Manhattans, and Whisky Sours all can be pre-mixed successfully and refrigerated till time to serve.

For more than twenty people, two bar areas are best. Two card tables, covered with a mattress pad for absorbency and then with a gay tablecloth, make a fine bar. Slide a big ice chest underneath for extra ice and supplies.

Limiting the variety of drinks served to guests is essential. Basically, the highball, Martini and Manhattan will be sufficient. After all, the host doesn't want to spend the entire evening, "Bar Guide" in hand, mixing everything from a Pink Lady to a Sazerac. An obvious answer to mass refreshment is punch, but it does have its drawbacks. Not everyone likes his alcohol too "doctored up", and punch tends to get watery as the evening progresses. One way to guard against its watering down is to freeze the non-alcoholic portion of the libation, and use it as you would a block of ice. This also works with eggnog, believe it or not.

(5) Food at a cocktail party: The variety of tidbits, munchables, spreadables, dipables, etc., that can be served for cocktails is practically limitless. However, hot foods should be kept hot and cold foods cold. Pass the right-from-the-oven hors d'oeuvres; don't allow them to sit around and turn to stone. If you do have something passed, it should be easily eaten. Passed hors d'oeuvres should not require assemblage, nor should they be drippy or hard to manage. It's very difficult to maneuver drink and cigarette while trying to spread a delicious pâté on a cracker. Spreads and dips should be sitting on a firm surface.

How much liquor and food to buy is a constant problem for the hostess entertaining at a cocktail party. One night friends will descend upon a party table and bar like a horde of locusts, demolishing everything in sight. That same group on another occasion will barely nibble at the feast. In between times, however, these rules of thumb may come in handy: **Liquor**—A fifth contains 25.6 ounces; a quart contains 32 ounces. A jigger holds 1½ ounces. There are 16 jiggers in a fifth and 20 jiggers in a quart. A bottle of wine will fill six 4-ounce wineglasses. A gallon of punch will fill 40 punch cups. Count on the average guest's having three drinks or three to four cups of punch. Light and heavy drinkers will balance out one another. **Food:** Figure about ten "bites" per person.

Rally Round the Flag

Old Glory will proudly wave over this Fourth of July celebration or election year party. Whether you are young or old, Democrat or GOP, all comers will enjoy this star-spangled, red-white-and-blue picnic.

INVITATIONS: Make invitations out of blue construction paper. Draw or glue an American flag in the center of the paper. Sprinkle a few gold stars here and about. Fold the paper in thirds; write party information inside in white ink on the side flaps. Seal with red sealing wax.

MENU:
> *Barbecued Ribs
> (see Barbecue Sauce)
> Smoked Brisket or Smoked Turkey
> *Papa's Farm Beans
> Potato Salad   *Roasted Corn
> Watermelon Cannon
> Homemade Peppermint Ice Cream
> Apple Cake   Chocolate Sheet Cake

DECORATIONS AND SERVING SUGGESTIONS: Make sure an American flag greets guests at entrance to party area. Cover buffet table with red and white striped cloth. Use large blue paper dinner napkins. Make a napkin ring out of red construction paper and glue a large white star on it. Use red paper plates, red or blue enamel coffee pots, platters, bowls, etc. Line a small produce basket (dime store variety) with your bright blue napkins and let it serve as a container for bread. For your centerpiece, buy a toy drum and attach small American flags around the rim. March children's toy soldiers down length of table. Tie together clusters of red, white, and blue balloons with crepe paper streamers of the same colors and hang them in the trees. Decorate a large cardboard carton with the words "Keep America Beautiful", and let it serve as a handy receptacle for disposable paper plates and napkins.

FUN AND GAMES: Hold the traditional relay races, sack races, egg rolls, etc.

Dive-In

When that summer daze is upon the land, entertain your fair-weather friends poolside. (Are you a tennis buff rather than a water baby? Substitute tennis courts for the pool, and there you have a "Love-Set".) A perfect way to christen a new pool or to entertain the college crew.

INVITATIONS: Make a two-dimensional flower by cutting a daisy from orange paper and overlaying it with a smaller yellow daisy. Write message in center of yellow flower with orange marker.

MENU: A couple shares a picnic box or basket which is filled with the following:

Small Wedge of Cheese, with Crackers
*Swiss Cheese and Bell Pepper Sandwich on Rye Bread
*Corned Beef Sandwich on Rye Bread
*Roast Beef Sandwich on French Bread
*Deviled Eggs   *Slaw   *Kosher Dill Pickles
Butterfudge Fingers or Butter Toffee

DECORATIONS: Cover tables around pool with a variety of brightly colored square paper tablecloths over long round yellow cloths. Cover pots holding ferns with a matching paper and insert slim tapers for lighting after sunset. Use a child's small plastic swimming pool for an ice-filled cooler. Line the drive with colored sacks filled one-quarter full of sand, inserting in sand a household candle. Outdoor ashtrays save policing the grounds.

SUGGESTIONS FOR SERVING: (1) Box suppers by the pool, served in cake boxes which have been sprayed to match the tablecloths and decorated with a flower on each lid. Line boxes with colored tissue and paper doilies. Paper napkins, plastic forks, the individually wrapped food, and a split of champagne go inside. (2) Great colored picnic baskets with tie-on name tags for each couple. (3) Pack your picnic in a knapsack made from material squares and knotted on a short cane pole. Garnish each with a flower. The ever-thoughtful hostess includes sealed packets of scented, pre-moistened hand towels in each picnic box.

FUN AND GAMES: Swimming (or tennis, if you please) is the main attraction. Have a juke box for dancing, filled with songs of the crowd's dating days. Paint two life-sized caricature figures (one male, one female) in bathing suits (any vintage) and leave headless. Have someone with a camera take snapshots. Great fun!

Sand-Trap

The wind from the sea blows and beckons landlubbers everywhere to come revel in sands warmed by the summer sun. This simple party is adaptable for lake or poolside, as well as seashore.

INVITATIONS: With magic marker write a note such as "Come for shrimp and suds in the sand . . . etc." on a piece of old newspaper. Mail, or put in an old bottle, and deliver to each cottage.

MENU: **New Orleans Barbecued Shrimp**
Roasted Corn   French Bread
Some-More's
Beer

DECORATIONS AND SERVING SUGGESTIONS: Cover table with old newspaper. Use any colorful paper plates, napkins, and cups. A rectangle of plywood atop two sawhorses, all painted gaily, makes a collapsible, easy-to-store table for beach or back yard. For place cards, paint a caricature of each guest on one side of a large shell or smooth rock and his name on the other side. The shells can be used later as ashtrays. Prepare shrimp ahead of time and transport to beach in insulated containers. Build grill in sand to roast corn, warm bread, and roast marshmallows. **Grill:** Dig a shallow pit about three feet long. Heat coals in the sand pit and place a flat mesh grill on top. Beverages should be kept frosty throughout the party in an insulated container filled with ice. **Roasted Corn:** Clean fresh ears of corn. Spread all sides with butter, salt or garlic salt, and pepper. Seal in aluminum foil and place on grill. Cook for 25 minutes, turning often. **Some-More's:** Break graham crackers and chocolate bars into individual squares. For each serving, cover one cracker with several chocolate squares. On skewers, roast marshmallows till soft and hot. Place marshmallow on chocolate-covered cracker and top with a second cracker. Press gently together.

FUN AND GAMES: Round up plenty of inflatable rafts for water fun. Make certain someone brings a guitar for singing after sundown. Hunt for full beer cans (like Easter eggs) before dinner!

The fall or early spring ushers in the perfect weather for an oyster roast in the great outdoors. Our country fare is well-suited for your week end retreat or farm-just-outside-the-city. Invite as many or as few as you wish. With its bonfire (and a few jack-o'-lanterns added), it's just meant for Halloween.

INVITATIONS: Use small paper bags with a map inside showing how to get to party, if any distance away. On one side of bag write poem, such as the following, and on other side write the address. Fold bag, staple, stamp and mail.

"We're having a party and want you all here.
(Place) is not far; it's really quite near.
The map in the bag will show you the way,
So please come early and have a long stay.
Beer, oysters, and music, too,
We hope that this will be fun for you."

Time   Date   Hosts

MENU: **Oysters**
                   French Bread
                        Beer

DECORATIONS AND SERVING SUGGESTIONS: Bushels of oysters from the coast can be ordered through a fish market. Serve approximately half the oysters on the half-shell and the rest roasted. Big skillets of butter and garlic salt can be placed over the fire for pan frying. **To roast oysters:** Make a large square with cement blocks and place charcoal inside the square. Place screens over the blocks. Wait till fire gets hot, about an hour, and put oysters on screens with a shovel. Cover the oysters with wet burlap and cook till oysters pop open, about one hour. Place bales of hay around the bonfire and elsewhere for seating. Set up long picnic tables with benches. If held at Halloween, use jack-o'-lanterns with candles inside for decorations and lighting. Put plenty of gloves and oyster openers on the tables so the guests can open the oyster shells. Also place crackers and bowls of oyster sauce on the tables. **For oyster sauce:** Mix chili sauce, horseradish, and lemon juice to taste. Help for handling the beer kegs and manning the oyster bar will be necessary. It also takes two men to roast the oysters. It's a good idea to have spaghetti on hand for those who don't care for oysters.

FUN AND GAMES: Hire a combo for the music and let guests dance on the grass.

Ed Giobbi's Sausage Stuffing

Edward Giobbi is a knowledgeable gourmet as well as an outstanding and well-known artist. One of the dreamy dinner parties given by the Giobbis features Ed's baked chicken . . . he covers the bird with clay, shaping the clay into a chicken. It is baked and then painted by the talented Mr. Giobbi. The following unusual party is a favorite of the artist and his wife. It's guaranteed to liven up a long winter evening.

INVITATIONS: Cut butcher's apron from paper. With magic marker write on it: "Wear me—to a Sausage Stuffing/ Time/ Place/ etc."

MENU: **Cocktail Tomatoes with Seasoned Salt**
Italian Sausage Marchigiana
Italian Sausages Black and Green
Sausages with Peppers and Onions
Italian Knot Bread
Fresh Pears with Bel Paese

DECORATIONS AND SERVING SUGGESTIONS: This party is ideally suited for taking place in a cozy kitchen . . . from the making of the sausage to eating dinner. It works best with a small group of intimate friends. Be sure to provide guests with large aprons. Cover the kitchen table with bright oilcloth, and set out wicker baskets. In one is a pile of cherry tomatoes for snacks. In the other is a "bouquet" of the flatware to be used, wrapped in brightly colored napkins. This party invites the use of heavy earthenware, large mugs for foaming beer, and tall wine glasses. If you have homemade wine on hand, serve it to this group.

FUN AND GAMES: Have a grinder set up on a table, and a keg of beer nearby. One guest grinds the seasoned meat, another holds the casing and another forces the meat into the casing. Someone else ties the strings as the sausage is stuffed. After the sausages are made, the host cooks them three different ways and serves them to his "helpers". **Making the sausages:** Have a pork butt or shoulder coarsely ground and season meat with freshly ground black pepper, salt, anise seeds, and chopped orange skins. A funnel, the right size for the pork casings, is needed. Casings may be purchased. They come salted, so must be soaked overnight before using. When stuffing the casings, tie with regular cord every three inches. Prick sausages before cooking.

Double Decker

Here is a party designed exclusively for bridge addicts, life masters, avid poker players, or other various and sundry card players.

INVITATION: Paste white paper on back of a playing card. Write party information on white paper. Invite enough guests to insure at least three tables of bridge.

MENU: **Marinated Ripe Olives   Assorted Nuts**
Celery Soup
Double Decker Sandwiches
(Guests make own from a tray of assorted
cold meats, cheeses and breads)
French Cream Tarts

DECORATIONS AND SERVING SUGGESTIONS: Make red or black corduroy bridge cloths for playing tables. Let one table be the jack, one the queen, and one the king. Center each table with block of Styrofoam and paste the appropriate cards on each side of block. Remove the jacks, queens and kings from an odd deck and have couples draw for tables. Set a red and black serving table. Make centerpiece of red flowers. Cut shapes of clubs and spades from black construction paper; wire these with florist wires and stick among the red flowers. Make the pastry for the dessert heart-shaped, if desired, and top with a red fruit (raspberry, strawberry, cherry).

FUN AND GAMES: At least two tables are necessary to play this game. Make four envelopes for each table, and number I, II, III, IV. After everyone is seated, open the first envelope. Four hands are played in each round with each player dealing once. After each round, open the next envelope.
Envelope I: "Play four hands, each player dealing once, then change tables."
Envelope II: "Play four hands; then pass your score for these hands only to the player on your left."
Envelope III: "Bid all four hands as usual, but after bidding has been completed, pass your hand to the person on your left."
Envelope IV: "All four hands **must** be played at three no-trump by the dealer."
Prizes may be awarded or not, as the hostess desires.

Health Party

Calories, calories! Who's got the calories!! Certainly not this fun party that proves weight-watching can be fun. An ideal party for those "oldsters" who are watching their waistlines. Invite guests for a late afternoon of not-too-strenuous games (croquet, badminton, etc.), followed by light supper. Or turn this into a birthday party for an "over-forty" spouse.

INVITATIONS: A prescription blank which reads, "Rx — For a Rejuvenating Evening of Fun." Guests are asked to dress in favorite exercise outfit (tennis, golf, jogging, etc.) or to come in a sporting outfit of a specified era (preferably guests' dating days).

MENU: Boiled Shrimp on Ice   Gazpacho
Steaks, cooked on the grill
Squash Casserole   Fresh Spinach Salad
Fake Watermelon or Watermelon Basket,
filled with fresh fruit

DECORATIONS AND SERVING SUGGESTIONS: For the table's centerpieces, use several small baskets or flower pots filled with bouquets of nature-perfect fresh vegetables. The following may be used (root ends forming the "bouquets"): radishes, carrots, mushrooms, purple and white turnips. Long-stemmed rhubarb, flawless and blushing, can be bunched, tied at top and bottom with ribbons, and stood upright (leafy end up) at intervals. Very slender, tall tapers may be used among the vegetable arrangements. Place cards are fortune cards from a penny weigh-yourself scale.

FUN AND GAMES: If this is a birthday party, have a football jersey ready to put on honoree, with his age as the numbers on the front and back. Music and dancing add to the party. Make certain that records from the honoree's heyday are played along with "now" music. Recruit two or three good-sport teenage couples to come for a while to teach the latest dances. For more fun, display some clothing of the honoree from a "few" years back (old Army uniform, wedding dress, etc.) See how it fits now! A jug of mineral water can be labeled "The Fountain of Youth". Have each guest bring a picture of himself at a specified point in yesteryear (say, twenty-five years ago). Make a showcase of the pictures on poster board or bulletin board. Gifts for the honoree should include funny things to keep one young—in spirit, as well as in body.

Young marrieds will welcome entertaining their contemporaries with this informal shower for the bride and groom, housewarming, or surprise birthday party. Fun is up to the maximum and spending is kept down to the minimum.

INVITATIONS: Write the following poem on gay stationery.
> The point of the party is this . . .
> To have fun in shirt sleeves and shift;
> But to make the night swing
> We'll ask you to bring
> A poem and minimum gift.
> Boys give to (bride's name), girls give to (groom's name)
> Some thrifty little household aid;
> A roll of Scotch tape or a ball of string
> Will patch up a fuss or most any old thing.
> Date   Time   Place

With some slight alterations in the wording, this invitation can also be used for a housewarming or surprise birthday party.

MENU: **Depression Cocktail**
Chicken Gumbo or Shrimp Gumbo or Ham Tetrazzini
Fresh Spinach Salad
Lemon Angel

DECORATIONS AND SERVING SUGGESTIONS: Decorate house with potted flowers or plants (geraniums, Jerusalem cherry, chrysanthemums, ivy, fern, etc.) which can be given at party's end to honorees for their new apartment or home. (Pots of fern make very effective centerpieces if studded with paper flowers on wire stems.) Hosts purchase a garbage can to hold the groom's or husband's (if this is housewarming) gifts and a large plastic wastebasket for the bride's or wife's gifts. These should be tied with wild ribbon or yarn. A bag of assorted rags is a wonderful additional gift for a bride who has had no chance to accumulate her own.

FUN AND GAMES: At the shower have best man and maid of honor read the poems aloud while presents are being opened. On other occasions let host and hostess read them.

Shower: Spread a nine-foot dish towel on floor and provide each guest with a threaded needle; have guests monogram or embroider names on towel. You will be surprised at how many men can do a creditable job. Toweling can be bought in most any fabric department.

Housewarming: Have guests plant a tree and/or put up a mailbox. It is absolutely essential to capture these moments with a camera.

Waffles on a Winter's Night

A crackling fire burns in the fireplace as close friends gather for old-fashioned country fare . . . it's a help-yourself party with guests doing their own cooking.

INVITATIONS: Use your telephone.

MENU: Perre's Waffles
or Turn-But-Once Pancakes or Pancake Crêpes
Turkey Hash
Cinnamon-Cream Syrup   Quick Cherries Jubilee Sauce
Variety of Syrups   Butter
Chopped Pecans   Berries   Chopped Apples
Baked Canadian Bacon
(surrounded with link sausages and bacon curls)
Coffee

DECORATIONS AND SERVING SUGGESTIONS: On the buffet table, use a wicker basket filled with apples and pine cones. This table contains the mounds of creamy butter or small pitchers of melted butter, the sauces and syrups, the meat platter, a chafing dish of hash, and the mugs for steaming coffee. Guests make own waffles or pancakes (or host can be the chief cook) on a "cooking" side table, then bring them to the buffet to add all the trimmings.
"Cooking" table: Set up a table to the side, well out of way of the buffet, and gift-wrap it with heavy aluminum foil (cover top and tuck foil under edges; secure with tape). Put waffle irons and portable flat grills on this table. Beside the grills, stand pitchers (ironstone would be great) of pancake and waffle batter and have chopped pecans and fruits close at hand. Guests add own choice of condiments to batter immediately after pouring batter on grill. Red and blue bandanas tucked into the coffee mugs could serve as napkins.
QUICK CHERRIES JUBILEE SAUCE: Stir ¼ c. brandy or port wine into a small jar of cherry preserves and warm; also excellent over ice cream. Serves 4.

MRS. C. WHITNEY BROWN

CINNAMON-CREAM SYRUP: Combine 1 c. sugar, ½ c. light corn syrup, ¼ c. water, and ½-¾ t. cinnamon. Bring to a boil over medium heat, stirring constantly. Cook and stir 2 minutes more. Cool 5 minutes and stir in ½ c. evaporated milk. Makes 1⅔ cups.

MRS. ROBERT G. ALLEN

The Cocktail Supper

(For twenty-five or more)

The cocktail supper differs from the cocktail party in that the food is heartier. The following menu is planned so that all the food can be put on the buffet and practically forgotten, save for occasional replenishing. Nothing need be passed, and there are no hot hors d'oeuvres that must be carefully watched and passed while still warm. The hostess is free to mingle and enjoy her guests. For more complete instructions for giving a cocktail party, see the introduction to this chapter.

MENU: **Liptauer**
Beef Tartare or Cold Steak Béarnaise
Mock Oysters Rockefeller   Crab Meat in Chafing Dish
Vegetables with Sour Cream Dressing
Salami Wedges   Cheese Straws
Rum Punch or Martini (or) Manhattan Bowl

SERVING SUGGESTIONS: The following are a few hints for a cocktail supper: Relocate or dispose of hazards when a large group will be present in your home. This means small children, pets, and any prized belongings that might be in a precarious spot. Provide plenty of readily identifiable ashtrays. Do have someone to empty the ashtrays and whisk away empty glasses and plates. A bar is needed if punch isn't served. See the introduction to this chapter for specific instructions for setting up a bar. One additional thought for this, however, is to fill a large punch bowl with ice, and stand in it all cocktails that need chilling . . . such as, a pitcher of Martinis, a bottle of dry sherry, tomato juice, etc. One of the greatest helps at a very large gathering is to have hanging over the doorknob a small sign which reads, "Please Come In". Guests will feel an immediate welcome (no more awkward front porch waits), and the doorbell doesn't ring over and over again. Of course, someone should be near the door to greet guests and take wraps.

Do your large entertaining at a once-a-year party, given at the same time or season of each year. Thus, you are able to accumulate, year by year, all the decorations and accessories needed for entertaining at that particular season. For example, Christmas party, Thanksgiving party, garden party, patio supper, October oyster roast, and on and on. Each year the entertaining will become easier for you and a much-looked-forward-to event by your guests.

Stock Your Larder

This sophisticated entertainment is a perfect welcome to new neighbors, a marvelous bachelor bash, or a lovely way to stock the larder of a friend's new home. A wine-tasting is a great party conversation-maker and ice-breaker.

INVITATIONS: (1) Cut the shape of a wine bottle from construction paper. In place of the label write:

"Drink Thy Wine With A Merry Heart."

Chateau de ─────────────

Vintage de ─────────────

Fête de Vin Honoring ─────────────

(2) Use a wine label and write party information on the back. Labels can be obtained at a liquor store. Indicate if guests are to bring a gift of wine by attaching a gift card to the bottle or writing on the label "Help the Smiths Stock Their Larder".

MENU:

TABLE I—FRENCH
Brie or Camembert   Boursault   Port Salut
English Water Biscuits   French Bread
Red Burgundy   White Burgundy   Loire   Red Bordeaux

TABLE II—ITALIAN
Bel Paese   Fontina   Provolone
Italian Bread
Soave Bolla   Valpolicella   Chianti

TABLE III—GERMAN
Tilsiter   Bianco
Rye Crackers   Pumpernickel
Liebfraumilch   Riesling   Moselle   Rhine

TABLE IV—AMERICAN
Monterrey Jack   Wisconsin Cheddar   Port Wine
Beaten Biscuit   Sourdough Bread
(All California Wines)
Pinot Noir   Rosé   Cabernet Sauvignon

GRAND FINALE
New York State Korbel Champagne

To gild the lily after the wine-tasting, serve a supper of Boeuf à la Bourguignonne, French bread, and a platter of fresh fruit.

DECORATIONS AND SERVING SUGGESTIONS: Use four card tables for wine-tasting, each representing a different country famous for its wine regions. These are French, Italian, German-Austrian, and American. On each table use a painter's laminated bucket (available at a paint store), and cover with felt, foil, contact paper or bright yarn wrapped around and around the bucket. Fill with ice and chill white wines in these. Cluster red and green grapes and leaves around the base of the buckets. Use a bright felt runner on the buffet table. Arrange wine bottles representing the different countries in either a straight or curved line. In front of each bottle, stand a miniature flag of the country. (Flags are available at a party or import store. Flag holder may be hidden with a small bunch of grapes.) Small placards, each skewered with a toothpick, are stuck into the cheeses to identify them by name. Use all-purpose wine glasses, two per person (one for white and one for red wine). Have wine coolers filled with water to rinse one's glass after each tasting. Serve red wines at room temperature, and open in advance to allow them to breathe. Serve white wines chilled. Wine tasting is traditionally done by pouring a small amount of wine in a tulip-shaped glass and swirling it around in the glass to catch the fragrance or bouquet. The wine is sipped or rolled on the tongue to get the little nuances of flavor. Before tasting the next wine, the palate should be "cleared" by eating a bit of cheese and bread. These are the classic accompaniments for wine-tasting.

FUN AND GAMES: On a special table, have a wine carafe marked "Brand X". Have guests try to identify the wine, its country and district on a ballot. After each guest has filled in a ballot and put it in a decorative box or tray, the host reads them and announces the winner. The winning prize is a bottle of champagne . . . of course. Have note pads and pencils available for those who want to make notes of wines to try at home.

For an unusual engagement, teenage, or poolside party, import a little bit of Spain or Mexico to your own yard and let the fiesta begin. Olé!

INVITATIONS: (1) Cut inexpensive straw mats into envelope size. Glue smaller rectangle of bright construction paper to mat and write party information with magic marker. Border invitations with yarn. (2) Draw a sun face on colorful construction paper and write party message on it. Fold over, seal with a sunburst decal, and mail without envelope.

MEXICAN MENU: *Margaritas
*Guacamole or Mexican Dip
Tamale Dip
*Chicken Yucatan with Saffron Rice
or
Marinated Roast Pork with Black Beans and Rice
Ceviche with Avocado Mousse
Mexican Cornbread
Fake Watermelon

SPANISH MENU: La Fonda Sangria
Marinated Ripe Olives   Empanditos
Gazpacho or Shrimp in Almond Sauce
Barbecued Butterfly Leg of Lamb
or
Steak in Spanish Marinade
Stuffed Mushrooms
Sesame Cheese Loaf
Spanish Flan or Chocolate Rum Cake

DECORATIONS AND SERVING SUGGESTIONS: Cover each table with brightly colored burlap cloths. Fringe edges (no hemming necessary). Or make a runner for each table using heavy, shiny wrapping paper. Place small, twinkling Christmas lights in trees. If there is a pool or fountain, place votive candles in foil pie plates, tuck a flower in each, and float in pool. Make lanterns from coffee cans: Perforate the sides of coffee cans around top and bottom with beer can opener; then punch holes with an ice pick to make designs. Spray-paint cans with bright colors and place a candle in each. Alternate suggestion for lanterns: Cover large glasses with colored cellophane and put candle inside. Pour several inches of sand into colored paper sacks, insert a candle in each, and use to line party area. Decorate doorways with garlands of bright ribbons, bells, and paper flowers. Place large potted plants on patio. For additional decoration, fashion different sized hoops from heavy duty foil and attach crepe paper streamers. Hang these by three light wires as you would a hanging basket. Decorate individual tables with coffee can lanterns or cellophane lamps and put one fresh flower at each place. You can also put castanets or maracas on each table. No fiesta would be complete without a large piñata hung in a prominent place. If extra lighting is needed, coffee can lanterns can be hung in trees. **Buffet table:** Wrap flatware in green napkins and tie with a large artificial poppy. Stand these upright in a clay pot to give the effect of a pot of flowers. Alternate suggestion: Fat colorful yarn may be used to tie napkins. Yarn may be braided into a "rope" and swagged around table edge. Make small hors d'oeuvre cacti by securing whole cucumbers in small clay pots and dotting them with toothpicks. Attach shrimp, cherry tomatoes, chili peppers and small paper flowers. **Centerpiece:** (1) Bank a small burro piñata with flowers and candles. (2) Invert a large, colorful, floppy hat and fill with flowers. Bright colors, lights, and music are essential to establish the fiesta mood!

FUN AND GAMES: Play mariachi and flamenco music to set mood of party. Invite guests to bring any musical instruments they may have and create own mariachi band. Guests with no instruments of their own use castanets and maracas found on dinner tables. Near end of party, guests break the large piñata.

Joyeux Noël

Capture the spirit and cheer of Christmas with this party for the entire family. Let one and all help plan and decorate for this Yuletide extravaganza.

INVITATIONS: Each member of your family is allowed to ask a designated number of his friends and their families to your party. Each person invites his or her guests personally or writes a note. A good time is from 5 p.m. to 7 p.m.

MENU:

Eggnog
For the children: Fruit Punch
or
Peppermint Eggnog Punch
Cucumber Dip   Cheese Rolls
Smoked Turkey, for sandwiches
Hot Curried Crab Dip   Sausage Stroganoff
Kentucky Bourbon Cake   My Grandmother's Brownies
Fruited Pecans   Russian Rocks   Sour Cream Fudge

DECORATIONS AND SERVING SUGGESTIONS: Decorate front door with a Christmas tree. To make base of tree, cut block of Styrofoam into flower pot shape. Line large candy canes side by side and wire together just below the crook of each, forming a long row. Stretch canes, crook ends out, around front and sides of base and attach; "tie" with red velvet ribbon. The canes will provide a complete covering for the base. Cover a yardstick with green felt to make trunk of tree. Fashion three graduated blocks of green Styrofoam and attach to yardstick. If green Styrofoam is not available, spray-paint white Styrofoam. Secure base to door with double-faced cellophane tape and wire yardstick to door knocker. Decorate "tree" with greenery, small candy canes, red bows and red birds. In the hallway, hang a jewel-studded Styrofoam ball and encircle it with a wreath of mistletoe. In the entrance hall, intertwine miniature white lights in a rope of greenery and outline a mirror. Place a silver compote of ribbon or rock candy on a table below the mirror. The focal point in your living room is your own "touch the ceiling" Christmas tree. Make a pair of peacocks and place them on the mantle facing each other. Mold chicken wire to form head and body of peacocks and stud with boxwood. Use longer pieces of boxwood for tails and let them hang over the mantle. Use jeweled hatpins for peacocks' eyes and for combs. Hang an Advent wreath of fresh greenery in a bay window, or over a table with red velvet ribbon. The wreath has three white candles and one purple for the Sundays before Christmas. Hang dozens of large candy canes from every branch or arm of the chandelier in your breakfast or family room. Decorations above eye level are most effective in a crowded room. Wrap juicy pink grapefruit in colorful tissue paper and pile in a large brass or copper container near your front door. As a small Christmas remembrance, give one to each guest as he leaves. Place hors d'oeuvre trees in several rooms. Use green oasis pyramids banked with parsley and studded with shrimp, cocktail tomatoes, radish roses and olives. Anchor trees on china or crystal platter with floral clay (do not use clay on a silver platter).

Children's room: The focal point is a manger scene. Surround the crêche with barnyard animals which have been made out of Christmas dough. (Recipe for dough: 4 cups flour, 1 cup salt, 1½ cups water. Mold dough and bake one hour at 350º.) Paint animals with tempera paint. Create an unforgettable winter scene with an enchanted gingerbread house by a mirror pond. Surround it with a forest of small green posterboard trees standing upright in giant gumdrop bases. Decorate a "favor tree" with cookie cutters and cookies for the children to take home. Add a personal touch by writing each child's name on a cookie with frosting. Tie tiny paper, wooden, or tin birds to tree also. As another favor, carve designs on citrus fruits and pile them in a golden basket. To carve fruits: Use a sharp paring knife to carve rind away, just down to white part of fruit. Result: A white design contrasted with the yellow, orange or green of rind.

Dining Room: Gift-wrap your table with a floor-length pink felt cloth. Across the top and down the sides, "tie" it with wide red velvet ribbon, and add a large stylized bow at one end of the table. Make an oversized tag saying "Merry Christmas" and attach to bow. For your centerpiece, make a carnation tree using a pyramid-shaped oasis for your tree form. Stud with small red velvet bows, greenery, and red and white striped carnations. Surround base of tree with tiny gifts wrapped in red and pink foil. For the Christmas punch: Freeze a fresh pineapple in a block of ice, allowing crown to be exposed. Float ice block in punch and decorate crown with tiny round ornaments. For the eggnog bowl: Brush edge with slightly beaten egg white and sprinkle edge with colored sugar crystals. Let dry.

FUN AND GAMES: Continuous playing of Christmas music. Perhaps children will sing carols for the grown-ups.

Ferocious beasts and man-eating cannibals lurk hungrily in the lush jungles of your own back yard, ready to pounce on the "great white hunter" on safari or unsuspecting camper in the wilds. This party could suit several themes . . . "Tarzan and Jane", "Noah's Ark", "Garden of Eden", "Return to Paradise" (South Seas idea).

INVITATIONS: Cut out a paw print of a jungle cat from black felt or other furry fabric; paste in center of a piece of brown construction paper. Fold paper in thirds. Write the following jungle chant on either side of paw:

"The natives are restless;
The drums are beating;
The spirits will be chanting at (your address).
The animals will be stampeding at eight;
(Name of host and hostess), your Tarzan and Jane.
Give the jungle yell. Go grab your spears, Your native masks, And dance the paths In your exotic dress."

MENU: **Banana Daiquiri   Rum Punch**
Stuffed Cocktail Tomatoes, with Seasoned Cream Cheese
Cantaloupe Balls Wrapped in Prosciutto
Cheese Pineapple
Roast Wild Boar (see Marinated Roast Pork)
Barbecued Chicken
Cauliflower with Garden Dressing
Monkey Bread
Bananas Flambé or Flaming Polynesian Ice Cream
Homemade Kahlúa

DECORATIONS AND SERVING SUGGESTIONS: For the swingers, hang a Tarzan rope in a large tree. Also hang a hammock, cages of birds (alive or fake), and baskets of jungle flowers. Place exotic plants everywhere. For a tablecloth, use an animal print cloth and cut jagged edges. Hang or drape mounted horns, masks, spears, stuffed animals, rubber snakes, etc., throughout. Provide drums for musical natives. Stake tiki torches strategically. For candle holders: Cut crown off a pineapple two inches deep; remove center leaves to make hole the size of a candle. Serve food in iron pots, wooden bowls, large natural shells.

FUN AND GAMES: Guests are costumed as hunters, natives, missionaries. Play background jungle music featuring birds, drums, etc. (The public library rents many recordings of exotic music).
Head Hunters: As guests arrive, give each a jungle animal headdress made from a paper sack. Make a male and female version. Have each guest find his or her headdress mate.

La Dolce Vita

For these two Italian menus the party colors are the Italian flag colors of red, white, and green . . . green and white checked cloths and red napkins. For a centerpiece, see the Bread Lanterns in "Ski-Bee". The bread sticks may be bunched together, tied with ribbon and stood on one end for a different serving trick.

MENU I:
Salami Chips
Lasagna or Pizza
Super Salad Bowl
Lemon Cheese Pie or Chocolate Cheese Cake
Valpolicella

MENU II:
Antipasto
Green Garlic Spaghetti
(the pasta; served as a separate course)
Scaloppine alla Marsala
or
Veal Cutlet Parmigiana
Zucchini   Insalata
Macaroon Tortoni
Bread Sticks
Chianti

Ski-Bee

Entertain your snow bunny buddies with this ápres-ski fondue party . . . or throw this bash for all the poor souls left behind when everyone else has departed for the slopes.

INVITATIONS: Work invitations around the theme of "Slide On In For Fondue Fun".

MENU:
> **Milk Punch or Gleu Vein**
> **Wheel of Cheese, with Crackers**
> **Meat Fondue (beef, liver, or chicken)**
> **Sauces: Duxelles, Onion, Pungent Peach, Mustard,**
> **Sour Cream-Horseradish**
> **Super Salad Bowl**
> **Bread Sticks or French Bread**
> **Gingerbread Men**

DECORATIONS AND SERVING SUGGESTIONS: If there's no snow, spray artificial snow around the front door. Use a cardboard snowman as a doorman. Inside, center the fun around a cozy fire. Use posters of ski countries. **Buffet Table:** Cover with a bold black and white plaid or striped tablecloth. Insert white candles in the tops of red apples and cluster them in two groups on the table. A second idea for candle holders is a "loaf lantern": For two lanterns, cut a foot-long loaf of unsliced bread in two. Using a long, sharp knife, hollow out the two pieces, leaving the crust ends intact. Stand each half upright on the crust end and cut narrow various-shaped "windows" in all sides. Place a pine or wood-scented votive candle inside. These lanterns can be made ahead and frozen; or use, then freeze for future entertaining, perfect for an Italian dinner. These can also be used as containers for bread sticks, instead of for candles. Serve milk punch from a wooden bucket (pail inside) and wheel of cheese on a cutting board or a butcher's block. Allow one fondue pot for every four guests.

FUN AND GAMES: Have a yodeling contest. First prize is a crutch with a tag attached reading, "A crutch for your failing spirits . . . since you're not on the slopes with everyone else!"

When in Rome

Do as the Romans did on a summer evening . . . Recreate the splendor that was Rome with lavish decorations and Epicurean food. Eliminate the elaborate trappings and you have left a marvelous cocktail supper menu.

INVITATIONS: Write party information on a scroll including "Togas Only". Give RSVP phone number in Roman numerals. Inform guests that prizes will be awarded for most unusual arrival conveyance, most beautiful couple, and funniest outfit.

MENU: Caesar's Bowl or Roman Punch
*Sunburst Artichoke   Broiled Shrimp
Volcano Cheese Ball
Patrician Pâté   *Venturian Chicken (Cold Fried Chicken Legs)
Romulus Ribs with Remus Sauce (see Barbecue Sauce)
Cold Marinated Vegetables
Italian Knot Bread
*Fresh Fruit and Cheese Platter

DECORATIONS AND SERVING SUGGESTIONS: Punch is served in goblets. Make certain paper frills cover ends of chicken legs for easy eating. To get the maximum effect of this party, these decorations should be done in a contained area. Make columns of heavy cardboard tubing painted white (tubes available at carpet or linoleum stores). Place columns everywhere to resemble Roman ruins. Drape purple ribbon from column to column and entwine with plastic ivy and grapes. Light party area with tiki torches. If available decorate with statuary. (Latter may be papier-mâché). Guests sit on chaise lounges or mattresses draped with sheets. Include lots of throw pillows.
Table: Use a golden cloth and decorate with various sized candles or candelabra grouped and entwined with ivy and grapes. Have a handy bird bath? Ice your punch container in it. Trumpet or sheepherder's horn is blown to herald arrival of feast. Waiters (recruit some of your guests) dressed in togas and with heads garlanded with ivy enter to Triumphal March from Aïda. Waiters carry food in large, ornate platters.

FUN AND GAMES: Present each guest with a laurel wreath and goblet of punch as he enters.

Midnight Supper

After the concert, theatre, or sporting event, bask in the "afterglow" of the evening with good friends and a divine midnight repast.

INVITATIONS: Use a playbill or show program, or simply say:
      "After our evening at the _____(event),
      Come to our place
      While the night is still young . . .
      Hosts
      Address."

MENU: **Broiled Grapefruit**
                            Eggs Hussarde
                        Macaroon Tortoni
                Demitasse   **Brandy**

DECORATIONS AND SERVING SUGGESTIONS: Create an intimate, relaxing atmosphere with lots of sparkle and candlelight. Capture the drama of an evening well spent by using a centerpiece apropos to the event . . . a playbill, show program, etc. Be sure to play the records of the music you have just heard, if a concert or musical was on your agenda.
BROILED GRAPEFRUIT: Cut grapefruit in half and cut around each section. This can be done well ahead. Just before serving, sprinkle generously with brown sugar and dot with butter. Run under the broiler and watch carefully till grapefruit heats through and sugar melts. Splash each half with sherry or cherry brandy before serving, if desired. Garnish center with a cherry, candied fruit or crystallized ginger.

FUN AND GAMES: If you don't wish to entertain after an event, entertain during! For instance, are you going to a Play-in-the-Park? An outdoor concert? Invite some friends along and pack a continental "Care Basket" for all . . . dessert cheeses, bread and wine . . . to be enjoyed while the band plays on.

Short and Sweet

Shrimp Spread
Easy Beef Stroganoff
Tomato and Artichoke Salad
French Bread
English Lemon Dessert

Candlelight and Champagne

Whether you are young marrieds celebrating your first anniversary with your former honor attendants, or a girl preparing a "velvet hammer" evening for her beau, whether you live in mansion or apartment, this intimate dinner with candlelight and champagne will cast the appropriate spell.

INVITATION: Write party information in black on silver paper.

MENU:
Champagne
Cheese-Bacon Puffs
Vichyssoise
Crab Stuffed Chicken Breasts or Chicken Supreme
Boiled Parsleyed Rice   Asparagus Vinaigrette
Rolls
Strawberry Soufflé or Black Forest Torte

DECORATIONS AND SERVING SUGGESTIONS: Concentrate on using your silver and crystal only. Place white candles in silver or crystal candlesticks of different heights and arrange on the table. Put a double old-fashioned glass filled with a votive candle at each place to create an atmosphere of warmth. Alternate silver and crystal candlesticks around your punch bowl. Fill the ice-filled silver or crystal punch bowl with splits of champagne. Tie with a velvet ribbon a pair of champagne glasses, upside down and stems crossed, to neck of each bottle. You can also use beautiful chunks of rock crystal to help decorate your table. Serve the cold soup in small glasses from a crystal pitcher and let guests help themselves.

FUN AND GAMES: Light your entire apartment or house with candles, and build a roaring fire in your fireplace. Invite guests to come in his or her favorite lounging outfit. Romantic music is a must!

Saturday Night on the Patio

24-Hour Cocktail
Avocado Crab Dip or Chutney Canapé Spread
Sirloin Tip Roast, cooked on the grill
Stuffed Potatoes   Caesar Salad
French Bread
Mocha Cake Kahlúa or Meade's Delight
Red Burgundy

Menu Ideas

Slightly Oriental

Bacon Wrapped Water Chestnuts
Chicken Breasts Piquant
or
Cen's Pork Chops, with Consommé Rice
Lima Beans in Sour Cream
Oriental Spinach Salad or Spinach and Mandarin Orange Salad
Rolls
Bananas Flambé

Slightly Eastern

Curried Shrimp or Seafood Curry
Hearts of Palm Salad
Sesame Seed Crackers, heated
Chocolate Cream Mint Pie

Slightly Greek

Avgholémono Soupa
Moussaká
Greek Salad   French Bread
Kolacky
Red Bordeaux

Slightly Southern

Avocado and Grapefruit Cocktail
Chicken with Sour Cream or Wild Rice and Chicken
French Style Green Beans
Rolls
Prune Cake or Chocolate Almond Dessert

Slightly Mexican

Avocados with Hot Cocktail Sauce
or
Bacon Wrapped Tamales (see Bacon Wraps)
Sopa Pollo
Sliced Fresh Tomatoes
Rum Pie

Country Game Dinner

Salmi of Duck or Country Smothered Venison
Stuffed Squash
Wild Rice
Spiced Peach Salad or Congealed Cranberry Salad
Rolls
Ruth's Bourbon Pie
Red Burgundy

Dinner Eden Isle

Breast of Chicken, Eden Isle
Mushroom-Stuffed Tomatoes
Green Salad with Vegetables
Angel Biscuits
Bing Cherry Parfait

Easy-Does-It Cocktail Party

The beauty of this party lies in the fact that all the food is simple to prepare or can be done ahead and frozen till party time. Mix up two cocktails, such as Martinis and Whiskey Sours, pour into pitchers or punch bowls and let guests serve themselves. See the introduction to this chapter for complete instructions for giving a cocktail party.

MENU: **Crab Meat and Ripe Olives**
or
Hot Clam Dip
Cream Cheese Consommé Mold
Poppy Seed Turnovers   Cocktail Meatballs
Cauliflowerets with Curry Dip Britton
(see Curry Dip Britton)
Assorted Relishes

For Cocktails Only

Often, a hostess entertaining with cocktails, has plans for later in the evening and does not want guests staying through the dinner hour. All the food in the following menu should be passed, so that guests cannot linger over a buffet laden with goodies. At a certain time the hostess can close the bar and stop passing hors d'oeuvres, hopefully eliminating the cocktail party guest who never knows when to depart.

MENU: **Cheese Squares**
Chipped Beef and Cream Cheese
Angels on Horseback   Sausage Hors d'Oeuvres
Stuffed Belgian Endive

One-Dish Dinner

Beef Stroganoff
or
Shrimp Creole En Bâteaux
or
Hamburger-Cheese Casserole
Mixed Green Salad
Hershey Bar Cake

At Eight

"At Eight"

Elegant Entertaining

"Come to dinner at 8 o'clock" will always have that magic ring of a treat in store . . . a convivial evening of good company, food, drink, and conversation. Your guests are thrilled to be invited, and you are charged with the responsibility of putting on "An Evening to Remember". The parties in this section can be done gracefully and successfully, even if you are bottle washer, cook, and waitress. Careful planning is the basic key to success. Assure your reputation as a host or hostess by preparing and freezing ahead as much food as possible. Carefully organize your courses and service. These precautions will help the dinner run smoothly and with apparent ease. Keep the following basic rules in mind and success is yours!

Do not invite more people than you can comfortably seat. Allow about a foot between each place setting to give the guests adequate elbow room. Set the table early, preferably the day before, so that there is no last minute silver polishing or glass washing. Remember to provide ash trays and cigarettes.

Plan the serving dishes and pieces to be used. If the dinner is being served by a waiter, this rule will make certain that he won't try to force a tea service-sized tray between the guests.

If the first course is being served at the table, there is usually a place plate with the napkin on it. After the guests sit down and remove the napkin, the plate is either taken away and replaced with a hot dinner plate or the soup course is brought in and put on top of it. To save time, slice meat in the kitchen and try to combine more than one vegetable on the same platter. Do not have long waits between dishes. There is nothing worse than sitting with a plate of congealing meat in front of you while waiting for the rice and gravy. To help eliminate serving everything at the table, have the soup and dessert passed by a maid and let the guests help themselves to the main course and vegetables from the sideboard. Pass the wine right after the meat. Otherwise you find yourself drinking wine when you have practically finished the meal. When serving more than one wine with water, place the glass for the first wine to the right of the water glass. The subsequent wine glasses are placed from right to left between the first wine glass and the water. Of course, champagne is always the most festive wine you can have at your special party, and it can also be served with every course.

Plan your seating arrangment ahead. If there are more than eight people, it is advisable to have place cards. The guest of honor sits on the right of her host, and it follows gentleman-lady all around the table. If you have a party of 8, 12, 16, etc., the hostess will have to move one place to her right. Under these circumstances, the hostess will not be seated at the foot of the table.

Be certain that the flowers on the table are low enough and do not block the flow of conversation across the table. Coffee is served at the table with dessert. Demitasse is more easily served with liqueurs on a tray away from the table. Also to make it easy for you, take a clue from this and serve your soup or first course in the living room.

Now that you have planned the perfect party, sit back, relax, and enjoy yourself!

One of the most elegant dinner parties yet is one with the enticing name "Demi-Dinner". Guests are invited for eight o'clock and are served hearty hors d'oeuvres in the living room . . . sliced roast beef on homemade rolls, chunks of lobster and crab, crudités, oysters on the half shell, etc. At ten o'clock the guests are invited into the dining room where coffee and a sumptuous array of sweets and pastries are waiting.

If your guest list is a gathering of those who see one another on a day-to-day basis, it will seldom be fascinating. Try throwing in a few people new to the area, or a couple involved in a worthy cause, or several people of varying points of view on a pressing issue. This will add certain distinction to your party (don't let it add to someone's high blood pressure). Anyway, this may jog you out of a personal chitchat rut.

A formal table setting doesn't have to be staid and stiff. Let it be as original in its way as the informal table that seems to have no limits or boundaries. Use a metallic or dark damask cloth rather than a white cloth. Mix Grandmother's antique flatware with your own up-to-date settings. Combine your china with those fascinating soup bowls picked up on one of your travels. Napkins can go most anywhere . . . in a water goblet, on a place plate, beside the forks. Practice folding or tying napkins in interesting shapes; or catch them with napkin rings.

Rehearsal Dinner

The impending marriage is an occasion for great excitement, anticipation and joy. To add to this general sense of euphoria, here are some ideas for a romantic prenuptial dinner.

INVITATIONS: Use formal engraved invitations.

MENU:

Champagne

*Marinated Oysters
Tomato Bouillon
Breast of Chicken Véronique
or *Chicken Cordon Bleu
*Herb Rice   *Broccoli with Lemon Butter
Rolls
*Crème de Menthe Bombe
or Raspberry Sherbet with Fresh Fruit Cassis

DECORATIONS AND SERVING SUGGESTIONS: Choose one basic color to be used throughout and complement this color with white; for example, yellow and white or pink and white, etc. Cover individual tables with floor length cloths of your basic color. Overlay long cloths with smaller squares of embroidered organdy or eyelet. Use white napkins and encircle them with velvet ribbon of your chosen color. Tuck a spray of lily-of-the-valley or orange blossoms into the ribbon. Use white place cards with the names written in your basic color of ink. For your centerpieces, invert a pilsener glass or wide mouthed stemmed goblet. Use floral clay to attach a small, inexpensive, green bowl to the inverted base. Soak an oasis the size of the bowl in water overnight. Place an oasis in each bowl and arrange centerpieces of fresh ivy and any flower of your choosing. A candle may be placed in the center of each oasis. The secret of this arrangement is to make certain that the bowl is covered by draping greenery. Be sure that the flame of the candle is not at eye level. To make extra seating for guests, have 48-inch round plywood circles cut to fit on top of card tables. This size table will seat six. If you want to cushion the plywood, glue white felt on the tops of the circles. Remember that many things such as tables, cloths, silver, etc. may be rented. Let strolling violinists or a pianist provide your dinner music. For additional decoration, fill the bottom of an ornate birdcage with flowers and place a pair of artificial lovebirds on the perches. Send out-of-town guests, who are immediately involved in the wedding, a list of the names of the wedding party and family. This is meant as a gracious gesture on the part of the mothers of the bride and groom to make the visitors feel more at home.

Great Lovers

This party would be a unique way to celebrate your anniversary or to honor an engaged couple. It would also be most appropriate for a Midsummer Night's fete, as this night is traditionally the most enchanted evening of the year for lovers.

INVITATIONS: On passionate pink paper write a torrid message in purple:

"Do a duet with Romeo and Juliet."

Time

Place

If you prefer, you may use a red and white invitation, since that color combination is often associated with lovers.

MENU I:
Crumbly Cheese Cookies
Mushroom Consommé
Lobster in Cardinal Sauce
or Fish in White Wine
Sautéed Asparagus   White Rice
Oriental Spinach Salad   Rolls
Frozen Lemon Cream (with sherry)
White Burgundy

MENU II:
Frosted Shrimp or Oysters Bienville
Curry Beef in Pastry
Eggplant and Tomatoes   Watercress Salad
Rolls
Chocolate Mousse
Rosé

DECORATIONS AND SERVING SUGGESTIONS: Create a romantic centerpiece of pink sweetheart roses and violets. Nestle purple napkins in goblets and insert nosegays of violets for the ladies. The color scheme for your decorations, like the invitations, may be changed to suit your own taste.

FUN AND GAMES: Match personalities of your guests to famous lovers. Make a tag naming one famous lover for each guest; pin this tag on the back of each person without letting him or her see the name written on it. Your guests can ask each person at the party three questions about himself or herself in hopes of finding out the identity of his or her famous lover. Your guests cannot be seated for dinner unless they know who they are. Place cards correspond to the names of the famous lovers written on your guests' tags. No fair husbands and wives being matched pairs!

Over the Limit

This game dinner could be served at Thanksgiving or Christmas, and would also be ideal for a bachelor's dinner or a husband's birthday. A dinner to make Tom Jones himself sit up and take notice!

INVITATIONS: No formal invitations are necessary and guests may be called on the telephone.

MENU:

Celery Soup
Chopped Oysters
Two Ducks or Quail in Grape Leaves or Pheasant
Mother's Cranberry Jelly or Cranberry-Horseradish Sauce
Buttered Peas and Pearl Onions
or
Green Beans with Water Chestnuts and Almonds
Consommé Rice
Hearts of Palm Salad
Rolls
Ruby Fruit with Mock Devonshire Cream
Chablis, Red Bordeaux or Red Burgundy

DECORATIONS AND SERVING SUGGESTIONS: Centerpieces: (1) Saw a circular piece out of the top of an understanding husband's heavy papier mâché decoy. Anchor a needlepoint flower holder inside with floral clay, and fill the make-believe waterfowl with gold and bronze chrysanthemums, reeds, or dried grass. (2) Fill copper or brass containers with beige strawflowers interspersed with cattails. (3) Place quail or any game bird figurine on the table with the centerpiece. If you have dinner plates or a platter featuring game birds (or perhaps a gravy boat or decanter in the shape of a duck), they would be handsome additions to the dining table. In place of a plain tablecloth, use one patterned with game birds; or drape the table with orange felt and use a centerpiece of pheasant feathers and yellow mums. Serve soup in mugs in the living room.

A teacart can assume many roles when you entertain. Let it be a traveling bar (the mountain came to Mohammed), a clearing cart for whisking away empty plates and glasses, or an extra side "table" from which the hostess serves coffee and dessert in the living room.

The Overture

There are two distinct and very different types of opera suppers. The first is a light meal for those going to the opera . . . the other is a combination of a Christmas dinner, Thanksgiving, a Greek wedding, an Italian funeral, and a world-wide meeting of the Chevaliers des Tastevins! Our elaborate after-the-opera feast is on the following page. The menus below are simply light overtures suitable for the gala evening ahead. They would serve well as suppers preceding not only the opera, but also the opening night of the theatre or the symphony season as well.

INVITATIONS: Because of the early hour and necessity of arriving on time at the special event, we suggest limiting this party to a small group and either sending your informals as invitations or calling your guests.

MENU I:

Champagne
Ham Mousse
Cold Marinated Vegetables
Cheese Squares
Petits Choux

MENU II:

***Champagne**
***Salmon Mousse, with Avocado Dressing**
***Garnishment of Fresh Vegetables and Hard-Cooked Eggs**
***Cheese Squares**
***Glazed Fruit Tartlets**

DECORATIONS AND SERVING SUGGESTIONS: Gear your decorations to the theme of the event you are going to see. For example, if the opera is "Madame Butterfly", run an obi down the center of your table and use Oriental arrangements such as Fuji mums and cherry blossoms. For "Carmen", create a Spanish atmosphere. For "La Traviata", float camellias in compotes. You may wish to be simpler by using a centerpiece of fresh flowers in a silver bowl. Because of the necessary brevity of this party, elaborate decorations are unnecessary. The menu is intentionally light to keep guests from falling asleep during the second act! And the dessert is such that it may be eaten on the run to make curtain time.

The Encore

"If music be the food of love, play on." There is just no way to have enough —or fine enough—food for opera stars. Most singers, whether or not their figures reflect it, are truly gourmets, and occasionally gourmands. Some are even exceptional and inventive cooks. Happily, they are usually very appreciative people. This after-the-opera supper is a celebration of sorts. Besides running the gamut of one's kitchen capabilities, it requires your old silver polished, bucket loads of fresh flowers, many candles, champagne, and a mood of elegance and gaiety.

INVITATIONS: (1) Send formal invitations. (2) Use libretto or program or blank music score sheet as invitation. Invitation reads: "Maestro and Mistress _____ Command your Presence at _____ Curtain Time _____."

MENU:

Champagne
Beluga Caviar
Honeydew Melon Wrapped in Prosciutto
Chicken Liver Mousse   Fresh Lobster Salad
Sliced Tenderloin of Beef with Béarnaise Sauce
(see Béarnaise Sauce)
Fresh Mushrooms in Garlic Butter
Creamed Shrimp and Artichoke Bottoms
Crudités with Curry Mayonnaise
French Bread   Imported Cheeses
Wine-Frosted Grapes   Strawberries Puccini   Mocha Cake

DECORATIONS AND SERVING SUGGESTIONS: Decorate according to the theme of the opera or play just seen. Don't spare the candlelight, and match the color of the candles to your linen, china, and flowers. **Centerpiece suggestions:** (1) Place spring flowers or roses in silver containers and arrange in the center of your table. (2) Incorporate a black silk top hat with white gloves, libretto, or a musical instrument into your table decorations.

Here is the first rule for the host-bartender: Stay on your feet, bright eyed and coherent. For parties, a temporary bar arrangement is usually preferable. For larger groups, place a good sized table—round or oblong—at one end of the room, but away from the wall so that you can stand behind it when bartending. This allows guests plenty of room to move up for refills.

Bon Voyage–For Travelers Going West

Le grand tour calls for this delightful party to further the anticipation of a long-awaited visit to the Continent.

INVITATIONS: Fold a 4 x 6-inch piece of heavy paper to resemble a passport and write message inside. Funny pictures of the traveling twosome could be pasted inside each "passport".

MENU:

Jellied Beef Consommé
(Consommé Gelée de Boeuf)
Veal Birds with Noodles and Green Peas
(Paupiettes de Veau et Nouilles avec Petits Pois)
French Bread
(Pain Francais)

Raspberry Mousse	or	Fresh Peaches in Champagne
(Mousse aux Framboises)		**(Pêches en Champagne)**

Red Bordeaux or Beaujolais

DECORATIONS AND SERVING SUGGESTIONS: Centerpiece: (1) A weathervane decorated at the base with boxwood or greenery. (2) A container of vivid flowers native to a European country i.e. tulips. **Place cards:** Border white cards with narrow ribbon in same colors as ribbons wrapping napkins. Tie napkins with a variety of striped grosgrain ribbons in flag colors of European countries. (For example, red-white-blue for France; green-red-white for Italy, etc.) Menu cards for the dining table are written in French and sit on a small easel.

FUN AND GAMES: Gifts for the voyager are pre-addressed post cards to be sent to friends. Ask each guest to bring a useful, small, amusing gift for the honoree to use while on the trip (sea sickness pills, aspirin, a calorie guide).

Watch for foods that are seasonal. It would be disappointing to plan a menu, buy most of the ingredients and then have everything fall to pieces because one item is out-of-season.

Bon Voyage—For Travelers Going East

An elaborate and authentic Oriental evening gives the honored guests and their friends a taste of what exotica is in store for them on a Far Eastern shore. The guest list should be limited to eight because of the nature of the food and its service.

INVITATIONS: Obtain small kites or parasols at an import or party store. Glue them to a card on which party information is written.

MENU:
Oriental Crab Balls
Corn Soup
Sweet and Sour Pork or Pork with Celery
or Sweet and Sour Beef Balls
Loquat Chicken or Walnut Chicken
Barbecued Ribs (see Barbecue Sauce)
Shrimp Foo Young
Chinese Fried Rice
Whale Melon, filled with Melon Balls in Wine
or Hong Kong Sundae

DECORATIONS AND SERVING SUGGESTIONS: Start your Oriental party right at the door by greeting guests with incense in the air. Place flowers around the house rather than on the dining table since there are a large number of serving dishes to be placed on the table. Use Fuji mums or flowering branches of blooms set in pebble-lined containers. Furnish kimonos and scuff-type slippers for guests. A low, round dining table and pillows on the floor to sit on are an authentic touch. Rice bowls, sake cups, obis, and chopsticks also add an Oriental flavor. The soup can either be served in the living room before dinner European style or can be eaten all through the meal Oriental fashion. In front of each guest are several small plates and a small bowl for the rice, which is eaten with a spoon. The other food is picked up with chopsticks. Good luck! Warm rice wine (sake) or hot tea is drunk throughout the meal and is a necessary accompaniment to the food. Pass scented rolled towels at the end of the meal. Scent the towels with jasmine, cologne, or after shave lotion. If you wish to serve a simpler dessert than these suggested above, skewer melon balls on wooden Oriental skewers available in variety or import stores. **Note:** To increase an Oriental recipe, make it twice; never double.

Hunting House Party

When your friends gather at your doorstep for a week end of hunting or merely congenial conviviality, welcome them graciously with these ideas for the perfect house party.

INVITATIONS: Invite your guests via a long distance phone call or a telegram.

Friday Night

Artichoke Bottoms with Cream Cheese and Caviar
Roast Veal with Sour Cream
Tomatoes Filled with Soufflé (Cheese)
Green Beans with Water Chestnuts
Bibb Salad
Rolls
Coffee Mousse or Crushed Toffee Meringue
Red Bordeaux

Saturday and Sunday Breakfast

Blueberry-Orange Muffins　　Banana Muffins
Turkey Hash　　Eggs　　Sausage
Individual Packets of Cereal
Basket of Fruits (Bananas, Grapefruit, Melon, Pears)
Fruit Juices　　Coffee

Saturday Noon

Black Bean Soup (with condiments)
Cheese Platter with Pumpernickel　　Fresh Fruit
Beer

Saturday Night

Cheese Wafers
Beef Tenderloin
Mushroom Pie　　Broccoli Soufflé
Rolls
Raspberry Bombe
Red Burgundy

Sunday Noon

California Tacos or Chili
Red Cabbage Slaw or Chinese Cabbage Salad
Pecan Apple Tartlets

DECORATIONS AND SERVING SUGGESTIONS: Place a small posy of flowers, two individual nut and fruit bowls, and a carafe of water in each guest bedroom to welcome them at their arrival. Put large fruit arrangements and nut bowls for nibbling in your den and living room. Decorate your house throughout by arranging autumn leaves and fall flowers in wooden or copper containers. Pheasant or other feathers will give these arrangements extra height and beauty. Create a centerpiece for your dining room table using fruit or vegetables which will last the entire week end. Refer to our game dinner for other ideas for a centerpiece.

For the early rising hunters, provide a kitchen counter laden with a hearty help-yourself breakfast in full trappings: coffee and tea in silver pots, turkey hash in a handsome silver server, sausages on a hot tray, and an electric skillet and a bowl of eggs for enterprising guests who want to cook their own. For the ladies who want to get their beauty sleep, provide a "ready-when-you-are" breakfast of muffins, individual packets of cereal, a basket of fruits and fruit juices.

Hints for the thoughtful hostess: Make up a schedule of events such as the hour of the hunt, mealtimes, cocktail hour, etc., and place a copy in each guest's room. For the avid morning coffee drinkers, have a coffee pot filled and ready to plug in on a small tray with cups, sugar, and non-dairy creamer in each guest's room. Be certain that you have a well-stocked guest bathroom providing dusting powder, bath oil, shower cap, aspirin, Alka Seltzer, a new toothbrush, safety pins and fresh soap.

The Fabulous Forties

Forty is as forty does . . . since forty is a state of mind. Help a friend pass this milestone, or millstone, however you choose to view it, with a gentle ribbing and a celebration dinner.

INVITATIONS: Send white invitations bordered with black. Write party information in black ink.

MENU:
Cheese Puffs (with olives)
Spinach Soup
Crown Roast of Pork with Cranberry-Apple Relish
Whipped Potatoes
Asparagus, Petit Pois, and Mushroom Casserole
Rolls
Ice Cream Balls   Birthday Cake
White Burgundy or Vin Rosé

DECORATIONS AND SERVING SUGGESTIONS: Decorate your table with a black and white color scheme. For your centerpiece, have the florist create a floral "fountain of youth" using white flowers. Flank your centerpiece with silver candelabra holding black candles. Use white place cards bordered with black. Instead of using names, write each guest's birth date on the place card in black ink. Give each guest who has already reached his or her fortieth birthday a gold crown as he or she arrives at the party. Those under forty receive nothing! Ask all guests to bring funny gifts to the honoree. The honoree can also turn the table and surprise everyone else by arriving in mourning garb, carrying an enormous bouquet of dead flowers.

For seated dinners in your home, renew the practice of using place plates. And rather than removing them with the soup course, leave them through-out the meal. Place plates may be silver, china, wood, stainless steel, or even decorative tinware. Rummage through the attic . . . Victorian cake plates, once a part of china coffee sets, make fine place plates. What you use depends upon your table setting and your whims.

Happy Easter

This joyful day, one which families traditionally spend together, calls for a dinner party including all the family, from grandparents to the smallest children.

INVITATIONS: Paste appropriate, gay, wrapping paper on folded colored cardboard or construction paper with the wrapping paper edge at the folded edge of the cardboard. Cut out Easter eggs so that a hinge is at the top of each egg. On the inside write party information, telling children to bring their Easter baskets.

MENU:

Cucumber Hors d'Oeuvres

Bacon-Cheese Rolls

*Roast Leg of Lamb with Rosemary

or Swedish Leg of Lamb

Chutney Peaches

Tomatoes Stuffed with Speedy Spinach,

Garnished with Bacon Curls

Butter-Steamed New Potatoes

Rolls

Cherries Jubilee or Frozen Orange Cups

*Ice Cream Filled Easter Eggs (for the children)

Red Bordeaux

*Photograph featured in "Our Parties" Section.

DECORATIONS AND SERVING SUGGESTIONS: Centerpiece: Place a pyramid of stone eggs of various hues in a tureen or basket. Tuck French violets between each layer of eggs and perch a butterfly on the topmost egg. Have an Easter egg hunt for the small ones before serving dinner. Give prizes for the child finding the most eggs and the golden egg. The adults can enjoy their cocktails during the egg hunt.

For special bunny napkins, lightly spray-starch and iron a square white dinner napkin. Fold diagonally and spray and iron again. Draw creased corners up for ears. Holding ears about 4 inches from points, bring up triangle point and fold forward to form face. Tie ribbon bow around "neck" below folded "face". Fill the base with goodies, if you like.

The children's dessert is an ice cream Easter egg made in plastic eggs that halve. Press softened ice cream into each half of egg and level off. Press halves together and freeze. To serve, dip top half of plastic egg in hot water and remove. Place plastic end of egg in an egg cup and serve one to each child. Ice cream may be sprinkled with jelly beans or colored coconut (made by stirring a few drops of food coloring into coconut).

Traditional Thanksgiving Dinner

Raise your own song of harvest home as you gather your dear ones close to the hearth's glow, and celebrate with this feast, the bounties of the year past. Thanksgiving can be made even more special by including at your gathering someone who may be far from home and family on this special day.

INVITATIONS: Since this dinner is designed primarily as a family affair, no formal invitations are necessary.

MENU: Clarence Moody's Holiday Punch
Cream of Clam Soup
*Roast Turkey in Foil   *Sausage-Pecan Dressing
Baked Ham with Raisin Sauce
(see Raisin Sauce)
Oysters Diablo or *Rosie's Oyster Casserole
Sweet Potato Balls   Stuffed Squash
*Green Vegetables with Sauce
*Cranberry-Apple Mold
Hot Rolls
Pumpkin Chiffon Pie   Easy Rum Cake
White Burgundy

DECORATIONS AND SERVING SUGGESTIONS: Decorate your front door with Indian corn. Use an ecru or white cutwork table-cloth with an undercloth of bittersweet. If the dinner is to be given at night, include candlelight with your table decorations. Fill your home with the scent of Clarence Moody's Holiday Punch. **Center-piece suggestions:** (1) Create a harvest of frosted fresh fruit placed on a large silver platter. Around an upright pineapple, mound tangerines, green and yellow apples, black and green grapes, and kumquats. To frost the fruit: Slightly whip egg whites; brush egg whites on the fruit with a pastry brush and let dry slightly. Sprinkle fruit with granulated sugar. Dry completely. (2) Have your favorite florist create a floral turkey out of feathers and flowers. (3) Hollow out a pumpkin and fill with frosted fruit. Surround the base of the pumpkin with garlands of mums and fall leaves. (4) Puncture a pumpkin at random with an ice pick. Make sure the ice pick enters at an angle and not straight in. Place small button mums in all the holes in the pumpkin, pushing stems all the way in so that only the flower head shows. Surround the base with additional flowers.

Dinner on Christmas Eve

On Christmas Eve a magical warmth spreads from a reddening hearth and a busy kitchen and descends on the home where loved ones gather to share gifts and a feast. Candles flicker, children giggle, grown-ups visit, and the absent and faraway cousins are phoned. The year's new crop of babies experiences its first Noël.

INVITATIONS: (1) Use dark green informals trimmed in silver; write information and address in white ink. (2) Use your best personal stationery. Seal invitations with legal seal or sealing wax.

MENU: ***Clarence Moody's Holiday Punch**
*Volcano Cheese Ball
Oyster Stew
Standing Rib Roast with Potatoes Romanov
*Quail Stuffed with Rice
Green Beans with Water Chestnuts
Cranberry Mold   **Rolls**
Eggnog Mousse or Mincemeat Pie with Rum Sauce
or
Syllabub
Red Bordeaux

*Photograph featured in "Our Parties" Section.

DECORATIONS AND SERVING SUGGESTIONS: Use a white damask or lace cloth. Put very small ornaments in boxes; wrap each box in silver foil and tie with green velvet bows. Tag each box with a guest's name and use as place cards. Put green candles in your best silver candelabra and arrange on your table.

Centerpiece: For a base use a block of Styrofoam inconspicuously set in a low bowl. Implant a graceful branch, sprayed white, in the base. Trim the boughs with crystal prisms, silver balls tied with small green velvet bows, tiny tinkling silver bells, and a sprinkling of silver stars. Make a "mountain" of rock candy to conceal your base.

Ladle eggnog, if you wish to serve it, into brandy snifters or mugs from a sugar crystal-ringed punch bowl. This is made by slightly whipping egg white and brushing it on rim of bowl. Dust rim with colored sugar crystals and let dry. Build a roaring fire, if you're fortunate enough to possess a fireplace, and toss a handful of hickory chips into the flames. Hickory logs set on warm floor furnace grates produce the same heady odor.

If you are tired of the usual New Year's bash or Fourth of July barbecue, here is an around-the-world tour of exotic places for a group of good friends. For a touch of mystery, no one knows who is giving the party!

MENU: **Martini Bowl   Manhattan Bowl**
                   Cream Cheese-Caviar Mold
                          Antipasto
                        Diane's Curry
Sacher Torte   Mazarin Torte   Wine-Frosted Grapes
                     Viennese Coffee

INVITATIONS: Create an "around-the-world" balloon using colored construction paper. Cut out five graduated circles using a different color for each circle and staple them together at the top. Make the basket from a burlap square and suspend from the largest circle with two strands of bright yarn. On the smallest circle write "Surprise!"; on the next largest circle write the following poem:
> Since you wouldn't think of this yourselves,
> We had to plan it for you,
> And think highly enough of you ourselves
> To know that this is what you'll do.
> At random have we parts assigned,
> So be a sport and stay resigned.

The next circle holds the schedule of events:
  (7:00)   Set sail from the "Burton's" on a luxury liner.
           Bon voyage and cocktails; nothing could be finer.
  (8:00)   Have some of the "Pucci's" antipasto at port No. I
           And soon you'll feel that Mediterranean sun.
  (9:00)   Farther east we'll travel for the "Aga Khan's" exotic curry.
           Take a lesson from the Indians, relish this and don't hurry.
  (10:00) We'll go to "Suzy Wong's" to end the day
           And celebrate the New Year the Chinese way.

On the next circle write the following:
> It has been decided in a bus we must load,
> To keep everyone off the road.
> This is a must . . . .
> Please cooperate.
> Parking and timing
> It will facilitate.

Park your car at the (name) at 6:30 time;
Get right on the bus and forget the wine.
As they are our hosts much later that eve,
When it's time to go home in your car you can leave.
On the last circle list the guests.

DECORATIONS AND SERVING SUGGESTIONS: First house:
The bus is a luxury liner filled with travel posters of foreign lands.
The first port of call is New York City. Line your walk with hurri-
cane lamps holding signs of famous New York bars, or hang the
signs over the doorways in your home. For atmosphere keep the
lights low and the music muted. Convert your table into a bar by
covering it with a shiny black plastic cloth and setting candelabra
at each end. At this "bon voyage" party serve Martinis and Manhattans from punch bowls placed on the table.
Second house: Disembark for Italy. Hang tambourines and red,
green, and white streamers on your doors. Serve the antipasto from
your table which has been covered with Florentine paper and swags
of fabric and gold cord. Gold candelabra and bunches of grapes
artistically arranged also help accentuate the feeling of Italy. Decorate a tea cart with boxwood and red, green, and white streamers
and load it with flowers (one for each lady).
Third house: Journey onward for your main course of East Indian
curry. Create a mosque at the doorway. Cut shape you desire out
of butcher paper and paint it in mosaic shapes. Stream this entrance with hanging beads and brass bells. Make low tables by
placing boards on bricks and cover them with paisley or tiger print
fabric. (Madras bedspreads make good tablecloths.) Surround the
tables with lavish cushions, enabling your guests to lounge around
and eat leisurely. String marigolds, chrysanthemums, or a combination of colored flowers and place in serpentine lines on the tables.
The flowered "leis" are made by stringing flowers back to back
with an upholstery needle and dental floss. These can be made two
days ahead and refrigerated. Intersperse with Divas (clay lamps
used in Divali, India) or "Aladdin lamps" filled with candles. At
each place put a tangerine, lemon, or lime studded at random with
cloves and topped by a hatpin holding a place card. Burn incense
and, if available, use Indian toe rings for napkin rings. Additional
table decorations may include small ivory elephants, peacocks, and
a liberal use of brass. Place appropriate horoscope books at each
guest's place and let each read aloud his or her horoscope for that
day. For added entertainment provide a Ouija board and a "guru"
(palmist or fortune teller).
Fourth house: Next on the itinerary is a visit to Vienna. Music fills
the air as your guests arrive and they can imagine waltzing to the
violin strings of the Viennese masters. Cover your table with lace
and set it to resemble the Baroque opulence of the old empire. Place

the sweets on cut crystal and silver tiered holders. If you have any white china or fine porcelain horses, arrange them in the center of your table to resemble the famous Lipizanner horses of Vienna. Place a large bowl of whipped cream on the table to accompany your sweets and the strongly brewed Viennese coffee. Serve coffee in demitasse cups, top with whipped cream and dust with nutmeg. **Fifth house:** The voyagers will usher in the New Year at their final port of call . . . Chinatown. Attach the animal of the New Year to the front door. Decorate with Japanese lanterns and paper fish. Fill a lacquer bowl with fortune cookies. Ward off the evil spirits and celebrate the New Year with a dazzling display of fireworks, sparklers, and firecrackers. For those men who feel the need for extra protection against the evil spirits, provide sprigs of juniper to pin to their lapels. All long sea voyages are apt to result in a touch of mal de mer. The wise hostess will put a tray in the entry on which individual packets of Alka Seltzer, wrapped and tied with ribbon, have been placed.

Veal Dinner

Mushrooms Stuffed with Crab Meat
Veal Vernon
Petits Pois Filled Peppers   Roquefort Tomatoes
Rolls
Peach Crisp or Crème Brûlée
Red Burgundy or Beaujolais

Cornish Game Hen Dinner

Sherried Crab Soup
Cornish Game Hens in Salt Clay
or
Cornish Game Hens with Wild Rice Stuffing
Vegetables with Mustard Sauce   Far East Celery
Bibb Lettuce with Caper and Egg Dressing
Rolls
Lemon Charlotte Russe
White Burgundy or Light Red Bordeaux

Menu Ideas

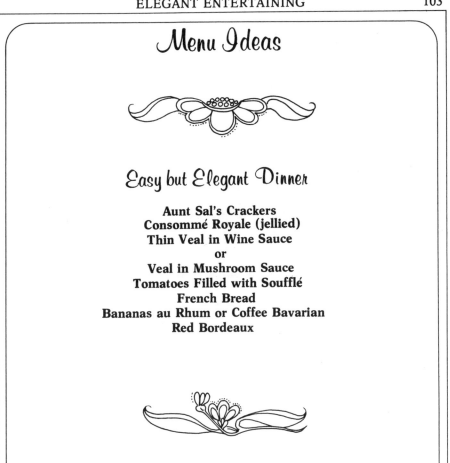

Easy but Elegant Dinner

Aunt Sal's Crackers
Consommé Royale (jellied)
Thin Veal in Wine Sauce
or
Veal in Mushroom Sauce
Tomatoes Filled with Soufflé
French Bread
Bananas au Rhum or Coffee Bavarian
Red Bordeaux

Mrs. Snowden Boyle's Dinner

Consommé
Dry Sherry

Fish Quenelles
White Burgundy

Tournedos Heloise
Fresh English Peas   Braised Celery
Red Burgundy

Rolls
Hot Apricot Soufflé

Dinner for Six

Marinated Ripe Olives
Consommé Royale
Lamb Chops Béarnaise with Green Minted Pears
Mushrooms Stuffed with Spinach   Potato Voisettes
Sesame Seed Rolls
Miss Hill's Apricot Soufflé or Chocolate Soufflé
Red Bordeaux or Beaujolais

Beef Wellington Dinner

Stuffed Artichoke Bottoms
Beef Wellington
Tomatoes with Peas   Mushrooms in Garlic Butter
Rolls
Baked Alaska in Pineapple Shells
or
Grapes with Brown Sugar Crust
Red Burgundy

Recipes

"Recipes"

Appetizers and Canapes

ANTIPASTO

Hard-boiled eggs, quartered
Artichoke hearts, rolled in olive
  oil and a little sugar
Quartered tomatoes
Cocktail tomatoes, rolled in olive
  oil and a little sugar
Olives: black, green, Greek
Sardines
Smoked salmon (or any smoked,
  canned fish)
Tuna fish
Spring onions
Radishes
Anchovies

Marinated mushrooms (marinate
  in Good Seasons Italian
  Dressing)
Green peppers: Bake in oven until
  skin blisters—cool, peel off
  skin; seed, devein; cut in
  manageable pieces, coat with
  olive oil in which salt has been
  dissolved
Hard salami, cut thin and rolled up
Prosciutto, cut thin and wrapped
  around thin slices of melon or
  fresh figs
Pickled shrimp
Pimientoes

Use a sectioned platter and select 6 or 8 of the above. Pass this as a first course, and let everyone select what he wants. When making the selection, keep in mind the color and texture of the food. A good combination would be: (1) hard-boiled eggs (2) tomatoes (3) artichoke hearts (4) black olives (5) sardines (6) mushrooms.

MRS. JAMES W. WRAPE, COLLIERVILLE, TENN.

CRUDITÉS

Behold this great mound of nature's handiwork . . . a delicious sight for the eye and treat for the palate.

Assorted raw vegetables
Head red cabbage

Curry Mayonnaise (see Index) or
Curry Dip Britton (see Index)

SUGGESTED FRESH VEGETABLES: Cherry tomatoes, yellow squash, cauliflower, carrots, celery hearts, small mushrooms, cucumbers, tiny beets, raw asparagus tips, giant pimiento-stuffed olives, radish "flowers", giant black olives. Cut or arrange vegetables in attractive serving shapes, such as: cauliflower broken into flowerets; carrot curls; celery stalks, leafy end left on; squash cut diagonally or left whole if very tiny; unpeeled scored cucumbers, cut diagonally; whole cherry tomatoes, beets and mushrooms. Hollow out center of well-shaped cabbage. Gently spread outer leaves (it should resemble a giant rose). Fill cavity with dip and surround with arrangements of raw vegetables (or toss vegetables at random for a mixed "bouquet").

VEGETABLES WITH SOUR CREAM DRESSING

Vegetables:

1 head cauliflower	Sharp French dressing
1 can artichoke hearts	

Separate cauliflower into flowerets and cook in boiling, salted water till just done. Drain and cool. Drain artichokes well. Marinate cauliflower and artichokes in French dessing at least 2 hours.

Sour Cream Dressing:

¼ c. sour cream	½ clove of garlic, crushed
½ c. mayonnaise	2 T. vinegar
1½ t. anchovy paste	1½ t. lemon juice
2 T. parsley flakes	Salt and pepper to taste

Combine above ingredients to make dressing. Drain French dressing from vegetables and arrange vegetables on a platter. Sprinkle vegetables with thinly sliced spring onions and paprika. Spear vegetables with toothpicks and dip in Sour Cream Dressing.

MRS. F. PEARSON ALLEN, JR.

SUNBURST ARTICHOKE

1 large fresh artichoke	1 t. Worcestershire
1 c. mayonnaise	3 hard-cooked eggs
2 t. dry mustard	

Cook artichoke in boiling water about 30 minutes and drain. Chill; then pull off leaves and trim off pointed ends. Mix mayonnaise, dry mustard and Worcestershire. Cut hard-cooked eggs into thin wedges. Place a dab of dressing at the base end of each leaf. Top mayonnaise with egg wedge. Arrange the leaves sunburst fashion on a large platter. Center platter with a bunch of fresh parsley. (Be sure to provide a receptacle for "eaten" leaves.) **Variation:** Following above instructions for cooking and arranging artichoke leaves, substitute Curry Dip Britton for above dressing and top with a tiny cooked shrimp.

MRS. JAMES GUY ROBBINS

STUFFED BELGIAN ENDIVE

Belgian endive will keep in a cool place for over a week and may have to be ordered from the grocer. Separate and stuff it as you would celery hearts. Mix cream cheese and bleu cheese; season to taste and thin with a little cream. Arrange on round trays like a flower.

MRS. J. B. INGLEHEART, EVANSVILLE, IND.

AUNT SAL'S CRACKERS

1 box Triscuit crackers	Bottled lemon-pepper marinade
1 stick butter	

Spread butter on crackers and sprinkle with lemon-pepper marinade. Heat in 350° oven until hot. Serve as hors d'oeuvres or with soup.

MRS. RONALD BYRNES

STUFFED COCKTAIL TOMATOES

½ lb. crab meat, picked and
  cleaned
½ c. finely diced celery
¼ c. grated onion

Salt and pepper to taste
Mayonnaise
40 cocktail tomatoes

Thoroughly mix crab meat, celery, onion, salt and pepper. Add enough mayonnaise to make mixture a thick paste. Wash and cap tomatoes. Cut out the inside of each tomato and fill with crab meat mixture. Arrange on tray and garnish with parsley. **Variations:** These may also be filled with tuna or chicken salad, or seasoned cream cheese (pipe through a cake decorator for ease in filling). Makes 40.

MARINATED RIPE OLIVES

1 can pitted ripe olives   1 small bottle Worcestershire

Drain olives. Place in a jar and cover with Worcestershire. Marinate in refrigerator for three days. Pour sauce off and serve.

MRS. J. T. MURFF, JR.

CHEESE STRAWS

3 c. sifted flour
1 lb. Cheddar cheese
2 sticks butter
1 T. paprika

½ t. celery salt
½ t. garlic salt
3 dashes Worcestershire
10 dashes Tabasco

Sift flour. Grate cheese. Set out butter and cheese to soften. Mix all ingredients. Using half of dough at a time, roll out ¼-inch thick between sheets of waxed paper. Cut into 1 x 3-inch strips, or put dough through a cookie press. Bake in 400° oven for 10 minutes on ungreased cookie sheet. Freezes well. Makes about 80.

MRS. T. GRIMES SNOWDEN

CRUMBLY CHEESE COOKIES

2 sticks soft oleo
2 c. flour
2 c. grated sharp Cheddar cheese

2 c. Rice Krispies
Red pepper

Mix and form balls; flatten slightly with fork. Bake at 375° for 10-12 minutes. Makes 50 small "cookies".

MRS. RALPH HON

SALAMI CHIPS

Salami, sliced wafer thin   Grated Parmesan cheese

Arrange salami slices on cookie sheet; sprinkle each slice lightly with cheese. Bake at 350° for 8 minutes. Drain on paper towels. Serve warm.

MRS. JAMES GUY ROBBINS

CHEESE WAFERS

1 lb. sharp Cheddar cheese (grated)	1 t. salt
½ c. butter	Dash red pepper
1½ c. flour	4 T. water
1 t. baking powder	Paprika

Grate cheese and mix well with softened butter (use hands). Sift dry ingredients, add to cheese and butter mixture. Add water and mix well. Pinch off bite-size pieces and shape into biscuits or roll dough ⅛-¼-inch thick and cut with biscuit cutter. Sprinkle with paprika. Bake in 400° oven about 15 minutes or until done. Dough freezes well before baking. **Variations:** Dough can be seasoned with Worcestershire or Tabasco. Chopped pecans may be added to dough. A salted pecan or pimiento stuffed olive can be placed in center of each cookie before baking. Makes 5-6 dozen.

MEMPHIS DAIRY COUNCIL

CUCUMBER HORS D'OEUVRES

1 cucumber, sliced	1 box onion round crackers
2 c. vinegar	Sour cream or homemade
½ c. olive oil	mayonnaise
1 t. seasoned pepper	Paprika
1 t. salt	

Marinate cucumber in mixture of vinegar, olive oil, pepper and salt for at least 6 hours. Put a little sour cream or mayonnaise on each cracker, top with drained cucumber slice and sprinkle with paprika. Makes about 30.

MRS. ROBERT C. BURLEIGH, JR.

ANGELS ON HORSEBACK

1 lb. bacon	2 12-oz. jars fresh oysters
2 oz. tube anchovy paste	

Cut bacon strips in two. Spread strips sparingly with anchovy paste. Wrap around oysters and secure with toothpicks. Broil until done. Drain. Yield: 3 dozen.

MRS. ALLEN COX, JR.

BROILED SHRIMP

1 lb. shrimp	½ c. melted butter
3 T. lemon juice	Salt
Red pepper	Paprika

Clean and peel shrimp. Split each shrimp down the back and place on baking sheet. Mix lemon juice, butter and seasonings and baste shrimp. Cook in oven at 400° for 8 minutes then turn to broil and place shrimp under broiler. May be passed with toothpicks or placed in chafing dish.

MRS. McDONALD THRASHER

CHEESE SQUARES

2 5-oz. jars Old English cheese
1½ sticks butter
1 egg

1 loaf unsliced bread
Paprika

Let cheese and butter come to room temperature. Blend together with well beaten egg. Trim crust from bread and cut into 1½-inch squares. Ice 5 sides of cubes with cheese mixture. Sprinkle with paprika. Bake at 350° for 10 minutes. Can be frozen now, baked later. Serve as an hors d'oeuvre or as an accompaniment for an aspic or mousse. Makes approximately 12 dozen.

MRS. THOMAS F. JOHNSTON

CHEESE TURNOVERS

1 jar Old English cheese
¼ lb. butter
1 c. sifted flour

2 T. cold water
Orange marmalade

Cut cheese and butter into flour. Mix with cold water. Shape into a ball and refrigerate overnight. Roll out dough very thin. Cut into 2-inch circles. Put scant ½ teaspoon of marmalade in center of circle, fold over edge and mash edges together with a fork. Bake at 375° for 10 minutes. Keep in covered tin. They freeze beautifully after being baked. Reheat before serving. Makes 2 to 3 dozen.

MRS. ROSS LYNN

EMPANDITOS
(Jamaican Patties)

PASTRY:
1 c. butter
2 3-oz. pkgs. cream cheese

2 c. flour

Cream the butter and cream cheese. Blend in flour and shape into ball. Wrap in wax paper and refrigerate overnight. Thirty minutes before using, take out of refrigerator. Flour board heavily. Roll the dough thin and cut with round cutter. Place a small spoon of filling on round. Moisten edges with water, fold over and press with fork. Bake on ungreased sheet for 12-15 minutes at 350° until bottom is golden. These may be frozen before baking. Allow 30 minutes to thaw and cook about 5 minutes longer. You may bake them before the party and keep warm until used. Makes 4½ dozen small meat pies.

FILLING:
½ lb. ground beef
½ c. chopped onion
3 T. chopped green pepper
Salt, pepper to taste
1½ t. garlic powder

3 T. chili powder
1 T. Worcestershire
½ t. Accent
½ c. tomato paste
1 bay leaf

Brown beef in skillet. Add onion and green pepper and cook till tender. Add remaining ingredients and simmer 10 minutes longer.

MRS. R. HENRY LAKE, HOUSTON, TEX.

CHEESE PUFFS

2 c. grated sharp cheese
½ c. butter
1 c. sifted flour
1 t. paprika
Dash of cayenne

½ t. salt
50 small stuffed green olives,
pearl onions or 35 pitted
dates

Blend cheese with soft butter. Stir in flour and seasonings which have been sifted together. Mix well. Wrap 1 teaspoon cheese mixture around each olive or onion, covering it completely (dates take more than 1 teaspoon). Arrange on a baking sheet and chill (or freeze) till firm. Bake at 400° for 15 minutes. Serve hot. Makes 50 puffs.

MRS. JAMES GUY ROBBINS

CHEESE-BACON PUFFS

2 eggs
1 c. finely grated Cheddar
cheese
2 t. grated onion or onion juice

½ t. dry mustard
6 slices white bread
24 (1-inch) bacon squares

Preheat oven to 375° In small bowl beat eggs with fork. Add grated cheese, onion, and dry mustard; stir until well blended. Trim crust from bread; cut each slice into quarters, making 24 squares in all. Arrange in shallow baking pan. Spoon a heaping teaspoonful of cheese mixture in center of each bread square. Top each with a square of uncooked bacon. Bake until bread is toasted and topping is slightly puffed, about 20 minutes. Makes 2 dozen.

MRS. JAMES GUY ROBBINS

BACON-CHEESE ROLLS

Thinly sliced white bread
1 jar pasteurized processed
sharp cheese spread

Bacon

Preheat oven to 400°. Trim crusts from bread; cut slices into 4 strips, then spread each with cheese spread. Roll up each bread strip; then wrap with ⅓ slice of bacon, and secure with a toothpick. Place roll-ups on cookie sheet and bake 10 minutes or until bacon is partially cooked. Remove from oven; cool; then wrap in foil and freeze. To serve: Open package of frozen roll-ups just enough to expose tops. Then bake at 400° for 10-12 minutes or until bacon is crisp and bread is golden.

MRS. TED LEWIS

FRESH MUSHROOMS IN GARLIC BUTTER

Heat butter. Press garlic with garlic press (amount depends upon taste). Sauté mushrooms in this garlic butter. Serve in chafing dish or over toast points. Allow 5 medium mushrooms per serving.

MRS. CHARLES TIFFANY BINGHAM

HAM-FILLED PARTY BISCUIT

3 oz. cream cheese (room
   temperature)
1 stick butter
1 c. flour

1 c. ground baked ham
Brown sugar
Dry mustard

Cream together butter and cream cheese until light and fluffy. Stir in flour until thoroughly mixed. Store in refrigerator an hour or so before rolling out. Roll about ½-inch thick and cut out in a rectangle. Sprinkle with ground baked ham. Dust lightly with brown sugar and dry mustard. Roll jelly roll fashion. Chill and slice. Bake 15-20 minutes on cookie sheet at 400°. Serve hot. Makes 16.

Can substitute: grated Cheddar cheese and chopped pimiento-stuffed olives; chopped bacon and onion which have been sautéed in bacon fat; or crumbled uncooked sausage.

MRS. ROBERT NORCROSS, FAIRVIEW FARMS
TYRONZA, ARK.

SAUSAGE HORS D'OEUVRES

24 sausage patties
24 small rounds of thinly
   sliced salt-rising bread
Catsup

Tabasco
Worcestershire
Dried parsley flakes

Place uncooked sausage patties on top of bread rounds. Make patties a little smaller than the bread. Put a generous spoon of sauce made from catsup, Tabasco, and Worcestershire on top of sausage. Sprinkle parsley flakes over sauce. Cook in a 225° oven about 1 hour or until well done. Drain on paper towel. Best served piping hot. Ground beef may be substituted for sausage. The bread-sausage patties may be put together and frozen on baking sheet. Defrost, put on sauce and bake. Makes 24.

MRS. J. HAL PATTON

POPPY SEED TURNOVERS

1 c. chopped onion
3 T. shortening
3 lbs. ground beef
2 cans mushroom soup
3 T. horseradish

1½ t. salt
2½ t. cracked pepper
6 sticks pie crust mix
6 T. poppy seeds

Brown onion in shortening. Add ground beef and brown. Add mushroom soup, horseradish, salt, pepper and any other seasonings you like. These need to be very highly seasoned. Cook until liquid is absorbed. When filling is ready, add 2 tablespoons poppy seeds to each 2 sticks pie crust mix. Roll out dough, cut in 3-inch rounds and put spoonful of meat on each circle of dough. Fold over and bake at 425° for 20 minutes. These freeze well. When frozen, increase cooking time by 10 minutes. Makes 100.

MRS. ROBERT M. LEATHERMAN, COLUMBIA, MISS.

ORIENTAL CRAB BALLS

1 T. butter	1 6½-oz. can crab meat
1 T. flour	½ t. salt
½ c. milk	½ c. cornstarch

Melt butter. Add flour to make a roux; then add milk slowly to make a thick cream sauce. Bring to a boil and add crab meat and salt. Chill. Form into small balls Roll in cornstarch and deep fry. Serve hot with dishes of soy sauce and hot mustard. Crab balls may be prepared a few hours in advance and then reheated in a 450° oven. Makes about 30.

MRS. JOHN E. LYON

ASPARAGUS FOLDOVERS

3 loaves sandwich bread	Butter
3 cans green asparagus spears	Parmesan cheese

Remove crusts from bread and roll each slice flat between two sheets of wax paper. (These may be done ahead and frozen.) Spread each slice with softened butter and sprinkle well with Parmesan cheese. Drain asparagus; then place on paper toweling to absorb all excess moisture. Place one spear on corner of each bread slice and roll up. Secure with toothpicks. These may be done the day before serving and refrigerated. Before baking, brush each roll with melted butter and sprinkle with more cheese. Bake 10-12 minutes at 400°. Serve piping hot. Makes approximately 75.

MRS. RODGERS MENZIES

BACON-WRAPPED WATER CHESTNUTS

2 10-oz. cans water chestnuts	Granulated sugar
1 5-oz. bottle soy sauce	1 lb. bacon

Marinate water chestnuts in soy sauce for at least 3 hours, turning often. Roll in sugar. Wrap each water chestnut in ½ strip bacon (don't stretch bacon). Secure bacon with toothpicks. Bake at 400° for 15-20 minutes, or until bacon is partially crisp. Serve hot. Can be made ahead and refrigerated until time to bake and serve. Chicken livers may be substituted for water chestnuts. Makes 35-40.

MRS. JOHN D. GLASS

BACON WRAPS

Large prunes, cooked, pits removed	Uncooked bacon

Wrap each prune in ⅓ or ½ slice bacon. Fasten with picks and bake on a broiler rack in a 375° oven until the bacon is crisp. Drain on paper towels before serving. Serve hot as an hors d'oeuvre or for brunch. **Note:** The following may be wrapped in bacon also and cooked as above . . . giant stuffed green olives, water chestnuts, pineapple chunks, chicken livers and chunks of tamale (cut whole tamale into 4 sections). Allow 3 per person.

MRS. MILTON LYMAN KNOWLTON, JR.

SAUSAGE ROLLS

2 c. packaged biscuit mix   1 lb. sausage

Make biscuit dough according to package directions on biscuit mix. Roll dough into a rectangle about ⅓-inch in thickness. Crumble uncooked sausage over dough. Roll as for jelly roll and seal edges. At this point, sausage rolls can be wrapped and frozen. Slice into pinwheels and bake at 450° on ungreased cookie sheet till sizzling and brown. Serve hot. Easy to slice if refrigerated first. Makes about 2 dozen.

MRS. RICHARD DIXON

ASPARAGUS ROLLS

1 T. frozen chives   1 can green asparagus spears,
½ c. mayonnaise   drained
Very thin slices of bread, rolled

Mix chives with mayonnaise. Spread bread with mayonnaise and roll each spear of asparagus diagonally in a piece of bread so that tip of asparagus shows at top of sandwich. Place in shallow pan, side by side, seam side down, until sandwiches will hold together by themselves. In case they pop open, secure with toothpicks.

HOT ASPARAGUS SANDWICH

1 small can asparagus tips,   ½ t. seasoned salt
   drained   16 slices sandwich bread
4 oz. cream cheese   Butter
Juice of ½ lemon   Parmesan cheese
2 sieved hard-boiled eggs

Mix well all ingredients, except butter and Parmesan cheese, and beat until smooth. Spread on 8 slices of trimmed bread. Cover with 8 additional slices of bread to make sandwiches. Spread the outside top and bottom of sandwiches with softened butter and sprinkle one side with grated Parmesan cheese. Cut sandwiches in half. Place under broiler until golden brown. Sprinkle the other side with cheese and broil as before. These may be cut into finger-sized sandwiches also. Makes 16 sandwich halves.

MRS. BEN C. ADAMS, JR.

AVOCADO FINGERS

1 ripe avocado   1 t. lemon juice
¼ t. salt   24 toast strips
⅛ t. paprika   12 bacon strips, halved

Mash avocado; add salt, paprika, lemon juice. Spread on 1 x 3-inch toast strips. Place narrow strips of bacon over avocado. Broil till bacon crisps. Serve for coffee or cocktails. Makes 24.

MRS. BEN C. ADAMS, JR.

LILY SANDWICHES

1 5½-oz. can boned chicken
½ c. finely chopped celery
1 t. grated onion
¼ t. dried tarragon leaves
¼ t. salt
⅛ t. pepper
¼ c. mayonnaise

18 slices white bread, crusted and
  flattened with rolling pin
¼ c. butter, softened
Chopped parsley
18 thin carrot sticks,
  about 1 inch long

Dice chicken and combine with celery, onion, tarragon, salt, pepper and mayonnaise. Cut bread into 2½-inch squares. Spread with softened butter and then roll up cornucopia fashion, overlapping the two adjacent edges. Secure with a toothpick. Spoon in chicken filling. Place close together in pan, cover with plastic wrap and chill for at least one hour. Before serving, remove toothpicks, sprinkle with chopped parsley and insert carrot stick for the stamen in each lily. Makes 18 sandwiches.

CUCUMBER TEA SANDWICHES

2 3-oz. pkgs. cream cheese
¼ c. milk or light cream or
  6 T. sour cream
2 T. garlic or bleu cheese salad
  dressing mix (Good Seasons)

2 cucumbers, scored and
  thinly sliced
1 dozen stuffed green olives,
  sliced
4 dozen cocktail rye bread slices

Soften cream cheese in small bowl. Add milk and salad dressing mix. Stir till blended. Spread on rye bread slices. Top with a slice of cucumber and garnish with a slice of olive. Makes 4 dozen sandwiches.

MRS. MILTON LYMAN KNOWLTON, JR.

OPEN-FACED CUCUMBER ROUNDS

Cucumbers, peeled and
  sliced very thinly
Vinegar
Ice water

Mayonnaise to spread
Bread rounds, crusted
Paprika
Salt

Use small biscuit cutter to cut cucumber slices and bread rounds the same size. Soak cucumber slices in refrigerator overnight in solution of ½ vinegar to ½ ice water. Just before serving, spread rounds with mayonnaise, top with drained cucumber and sprinkle with paprika and a little salt.

EGG AND ANCHOVY SANDWICHES

Whole wheat bread
12 hard-boiled eggs,
  chopped well

4 T. anchovy paste
Mayonnaise to spread

Cut whole wheat bread into rounds with a large biscuit cutter. Mix remaining ingredients well and spread on round sandwiches. May be served open-faced with a sprig of parsley or closed.

MRS. W. D. GALBREATH

AVOCADO SANDWICH

Bakery bread
Durkee's dressing
Thin slices of avocado

Thinly sliced bacon, cooked
Seasoned pepper (optional)

Spread toasted bread with Durkee's dressing. Make sandwich with remaining ingredients. If avocado is sliced ahead of time, sprinkle with lemon juice to keep it from turning dark. Good with aspic salad.

MRS. FRED TARKINGTON, JR.

PARSLEY-BACON SANDWICH FILLING

2 bunches fresh parsley or
   watercress, chopped
1 lb. crisp bacon, drained
Mayonnaise
Worcestershire

Garlic powder
Butter, softened
1 loaf very fresh sandwich
   bread, trimmed

Combine parsley, finely crumbled bacon, mayonnaise and Worcestershire to a spreading consistency. Mix garlic powder and butter and spread on bread, which has been rolled lightly with rolling pin. Spread parsley mixture over butter. Roll slices up in waxed paper and twist ends. Freeze. To serve: Unwrap and slice 4 to a roll. They thaw immediately. These may also be made into closed sandwiches, frozen, then sliced into fingers or triangles. Makes 9 dozen.

MRS. KIMBROUGH VOLLMER

GINGER-CHICKEN SANDWICHES

2 3-oz. pkgs. cream cheese,
   softened
2 4¾-oz. cans chicken
   spread

4 t. finely chopped
   candied ginger
¼ c. slivered almonds

Combine all ingredients and blend well. Chill at least 1 hour. Spread onto crusted, rolled bread; cut into finger sandwiches.

MRS. JAMES GUY ROBBINS

NUT BREAD FINGER SANDWICHES

6 c. flour
6 t. baking powder
1 c. sugar
¼ t. salt

3 eggs
2 c. milk
1 pkg. chopped dates
2 c. chopped nuts

Sift dry ingredients. Add beaten eggs and milk to form a batter; then add dates and nuts. Bake in greased loaf pan 40 minutes at 350°. When cool, slice thinly, cut into finger-sized and spread with butter or cream cheese.

MRS. WILLIAM B. FONTAINE, JACKSON, MISS.

GROUND CHICKEN SANDWICHES

2 c. ground chicken	Salt and pepper to taste
¾ c. mayonnaise	Bread rounds
1 T. lemon juice	Capers, drained

Boil chicken breasts, remove bone and skin, and put through a grinder. Mix with mayonnaise and seasonings. Spread on firm bread rounds and garnish with capers. Makes about 3 dozen.

JAM HEARTS

Cut firm bread into heart shapes with a cookie cutter. Spread with strawberry jam (or any red jam). Soften cream cheese and thin with milk. Pipe cream cheese through a cake decorator to form a decorative border around each heart. Cheese may be tinted pink, if desired.

HOT MARMALADE ROLLS

Thinly sliced bread	Orange marmalade
Butter, softened	

Remove crusts from bread and spread bread lightly with butter. Spread next with marmalade; then roll up, secure with toothpicks, and toast under the broiler. Serve hot.

MRS. JAMES W. WRAPE, COLLIERVILLE, TENN.

CHIPPED BEEF AND CREAM CHEESE

2 8-oz. pkgs. cream cheese	Dash Tabasco
½ medium onion, grated	1 pkg. smoked dried beef
Juice of 1 or 2 lemons	

Soften cream cheese and season with grated onion, lemon juice and Tabasco. Spread dried beef on waxed paper, overlapping edges. Spread cream cheese thinly over beef. Roll tightly and refrigerate. Makes 2 rolls. Cut into thin slices when serving.

MRS. T. GRIMES SNOWDEN

SALAMI WEDGES

36 thin slices of Hard	2 T. horseradish
Genoa salami	Dash of Tabasco
8 oz. cream cheese, softened	

Combine cream cheese with horseradish and Tabasco. Make three-decker sandwiches by spreading 1 slice of salami with about 2 teaspoons of the cheese mixture. Top with another slice of salami; spread with cheese and put a final slice of salami on top. Chill for at least 1 hour. Cut into quarters and spear with toothpicks. Makes 4 dozen.

MR. JOHN J. FITZMAURICE

SHRIMP SANDWICHES

1 c. finely diced shrimp	Mayonnaise
1 T. lemon juice	Salt and pepper to taste
⅓ c. finely chopped celery	Trimmed bread slices

Sprinkle shrimp with lemon juice. Mix well with celery. Add enough mayonnaise to spread and salt and pepper to taste. Spread on bread which has been rolled with a rolling pin. Cut into finger sandwiches. **Note:** These may be additionally seasoned with chopped chives or capers and lemon-pepper seasoning.

MRS. CHARLES L. PIPLAR

TOMATO SANDWICHES

2 to 3-in. size bread rounds	Small peeled tomatoes, sliced
Butter	Salt and pepper to taste
Mayonnaise	Basil

To assure ease in preparing, freeze bread. Cut rounds from frozen bread and spread with butter, then mayonnaise. Using half the bread rounds, place a tomato slice on each. Sprinkle tomato slice with salt and pepper and a little basil. Top each sandwich with one of the remaining bread rounds. **Note:** Butter keeps bread from becoming soggy.

WATERCRESS SANDWICHES

1 3-oz. pkg. cream cheese	1 c. finely chopped watercress,
1 t. lemon juice	lightly packed
⅓ c. sour cream	18 slices fresh white bread, crusted
Salt to taste	and flattened with rolling pin
1 t. finely cut chives	2 T. softened butter
Dash of Worcestershire	Sprigs of watercress

Blend together cream cheese, lemon juice, sour cream, salt, chives, and Worcestershire. Stir in watercress. Spread bread with softened butter, then with watercress mixture. Roll up in jelly roll fashion and arrange seam side down in a shallow pan. Cover pan and chill at least 1 hour. To serve: Slice each roll-up into two lengths, about 1½-inches long. Stand each roll-up upright and insert a sprig of watercress in top of each. If serving on a tray, garnish with additional watercress sprigs. Makes 36 sandwiches.

COLD STEAK BÉARNAISE

5 thick sirloin steaks	3 c. Béarnaise sauce

Cook steaks rare, cool, and wrap in plastic wrap. Refrigerate. To serve: Cut paper thin slices across the grain, cut away all fat and cut slices into bite-sized pieces. Arrange on a platter and serve with Béarnaise sauce (see Index). Serves 25.

MRS. FRANK T. DONELSON, JR.

SAUSAGE STROGANOFF

1 clove garlic
2 lbs. country sausage
3 T. flour
2 c. milk
2 large onions, sliced
then chopped
1 large can mushrooms

⅛ lb. butter
2 t. soy sauce
2 T. Worcestershire
Salt, pepper, paprika to taste
1 pt. sour cream

Rub large skillet with garlic and heat. Brown sausage well. Pour off grease as it accumulates. Dredge sausage with flour. Add milk and simmer until slightly thickened. Set aside. Sauté onions and mushrooms in butter. To the sausage-cream sauce mixture add soy sauce, Worcestershire, onions, mushrooms and seasonings. When mixture bubbles, add sour cream. Keep hot in chafing dish. Heap upon biscuits or pastry shells or use as a dip with Melba toast. Wonderful served in chafing dish for cocktail parties, large or small! For 50 people or over, double recipe. When doubling, add only 3 onions. May be made in advance and frozen, eliminating sour cream. On day of party, thaw and heat in electric skillet, adding sour cream as called for in recipe. Remains from party can be served over rice for dinner. Served with rice, this will serve 6.

MRS. EUGENE R. NOBLES, JR.

TAMALE DIP

2 medium onions, chopped
1 28-oz. can tomatoes
1 14-oz. can tomato sauce
2 large cans tamales,
chopped

1 clove garlic, minced
Dash Tabasco
1½ T. chili sauce
1 can ripe olives, drained and
chopped
Salt, pepper, and chili powder
to taste

Mix first 3 ingredients and simmer covered for 3 hours. Add chopped tamales with sauce from can and other ingredients. Serve hot from a chafing dish with corn chips or bread sticks. Sprinkle top of dip with grated cheddar cheese, if desired. Serves 12.

MRS. LAWRENCE L. CRANE, JR.

COCKTAIL MEATBALLS

1½ lbs. ground chuck,
seasoned to taste

1 12 oz- bottle chili sauce
1 12-oz. jar red currant
jelly

Make bite-sized meatballs and brown well in a small amount of fat. Drain well. Mix chili sauce and jelly in a saucepan; heat and add meatballs. Simmer till sauce thickens. Keep warm in chafing dish and use toothpicks to spear balls. Meatballs may be made ahead and frozen. Cooked cocktail franks or regular franks, sliced diagonally, or sausage balls may be substituted for the beef balls. Makes 40-45 meatballs.

MRS. DONALD BERUBE, JR.

CREAMED SHRIMP AND ARTICHOKE BOTTOMS

4½ T. butter
4½ T. flour
½ c. milk
¾ c. whipping cream
Salt and freshly ground
  pepper to taste
¼ c. dry vermouth

1 T. Worcestershire
1½ lbs. shrimp, cooked, shelled
  and deveined
2 #2 cans artichoke bottoms,
  drained
¼ c. freshly grated Parmesan
  cheese

Melt butter and stir in flour. When blended, gradually add milk and cream, stirring constantly with a wire whisk. When the mixture is thickened and smooth, season with salt and pepper. Add vermouth and Worcestershire to cream sauce. Combine with shrimp and artichokes. Heat through. Pour into chafing dish. Sprinkle Parmesan cheese on top. Serve with buttered toast rounds. **Variations:** (1) Gruyère cheese can be added to the cream sauce to make the sauce very similar to Mornay sauce. (2) Artichoke hearts, drained and sliced, may be substituted for the artichoke bottoms. (3) Substitute artichoke hearts for both shrimp and artichoke bottoms. Serves 50 as an appetizer.

MRS. CHARLES TIFFANY BINGHAM

MOCK OYSTERS ROCKEFELLER

2 pkgs. frozen chopped
  broccoli
1 medium onion, grated
1 stick margarine
1 can mushroom soup

1 small can chopped mushrooms,
  drained
1 roll garlic cheese
Sliced almonds, optional

Boil chopped broccoli and drain. Sauté onion in margarine until soft. Combine soup, onion, mushrooms, and mix with broccoli and crumbled cheese in pan. Keep hot and allow cheese to melt. Add almonds and stir well. Serve hot from a chafing dish. May be made up ahead of time, refrigerated and heated before serving. Serves 25 as a cocktail dip. To serve as a vegetable casserole: Bake in casserole in 350° oven for 30 minutes, or until hot and bubbling. Serves 8-10.

MRS. RONALD BYRNES

HOT CLAM DIP

12 oz. cream cheese
1 small jar sharp Old
  English cheese
½ large onion

2 cans minced clams
Tabasco, Worcestershire, black
  pepper, and red pepper to taste

Melt cheeses in double boiler. Dice onion; add onion and its juice to 2 cans of drained and washed minced clams. Combine all ingredients in a chafing dish and serve.

MRS. EDWARD LABRY, HUMBOLDT, TENN.

VOLCANO CHEESE BALL

1 lb. Tally-ho cheese	2 T. Worcestershire
1 8-oz. pkg. cream cheese	¼ c. sauterne
½ c. butter	Dash of Tabasco
½ small onion, grated	

Place all ingredients in mixer and blend at medium speed until smooth. Work into a ball and refrigerate until firm. Make a hole in the center of the ball and fill with Heinz 57 Sauce. Smooth cheese over and cover hole. Return to refrigerator. The cheese ball may be covered with ground nuts or sprinkled with paprika. Serves 30 or more.

MRS. ROBERT ARCHER

HOW TO SERVE CAVIAR

Caviar	Chopped egg yolk
Chopped onion	Chopped egg white

Place caviar in a bowl over crushed ice. Place onion, egg yolk, and egg white in individual bowls and set around caviar. Guests spread caviar on toast rounds and add condiments as they choose.

CREAM CHEESE — CAVIAR MOLD

1 8-oz. pkg. cream cheese	Dash Tabasco
2 T. mayonnaise	Dash Worcestershire
2 T. sour cream	Caviar, black or red
1 T. lemon juice	

Mix all ingredients, except caviar, and form into round ball. Spread ball with caviar. Serve with crisp crackers or buttered toast rounds. Serves 8-10.

MRS. C. NILES GROSVENOR, III

LIPTAUER

2 8-oz. pkgs. cream cheese	Cucumbers, chopped
3 T. whipping cream	Green onions, chopped
½ stick butter	Capers
Paprika	Lettuce cups
Anchovies, chopped	

Combine softened cream cheese with cream, butter and enough paprika to make the mixture pink. Beat it slightly till well mixed. Form into a ball. Place ball in center of a large tray and place anchovies, cucumbers, green onions, and capers in individual lettuce cups around the cream cheese ball. Serve with thinly sliced pumpernickle. Each guest spreads the pumpernickle with some of the cream cheese mixture, then adds any condiment he chooses. Beautiful and tasty. Serves 10.

MRS. EVERETT B. GIBSON

CRAB MEAT AND RIPE OLIVES

1 can crab meat
1 8-oz. pkg. cream cheese,
 softened
2 cans celery soup

1 small jar chopped ripe olives
Tabasco
Curry powder

Mix all ingredients. Heat until cheese melts. Serve from a chafing dish with Melba toast. Serves 15.

MRS. HALLAM BOYD, JR.

CRAB MEAT DIP

1 8-oz. pkg. cream cheese
1 c. crab meat
2 T. finely chopped onion
1 T. milk

½ t. horseradish
¼ t. salt
Pepper to taste
⅓ c. toasted blanched almonds

Mix all ingredients, except almonds. Put in baking dish and sprinkle with almonds. Heat at 375° for 30 minutes. Can be made ahead and heated in chafing dish.

MRS. ROBERT C. BURLEIGH

CHEESE PINEAPPLE

1½ lb. sharp Cheddar cheese,
 grated (6 c.)
½ lb. Swiss cheese,
 grated (2 c.)
1 8-oz. pkg. cream cheese,
 softened
¼ lb. bleu cheese, crumbled
½ c. butter or margarine,
 softened

½ c. apple juice
2 T. lemon juice
1 T. Worcestershire
Whole cloves
Paprika
1 leafy crown from a large,
 fresh pineapple

Day ahead of serving: Combine cheeses with butter or margarine in the large bowl of an electric mixer. Slowly beat in apple and lemon juices and Worcestershire. Continue beating, scraping down sides of bowl often, for 5 minutes or until well blended. Cover and chill several hours or until firm enough to handle. Shape cheese mixture with your hands into a "standing pineapple" on a plate. Smooth top flat and cover whole with foil or waxed paper. Chill several hours or until very firm. Allow ample time for the following: Before serving, mark cheese with the tip of a teaspoon or toothpick to resemble a pineapple. This requires crisscross lines which form diamond shapes. Center each diamond with a whole clove and lightly sprinkle cheese with paprika. Lift mold onto a serving plate with a spatula. Place pineapple crown on top of mold; hold in place with several toothpicks, if needed. Frame with various crackers and parsley. **Note:** Slices of pimiento-stuffed olives may be substituted for the cloves. Serves 50.

MRS. E. J. JOHNSON, JR.

CRAB MEAT IN CHAFING DISH

2 cans crab meat
1 can mushroom soup
1 can sliced mushrooms
1 can artichoke hearts

½-1 c. grated Cheddar cheese
¼ c. sherry
Dash Tabasco

Slice artichoke hearts. Combine all ingredients and heat. Serve hot from a chafing dish with Melba toast points or patty shells. If mixture seems too thick, add more soup or mushroom liquid. Serves 12.

MRS. C. NILES GROSVENOR, III

HOT CURRIED CRAB DIP

2 8-oz. pkgs. cream cheese
2 cans crab meat
½ c. sherry

Juice of 3 lemons
Curry powder, salt and pepper
to taste

Let cream cheese come to room temperature. Drain crab meat. Combine all ingredients and heat in a 300° oven till bubbly. Set out to cool and thicken a bit before serving. Serve with Melba toast rounds. Serves 10.

MRS. HENRY T. V. MILLER, JR.

AVOCADO CRAB DIP

1 large avocado, peeled
and seeded
1 T. lemon juice
1 T. grated onion
1 t. Worcestershire

1 8-oz. pkg. cream cheese
½ c. sour cream
¼ t. monosodium glutamate
¼ t. salt
1 7½-oz. can crab meat, drained

Blend together all ingredients, except crab meat. Stir crab meat into mixture. Chill. Serve with crackers or chips. Serves 6-8.

MRS. FRED C. WOLFF

CREAM CHEESE CONSOMMÉ MOLD

2 cans chicken or beef consommé
2 envelopes gelatin
1 8-oz. pkg. cream cheese

1 tin anchovies
1½ T. bourbon

Heat 1½ cans consommé. Dissolve gelatin in other half can. Combine the two mixtures. Mix cheese, drained anchovies, which have been patted dry, and bourbon. Let this mixture stand for a short time. Place the consommé-gelatin mixture in a **lightly** oiled 10-inch pie plate, and congeal in refrigerator. Form cheese mixture into approximately 3-inch diameter patty and place in center. When ready to serve, turn out on a silver tray and garnish with lemon slices and sprigs of parsley or watercress. Serve with Melba rounds or wheat thins. This cannot be made more than 24 hours in advance. Makes 25 servings.

MRS. WILLIAM M. PREST

PATRICIAN PÂTÉ

½ lb. smoked liverwurst
3 oz. pkg. cream cheese
¼ lb. softened butter

1 t. Worcestershire
Dash Tabasco or cayenne
1 slice truffle (optional)

Mash all ingredients and beat with a fork until thoroughly mixed. Refrigerate in small mold until set. Unmold, garnish with truffle, and serve with crackers. Serves 12 for cocktails.

This pâté can be iced with cream cheese softened with mayonnaise and sour cream, then topped with caviar.

MRS. ROANE WARING, JR.

CHICKEN LIVER MOUSSE

1 lb. (2 c.) chicken livers
2 T. minced shallots or
   green onions
2 T. butter
⅓ c. Madeira or Cognac
¼ c. whipping cream

½ t. salt
⅛ t. allspice
⅛ t. pepper
Pinch of thyme
½ c. melted butter

Cut livers in ½-inch pieces. Sauté with the shallots or green onions in hot butter for 2-3 minutes until livers are just stiffened but still rosy inside. Scrape into an electric blender jar. Pour the wine or Cognac into the saucepan and boil it rapidly until it has been reduced to 3 tablespoons. Scrape into blender. Add cream and seasonings to blender jar. Cover and blend at top speed until the liver is a smooth paste. Then add the ½ cup melted butter and blend several seconds more. Force the mixture through a fine meshed sieve with a wooden spoon and taste carefully for seasoning. Add salt and pepper to taste. Pack into a 2-cup decorative bowl or jar and chill at least 3 hours. Use as a spread for appetizers.

MRS. JOHN APPERSON, JR.

BEEF TARTARE LOAF

5 lbs. sirloin, trimmed and
   ground twice
4 or 5 egg yolks, slightly
   beaten
3 medium onions, finely
   minced
5 t. salt

1 t. freshly ground pepper
½ c. minced parsley
Chives
Capers
Tabasco and Worcestershire
   to taste

Mix beef with egg yolks, onions, seasonings and some of the parsley. When thoroughly blended, form in a loaf or long roll, sprinkle with minced chives and stud with whole capers. Press with rest of parsley, adding more, if you like, to the sides. Beef Tartare can also be pressed into a decorative mold and unmolded at serving time. Serves 50.

MRS. GEORGE T. LEE, DALLAS, TEX.

SMOKED SALMON BALL

1½-2 lbs. salmon steaks	2 t. grated onion
1 8-oz. pkg. cream cheese	1 t. horseradish
1 T. lemon juice	¼ t. liquid smoke

Cover 1½-2 pounds of salmon steaks with salted water in a skillet. Add a few peppercorns and slice of lemon. Bring to a boil and then simmer very gently 20-25 minutes until fish just begins to flake. Drain and discard skin and bones and flake. Mix with rest of ingredients.

Chill several hours in small mold lined with plastic wrap. Unmold on platter and pat chopped parsley and pecans into surface. Serve with crackers.

MR. JOHN J. FITZMAURICE

SHRIMP SPREAD

2 lbs. boiled shrimp	¼ t. lemon juice
¼ lb. butter	Salt and pepper to taste
3 T. mayonnaise	1 t. Worcestershire
Mace	Few drops Tabasco

Put shrimp through meat grinder twice. Rub butter and shrimp well together and add enough mayonnaise to soften slightly. Season with ground mace, lemon juice, salt, pepper and sauces to taste. Chill mixture and serve with crackers or thin crisp toast. Mayonnaise may be omitted and celery seed may be used instead of mace.

MRS. WILLIAM T. BLACK, JR.

GUACAMOLE

2 avocados, mashed	¼ t. chili powder
1 T. lemon juice	Dash cayenne
2 T. lime juice	⅓ c. mayonnaise
1 T. grated onion	¼ c. chopped ripe olives
1 t. salt	4 slices crisp bacon, crumbled

Mix all together well. Serve with warmed corn chips. Serves 6.

This may be spooned over shredded lettuce and served as Guacamole salad.

MRS. RICHARD DIXON

MEXICAN DIP

1 8-oz. pkg. cream cheese, softened	1 T. capers
½ stick soft butter	1 t. dry mustard
1 T. grated onion	½ t. cayenne
	1 T. mashed anchovies

Mix all together well. Serve with warm corn chips. Serves 6.

MRS. RICHARD DIXON

CUCUMBER DIP

1 c. unpeeled grated cucumber
2 8-oz. pkgs. cream cheese
2 T. grated onion
1 T. Worcestershire

3 T. mayonnaise
Dash of salt, pepper, Accent
2 T. lemon juice

Drain all the "water" from the cucumber, making certain there is no moisture left in it. Mix well all ingredients in blender. Serve cold with corn chips or potato chips. Makes 3 cups. Serves 12 amply.

MRS. ALLEN HOLT HUGHES

DILL SHRIMP DIP

1 8-oz. pkg. cream cheese
¼ c. chopped cucumber
2 T. chopped onion
⅛ t. dill weed

Dash Tabasco
1 10-oz. can frozen cream of
shrimp soup

Soften cream cheese and add seasonings. Blend thoroughly and add thawed soup. Serve with potato chips, pretzels, celery sticks or carrot sticks. Pretty served in a large shell or hollowed head of red cabbage (outer leaves spread petal fashion) and surrounded by raw vegetable sticks. Serves 6-8.

MRS. BILL R. BOBBITT

CURRY DIP BRITTON

An excellent accompaniment for shrimp or cauliflower

1 c. mayonnaise
3 T. catsup
1 T. Worcestershire
2 T. grated onion

1 T. curry powder
Salt to taste
½ t. Tabasco

Mix well all ingredients and chill. (Should be made several days ahead.) Makes enough dip for 1 large head cauliflower.

MRS. WILLIAM J. BRITTON, III

CHUTNEY AND HOT BACON

8 slices bacon
¾ c. mango chutney

24 toast fingers

Cut slices of bacon into ½-inch squares and fry until they start to brown. Pour off most of drippings and add ¾ cup mango chutney, cutting large pieces of mango into small squares. Let this bubble over low heat until you are ready to spread it on crisp toast fingers. Serve hot. May be served from a small chafing dish. Covers about 2 dozen toast fingers.

CHUTNEY CANAPE SPREAD

4 hard-cooked eggs	1 T. curry powder
1 3-oz. pkg. cream cheese	Dash cayenne and Tabasco
2 T. mayonnaise	Black pepper and salt to taste
1 T. Worcestershire	2 T. chopped chutney

Mash hard-cooked eggs with cream cheese. Add mayonnaise and seasonings and mix well. Add chutney and chill. Take out of refrigerator in time to soften. Serve on a large lettuce leaf or in a large hollowed bell pepper shell with cocktail crackers. Serves 10.

MRS. JAMES GUY ROBBINS

CHEESE ROLL

½ lb. New York State cheese	2 3-oz. pkgs. cream cheese
½ lb. pimiento cheese	4-5 garlic cloves, pressed
Red pepper or Tabasco to taste	Pinch of salt

Grate cheese, mix all ingredients and shape into logs about 1½-inches in diameter. Roll logs in mixture of chili powder and paprika (may also be rolled in chopped parsley or chopped pecans). Slice and serve with crackers. Improves with age.

MRS. CLAUDE E. GRIMES, VICKSBURG, MISS.

First Courses

SHRIMP REMOULADE (IN TOMATO ASPIC RING)

SHRIMP REMOULADE:

½ c. vinegar
1 c. olive oil
6 T. Creole mustard
1 t. paprika
10 sprigs chopped parsley
4 T. anchovy paste (about 3 oz.)
1 T. horseradish

2 bunches shallots
6 small stalks celery
4-5 drops Tabasco
1 large head lettuce, shredded
3 lbs. shelled cooked shrimp,
   chilled

To make sauce: Place vinegar and oil in blender. Add other ingredients, except lettuce and shrimp, and blend well. Pour in a jar and refrigerate for a day. To serve: Place shrimp on a bed of shredded lettuce and pour sauce on top. Lovely served in baking shells or silver shells. Serves 10 as first course, 6 as main dish.

To serve in Aspic Ring: See Index for Tomato Aspic recipe. Omit the chopped celery from the basic aspic recipe and add instead: 1 cup chopped artichoke hearts or 1 cup chopped all-green asparagus. Unmold aspic ring on shredded lettuce on large serving platter. Fill center of aspic ring with shrimp and pour some of Remoulade sauce over shrimp. Surround aspic with additional shrimp tossed with sauce, and garnish with avocado wedges, tomato wedges and hard-cooked egg slices. Sprinkle with chopped fresh dill. Garnish with home-made mayonnaise, if desired. Serves 6-8.

MRS. CHESTER GELPI, NEW ORLEANS, LA.

AVOCADO AND GRAPEFRUIT COCKTAIL

ANCHOVY DRESSING:

½ c. mayonnaise
1 T. tomato catsup
1½ t. anchovy paste

1 t. lemon juice
1 t. Worcestershire

Combine diced avocado and grapefruit segments. Pour anchovy dressing over cocktail and top with teaspoon of grated hard-boiled egg. Serve with crackers or saltines. Serves 6.

This sauce is also delicious with shrimp cocktail. Add a little more catsup and a small amount of onion juice.

MRS. JAMES W. MOORE

FISH QUENELLES

½ lb. white fleshed fish
    fillet, cut in ½-in. strips
½ t. salt
1 egg white

1 ice cube, cracked
1 c. whipping cream
Fish court bouillon or clam
    juice and white wine

Into a blender container put fish, salt, egg white and ice cube. Cover and blend on high speed for 10 seconds, flicking motor on and off several times. Remove cover and with motor on, gradually pour in whipping cream. The mixture will be smooth and creamy. Drop 2 tablespoons of mixture from a spoon dipped in cold water into a large frying pan containing 1-inch of fish court bouillon. Poach gently for 8-10 minutes, basting constantly. Remove quenelles with a slotted spoon and place on paper towel to drain. Serve garnished with tiny shrimp and Sauce Normande.

SAUCE NORMANDE:

½ c. butter
2 T. clam juice
¼ c. hot coffee cream
4 egg yolks
1 t. lemon juice

¼ t. salt
Pinch of cayenne
½ T. brandy
2 mushroom caps, cooked

In a small saucepan, heat butter, clam juice and cream to bubbling. Put remaining ingredients, except mushroom caps, into a blender container. Cover and turn motor on high. Immediately uncover and pour in the mixture from the saucepan in a steady stream. Turn off motor, add mushroom caps, flick motor on and off twice, set container into saucepan holding 1-inch of very hot water and let stand 6 minutes before serving. Serves 4.

MRS. SNOWDEN BOYLE, JR.

CHOPPED OYSTERS

1 qt. oysters
1 onion, chopped
½ c. cracker crumbs
2 hard-boiled eggs
2 egg yolks

1 t. lemon juice
1 t. Worcestershire
4 T. butter
Seasoning to taste; salt, pepper,
    Tabasco, nutmeg

Mince hard-boiled eggs finely and set aside. Chop oysters. Press onion through meat grinder to extract juice, or grate onion finely. Place oysters and all the oyster liquor in a large pan, adding to this the onion, hard-boiled eggs and remaining ingredients. Mix well and taste for seasoning. Cook and stir till hot. Remove from stove and divide mixture among baking shells, sprinkling a few more cracker crumbs on each. Place shells in 350° oven and bake 30 minutes. Serves 8-10.

MRS. THOMAS H. TODD, JR.

MARINATED OYSTERS

2 8-oz. cans oysters	1 t. lemon pepper
½ c. olive oil	1 t. salt
¼ c. lemon juice	½ t. mustard seed
2 t. Worcestershire	¼ t. thyme
2 T. parsley	8 thin slices onion
¼ c. white wine	Tabasco to taste

Drain oysters. Make a marinade of the other ingredients. Marinate oysters in sauce for 12 hours or more in refrigerator. Toss lightly occasionally with a fork. Serve cold with small Melba toast rounds. Serves 8.

MRS. JOHN M. MAURY, JR.

FROSTED SHRIMP

1 12½-oz. can madrilene consommé	¼ t. salt
6 large cooked, cleaned shrimp	½ c. rosé wine
½ t. Worcestershire	Shrimp and lemon wedges for garnish
¼ c. tomato juice	

Put consommé, shrimp, and Worcestershire into blender. Cover and blend at high speed. Add tomato juice, salt and wine. Mix and pour into refrigerator tray to freeze. When almost firm, whip and spoon into sherbets, all-purpose wine glasses or icers. Garnish with shrimp and lemon wedges. Serve at once. **Note:** If blender is not available, whip consommé and Worcestershire well. Stir in grated shrimp, and proceed as above. Serves 6-8.

MRS. MILTON LYMAN KNOWLTON, JR.

ARTICHOKE BOTTOMS WITH CREAM CHEESE AND CAVIAR

1 pkg. Good Seasons Old Fashioned French Dressing Mix	1 t. grated onion
	Lemon juice
	Dash Tabasco
1 large can artichoke bottoms	Caviar
3 oz. pkg. cream cheese	

Make salad dressing according to package directions, cutting oil in half. Drain artichokes and marinate in dressing at least 4 hours. Mix cream cheese with onion, lemon juice and Tabasco. Add to the cheese some of the marinade. Drain bottoms and fill with cheese mixture. Cut into quarters, top each with caviar, and spear with toothpicks. Pass on tray as an hors d'oeuvre or first course. Serves 6 as first course, 12 as hors d'oeuvres.

MRS. ROBERT M. LEATHERMAN, COLUMBIA, MISS.

MUSHROOMS STUFFED WITH CRAB MEAT

24 large, fresh mushrooms	Salt and pepper to taste
12 green onions, chopped	1 T. flour
4 sprigs parsley, chopped	½ c. sherry or white wine
5 T. oleo	2 cans crab meat
¾ t. Worcestershire	1 lb. sharp cheese, grated

Wash mushrooms gently under running water and drain in colander. Trim stems; then cut off stems and chop along with onions and parsley. Sauté mushroom stems, onions and parsley in oleo in small skillet, adding Worcestershire and salt and pepper, for about 10 minutes. Stir in flour and then wine. Add crab meat last. Put mushroom tops in large shallow pan and salt lightly. Use a teaspoon to divide mixture among mushrooms. Top with grated cheese and run into 400° oven for about 10 minutes, or until cheese is melted. Excellent as appetizer, entrée for luncheon or garnish for filet of beef! Serves 8.

MRS. FRED BEESON

OYSTERS BIENVILLE

4 T. butter	2 egg yolks
8 small shallots, finely chopped	½ c. white wine
2 T. flour	Salt and pepper to taste
1 c. chicken broth or fish stock	2 doz. oysters on the half shell
1 c. cooked shrimp, finely chopped	½ c. bread crumbs
1 7-oz. can mushroom pieces, finely chopped	2 T. Parmesan cheese
	Paprika

Heat butter in skillet. Add shallots and sauté until soft. Add flour and stir until lightly browned. Stir in chicken broth or fish stock, stirring until blended. Add shrimp and mushrooms. Beat egg yolks with wine and add to mixture, stirring until blended and slightly thickened. Remove from heat and season to taste with salt and pepper. Remove oysters from shells and set aside. Scrub shells thoroughly. Arrange 6 shells on each of 4 pie pans half filled with rock salt. Heat in 450° oven for 10 minutes. Remove pans from oven, place oysters in shells and top each with a spoonful of the prepared mixture. Combine bread crumbs and Parmesan cheese and sprinkle atop mixture. Then lightly sprinkle with paprika. Bake in a 450° oven 15 minutes or until tops are lightly browned. **Note:** The sauce can be made a day ahead. Once you have the oyster shells, they can be filled with oysters purchased in a jar, rather than with fresh oysters. Serves 4 as a main course, 8 as an appetizer.

MRS. PETER L. BALLENGER

AVOCADOS FILLED WITH HOT COCKTAIL SAUCE

6 T. butter or margarine	2½ t. Worcestershire
6 T. catsup	½ t. salt
2½ T. vinegar	Dash Tabasco
2½ T. water	4 small ripe avocados
4 t. sugar	

In top of a double boiler, mix together all ingredients except avocados. Heat over boiling water until butter has melted and sauce is smooth. Cut **unpeeled** avocados in half, lengthwise; separate halves and remove seeds. Ladle hot sauce into avocados and serve with spoons as appetizer or first course. Large avocados may be sliced in chunks or scooped into balls with a melon ball cutter, speared with toothpicks, and dunked into hot sauce. Serves 8.

MRS. DAVID B. MARTIN

STUFFED ARTICHOKE BOTTOMS

6 artichoke bottoms, canned or fresh	1 lb. crab meat
	¾ c. Hollandaise sauce

Fill bottoms with crab meat and ladle Hollandaise over all. Serves 6.

The bottoms can also be soaked in vinaigrette dressing, garnished with pimiento strips, and served on a bed of lettuce.

MRS. CHESTER GELPI, NEW ORLEANS, LA.

Soups

BEAN SOUP

2 ham shanks
2 c. dried Navy beans
2 onions, chopped

6 celery ribs, chopped
2 c. tomatoes, canned or fresh

Soak beans overnight in water to cover. Cover shanks with water in large cooking pot and simmer 2-3 hours. Add drained beans, celery, onion and tomatoes to pot in which shanks have been simmering. Cook 1½ hours longer and season to taste. Serves 8.

MRS. JAMES C. RAINER, III

BLACK BEAN SOUP

2 pkgs. black beans (soaked
  4 hrs. or overnight)
Ham bone
Piece of salt pork (optional)
2 onions, chopped
2 bay leaves
Celery tops
1 can tomato sauce or purée

Tabasco, few drops
Salt and pepper to taste
Worcestershire (optional)
Condiments:
  Chopped onion
  Oil and vinegar
  Chopped hard-boiled egg
  Steamed rice

Add enough water or broth to cover washed and soaked black beans. Add ham bone, with fat removed. and salt pork. Cook slowly "all day" (actually about 6 hours of simmering is sufficient). During last 2 hours of cooking, add onions, bay leaves, celery tops, tomato sauce or purée, Tabasco, salt and pepper and several large dashes of Worcestershire. Before serving, remove ham bone, skin, and celery tops. Do not strain. Serve with condiments of onion, oil and vinegar, hard-boiled egg and rice. Black Bean Soup is served at the fine Spanish restaurant, Las Novedades, in Tampa, Florida. As a soup course, this serves 24; as a main course, 12-14.

MRS. W. HAMILTON SMYTHE, III

JELLIED BEEF CONSOMMÉ

2 cans consommé
½ pt. sour cream

1 small jar caviar

Jell consommé in refrigerator. Fill bouillon cups or sherbet glasses with consommé. Top with 1 tablespoon sour cream and 1 teaspoon or more caviar. Serves 8.

MRS. HUGH WYNNE

CONSOMMÉ

2 cans consommé	Lemon slices
2 T. vermouth	Parsley
1 T. sherry	

Add vermouth and sherry to consommé. To serve: Place a thin slice of lemon, sprinkled with parsley, in each bowl. Serves 4-6.

MRS. SNOWDEN BOYLE, JR.

CONSOMMÉ ROYALE

2 c. beef consommé	1 t. Fines Herbes
2 c. V-8 Juice	1 t. seasoned salt
½ c. Burgundy	

Combine ingredients and heat thoroughly. Add twist of lemon in each serving.
Note: For jellied consommé, add 1 tablespoon gelatin and chill. Serves 6.

MRS. C. NILES GROSVENOR, III

MUSHROOM CONSOMMÉ

½ lb. fresh or canned mushrooms	Juice of ½-1 lemon
2 T. butter	1 T. or more sherry
2 cans consommé	2 T. or more vermouth
	Salt and pepper to taste

Chop mushrooms; sauté in butter 3-4 minutes. Add 3 tablespoons consommé and lemon juice. Put in blender, but do not purée too finely. Add purée, sherry, and vermouth to remaining consommé. Season with salt and pepper. Serve hot or cold. If cold, spoon sour cream on top. Serves 6.

MRS. J. FRED SCHOELLKOPF, JR., DALLAS, TEX.

AVGHOLÉMONO SOUPA
(Greek Chicken Soup)

4 c. chicken stock, preferably homemade	2 eggs, well beaten
½ c. uncooked rice	Juice of 1 lemon

Bring stock to boiling point. Stir in rice, reduce heat and cover pan. Simmer till rice is soft. Slowly beat lemon juice into beaten eggs. Add about one cup hot stock to the egg mixture, then return warmed eggs to body of soup. For a heartier soup add small chunks of cooked chicken. Serves 6.

COLD ORANGE TOMATO SOUP

2 c. tomato juice	1 t. sugar
2 c. orange juice	1½ t. salt
½ c. white wine	3 dashes cayenne pepper
Juice of 1 lemon	Chopped parsley

Combine first seven ingredients. Serve very cold, sprinkled with chopped parsley. Serves 8.

MRS. J. FRED SCHOELLKOPF, JR., DALLAS, TEX.

TOMATO BOUILLON

2 large cans tomatoes	Sherry
2 cans beef bouillon	Salt and pepper to taste

Strain the seeds from the tomatoes. Put juice and pulp in blender to purée. Pour into a saucepan along with bouillon. Heat and add sherry and seasonings to taste. Serve hot or cold. Serves 8.

MRS. JAMES GUY ROBBINS

HOT TOMATO BOUILLON

1 can condensed tomato soup	¼ t. horseradish
1 can condensed beef broth	Dash Tabasco
1 c. water	Sour cream

Combine all ingredients except sour cream. Simmer uncovered for 5 minutes and blend well. Pour into bowls or mugs and float a spoonful of sour cream in each. Serve with warm crackers, if desired. Serves 6.

HEARTY VEGETABLE SOUP

Combine:

3 qts. boiling water	Leftover roast beef or steak, cubed
uncooked soup meat (any amount)	2 pkgs. dried onion soup mix

Let boil 25-30 minutes. Then add:

1 lb. can tomato sauce	1 t. garlic powder
1 lb. can tomatoes, cut up	1 T. salt
1½ t. marjoram	2 bay leaves
1½ t. basil	1½ t. parsley flakes
1½ t. pepper	

Let this cook 15 minutes. Then add:

1 large bag frozen mixed vegetables	1 box frozen cut okra

Let all cook covered 2-2½ hours. Sprinkle Parmesan cheese over top to serve. Serves 12.

MRS. BRUCE E. CAMPBELL, JR.

GAZPACHO

1 large can tomatoes and
  6 very ripe tomatoes,
  peeled and chopped
3 T. finely chopped parsley
3 T. olive oil
1 clove garlic
1 medium onion, chopped

2 T. vinegar
1 c. beef stock or consommé
Salt and pepper to taste
2 medium cucumbers
2 medium tomatoes
1 green pepper
1 medium onion

Purée tomatoes, parsley, olive oil, garlic, onion, and vinegar in a blender; then pour into a mixing bowl. Mix the beef stock, salt, and pepper with the purée. Finely chop cucumbers, tomatoes, green pepper, and onion. These ingredients may be added to the soup itself or served separately as condiments. Croutons or sour cream seasoned with curry may be placed on top each bowl of soup. If seasoning with the curry, wait until the very last minute to add it to the sour cream. Serve icy cold. Serves 16.

MRS. WILLIAM HENRY HOUSTON, III

VICHYSSOISE

6 green onions or 4 leeks
1 medium onion
2 T. butter
5 medium potatoes
1 qt. chicken broth
  (homemade best, but
  canned may be used)

1 T. salt
2 c. milk
2 c. coffee cream
1 c. whipping cream
Chopped chives

Slice finely the white part of the leek. Slice onion and cook with leeks in butter until golden. Slice and peel potatoes. Add potatoes, chicken broth (this may be diluted with water to make 1 quart) and salt to leeks and onions and boil for 35-40 minutes. Rub liquid through fine sieve, return to fire and add milk and coffee cream. Season to taste and bring to a boil. Cool and rub mixture through very fine sieve. When cold, add the whipping cream. Chill thoroughly. May be served in tea cups and sprinkled with chives or a parsley sprig. Vichyssoise is very nice served at a buffet from a tall crystal pitcher. Guests help themselves by pouring the cold soup into small on-the-rocks type glasses . . . clear plastic glasses are great for this. Serves 8.

MRS. E. JAMES HOUSE

CHILLED GREEN SOUP

2 cans green pea soup
2 cans beef bouillon
1 can red madrilene

1 t. curry powder
1 T. Worcestershire
½ c. sherry

Mix above ingredients. Serve cold with dollop of sour cream to each cup. Serves 6-8.

MRS. JAMES W. MOORE

SPINACH SOUP

2 large jars of junior baby
   food spinach
4 c. chicken broth
2 c. white sauce

2 c. very finely chopped
   chicken (optional)
Salt and pepper to taste
⅔ t. curry powder

Mix all ingredients well and heat in a double boiler. Serve hot, garnished with
sieved egg or croutons. Serves 8.

MRS. CHARLES L. PIPLAR

CORN SOUP

¼ c. minced onion
¼ c. butter
1 T. lemon juice
½ t. dry mustard
1 t. sugar
1 t. salt

Freshly ground black pepper
2 c. fresh raw corn (about 4 ears)
2 c. chicken stock
2 c. coffee cream
Tabasco

Sauté onion in butter until transparent. Mix in lemon juice, mustard, sugar,
salt and pepper. Add corn and chicken stock. Bring to a boil, cover, reduce
heat and simmer for about 10 minutes. At serving time, add cream and dash
of Tabasco and heat (do not boil). Even better cold, in which case, add cream
and Tabasco to warm soup. Refrigerate overnight. Serves 6.

MRS. JAMES W. WRAPE, COLLIERVILLE, TENN.

WATERCRESS SOUP

⅓ c. minced onion
3 T. melted butter
3-4 c. watercress with
   stems, (tightly packed)
½ t. salt

3 T. flour
5½ c. chicken broth
½ c. whipping cream
2 egg yolks

Sauté onions in butter 5-7 minutes, until tender and transparent, but not
brown. Stir in watercress and salt and cook slowly until tender, about 5 minutes. Sprinkle flour into watercress mixture. Stir over moderate heat for 3
minutes. Add chicken broth and bring to boiling point. Simmer 5 minutes.
Strain watercress mixture. Place strained watercress in blender and purée.
Return purée to chicken broth, correct seasonings, and stir in whipping cream,
into which egg yolks have been beaten. Place saucepan over heat for a few
minutes, simmer, but do not let boil. Cool and refrigerate. Can be served hot
or cold. Garnish top with unsweetened whipped cream and watercress sprigs.
Watercress soup may be garnished with French roll croutons, if desired. **To
make croutons:** Cut French rolls into ½-inch slices. Toast slices in a 300° oven
for 15-20 minutes, turning once. Make a hole ¼-inch wide in center of each
crouton and insert several watercress sprigs through each hole. Float crouton
on each serving of soup. Serves 12.

MRS. FLOYD HUMPHREYS DUNCAN

CELERY SOUP

4 cans cream of celery soup   Parsley
8 strips crisp bacon   Paprika
4 grated hard-boiled eggs

Pour soup in saucepan. Add 4/5 can of water for each can of soup. Add water slowly, stirring constantly. Break bacon into small bits and add to soup along with egg. To serve: Float parsley on the top and sprinkle with paprika. Serves 12.

MRS. CHARLES H. McGEE, BRUIN PLANTATION,
HUGHES, ARK.

CREAM OF PEANUT SOUP

2 stalks celery   ½ gal. chicken broth
½ onion   1½ c. peanut butter
¼ lb. butter   ½ qt. cream
1 T. flour   Crushed peanuts (optional)

Chop celery and onion and sauté in the butter. Add flour and cook till well blended. Add the chicken broth and bring to boiling. Stir in the peanut butter. Add the cream, heat thoroughly, and serve. If desired, garnish with crushed peanuts. Serves 8.

MRS. EDWARD J. LAWLER

SOUP VIRGINIA MCKINNEY

2 cans cream of celery soup   ½ t. salt
2 c. coffee cream   ½ t. pepper
2 t. grated onion   2 cans crab meat
2 t. shredded parsley   2 small, ripe avocados, diced

Heat all ingredients, except avocado, till bubbling around edges. When ready to serve, add avocado. Serves 6.

MRS. JAMES W. WRAPE, COLLIERVILLE, TENN.

SHERRIED CRAB SOUP

2 c. cooked crab meat,   3 c. coffee cream
   fresh or canned   4 T. chopped parsley
1 c. sherry   Dash of curry powder
2 cans pea soup   Salt and pepper to taste
2 cans tomato soup

Soak crab meat in sherry for 1 hour. Combine soups and cream in top of double boiler. Heat just to simmering, stirring occasionally. Add crab meat, sherry, parsley and seasonings. Serve piping hot. Serves 8.

MRS. JACK M. DALY

CREAM OF CLAM SOUP

¾ lb. diced lean salt pork
4 7-oz. cans minced clams,
   undrained
4 c. whipping cream

6 T. butter
Salt and freshly ground pepper
Tabasco

To make pork croutons: Fry pork slowly in skillet until each piece is golden and crunchy. Drain. Purée undrained clams in blender. Add cream and butter to clam mixture. Heat and season to taste with salt, pepper and Tabasco. Serve steaming soup with croutons sprinkled on top. Serves 8.

MRS. J. TUNKIE SAUNDERS

SHRIMP GUMBO

6 onions
4 green peppers
Bunch of celery
1 bunch parsley
4 garlic pods
1 1-qt. 14-oz. can tomato
   juice
2 28-oz. cans tomatoes
2 6-oz. cans tomato paste
1 pouch of seafood seasoning

1 T. salt
5 T. Worcestershire
6 drops Tabasco
1 T. pepper
3 lbs. cleaned and deveined
   fresh shrimp
1 sack frozen chopped okra
1 lb. regular or lump fresh
   crab meat

Chop onions, green peppers, celery, parsley and garlic. Sauté in bacon grease until transparent. Add tomato juice, tomatoes broken into pieces and their juice, tomato paste and seasonings. Cook slowly for 2 hours. Remove pouch. Add shrimp and cook for 30 minutes. Add okra and cook slowly for another hour. Stir in crab meat and mix thoroughly. Set aside to cool before refrigerating overnight. Reheat next day and serve over a bed of rice. If consistency is too thick, add a can of consommé. Taste to see if more seasoning is needed. Serves 12.

MRS. HYDE BOONE

CHICKEN GUMBO

1 roasting chicken (2½-3 lb.)
1 slice ham
½ lb. shrimp
1 28-oz. can tomatoes, well
   drained
1 14-oz. can okra or 1 pkg.
   frozen okra

1 T. chopped parsley
½ t. thyme
Salt and pepper to taste
1 qt. chicken stock
½ t. filé powder

Stew chicken. Cut from bones into bite-size pieces. Slice ham in small bits. Sauté lightly. Combine rest of ingredients and cook about 30 minutes. Do not put filé powder in if you freeze; add later. Serves 6-8.

MRS. JOHN HART TODD

OYSTER STEW

2-4 T. butter
1 pt. oysters with liquor
1½ c. milk
½ c. coffee cream

½ t. salt
⅛ t. pepper or paprika
2 T. chopped parsley

In top of a double boiler melt butter; then add oysters and liquor. Bring just to boiling, but do not allow to boil. Add milk, cream and seasonings. Place pan over boiling water to heat. When oysters rise to top, add 2 tablespoons chopped parsley. Place a thin slice of lemon in bottom of each soup bowl and serve. Makes 4 cups.

MRS. THOMAS F. JOHNSTON

IVORY COAST CURRY SOUP

2 T. butter
½ c. sliced leeks
2 10½-oz. cans cream of
 chicken soup
2 10½-oz. cans water
½ c. cooked, sliced carrots

2-3 drops Tabasco, optional
1 T. curry powder
For Cold Soup:
 ½ c. julienne apple strips
 1 c. cooked chicken, cut in
 julienne strips

In butter, sauté sliced leeks about 5 minutes or until soft but not browned. Set aside. Combine in a saucepan chicken soup, water, carrots, Tabasco and leeks. Blend in curry powder with fork or wire whisk; place on heat and bring to gentle boil. Reduce heat; cook 3-4 minutes longer. For hot soup: Serve immediately. For cold soup: After soup has cooled, whiz in blender, 1 cupful at a time, for 30 seconds. Place apple strips and chicken strips in cooled soup when ready to serve. Serves 6-8.

MRS. TOM KIMBROUGH

Cheese and Egg Dishes

CHEESE ENTREE

Prepare 24 hours ahead.

8 slices stale white bread	¼ t. paprika
Butter	1 finely minced green onion
1½ lbs. sharp Cheddar	½ t. dry mustard
cheese, grated	½ t. salt
6 eggs, slightly beaten	⅛ t. pepper
2½ c. half and half	½ t. Worcestershire
1 rounded t. brown sugar	⅛ t. cayenne

Remove crust from bread, butter generously, and cut in tiny ½-inch squares. Butter well a 2-quart shallow baking dish. Arrange diced bread on bottom. Put generous layer of cheese over bread, using half of cheese, then add another layer of bread squares. Put remaining grated cheese over second layer of bread. Add remaining ingredients to beaten eggs and blend briefly; pour over cheese and bread. If half and half does not show around edges, add more. Cover with wax paper and put dish in plastic bag in refrigerator. Two hours before serving, remove from refrigerator and let stand for ½ hour. Set dish in shallow pan in which flat brown paper bag has been placed. Put ½-inch cold water in baking pan. Bake at 300° for 1 hour. Leave in oven, heat turned off, for 20 minutes after done. Bread and cheese mixture can be kept in covered container in refrigerator as long as one week before being used. The night before serving, pour egg and half and half over and proceed as directed. Serves 8.

MRS. GAITHER HATCHER

CHEESE GRITS

1 qt. milk	½ t. white pepper
½ c. butter or margarine	⅓ c. butter or margarine
1 c. grits	4 oz. Gruyère cheese, grated
1 t. salt	½ c. grated Parmesan cheese

Bring milk to a boil. Add ½ cup butter and stir in grits. Cook, stirring constantly, until the mixture is the consistency of oatmeal (about 5 minutes). Remove grits from heat, add salt and pepper, and beat the mixture well with an eggbeater. Add the ⅓ cup butter, stir in the grated Gruyère cheese, and pour into a greased 2-quart casserole. Sprinkle with Parmesan cheese. Bake at 350° for 1 hour. This can be made the day before and cooked when ready to serve. The Gruyère and the Parmesan give this dish a very unique taste . . . complements game beautifully. Serves 10.

MRS. CHARLES McGEE, BRUIN PLANTATION,
HUGHES, ARK.

GARLIC CHEESE GRITS

1 c. quick-cooking grits	2 eggs, beaten
1 roll garlic cheese	¾ c. milk
1 stick butter	

Cook grits as package directs. Add cheese and butter. Cool. Combine eggs and milk. Put grits in 2-quart buttered casserole and pour egg-milk mixture over grits. Bake uncovered for 1 hour in 375° oven. Can be made ahead. **Note:** Egg-milk mixture can be stirred into the cooled grits, if desired, and top dusted with paprika. Serves 8.

MRS. ROBERT C. BURLEIGH

MAKE-AHEAD CHEESE SOUFFLÉ

12 oz. sharp Cheddar cheese	To taste: cayenne, onion salt,
6 T. butter	dry mustard, Worcestershire
6 T. flour	1½ c. milk
1 t. salt	6 large cold eggs, separated
½ t. paprika	

Grate cheese. Butter a 2-quart soufflé dish. In double boiler, melt butter and blend in flour and seasonings. Add milk and cook, stirring constantly, until smooth and thickened. Add cheese and stir until melted. Remove from stove. Beat yolks with electric mixer until thick and lemon colored. Gradually stir yolks into cheese mixture. With a clean, dry mixer, beat whites until very stiff, but not dry. Slowly pour cheese mixture into whites, folding carefully with a rubber spatula until well blended and no large lumps of white remain. Bake, uncovered, in preheated oven at 325° for 45 minutes or until puffed and golden brown. Do not open oven door until time is up! Serve at once with a shrimp sauce made by heating undiluted frozen shrimp soup. **Note:** Soufflé can be made up ahead and refrigerated as long as 18 hours. Put soufflé in cold oven and bake 50 minutes. This can be frozen up to 7 days. Allow 50-60 minutes to bake frozen soufflé. Fill bowl almost to top when freezing; otherwise fill ¾ of bowl depth. Frozen soufflé will not rise as high as when baked right away. The frozen soufflé will be more moist after baking than one baked immediately, but the appearance and taste are marvelous. Serves 6.

MRS. ROBERT G. ALLEN

CHEESE FONDUE

1 lb. aged hoop cheese	Dash salt and pepper
1 lb. Swiss cheese	¼ c. brandy
¾ c. Madeira or white wine	1 large loaf French bread or
Dash nutmeg	2 small loaves

Break cheese into pieces in fondue dish (pottery) or chafing dish. Add wine, nutmeg, salt and pepper. Let stand for several hours. When ready to use, heat on stove until cheese has melted and add brandy. Transfer fondue dish to its burner. Break French bread into bite-sized pieces and dip into cheese with fondue forks. Serves 6.

MRS. WALLACE WITMER, JR.

SPINACH QUICHE

1 pie crust recipe	½ lb. boiled ham, cut into
1 egg white, slightly beaten	¼-inch cubes, or cooked
1 envelope (1⅜-oz.) dry	and drained bacon
onion soup mix	½ lb. natural Swiss cheese,
3 T. flour	grated
2 9-oz. pkgs. frozen creamed	1 whole egg
spinach, thawed	1 egg yolk
	⅔ c. coffee cream

Make pie crust and fit into a 10-inch pie pan or 6 five-inch fluted tart pans. Lightly brush shell(s) with egg white. Cover and refrigerate. Preheat oven to 375º. In a large bowl, blend onion soup mix with flour. Add spinach, ham, and 1 cup cheese. Mix well. In a small bowl, beat whole egg, yolk and cream until well combined. Add salt, if needed, to spinach mixture. Spoon spinach mixture into pastry; top with remaining cheese. Spoon on egg mixture. Bake the individual tarts about 30 minutes, the larger pie about 45 minutes. When done, the quiche will be nicely browned on top and will puff slightly. To serve, let cool slightly. For tarts, loosen edges with knife, and turn out of tart pans. Larger quiche must be served from its baking pan. Garnish with watercress, if desired. **Note:** The pastry, the egg mixture, and the spinach mixture can be made separately a few hours ahead of time. Just before baking quiche, assemble. Serves 6.

MRS. MILTON LYMAN KNOWLTON, JR.

QUICHE LORRAINE

1 9-in. pie shell	4 eggs
4 slices bacon, cooked and	1 c. half and half cream
crumbled	½ t. salt
½ c. diced ham	¼ t. nutmeg
½ c. diced Swiss cheese	¼ t. white pepper

Sprinkle bacon in bottom of unbaked pie shell. Cover with ham and Swiss cheese. Put eggs, cream and spices in blender and blend until mixed. Pour over ham, cheese, and bacon in pie shell and bake at 350º for about 45 minutes or until mixture is set. Serve hot. Serves 6.

MRS. WILLIAM M. BELL, JR.

CHEDDAR CHEESE SCRAMBLED EGGS

12 eggs	1 t. salt
½ c. milk	¼ t. pepper
2 c. grated Cheddar cheese	4 T. butter
2 t. chives	

Beat eggs well. Add other ingredients, except for butter. Heat 2 tablespoons butter in 10-inch skillet over low heat. Scramble half of egg mixture. Repeat with other half. Serves 6.

MRS. W. G. WESCHE

CRÊPES
(To Be Filled with Meat or Seafood Filling)

1 c. cold water	½ t. salt
1 c. cold milk	2 c. sifted all-purpose flour
4 eggs	4 T. melted butter

Put liquids, eggs and salt into blender. Add flour, then the butter. Cover and blend at top speed 1 minute. Scrape sides and blend again. Refrigerate at least 2 hours. Rub a crêpe pan (or small skillet 5 inches in diameter) with bacon fat or oil. Place on fairly high heat till it begins to smoke. Remove from heat. Hold pan in right hand and quickly pour 3-4 tablespoons of batter (easier to pour from measuring cup) into pan and tilt in all directions. Batter should cover bottom of skillet in a thin layer. Return pan to heat for 60-80 seconds, then loosen crêpe and turn over to brown lightly on the other side. Turn out on waxed paper. Repeat process. Makes 24 5-inch crêpes. When ready to serve, make certain "pretty side" of crêpe is showing. It is advisable to make these ahead and freeze, as they are time consuming. To freeze: Cool and stack between layers of waxed paper. Fill with Crab Meat Filling for Crêpes or Chicken Filling for Crêpes.

MRS. FRANK T. DONELSON, JR.

CHICKEN FILLING FOR CRÊPES

An elegant, yet inexpensive, entrée . . .

24 average sized, tightly closed fresh mushrooms	1 c. plus 5 T. sour cream
6-8 T. butter	1 T. chopped fresh parsley
2¼ c. shredded, cooked chicken	¾ c. grated Parmesan cheese
6 hard-boiled eggs, chopped	Salt to taste
	Pinch red and black pepper

Topping:

Sour cream	Parsley sprigs
Parmesan cheese	

Slice mushrooms. Sauté in butter for 4-5 minutes. In top of a double boiler, combine sautéed mushrooms with rest of ingredients. Heat. Place about 2 tablespoons chicken mixture in center of each crêpe and roll up. In a greased oven-to-table dish or dishes, line filled crêpes, cover tightly and heat in a very low oven until hot. All ingredients may be cooked or chopped the day before. Combine ingredients just before heating. When ready to serve, place dollop of sour cream on each, sprinkle generously with Parmesan cheese and garnish with parsley sprigs. Allow 2 crêpes per serving. Fills 30, 4 to 5-inch crêpes.

MRS. PHILIP FOX SOUTHALL

CRAB MEAT FILLING FOR CRÊPES

4½ T. minced green onion	¾ c. white wine or sherry
6 T. butter	Salt and pepper to taste
3¾ c. fresh crab meat	

Cook onions in butter over low heat for a minute. Stir in crab meat and cook slowly for 2 minutes. Add wine, cover, and simmer 1 minute. Uncover, raise heat and boil rapidly until liquid is almost gone. Season with salt and pepper and set aside.

Sauce:

6 T. butter	Salt and pepper to taste
7½ T. flour	3 egg yolks
4 c. liquid (milk, chicken,	¾ c. whipping cream
fish or mushroom stock)	¾ c. Swiss cheese

In double boiler, melt butter and add flour. Cook 2 minutes. Remove from heat and beat in boiling liquid. Season with salt and pepper. Heat again for 1 minute. Beat egg yolks and cream until well mixed. Remove double boiler from heat and beat into egg-cream mixture by the tablespoonful. Correct seasonings. To assemble: Use a very little of the sauce to hold the crab meat together. Put a little crab meat mixture on each crêpe and roll up. Place in a buttered shallow pan (not stacked). Cover with rest of sauce and sprinkle grated Swiss cheese over all. Bake at 350° for 20-25 minutes, then run under broiler to brown.

To prepare the day before: Make and fill crêpes. Cover pan securely and refrigerate. Refrigerate sauce separately. When ready to serve, heat sauce in double boiler; then pour over crêpes. Grate cheese and proceed as above. Allow 2 crêpes per serving. Filling and sauce are enough for 25 crêpes.

MRS. FRANK T. DONELSON, JR.

POACHED EGGS BRITTANY

8 small onions	½ c. cream
Chicken stock	1 egg yolk
4 eggs	Salt
4 slices French bread	Pepper
4 cooked mushroom caps,	
quartered	

Peel onions and simmer in enough seasoned chicken stock to cover. While onions are simmering, poach eggs and fry bread on both sides in butter. When onions are tender and liquid is reduced to syrup consistency, add mushroom caps and cream beaten with egg yolk. Season sauce with salt and pepper and stir until slightly thickened. **Do not boil.** Place an egg on each piece of bread and spoon sauce over each. Serve immediately. **Note:** French bread may be fried ahead and frozen; then reheated at serving time. Recipe is easily doubled. Serves 4.

MR. AND MRS. JOHN LARY

POACHED EGGS FLORENTINE

1½ T. butter
1 T. minced shallots
1 pkg. frozen chopped spinach, cooked and drained
1 T. flour
Salt and pepper

Nutmeg
1 c. whipping cream
6 soft poached eggs, cold
6 3-in. bread rounds, sautéed in butter

Melt butter, stir in shallots, then spinach. Sprinkle in flour and cook slowly for 2 minutes. Add salt, pepper, pinch of nutmeg. Stir in half of cream. Cover pan, cook slowly 5-6 minutes, stirring frequently. Slowly stir in rest of cream. Spinach sauce, poached eggs, bread rounds may be done day ahead.

Meringue:

¼ c. all-purpose flour
¾-1 c. milk
Salt and pepper
Nutmeg
3-4 egg yolks

4-5 egg whites, room temperature.
¼ t. cream of tartar
½ c. coarsely grated Swiss cheese

Preheat oven to 375°. Put 2-3 spoonfuls of spinach sauce on each bread round; arrange in buttered baking dish. Top each with a poached egg. Place flour in saucepan; gradually beat in ¾ cup of milk with wire whisk. Beat over high heat till sauce thickens and comes to a boil. Beat in 4 egg yolks, salt, pepper and nutmeg to taste. Beat whites in bowl until they foam. Beat in pinch of salt and cream of tartar. Increase speed till stiff peaks are formed. Stir ¼ of egg whites into sauce; gently fold in rest along with ¾ of the grated cheese. Mound soufflé mixture over each egg and top with a big pinch of reserved grated cheese. Set immediately in upper third of oven and bake about 25 minutes until puffed and browned. Serve at once. Makes 6 servings.

MRS. ROBERT G. ALLEN

CURRIED EGGS

2 small onions, minced
½ c. margarine
2 T. flour
1 T. curry powder
1½ c. hot water

2 chicken bouillon cubes
Salt and pepper
½ c. whipping cream
12 hard-cooked eggs, quartered
1 pimiento, chopped

In top of double boiler, cook onion in margarine until soft. Stir in flour and curry. Add hot water slowly; then add bouillon cubes. Cook and stir constantly until smooth and thickened. Season with salt and pepper to taste. Blend in cream; add eggs and pimiento. Heat over boiling water about 10 minutes and serve over pastry shells or rice. Garnish with paprika and serve with the usual condiments: chopped peanuts, chutney, coconut, candied orange peel, etc. Serves 8.

MRS. C. WHITNEY BROWN

ANCHOVY-STUFFED EGGS

6 hard-cooked eggs
6 flat anchovies, drained
   and chopped
3 T. mayonnaise or salad
   dressing

2 t. lemon juice
Dash pepper
2 T. chopped parsley
1 small jar pimientos, drained
Bottled capers, drained (24)

Cut eggs in half lengthwise. Remove yolks to a small bowl. Add anchovies, mayonnaise, lemon juice, pepper and parsley. Mix well with a fork. Stuff egg whites with yolk mixture, mounding it with a fork. Cut pimientos into 24 strips, 1 inch long. Arrange 2 strips crisscross on each egg half. Garnish with 2 capers, one at each end. Cover with plastic wrap; refrigerate. Serves 6.

MRS. MILTON LYMAN KNOWLTON, JR.

EGGS HUSSARDE

Canadian bacon
English muffins
Marchand de Vin Sauce
Tomato slices

Poached eggs
Hollandaise sauce (see Index)
Paprika

Lay slices of grilled Canadian bacon cut ¼-inch thick on buttered and toasted English muffins, split. Cover with Marchand de Vin Sauce. Top with uncooked, or grilled tomato slices, then soft poached eggs. Ladle Hollandaise sauce over all and garnish with paprika. Two servings each will satisfy even the hungriest of men. **Note:** You can poach a number of eggs at a time by placing eggs in well-greased muffin tins. Place muffin tins over large pan of boiling water and seal tightly with an aluminum foil tent. Watch closely or eggs will cook hard. Or, break eggs into greased ramekins, place ramekins in utensil containing 1 inch of boiling water, and cover.

Marchand de Vin Sauce:

½ c. butter, no substitutes
⅓ c. finely chopped
   mushrooms
½ c. minced ham
⅓ c. shallots, finely
   chopped, or green onions
½ c. finely chopped onion

2 or 3 cloves garlic, minced
2 T. flour
⅛ t. pepper
Dash of cayenne
¾ c. beef stock
½ c. claret

In a large skillet, melt butter and lightly sauté the mushrooms, ham, shallots, onion and garlic. When the onion is tender, add the flour, pepper and cayenne. Brown about 7-10 minutes, stirring constantly. Blend in the stock and wine. Cover and simmer over low heat about 30 minutes, stirring now and then. Makes 1½ cups. The sauce can be made ahead and reheated very slowly. Eggs Hussarde can be cooked and assembled in about 30 minutes if the Marchand de Vin Sauce is made ahead. It is possible to poach your eggs ahead of time (do not poach "hard"), refrigerate (tightly covered) then let come to room temperature before assembling. Serves 10.

MRS. MILTON LYMAN KNOWLTON, JR.

EGGS IN ASPIC

6 eggs
2 T. tarragon vinegar
1 12½-oz. can chicken
  consommé
1 pkg. unflavored gelatin

6 sprigs tarragon (if unable to
  buy fresh, use kind that
  comes in bottled tarragon
  vinegar and blot dry)

Poach eggs, three at a time, in simmering water with tarragon vinegar in it or cook them in an egg poacher until the whites are firmly set and the yellows still a little soft. Drain. Cut them to a perfect circle. Cool on a paper towel. Add to chicken consommé enough water to make 2 cups in all. In a small bowl, blend gelatin with ½ cup chicken liquid. Let soften 5 minutes. Stir in the remaining liquid, heated to boiling point. Place 2 tablespoons of mixture in each of six 4-ounce individual ramekins. In each, place a sprig of tarragon. Chill in refrigerator, or 5 minutes in the freezer, until jellied. Remove and place 1 egg face down in each mold. Fill with rest of liquid, about ¼ cup each. Cover with plastic wrap and chill until set. Unmold to serve. This can be served atop a slice of prosciutto, ham, or pâté, if you choose. Serves 6.

MRS. B. PERCY MAGNESS, JR.

EGGS BAKED IN MUSHROOM SAUCE

1 lb. fresh mushrooms,
  washed and sliced
4 T. butter
3 T. flour
2 c. coffee cream
1 beef or chicken
  bouillon cube

1 T. grated onion, optional
Salt and pepper to taste
1 t. dried parsley
1 egg yolk, slightly beaten
Grated Parmesan cheese
6-8 eggs

Sauté mushrooms in butter for 5 minutes. Remove mushrooms from skillet. Stir flour, cream, bouillon cube (dissolved in 1 tablespoon hot water), and onion into the liquid left in skillet. Cook, stirring till thick. Add mushrooms, salt and pepper, and parsley. Add some of the hot sauce to the yolk; stir and return to mushroom sauce. Cook a little longer. Pour hot sauce into individual buttered ramekins or into a large buttered baking dish (sauce should be about 1 inch deep). Drop eggs into sauce, slipping a spoon under each egg so that it will sink slightly into sauce. Sprinkle with cheese and bake at 350° until whites of eggs are firm (yellow should be soft), about 15 minutes. Serves 6.

MRS. MILTON LYMAN KNOWLTON, JR.

Seafood

SHRIMP IN ALMOND SAUCE

1½ c. water
1 stalk celery
½ t. pickling spice
2 t. salt
2 lbs. raw shrimp, shelled
 and deveined
1½ c. diced white bread
1½ c. milk
4 T. butter

1½ c. finely chopped onions
2 cloves garlic, minced
½ t. ground black pepper
¼ t. chili pepper
1 t. Spanish paprika
½ c. olive oil
1 c. ground almonds

Bring water, celery, pickling spice and 1 teaspoon salt to boil. Add shrimp; cook over medium heat 7 minutes. Drain, reserving 1 cup stock. Soak bread in milk 10 minutes and mash smooth. Do not drain. Melt butter in skillet; sauté onions and garlic until soft and browned. Mix in pepper, chili pepper, paprika and undrained bread; sauté 5 minutes, stirring frequently. Gradually mix in olive oil, then the almonds and remaining salt. Cook 2 minutes. Blend in stock and add shrimp. Cook over low heat 5 minutes. Taste for seasoning. Serve in individual shells. Serves 8.

MRS. JAMES GUY ROBBINS

CURRIED SHRIMP

2 chicken bouillon cubes
2 c. boiling water
2 T. curry powder
¾ c. flour
1 c. butter
1 c. chopped onion
2 cloves garlic, minced
2 apples, chopped
1 c. chopped celery (optional)

½ c. chopped green pepper
 (optional)
Dash of chili powder
1 t. (scant) ginger
4 t. lemon juice
2 c. coffee cream
1½ t. salt
Dash of pepper
7-8 c. cleaned and cooked shrimp

Dissolve bouillon cubes in water. In a heavy skillet over low heat, cook curry powder and flour in 3 tablespoons of the butter. In another pan, cook onion, garlic, apple, celery and green pepper in rest of butter until tender but not brown (about 5 minutes). Add chili powder and ginger. Remove from heat and add bouillon and lemon juice. Add to flour and curry mixture. Add cream and mix well. Cook uncovered over low heat until thick (about 2 hours). Add salt, pepper, and shrimp. Simmer 15 minutes more. Serve over plain or saffron rice with small dishes of condiments. See Diane's Curry for Condiments. Serves 12.

OYSTERS DIABLO

3 pts. oysters
4 T. olive oil
6 stalks celery, chopped
6 spring onions
3 c. crumbled crackers (30)
4 T. Worcestershire

6 T. catsup
½ lemon rind, grated
16 dashes Tabasco
Parsley, finely chopped
½ t. Accent
Salt to taste

Clean and plump oysters and save 1½ cups oyster liquor. In a skillet put olive oil, celery, and white part of onions. Cook until clear. Add green part of onions. To the oyster juice add cracker crumbs, Worcestershire, catsup, grated lemon rind, Tabasco, finely chopped parsley. Add celery and onion, Accent, oysters and salt to taste. Grease casserole with butter, add mixture, cover lightly with bread crumbs and dot generously with butter. Bake at 300° until hot.

DR. AND MRS. BENSON MARTIN

OYSTERS FLORENTINE

3 10-oz. pkgs. frozen chopped
    spinach
Salt to taste
1½ c. grated medium sharp
    Cheddar cheese

3 c. medium white sauce
1½ lbs. drained oysters, chopped
Additional grated cheese
Cracker crumbs (Saltines, Waverly
    Wafers, or Ritz)

Cook spinach according to package directions. Drain and add salt to taste. Add cheese to white sauce, stirring until cheese melts. Add chopped oysters to the sauce. Salt to taste. Layer cooked spinach over the bottom of a greased flat baking dish. Pour white sauce with oysters over spinach. Top with additional cheese and cracker crumbs. Bake at 300° for 20-30 minutes. This may also be baked in ramekins. Serves 12.

MRS. ARTHUR C. CLARKE, VANCOUVER, BRITISH COLUMBIA

CREAMED SALMON AND RIPE OLIVES

1 T. flour
1 T. butter
¾ c. milk
Salt to taste
Worcestershire
Pinch of tarragon

Pinch of basil
¼ t. lemon juice
1 large can salmon
1 c. sliced ripe olives
Buttered bread crumbs

Make a thin cream sauce by combining the flour, butter and milk in saucepan over moderate heat. Remove from heat, and season white sauce with the spices. Remove bone and skin from salmon, saving juices to thin cream sauce if too thick. Break salmon into small pieces. Mix with olives and cream sauce. Put in ramekins and sprinkle with buttered bread crumbs. Bake at 400° about 10 minutes or till hot. Makes 6 servings.

MRS. ERIC BABENDREER

FISH IN WHITE WINE

An easy dish.

1 T. butter	A lavish ½ c. dry white wine
5 sliced mushrooms	or dry vermouth
2 chopped green scallions	Roux sauce: 2 T. butter
6 fillets of any white fish	1 T. flour
Salt and pepper to taste	Chopped chervil or fresh dill

Melt butter in skillet; add mushrooms and scallions. Lay the fillets on top. Salt and pepper well and add wine. Cover tightly and simmer for 12 minutes. Remove fish to a **hot** serving platter. Make a roux of flour and butter, and add to sauce in skillet to thicken. Add plenty of pepper to sauce, then pour it over fish on platter and sprinkle with chervil or fresh dill. Serves 4 (or 6 people with average appetites).

LETITIA BALDRIGE HOLLENSTEINER, NEW YORK, N.Y.

SHRIMP CREOLE EN BATEAUX

2 T. butter	Salt and pepper to taste
1 T. flour	2 lbs. raw shrimp, peeled and
1 large onion	deveined
1 stalk celery, minced	3 or 4 drops Tabasco
1 can tomatoes	1 t. cornstarch

In a heavy pot melt butter, then mix in flour. Add onion and celery. When they start to brown, add tomatoes, salt and pepper, shrimp, Tabasco, and enough water to cover. Cook gently for about 20 minutes. Just before serving, add cornstarch to thicken sauce and add a glaze. Serve in Bateaux or over white rice. Serves 6.

Bateaux (boats):

6 individual loaves French bread (or) 1 pkg. Pepperidge Farm club rolls

Cut off top and scoop out bread, leaving a crust shell. Butter inside well and place on cookie sheet in 250° oven for 20-25 minutes, or till very crisp.

MRS. CHESTER GELPI, NEW ORLEANS, LA.

EASY CREAMED SHRIMP

3 cans frozen cream of shrimp	1½ t. curry powder
soup	1½ lbs. shrimp
3 c. sour cream	

Combine all ingredients and heat in top of double boiler. Serve over rice or in patty shells. This dish has a very distinct curry flavor. Serves 12.

MRS. R. HENRY LAKE, HOUSTON, TEX.

SHRIMP IN CHEESE SAUCE

2 rolls garlic cheese
2 cans frozen cream of shrimp
  soup
2 cans mushrooms (reserve
  liquid)
1 t. onion juice

2 t. Worcestershire
2 T. lemon juice
Dash Tabasco
2 cans small shrimp
Salt to taste

Combine all ingredients, except canned shrimp and salt, in top of double boiler. Cook until thick (about 1 hour), stirring occasionally. If too thick, thin with mushroom liquid. Season with salt to taste. Add shrimp. Serve in chafing dish with Melba toast rounds as an appetizer or over Melba toast or patty shells for lunch. Serves 12 as an entrée or 50 as an appetizer.

MRS. ERNEST W. FARRAR

SHRIMP FOO YOUNG

5 eggs
1 c. shrimp, shredded
1 c. onions, shredded

¼ c. water chestnuts, sliced thin,
  or bean sprouts
½ c. mushrooms, sliced thin
2 T. soy sauce

Beat eggs till thick. Add shrimp, onions, chestnuts, mushrooms, and soy sauce to eggs and continue beating. Heat small amount of oil in a heavy shallow pan or skillet. Carefully ladle shrimp mixture into pan. Cook until brown and then turn. This will resemble an omelet. Serve with sauce. Serves 6.

Sauce:

1 T. cornstarch
1 T. soy sauce

¾ c. bouillon
¼ t. sugar

Mix ingredients and cook till slightly thickened. **Note:** This recipe cannot be doubled. To increase, it must be made twice.

MRS. JOHN HART TODD

NEW ORLEANS "BARBECUE SHRIMP"

5 lbs. shrimp in shells
1 lb. oleo
2 oz. can black pepper

Large bottle Italian dressing
Juice of 4 lemons

Put shrimp in large roasting pan. Melt oleo; add pepper, salad dressing, and lemon juice. Pour over shrimp and cook covered for 45 minutes in 350° oven. Serve on large platters. Pour pepper and butter sauce from pan over shrimp. Give guests large napkins and bibs and invite them to "Peel'em and eat'em". Serves 8-10.

MRS. EUGENE J. PIDGEON

SHRIMP, MUSHROOM, AND ARTICHOKE CASSEROLE

2½ T. butter
½ lb. mushrooms
1½ lbs. shrimp
1 #2 can artichoke hearts
4½ T. butter
4½ T. flour
¾ c. milk

¾ c. whipping cream
½ c. dry sherry
1 T. Worcestershire
Salt, pepper to taste
½ c. Parmesan cheese
Paprika

Melt 2½ tablespoons butter and sauté mushrooms. Set aside. Boil and shell shrimp. In a 2-quart casserole, make one layer each of artichoke hearts, shrimp, and mushrooms. To make sauce: Melt 4½ tablespoons butter. Stirring with a wire whisk, add the flour, then the milk and cream. Stir until thick. Add sherry, Worcestershire, salt and pepper to cream sauce. Pour sauce over layered ingredients. Sprinkle top with grated cheese; then sprinkle with paprika. Bake in 375° oven for 20-30 minutes. Serve over rice. This is better if made the day before. Serves 6.

MRS. RONALD BYRNES

CRAB MEAT CASSEROLE

2 c. white crab meat
4 c. fresh bread, torn into
   tiny pieces
1 c. melted butter
1 T. Worcestershire
1 t. salt
4 hard-cooked eggs, mashed
2 raw eggs

2 c. milk
Juice of 2 lemons
2 T. minced green pepper
4 T. Milani's mustard-flavored
   dressing
½ t. red pepper
½ t. black pepper

Mix all ingredients and bake in 2-quart greased casserole or in individual baking shells at 400° for 30 minutes. Serves 8.

MRS. ROSS LYNN

ROSIE'S OYSTER CASSEROLE

1 pt. oysters
Salt and pepper
Cayenne to taste

Buttered bread crumbs
½ c. butter

Butter casserole and sprinkle lightly with flour. Place in the casserole half of oysters in their juice. Sprinkle oysters with salt, pepper and cayenne; top with bread crumbs; then dot with half of butter. Repeat with another layer. Do not make more than two layers. To increase, make twice; do not double. Bake at 350° for 15 minutes. Serves 6.

MRS. E. JAMES HOUSE

LOBSTER IN CARDINAL SAUCE

4 pkgs. frozen lobster tails or
2 pkgs. frozen lobster tails and
2 pkgs. frozen king crab meat
¼ c. butter
¼ c. flour
1½ c. coffee cream
¼ c. tomato paste
1 t. salt

½ t. garlic salt
Few drops hot pepper sauce
Pinch saffron
¼ t. curry powder
¼ t. ginger
2 t. brandy (optional)
1 t. lemon pepper

Cook lobsters in boiling salted water for 10 minutes. Remove and drain; strain stock and reserve. If using frozen crab meat, thaw and break into small pieces. Cut cooled lobster meat into bite-sized pieces. For sauce, melt butter and blend in flour, stirring constantly. Add ⅔ cup lobster stock and the cream. Cook, stirring, until thick and smooth. Add tomato paste, salt, garlic salt and remaining seasonings. Add seafood and simmer until hot. If you like, add brandy to the sauce. Keep warm over hot water in chafing dish and serve over hot rice. Serves 4-6.

MRS. DENNIS COUGHLIN, KNOXVILLE, TENN.

SEAFOOD CURRY

3 large onions, sliced thin
2 cloves garlic, minced or mashed
¾ c. butter or margarine
1½ T. curry powder
5 medium tomatoes
1 10-oz. pkg. frozen peas, cooked

3½ c. fish or chicken stock
4 lbs. assorted seafood (crab meat;
peeled, cleaned shrimp; baby
lobster tails, cut in sections;
scallops; clams or oysters)

Cook onions and garlic in half the butter until golden. Add curry powder and sauté for another 5 minutes. Peel the tomatoes, cut in pieces and stir into onion mixture. Purée the peas or whirl them in a blender with 1 cup of the stock. Add the peas, along with the remainder of the stock, to the curry, and simmer for 20 minutes. Sauté the seafood lightly in the remaining butter, but do not overcook. Combine with the curry sauce; correct seasonings, adding salt to taste and more curry powder, if desired. Before serving, reheat thoroughly. This curry does not have as much sauce as some, and the peas are its only thickening. If you prefer, thicken it further with a flour paste. Serve over rice and pass small bowls of condiments. Suggestions for condiments are listed under Diane's Curry. Serves 12-14.

Game and Poultry

BARBECUED CHICKEN

**6 (2-2½ lb. size) broiler-fryers, split, or 4-5 lbs. of chicken legs
or second joints of wing (part that resembles small chicken leg).**

Marinade:

¾ c. salad oil	1½ t. salt
¾ c. lemon juice	1 chicken bouillon cube, crushed
¼ c. cider vinegar	1 clove garlic, crushed
¼ c. dry vermouth or tomato juice	1 t. dried oregano leaves

Wash chicken well; dry with paper towels. Arrange chicken in two large
shallow baking dishes. Make marinade by combining all ingredients and shaking well. Pour over chicken. Refrigerate, covered, overnight, turning occasionally. Either grill over coals 50-60 minutes, turning often and brushing
with marinade, or broil in oven on broiler pan rack 6 inches from heat for
45 minutes, turning and brushing frequently with marinade. (The smaller
cut pieces of chicken require less cooking time.) Serves 12.

MRS. JAMES GUY ROBBINS

CHICKEN CHAUDFROID

8 chicken breast halves, boned	2 T. lemon juice
2 cans chicken broth	½ t. grated lemon peel
3 oz. pkg. cream cheese	¼ t. salt
4 T. mayonnaise	2 T. snipped dill

Place chicken breasts and broth in saucepan and simmer, covered, 30 minutes
or until fork tender. Refrigerate in broth until cool. Thirty minutes before
serving, remove breasts from refrigerator and pour off broth. Remove any
skin. Make a paste of the remaining above ingredients and coat the rounded
side of each breast.

To assemble:

8 very thick slices peeled tomato	Snipped dill
Romaine lettuce	Avocado, sliced in strips
Seasoned salt	French or Italian dressing
Toasted slivered almonds	

Place one slice tomato on each bed of romaine. Sprinkle with seasoned salt.
Place chilled, coated breast over tomato. Sprinkle with almonds and dill.
Garnish long edges of breast with avocado slices. Serve with French or Italian
dressing. Serves 8.

MRS. RAYMOND E. MANOGUE

CHICKEN YUCATAN

The Yucatans do this with a spice called pibil. They wrap the chicken in banana leaves and cook it all day over hot coals. This is the Memphis version . . .

8 large chicken breast halves	2 large tomatoes, chopped
Salt and pepper	3 large stalks celery, chopped
Chili powder, sprinkled thickly	1 large green pepper, chopped
Curry powder, sprinkled thickly	1 qt. orange juice
1 large onion, finely chopped	

Season chicken breasts with spices. Line a flat pan with aluminum foil. Put the breasts in, distribute onion, tomato, celery, and pepper over breasts. Pour in orange juice and marinate several hours. It's convenient to do this in the morning and forget it until mid-afternoon. Cover with foil and cook at 300° for 4 hours. Serve over saffron rice. The slow long cooking is very important. Serves 8.

MRS. B. PERCY MAGNESS, JR.

BREAST OF CHICKEN VÉRONIQUE

9 T. butter	1½ c. coffee cream
3 large chicken breasts, split	¾ c. white wine
18 medium mushroom caps,	1 c. diced ham
quartered	Salt and pepper to taste
3 T. flour	1½ c. seedless grapes

Melt 6 tablespoons butter in large heavy pan and brown chicken breasts over medium heat. Remove to a casserole. Melt 3 tablespoons butter in same pan. Sauté mushrooms over high heat for 3 minutes. Remove with a slotted spoon and scatter over chicken. Reduce heat and stir flour into skillet. Cook the roux 1 minute. Gradually add cream and wine, stirring constantly. Cook until sauce is thick. Add diced ham and season with salt and pepper. Pour sauce over chicken. Bake covered in a 350° oven 35-40 minutes. Uncover and scatter grapes over chicken and bake another 10 minutes. This can be prepared ahead and refrigerated until baking time, but grapes should not be added until last 10 minutes of cooking. Serves 6.

MRS. JAMES GUY ROBBINS

CHICKEN BREASTS PIQUANT

3 c. dry red wine	4 t. ground ginger
1 c. soy sauce	1 t. oregano
1 c. salad oil	4 T. brown sugar
8 T. water	8 chicken breast halves
4 cloves garlic, sliced	

Combine all the ingredients and pour over the breasts arranged in a 3-quart rectangular baking dish. Cover and bake at 375° about 1 hour. Serve over rice. Can be made with cut-up pieces of a whole chicken. This may be made the day before. Serves 8.

MRS. EPHRAIM B. WILKINSON, JR.

CRAB STUFFED CHICKEN BREASTS

¾ c. seasoned stuffing mix
1 egg
½-¾ c. undiluted mushroom soup
6 oz. pkg. crab meat

1 T. lemon juice
2 t. Worcestershire
1 t. prepared mustard
½ t. salt
6 whole chicken breasts

Combine stuffing mix with lightly beaten egg, undiluted mushroom soup, crab meat, lemon juice, Worcestershire, mustard and salt. Spoon stuffing down center of each chicken breast. Roll up and fasten with metal skewer or toothpicks. Preheat broiler and broil stuffed breasts 6-inches from heat for about 15 minutes. Turn and broil 15 minutes more. Do ahead of time and reheat. Serves 6.

MRS. JAMES GUY ROBBINS

CHICKEN DIVAN

4 whole chicken breasts
2 c. water
1 T. salt

1 onion, quartered
2 pkgs. frozen asparagus

Cook chicken in water with salt and onion. Skin, bone, and pull apart in large pieces. Cook asparagus according to package directions.

Cream Sauce:

4 T. butter
4 T. flour
1 c. milk
1 c. chicken stock

Juice of 1 lemon
4 egg yolks, beaten
2 T. sherry
Grated Parmesan cheese

Melt butter in saucepan and stir in flour. Add the milk and stock. Cook till thickened and add lemon juice. Add some of the hot sauce to the yolks, then return the yolk mixture to the rest of the sauce. Cook over low heat for a few seconds. Remove from heat and season sauce with sherry. Pour ½ the sauce over the asparagus, which have been arranged in a buttered baking dish, and sprinkle with Parmesan cheese. Arrange chicken on top, cover with rest of sauce and sprinkle with more cheese. Refrigerate. To serve, heat 20 minutes at 400°. Serves 8.

MRS. FRANK T. DONELSON, JR.

CHICKEN WITH SOUR CREAM

2 c. sour cream
2 t. paprika
2 t. celery salt
2 T. lemon juice

1 t. salt
4 cloves garlic, sliced
2 T. Worcestershire
6 chicken breast halves

Mix all ingredients except chicken and let stand at least 1 hour. Press the garlic a little, then remove. Dip pieces of chicken in mixture until well coated. Lay in shallow, foil-lined pan, sprinkle with cracker crumbs, and bake at 350° in oven for 1 hour. Serve with rice. Serves 4-6.

MRS. JAMES K. POLK, INVERNESS, MISS.

CHICKEN IN FOIL

Chicken breasts   Butter
Salt and pepper to taste   Tiny whole mushrooms
Poultry seasoning

For each serving, place half a chicken breast on a piece of heavy duty foil. Sprinkle with salt, pepper, and poultry seasoning. Place 6 mushrooms on each breast and dot each with 3 pats of butter. Seal air tight. Place on cookie sheet, and bake at 350° for 1½ hours. These may be frozen "ready for the oven".

MRS. F. PEARSON ALLEN, JR.

DIANE'S CURRY

5 c. cooked turkey or chicken   Handful of raisins
  (about 5 lb. hen)   2 t. sugar
8 T. poultry fat or oleo   2 T. chutney, diced
3 medium onions, chopped   ¼ c. almonds, finely chopped
½ clove garlic, pressed   ½ c. cream
1¼ T. curry powder   1 cucumber
1½ c. poultry stock   Salt to taste
8 whole peppercorns   Juice of 1 lemon
½ t. ginger

Cook fowl till **just done**, remove skin and bones, and cut meat in large bite-sized pieces. Brown fowl till golden in fat in skillet. Remove to a large kettle. In same fat, brown till golden, the onions and garlic. With slotted spoon, remove to kettle. Stir curry powder till smooth into fat remaining in skillet. Add the following to the curry-fat mixture: stock, peppercorns, ginger, raisins, sugar, and chutney. Add this mixture to the kettle, cover and simmer gently. While mixture is simmering, fry almonds in additional fat till light brown. Add cream to almonds and cook 5 minutes. Remove almond mixture and kettle from heat and cook 30 minutes. Add almond-cream to contents of kettle. Cut cucumber in ½-inch cubes and add to kettle. Add more stock, if needed, to cover mixture. Uncover kettle and simmer till gravy is thick and rich (about 4 hours). East Indian curry does not depend on flour for thickening but on reduction by cooking. After mixture has thickened, taste for intensity of curry. Add salt and lemon juice. Serve over white or saffron rice. **Note:** Freezes well. To serve frozen curry: Place in pan and reheat slowly. Serves 6-7.

Suggested Condiments:

Poppadoms, toasted, or crushed   Chopped onions
  potato chips   Chopped peanuts, or cashews
Crumbled bacon   Sieved egg yolk
Chopped green pepper   Grated coconut
Chopped egg white   Raisins, soaked in whiskey
Chopped tomato   Chutney
Chopped preserved ginger   Preserved kumquats
Chopped, unpared cucumber

MRS. J. B. IGLEHEART, EVANSVILLE, IND.

CHICKEN SUPREME

6 chicken breast halves	3 egg yolks
Salt and pepper to taste	½ c. crab meat
¼ t. marjoram	1 T. parsley
¼ c. butter	6 large fresh mushrooms
½ c. sherry	½ c. grated Swiss cheese
2 c. cream	

Remove skin from chicken breasts. Sprinkle with salt and pepper and rub with marjoram. Sauté chicken in butter over low heat until done. Remove chicken and add sherry to pan juices. Cook until almost evaporated. Add cream and egg yolks. Cook over low heat until thickened. Combine crab meat and parsley and add enough of the sauce to hold crab meat together. Sauté mushrooms and fill with the crab meat mixture. Place chicken breasts in a buttered shallow casserole and place a stuffed mushroom on top of each. Cover with remaining sauce. Sprinkle with Swiss cheese and place in a 425° oven for 5-10 minutes to brown. Serves 6.

GROVEL ROAD, ST. MARY'S EPISCOPAL GUILD

SOPA POLLO

(Chicken Casserole)

1 large onion, chopped	1 10½-oz. can enchilado sauce
8 oz. can chili peppers	1 can cream of chicken soup
1 pkg. frozen tortillas	1 small can evaporated milk or
4 c. cooked, boned and diced	1 c. whole milk
chicken	2 c. chicken broth
2 c. grated Cheddar cheese	

Sauté onion in small amount of margarine; add chopped chili peppers and set aside. Line 3-quart casserole or baking dish with about 5 uncooked tortillas. Next, layer chicken, cheese, sautéed onion and chili peppers and broken tortilla pieces. Repeat layers, topping with cheese. Combine liquid ingredients and mix thoroughly. Pour over casserole and refrigerate overnight. Cook uncovered for 1 hour at 350°. Serves 8-10.

MRS. CHARLES G. SWINGLE, MARKED TREE, ARK.

CHICKEN LIVERS IN MADEIRA

2 lbs. chicken livers	1 t. Worcestershire
Seasoned flour	Salt, pepper to taste
2 c. dry Madeira	Thin sliced toast
6 T. sweet butter	

Shake livers in paper bag filled with seasoned flour. Heat butter until foamy. Cook livers quickly in butter, about 5 minutes, shaking pan. Gradually add Madeira and Worcestershire; season to taste. Cover and simmer about 10 minutes. Serve over thin slices of toast. This can be served as a luncheon, brunch or supper dish over thin slices of toast with butter-browned mushroom caps, or as an hors d'oeuvre in a chafing dish. Serves 8.

CHICKEN CORDON BLEU

6 whole chicken breasts	1 c. bread crumbs
½ lb. thin sliced ham	1 t. salt
½ lb. thin sliced Swiss cheese	1 t. pepper
1 stick butter	1 t. paprika

Have butcher remove center bone from chicken breasts. Open breasts under ribs to make a pocket. Place 1 slice ham and 1 slice cheese in each pocket. Roll up and secure with toothpicks. Melt butter in pie plate. Mix crumbs, salt, pepper and paprika in second plate. Roll chicken in butter, then in crumbs. Place in buttered baking dish and store in refrigerator for several hours. Bake uncovered in 400° oven for 40 minutes. Serves 6.

MRS. CHESTER GELPI, NEW ORLEANS, LA.

BREAST OF CHICKEN, EDEN ISLE

6 chicken breasts, boned	2 cans cream of chicken soup
Pepper	1½ c. sour cream
6 slices bacon	1 8-oz. pkg. cream cheese
1 pkg. dried beef	

Pepper, but do not salt, chicken breasts. Wrap slice of bacon around each. Place layer of dried beef (not corned beef) in bottom of baking dish. Place bacon-wrapped breasts in dish. Cover with mixture of chicken soup, sour cream and cream cheese. Cover lightly with foil. Place in 325° oven for 2 hours. When tender, remove foil and let brown slightly. Serve on bed of rice. Serves 6.

RED APPLE INN, EDEN ISLE, ARK.

LOQUAT CHICKEN

1 lb. raw chicken, ground	2 T. soy sauce
10 water chestnuts, chopped fine	2 T. wine
6 mushrooms, chopped fine (⅓ c.)	2 egg whites, beaten
2 T. onion, chopped fine	1 can loquates or apricots
2 T. cornstarch	3 c. oil
½ t. salt	

Paste Mix:

1 T. oil	1-2 T. soy sauce
1 c. apricot juice	4 t. cornstarch
½ c. chicken stock	

Mix chicken, water chestnuts, mushrooms and onion together. Add cornstarch, salt, soy sauce, wine and egg whites. Form into balls the size of walnuts. Heat pan and add oil. Fry chicken balls until brown. Remove from oil and drain. Pour off remaining oil in skillet and reheat pan. Add 1 tablespoon strained oil, apricot juice, chicken stock, soy sauce and cornstarch and cook a few seconds. Add chicken balls and apricots. Heat and serve. Serves 6.

MRS. JOHN HART TODD

WALNUT CHICKEN

½ lb. (2 c.) walnut meats or
    blanched almonds
8 water chestnuts
½ c. cooking oil
1 c. bamboo shoots, diced
1 c. celery, chopped
1 c. chopped onion

1 lb. boned chicken, cubed and
    dredged with:
¾ t. salt
2 T. cornstarch
2 T. wine
1 t. sugar
3 T. soy sauce
¼ c. soup stock

Sauté nuts in hot oil, stirring often, until just brown. Remove and drain well. In same oil, sauté bamboo shoots, celery, and onion, until slightly tender. Remove vegetables and drain on absorbent paper. Strain oil if necessary, reheat, and sauté in it the dredged chicken until tender. It may be necessary to add a little more oil. Remove chicken and pour oil from skillet. To the soup stock, add the cooked chicken, nuts and vegetables and heat. Serves 6.

MRS. JOHN HART TODD

WILD RICE AND CHICKEN

1 c. wild rice
2 c. chicken broth
Butter
Salt and pepper to taste
3 oz. can mushrooms

6 chicken breast halves
½ pkg. dry onion soup mix
1 can mushroom soup
Paprika

Soak wild rice overnight. Drain rice. Pour chicken broth over rice in large flat casserole. Dot with butter, salt and pepper. Drain can of mushrooms and add mushrooms to casserole. Place chicken breasts over rice. Sprinkle onion soup mix over all. Dilute mushroom soup with a little water and spoon over each breast. Sprinkle with paprika. Cook uncovered at 350° for 1 hour; then cook covered ½ hour longer. A more economical, but very tasty, change is to use Uncle Ben's long grain and wild rice mix instead of the wild rice. Do not soak the Uncle Ben's rice mixture overnight. Serves 6.

MRS. J. HAY BROWN, III

CHICKEN LIVER AND MUSHROOM CASSEROLE

2 lbs. chicken livers
3 lbs. fresh or frozen mushrooms
Butter for sautéeing
2 pkgs. frozen peas, cooked
½ c. butter

½ c. flour
1½ c. cream
1½ c. chicken stock
Sherry
Salt

Sauté chicken livers and mushrooms together in butter and add peas. In a separate pan, make a sauce of ½ cup butter, flour, cream and stock. Add sherry and salt to taste. Fold in livers, mushrooms and peas. Bake in a casserole at 350° for 15 minutes. Serve with curried rice. Can be prepared for oven the day before. Serves 8-10.

MRS. HERRICK NORCROSS, FAIRVIEW FARMS, TYRONZA, ARK.

CHICKEN LIVERS STROGANOFF

2 lbs. chicken livers
½ c. butter
2 small onions, cut finely
2 T. flour
4 oz. can sliced mushrooms
2 t. chicken seasoned stock base

1 c. hot water
2 c. sour cream
2 t. Beau Monde seasoning
¼ t. Fines Herbes
2-4 T. sherry
2 t. parsley or chervil

Wash livers and cut in half or quarters. Brown in butter for 5 minutes, turning frequently. Remove livers. Add onions and cook 3-4 minutes. Do not let them brown. Stir in flour. Mix drained mushrooms, stock base and hot water. Add to onions. Stir in sour cream, Beau Monde, and Fines Herbes. Add chicken livers and sherry. Heat thoroughly, but do not let boil. Sprinkle with parsley or chervil. Serve over noodles as a main course or with toast rounds from a chafing dish for coffee or cocktails. Makes 8 large main course servings. Serves 25 for cocktails.

MRS. ROBERT G. ALLEN

CHICKEN LIVERS IN WINE

12 slices bacon
4 T. finely chopped onions
4 T. finely chopped green pepper
1 lb. chicken livers

1 c. Burgundy cooking wine
1 T. parsley flakes
⅛ t. thyme
¼ t. salt
Dash pepper

Fry bacon until crisp and drain. Add onions and green pepper to drippings and cook until tender, but not brown. Dredge chicken livers in flour, add to drippings and cook 10 minutes. Add wine, parsley flakes, thyme, salt and pepper. Serve on buttered, toasted Holland Rusks. Crumble bacon on top of each serving. Serves 4-6.

CORNISH GAME HENS WITH WILD RICE STUFFING

Stuffing:

Giblets out of hen
1 c. water
¼ c. oleo
½ lb. chopped mushrooms

1 large onion, chopped
1 c. wild rice, cooked
Salt and pepper
1½ t. poultry seasoning

Cook giblets in water; drain. Add oleo, mushrooms and onion. Cook over low heat for 5 minutes. Remove from stove, stir in drained rice. Add seasonings. This will stuff 6 cornish hens or 2 4-pound chickens.

Cornish hens:
Season each bird with salt and pepper or lemon pepper. Stuff with wild rice mixture. Close neck and body cavities with a toothpick. Place hen, breast down, on rack in roasting pan. Brush with melted oleo. Cook covered in 400° oven for 20 minutes, then reduce heat to 325° for 30 minutes or until breast is fork tender. Uncover roaster last 10 minutes of baking to allow hens, to brown. Baste 2 or 3 times while cooking. Serves 6.

MRS. JEROME TURNER

TURKEY HASH

2 T. butter
2 T. flour
2 c. turkey broth or chicken stock
3 c. cubed turkey
1 c. boiled, cubed potatoes

3 stalks celery, chopped
1 onion, chopped
1 t. sage
Salt and pepper to taste

Melt butter in skillet and stir in flour. Slowly add broth or stock to make gravy. Add other ingredients to gravy and mix well. Simmer covered over low heat for 1-1½ hours. Add more stock if needed. Serve over waffles or grits. Serves 8.

MRS. WILLIAM K. STODDARD, RIVERDALE PLANTATION, HUGHES, ARK.

TWO DUCKS

2 wild ducks
Bacon drippings
2 chicken bouillon cubes
Garlic salt
1 t. salt

Dash pepper
2 T. Worcestershire
¾-1 c. light cream
½ c. sherry
Chopped apple, onion, celery

In a large seasoned iron skillet or Dutch oven, brown ducks on all sides in bacon drippings or oleo. Fill a second large skillet ½ full of water and heat. Dissolve chicken cubes in this and sprinkle generously with garlic salt. Add next 5 ingredients and heat to boiling, but do not boil. Stuff ducks with apple, onion and celery and place breast down in Dutch oven. Pour sauce over ducks. Cover tightly and cook at 350° for 2-2½ hours. Baste or turn ducks in sauce every 30 minutes. Gravy may be thickened and served over duck or rice. Do not eat stuffing. Other wild fowl may be substituted for ducks. Serves 3-4.

MRS. JEROME TURNER

SALMI OF DUCK

3-4 ducks
¼ c. butter
1 T. finely chopped onion,
  or more to taste
1 stalk finely chopped celery
1 carrot, finely chopped
¼ c. flour

2 c. consommé
1 bay leaf
Parsley
2 whole cloves
Salt and pepper to taste
½ c. sherry
Green olives or mushrooms,
  optional

Boil ducks in salt water for 3 hours. Remove and cut off breasts and legs. Melt butter in pan, adding onion, celery, carrot. Cook until butter is brown. Add flour and brown. Add consommé and all seasonings. Cook 30 minutes. Add duck meat and sherry. Remove from heat and let duck sit in sauce all day. When reheating to serve, add more consommé, if necessary. Green olives or chopped mushrooms may be added, if desired. Serves 6.

MRS. JOHN APPERSON, JR.

ROAST TURKEY IN FOIL

Turkey   ¼ lb. melted butter or margarine
Salt and pepper   2 t. Kitchen Bouquet
Stuffing

Rub turkey cavity with salt and pepper. Fill with favorite stuffing, allowing ½ cup stuffing for each pound of bird; truss. Rub turkey with salt and pepper, brush with mixture of melted butter and Kitchen Bouquet. Wrap tightly in foil. Roast breast side down in pan for first hour. Turn turkey breast side up for remaining roasting time. Roast in 350° oven, allowing 22 minutes per pound. Remove foil last ½ hour and baste bird every 10 minutes with butter mixture. Make gravy from pan drippings.

MRS. CHARLES H. McGEE. BRUIN PLANTATION, HUGHES, ARK.

PHEASANT

4 pheasants   Pheasant or chicken stock
Salt and pepper to taste   Sherry to taste
4 cinnamon sticks   2 sticks of butter, melted

Place pheasants, breast side down, on rack in roasting pan after cleaning and washing thoroughly. Grease well (preferably with olive oil) and rub in salt and pepper. Add stock. Put cinnamon in cavity of each bird. Cover and roast at 325° for 2½ hours or less (depending on tenderness of pheasant). During roasting, pour off stock and add sherry and butter to it, stirring together. Baste pheasant with this every 10 minutes until brown and done. Garnish with parsley. Serves 8.

MRS. HARRY W. LAUGHLIN

QUAIL IN GRAPE LEAVES

6 quail, including giblets   1 T. butter
Olive oil   1 T. flour
Unsalted pork fat   1 t. salt
12-15 fresh or preserved grape   ½ t. freshly ground pepper
  leaves   2 oz. Cognac
Cooking parchment or foil
Toast rounds
1½ c. chicken stock

Rub quail with olive oil and wrap each in a thin layer of unsalted pork fat, then in 2 or 3 grape leaves. Tie each bird firmly with twine or heavy thread and wrap in lightly oiled cooking parchment or foil. Roast quail at 375° for 40-45 minutes. Unwrap and serve on thick toast rounds which have been fried in butter until golden brown. Serve with a sauce made from the giblets: Cook giblets in chicken stock until tender. Remove giblets and chop. Thicken broth with a little beurre manié (1 T. butter kneaded with 1 T. flour). Add to sauce the giblets, salt, pepper, and Cognac.

MRS. SNOWDEN BOYLE, JR.

SMOKED TURKEY

1 12-16 lb. turkey	Hickory chips
Briquettes	

A smoking accessory for the grill is necessary. Place accessory on grill according to directions. Build a fire with briquettes on one side of smoking accessory. Soak **real** hickory chips (**not** hickory-flavored) in water and place 2 handfuls on fire. Put turkey on grill, not directly on top of coals but to one side. Cover lid of smoking accessory and let cook for 3 hours or until coals need replenishing. Add more briquettes and hickory chips and cook for 4 hours more.

MRS. EPHRAIM B. WILKINSON, JR.

DOVE AU VIN

12 doves	1 c. chopped onion
Salt and pepper to taste	1 small bell pepper, chopped
Flour	1 can consommé
¾ stick butter	½ c. red wine
1 c. chopped celery	

Season doves with salt and pepper and roll in flour. In a skillet brown doves slowly in butter till brown on both sides. Transfer to a casserole and add celery, onions, bell pepper and consommé. Put top on casserole and cook in 350° oven for 2 hours. Add wine last 30 minutes of cooking time. Serves 6.

MRS. JOHN APPERSON, JR.

DOVES FOR BRUNCH

12 strips of bacon, or more	Salt and pepper
12-16 dove breasts	Lowry's seasoned salt
Flour	1-1½ c. water

Fry 12 or more strips of bacon. In same grease, brown breasts which have been floured, salted and peppered. When brown on all sides, sprinkle with Lowry's salt, add water and simmer covered for 1 hour. More water may need to be added. This is best if done in an iron skillet and may be cooked ahead and warmed. Serve with the bacon strips. Allow at least 3 birds per person.

MRS. WILLIAM J. BRITTON, III

QUAIL

12 quail, 1 bird per person	Bacon
Salt and pepper	Margarine
1 pkg. Chung King Fried Rice	
with Pork or Chicken	

Salt and pepper birds, then stuff with rice (loosen rice in a bowl first). Wrap each bird with bacon. Pour 3 tablespoons melted margarine over each. Cover with foil and bake in 350° oven for about 1 hour. Open foil and brown. Serves 12.

MRS. JEROME TURNER

CORNISH GAME HENS IN SALT CLAY

As old as cookery, probably, is the idea of baking birds in clay. Generations of chefs have used sculptors' clay. This version is made from ordinary table salt and flour.

Stuffing:

2 c. French bread cubes	¼ t. pepper
(¼ inch), crust removed	½ c. water
1 c. diced dried apricots	¼ c. butter or margarine
1 c. golden raisins	6 small Cornish game hens
1 T. basil	Salt and pepper
1½ t. powdered sage	¼ c. oil
1 t. salt	

For 1 batch of clay (make each batch separately; you will need one per bird):

1¼ c. salt (½ box)	½ c. water
1 c. unsifted all-purpose flour	

Prepare stuffing: Combine in a large bowl the bread cubes, apricots, raisins, basil, powdered sage, salt and pepper. Heat water and butter or margarine until butter is melted. Pour into dry stuffing and toss to combine well. Wash game hens and pat dry. Use approximately ⅓ cup stuffing for each bird. Fold wings under body and tie legs together. Season each bird inside and out with salt and pepper. Brush each well with a little oil. Wrap each completely in layer of aluminum foil. Press foil tightly against body of bird to eliminate air pockets. Make each batch of clay by combining table salt, unsifted flour and water in a large bowl. Knead in bowl, then in your palms. Sprinkle on more water if clay is too stiff. Roll out on floured pastry cloth to 9-inch square. Set foil-wrapped bird in center. Bring up clay around bird to seal completely. Repeat this process for each bird. (Preparation of each bird takes about 15 minutes.) Bake at 475° for 1½ hours. Cover with foil last 30 minutes of cooking to prevent over-browning. Let cool 10 minutes. Set each in napkin-lined basket. Cover with another napkin. Provide guests with a mallet to break clay. Keep bird covered with napkin so it won't splatter. Peel away clay and foil and lift bird from basket onto dinner plate. Serves 6.

Note: (1) Because the salt clay sets so quickly it is best to make only enough to cover 1 bird at a time. They can be done ahead and refrigerated until cooking time . . . but only if they are to be cooked the same day. (2) To do a day ahead: Do not stuff the birds but proceed as above for wrapping in foil and clay. Refrigerate overnight. Make stuffing separately. Place in a 9-inch pie plate. Cover with foil and bake at 375° for 20 minutes. Remove foil. Bake 10 minutes longer. (3) If you are really in a fun mood, decorate your clay birds (while clay is **still damp**) with water-based paints. Bright colors best, as clay bakes to a pale brown. Paint name of guest on each bird (takes place of place cards), or, if you have the soul of an artist, paint seasonal or holiday motifs on clay. For a family party let your children paint birds.

MRS. J. TUNKIE SAUNDERS

Meat

BEEF STROGANOFF

A marvelous recipe for serving a crowd . . .

8 lbs. sirloin tip	4 10½-oz. cans beef bouillon
Adolph's meat tenderizer	¾ c. flour
4 lbs. fresh mushrooms	1½ pts. sour cream
5 large onions	1 c. Rhine wine
½ lb. butter	2 c. tomato juice

Slice meat into thin strips about 1½-inches wide and 2-3 inches long. Sprinkle **lightly** with tenderizer, toss and refrigerate. Cut off mushroom stems even with the cap and slice mushrooms. Chop onions. Sauté ¼ of the onions in 3 tablespoons butter until almost clear, but not brown. Add ¼ of the mushrooms and sauté until just tender. Remove to a 12-quart enamel roasting pan. Sauté remaining onions and mushrooms in same manner, i.e. in four batches. You may need to add a little butter each time, but not too much. In same skillet in which vegetables have been cooked, brown meat a little at a time with a minimum of butter, removing it to the roasting pan as it browns. Put 2 cans of bouillon and the flour in a blender and blend until smooth. (Or add bouillon a little at a time to the flour, stirring to keep it smooth.) Set aside. Pour remaining cans of bouillon into skillet and stir and scrape to deglaze the pan. Add bouillon and flour mixture, stirring as you add to keep smooth. Add tomato juice and Rhine wine. Pour over the meat and vegetables in roasting pan. Season to taste. About 1½ hours before serving, place in a 375° oven and bring to a simmer, stirring occasionally. Just before serving, add sour cream and a splash of Rhine wine. Serve with buttered noodles or long grain and wild rice. This recipe can easily be halved. Serves 20.

MRS. HENRY H. HANCOCK

EASY BEEF STROGANOFF

4 lbs. top round	1 t. crushed garlic
Butter	¼ t. thyme
1 onion, chopped	¼ t. basil
1 can mushroom soup	¼ t. marjoram
1 c. grated Cheddar cheese	Mushrooms, if desired
1 c. Burgundy	1 c. sour cream

Cut meat into thin strips and brown in butter. Remove meat and brown onion. Put meat and onion in large casserole. Add remaining ingredients, except sour cream. Bake covered at 325° for 2 hours. Add sour cream and bake 20 minutes longer. Serve over rice, wild rice or noodles. Serves 6-8.

MRS. LAWRENCE L. CRANE, JR.

BEEF WELLINGTON

This is a real job, but for a true culinary masterpiece this is it. Many good cooks, once they have mastered this beef in pastry, will come back to it frequently because the time put into it is so rewarding.

Pastry:

4 c. all-purpose flour
1 t. salt
½ c. butter

½ c. shortening
1 egg lightly beaten
½ c. ice water, approximately

Filling:

1 tenderloin of beef,
2½-3 lbs.
2 T. Cognac
Salt and freshly ground pepper
6 slices of bacon

8 oz. pâté de foie gras or
chicken liver pâté
3 or 4 truffles (optional)
1 egg, lightly beaten

Place the flour, salt, butter and shortening in a bowl and blend with the tips of fingers or a pastry blender. Add egg and enough ice water to make a dough. Wrap in wax paper and chill. Preheat oven to 450°. Rub the beef all over with Cognac and season with salt and pepper. Lay the bacon over the top, securing with string if necessary. Place the meat on a rack in a roasting pan and roast 15 minutes per pound for rare, 20-25 minutes per pound for medium. Remove from oven, and remove bacon. Cool to room temperature. Spread the pâté over the sides and top of the beef. Cut the truffles into halves and sink the pieces in a line along the top of beef. Preheat oven to 425°. Roll pastry into a rectangle (about 18 x 12 inches), ¼-inch thick. Place the beef, top down, in the middle. Draw the long sides up to overlap on the bottom of the beef; brush with egg to seal. Trim ends of pastry and make an envelope fold, brushing again with egg to seal. Transfer the pastry wrapped meat to a baking sheet, seam side down. If you have some tiny decorative cookie cutters, take the left-over pieces of pastry and cut out some decorations and put on top. Brush all over with egg. Bake for about 30 minutes, or until the pastry is brown. Slice with a sharp knife. Puff pastry can be used to wrap the beef but care should be taken to roll it very thin. Puff pastry can be purchased at many delicatessens. Serves 6-8.

MRS. CHARLES H. MCGEE, BRUIN PLANTATION,
HUGHES, ARK.

ROAST BEEF BAKED IN SALT

Large box table salt
Sirloin tip steak, 2-2½-in. thick

Sour Cream-Horseradish Sauce

Place meat in pan and cover with 1-inch of salt. Preheat oven to broil. Place steak under broiler till salt is crusty, about 10-15 minutes. Turn meat and repeat first procedure. Brush away salt at end of cooking time. Meat should be seared on outside and pink inside. If not done to suit you, cook longer. Slice and serve hot or cold with Sour Cream-Horseradish Sauce (see Index). Figure ¼-½ pound meat per person.

MRS. JOHN C. BARTON

BOEUF a la BOURGUIGNONNE

6 strips bacon, cut in ½-in.
   pieces
3 lbs. beef chuck, cut in
   1½-in. cubes
1 large carrot, sliced
1 medium onion, sliced
2 t. salt
¼ t. pepper
3 T. flour
2 cans condensed beef broth

2 c. red Burgundy wine
1 T. tomato paste
2 cloves garlic, minced
½ t. thyme
1 bay leaf
1 qt. (about 1 lb.) mushrooms
1 lb. (18-24) small white
   fresh onions
Beurre manié

In Dutch oven, cook bacon until crisp; remove from pan. Brown the meat in small batches in bacon fat, turning often. Remove meat. In pan drippings, brown sliced carrot and onion. Spoon off fat and return bacon and beef to pan with vegetables. Add salt, pepper, flour, stirring to coat meat lightly. Reserve ½ cup broth; add remainder to stew along with wine, tomato paste, and herbs. Cover; simmer (do not boil) about 3 hours or until meat is fork-tender. Quarter large mushrooms (leave small ones whole). In large skillet, sauté mushrooms in 3 tablespoons butter and 2 tablespoons salad oil about 5 minutes; lift out mushrooms and set aside. In the same skillet, brown the small whole onions (add a little more butter and oil if needed), about 10 minutes, shaking skillet occasionally. Add reserved broth to onions, cover and simmer till onions are tender but still hold their shape, about 10 minutes. Beurre manié: used to thicken the stew. Cream together ¼ cup flour and 2 tablespoons of butter; roll into tiny balls the size of a pea. Skim fat from stew, then drop in the tiny balls. Stir over very low heat until gravy thickens. Add the cooked mushrooms and onions; bring just to bubbling and serve at once. (Remove bay leaf before serving.) Serve with parsleyed potatoes, rice, or buttered noodles. Serve 8-10.

MRS. MILTON LYMAN KNOWLTON, JR.

CHISM MARINATED STEAK

1⅔ c. Burgundy wine
½ c. salad oil
2 T. minced onion
2 t. thyme leaves
2 t. salt

¾ t. instant minced garlic
¼ t. ground black pepper
3 lbs. round steak, 2½-in. thick
1 ⅞-oz. pkg. brown gravy mix
   (optional)

Combine wine, oil, onion, thyme, salt, garlic and pepper. Mix well. Place meat in plastic bag or pan that fits snugly around meat. Pour marinade over meat. Marinate at least 18 hours, turning occasionally. Broil meat over hot coals 15-20 minutes on each side, or until desired doneness is reached. If desired, make gravy from marinade. Strain marinade and combine with 1 cup water and 1 package brown gravy mix. Bring to a boil, stirring constantly until thickened slightly. Serves 4.

MR. DOUGLAS CHISM

SMOKED BRISKET

1 c. sugar	½ c. paprika
¼ c. black pepper	2 T. Accent
2½ T. garlic powder	4-4½ lb. beef brisket
⅓ c. salt	

Mix together sugar, pepper, garlic powder, salt, paprika and Accent. Rub dry sauce generously all over brisket. Smoke in hooded charcoal grill for 2½ hours. Rub with sauce again. Wrap brisket in foil and bake in oven for 2½ hours at 250°. The beef may be smoked the day before and oven-cooked later. Serves 8.

MRS. W. G. LOGAN

SIRLOIN TIP ROAST
(Cooked on the Grill)

⅓ c. wine vinegar	1 onion, chopped
⅓ c. red wine	Salt and pepper to taste
3 T. soy sauce	Garlic salt to taste
⅓ c. Worcestershire	5 lb. sirloin tip, tied to fix
¼ c. olive oil	on rotisserie

Mix all ingredients and marinate roast overnight in the marinade. Heat fire to at least 600° on the grill. Cook the roast 20-25 minutes per pound. A 5 pound roast cooks in 1½-2 hours. Delicious! Serves 6-8.

MRS. BILL R. BOBBITT

MEAT FONDUE

Plan on 8 ounces of meat per guest, for example, 2 pounds for 4. Use any 1 or a combination of the following suggested meats:
Beef: Tenderloin, short loin, or sirloin, cut in ¾ to 1-inch cubes.
Calves' Liver: Cut in ¾ to 1-inch cubes. Cook as for beef.
Chicken: Breasts, boned and skinned, cut into ¾-inch cubes. Pat dry; cook as for beef.
Marinated Chicken: Combine ⅓ cup soy sauce, ¼ cup dry sherry and ¼ teaspoon ground ginger. Bone, skin and cube breasts; place in bowl. Pour marinade over chicken; cover. Chill 1 hour. Just before serving, drain and dry on paper towels. Cook as for beef.

Guests spear and cook meat in hot peanut oil to desired degree of doneness: 20 seconds for rare to about 1 minute for well done. Allow 1 cooking pot for every 4 guests. The meat is then dipped into a sauce and eaten. Serve fondue with 1, or a combination of the following sauces: Duxelles, Onion, Pungent Peach, Mustard, Sour Cream-Horseradish (see Index). If you wish to make your fondue party very colorful and more interesting, serve condiments for the meat along with the sauces. Same condiments can be used as with curry.

MRS. JAMES GUY ROBBINS

STANDING RIB ROAST

This recipe is for a standing rib roast of any size.

Meat should be at room temperature. Preheat oven to 375°. Cook roast, seasoned to taste, in shallow pan, fat side up, for 1 hour. NEVER OPEN OVEN DOOR. Turn oven off. Before serving, turn on oven again for 40 minutes at 375°. Cook in the morning the first time or at least 3 hours before the second cooking. (If the roast is small, cook only 35 minutes for the second cooking.) This makes a rare to medium rare roast. "Foolproof with delicious texture and flavor." Allow 2 servings per rib.

MRS. J. HAL PATTON

GRILLADES

This is pronounced "gree-yods".

2 beef or 3 veal round steaks,
    about ¼-in. thick (about 2 lbs.)
½ c. flour
2 T. shortening
2 chopped onions
6 stalks chopped celery

2 T. chopped green pepper
1 clove garlic, pressed
1 lb. 12-oz. can tomatoes
Salt and pepper to taste
3-4 drops Tabasco

Beat meat well and cut grillades about 4-inches square. Season highly with salt and pepper. Dredge meat in flour. In a heavy pot, melt shortening, drop in meat and sear until brown. Remove and reserve. Place onions, celery, green pepper and garlic in pot and cook until just brown. Add tomatoes and put meat and drippings back into pot. Add water to cover, salt, pepper, and Tabasco and cook uncovered over low heat for about 1½ hours. Serve over yellow or white grits or rice. Serves 4-6.

MRS. CHESTER GELPI, NEW ORLEANS, LA.

TOURNEDOS HELOISE

4 filets, 1-in. thick
4 artichoke bottoms, cooked
Foie gras
Truffles, optional
¾ lb. mushrooms, sliced
Lemon juice

½ c. whipping cream
1 t. meat extract
½ t. potato flour
3 T. water
¼ c. Madeira

In a heavy skillet, sauté filets in butter for 3-4 minutes on each side. Place each filet on an artichoke bottom which has been heated in butter. Place a slice of foie gras and a slice of truffle on each filet. Arrange the meat around the edge of a round platter and fill the center with the mushrooms which have been sprinkled with lemon juice, sautéed in butter until soft and heated with whipping cream. Over the filets, pour a little Madeira Sauce: Make by adding to the pan, in which the filets were cooked, meat extract, potato flour, water and Madeira. Simmer sauce 2-3 minutes and strain. Serves 4.

MRS. SNOWDEN BOYLE, JR.

CORNED BEEF IN FOIL

3-4 lbs. corned beef	1 onion, sliced
¼ c. water	1 stalk celery with leaves
2 T. pickling spice	1 carrot, sliced
1 small orange, sliced	

This recipe calls for beef already corned, just as it comes from the market. Soak beef in cold water to cover for ½ hour, or longer if deeper corned. Place large sheet of heavy duty foil in a shallow pan. Pat meat dry and place in center of foil. Pour ¼ cup water over it. Sprinkle with the spice and arrange orange slices and vegetables over and around meat. Bring long ends of foil up over meat and seal with a tight double fold. Seal other ends, turning them so liquid cannot run out. Bake 4 hours in 300° oven. Drain and cool. Slice paper thin. Serve for sandwiches with Hot Mustard (see Index).

A time-saver: Return your cooked meat to your friendly neighborhood butcher and have him slice it for you!

MRS. BEN C. ADAMS, JR.

SPICY BEEF

1 lb. ground beef	¼ c. catsup
½ c. chopped onion	¾ t. oregano
1 clove garlic, minced	1 t. sugar
4 T. margarine	1 8-oz. pkg. cream cheese
Salt and pepper to taste	⅓ c. Parmesan cheese
1 8-oz. can tomato sauce	Small hamburger buns

Cook beef, onion, and garlic in margarine till beef is slightly browned and tender. Season with salt and pepper. Stir in tomato sauce, catsup, oregano, and sugar. Cover; simmer 10 minutes. Spoon off excess fat. Remove from heat and add cream cheese and Parmesan. Stir till cheese melts and blends. Serve in chafing dish with small hamburger buns. Makes 3 cups.

MRS. BEN C. ADAMS, JR.

CALIFORNIA TACOS

1 lb. sausage	½ c. stuffed olives, sliced
1 lb. ground beef	1 10-oz. can mushroom soup
1 c. coarsely chopped walnuts	1 t. chili powder
2 c. coarsely grated American cheese	12 tortillas

Brown beef and sausage separately; drain on paper towels. Reserve fat. Add walnuts, cheese, olives, soup, and chili powder to beef fat and cook for 5 minutes. Lightly brown 12 tortillas on both sides in the sausage fat. Drain on paper towels and fill with meat mixture. Filling may also be put in hollowed French rolls. Wrap in foil and bake at 400° for 10 minutes. To serve: Sprinkle each with shredded lettuce and chopped tomatoes. Makes 12.

MRS. JAMES GUY ROBBINS

SWEET AND SOUR BEEF BALLS

1 lb. ground beef	4 slices pineapple
1 egg	3 large green peppers, cut in strips
1 T. cornstarch	3 T. cornstarch
1 t. salt	1 T. soy sauce
1½ T. finely chopped onion	½ c. mild vinegar
Few grains pepper	½ c. sugar
¾ c. cooking oil	⅔ c. bouillon
⅓ c. pineapple juice	

To ground beef, add egg, 1 tablespoon cornstarch, salt, onion and pepper. Mix well and form into 18 balls. Fry the meat balls in hot oil until brown. Drain. Add pineapple juice, pineapple slices cut in pieces, and peppers to 1 tablespoon oil in skillet. Cook over low heat a few minutes. Add mixture of cornstarch, soy sauce, vinegar, sugar and bouillon. Stir constantly until juice thickens and add meat balls. Heat and serve hot. **Note:** Do not fry beef balls in deep fat. May substitute shrimp, chicken or pork for beef. If no bouillon is on hand, use pineapple juice or tangerine juice. Serves 6-8.

MRS. JOHN HART TODD

MOUSSAKÁ

3 medium eggplants (about 2 lbs.)	Salt and pepper to taste
	6 T. flour
2 sticks butter	1 qt. milk, heated
3 onions, chopped	4 eggs
2 lbs. ground lamb or beef	Nutmeg to taste
3 T. tomato paste	2 c. ricotta or cottage cheese
½ c. dry red wine	Bread crumbs
Minced parsley	Parmesan cheese
⅛-¼ t. cinnamon	

Peel eggplants and cut into ½-inch slices. Heat 4 tablespoons butter in skillet and brown slices. Drain on paper towel. Add 4 more tablespoons of butter to skillet. When hot, add onions; cook until nicely browned. Stir in ground beef or lamb (or half and half) and cook 10 minutes. Combine tomato paste, wine, parsley, cinnamon, salt and pepper; stir into meat mixture. Bring to a boil; reduce heat and simmer until all liquid has been absorbed. Take off heat. Heat 1 stick of butter in a saucepan. Stir in flour until smooth and cook 3 to 4 minutes. Add milk, stirring constantly until smooth and thick. Cool slightly; add eggs, one at a time, beating each in thoroughly. Stir in nutmeg and ricotta or cottage cheese. Grease an 11 x 16-inch pan and sprinkle enough bread crumbs over bottom to cover lightly. Arrange alternate layers of eggplant and meat mixture in pan, sprinkling each layer with Parmesan cheese and bread crumbs. Pour cheese sauce over top and bake at 350° for 1 hour. Take out and cool 20-30 minutes before serving. Can be baked a day ahead. To reheat, bake for about 15 minutes. Serves 10.

MRS. JAMES GUY ROBBINS

CURRY BEEF IN PASTRY

3 T. oil	2 t. salt
½ c. chopped onion	½ t. pepper
1 lb. ground round steak	1 T. curry powder
2 c. chopped mushrooms	1 c. thick cream sauce

Heat oil in skillet. Sauté onion, beef, and mushrooms 10 minutes. Add salt, pepper, curry powder and cream sauce. Mix well and set aside to cool.

Pastry:

2 c. sifted flour	4 T. butter
2 t. baking powder	½ c. (scant) white wine
½ t. salt	1 egg yolk, beaten

Sift flour, baking powder and salt into bowl. Cut in butter; stir in wine gradually till ball of dough is formed. Roll out dough into a rectangle ⅓-inch thick. Spread beef mixture down center. Bring edges together on top and seal. Brush with beaten egg. Bake in 400° oven about 35 minutes or till browned. Serve with 1 cup sour cream mixed with ¼ cup chopped chutney. Serves 8.

MRS. ROBERT G. SNOWDEN

HAMBURGER-CHEESE CASSEROLE

1 8-oz. pkg. noodles	¼ c. sour cream
1 lb. ground beef	1 c. cream style cottage cheese
1 T. margarine	1 8-oz. pkg. cream cheese
1 T. chopped green pepper	½ c. chopped onions
2 8-oz. cans tomato paste	Seasoned salt and pepper to taste

Cook noodles. Brown meat in margarine, then add green pepper and tomato paste. Let simmer 10 minutes. Mix sour cream, cottage cheese and cream cheese together. Put ½ of noodles in a layer on bottom of 3-quart casserole and put all of the cheese mixture over noodles. Put chopped onions over cheese layer, and then ½ of meat sauce. Put last of noodles on meat sauce and follow with remainder of meat sauce. Bake in 400° oven for 40-50 minutes or until bubbly. Serves 8.

MRS. JOHN H. SHUTE, JR.

BAKED CANADIAN BACON

2 lb. piece Canadian bacon	1 c. cider
½ c. beer	1 c. brown sugar
¾ c. sugar	1 t. mustard
½ t. dry mustard	½ t. ground cloves

Cook bacon, fat side up, on rack and add beer. Bake at 350° for 15 minutes, basting occasionally with juices in pan. Combine sugar with dry mustard and enough beer to make a paste. Spread paste over bacon and bake 1 hour longer; or combine cider, brown sugar, mustard, ground cloves and pour mixture over bacon, basting frequently. Serves 5-6.

MRS. JAMES GUY ROBBINS

LASAGNE

1 onion, chopped
Cooking oil
1½ lbs. ground beef
1 large can tomato paste
1 large can tomatoes
1 c. water
3 T. chopped parsley
1 t. oregano
1 t. sweet basil
1 garlic clove, chopped

2 t. salt
1 pt. cottage cheese
1 egg
1 pkg. lasagne noodles
1 6-oz. pkg. Mozzarella cheese, sliced
1 8-oz. pkg. American cheese, grated
Parmesan cheese

Sauté onion in cooking oil. Add ground beef. When brown, add tomato paste, tomatoes, water, and spices. Simmer 30 minutes or until thick. Add cottage cheese to slightly beaten egg. Set aside. Boil noodles in salted water until done. Drain. In a 3-quart greased rectangular casserole, layer the noodles, cottage cheese mixture, sauce, and sliced cheeses, into two or three layers. Top layer should be sliced cheese. Sprinkle Parmesan cheese over all. Return to 375° oven 20 minutes or until cheese is melted. May be frozen. Serves 8 generously.

MRS. LARRY B. CRESON, JR.

BARBECUED FRANKFURTERS

3 medium onions
6 T. vinegar
3 T. flour
4½ T. Worcestershire
2 T. salt
3 pinches red pepper
1 T. paprika

¾ t. black pepper
1 T. chili powder or dry mustard
1½ c. tomato catsup
2 T. brown sugar
6 T. hot water
20-25 frankfurters
Hot dog buns

Chop onions; blend vinegar and flour and combine with onions, seasonings, sugar, and water. Pierce each frank 5 or 6 times with a fork and dip into sauce. Arrange franks in well-greased roaster and pour remaining sauce over them. Cover and bake 1 hour at 350°. Serve from roaster putting frank and some sauce in each hot dog bun.

MRS. ROSS LYNN

LASSOED HOT DOGS

1 8-oz. pkg. refrigerator crescent rolls
2 T. softened butter

¼ t. dry mustard
1 lb. pkg. hot dogs

Separate refrigerator rolls into triangles. Spread butter and mustard thinly on triangles. Place a hot dog at broad end of triangle; roll up to pointed end. Place on ungreased cookie sheet and bake at 375° for 10 minutes. Cheese may be placed inside hot dogs. Makes 8.

MRS. EDWIN P. VOSS

PIZZA

Sauce (make day ahead):

1 lb. mild sausage	1 t. oregano
Cooking oil	1 t. salt, to taste
1 large onion, chopped	1 t. chili powder
½ green pepper, chopped	1 t. sweet basil
1 clove garlic, minced	1 large can mushrooms, drained
1 lb. ground beef	Grated American cheese
1 large can tomatoes	Sliced Mozzarella cheese
1 large can tomato paste	

Cook sausage. Remove from pan and drain. In iron skillet, heat enough oil to sauté onion, green pepper and garlic. Cook until tender. Add ground beef and brown. Drain off most of liquid. Add tomatoes, tomato paste, spices and mushrooms. Simmer uncovered for 1 hour. This makes enough sauce for 3 12-inch pizzas or 4 10-inch pizzas.

Crust for 1 pizza:

⅓ c. oil	1 t. salt
2 c. flour	⅔ c. buttermilk
1 t. baking powder	

Add oil to flour, baking powder, and salt. Blend until mixture resembles corn meal. Add buttermilk and blend. Roll out to fit a 12-inch round pan. Cook at 450° until done. Watch until crust turns golden brown. Cover baked crust with sauce and top with grated American cheese and sliced Mozzarella cheese. Bake at 450° until cheeses melt. When serving, put bowls with anchovies, sausage, shrimp, black olives, chopped onion, etc. on table. Let each guest make his own. Great for an after theater supper, midnight supper, or stag supper.

MRS. LARRY B. CRESON, JR.

CHILI

2 large onions, chopped	2 cloves garlic or
1 lb. ground chuck	¼ t. garlic powder
2 t. salt	1 10-oz. can tomato purée
⅛ t. cayenne	1 1-lb. 12-oz. can
1 t. monosodium glutamate	peeled whole tomatoes
4 t. oregano	1 6-oz. can tomato paste,
1 t. basil	plus 6 oz. water
2 T. parsley	1 c. Burgundy
2 bay leaves	1 1-lb. 14-oz. can
2 T. chili powder	red kidney beans
2 T. paprika	

Cook onions and chuck till lightly browned, stirring frequently. Add remaining ingredients (except beans), simmer 2 hours. Add beans and simmer ½ hour longer. **Note:** For a different touch, place a thin slice of Cheddar cheese in bottom of each bowl of chili. Freezes well. Serves 8.

MRS. C. P. J. MOONEY, III

ITALIAN SAUSAGES MARCHIGIANA

1 large cauliflower, broken
   into flowerets
9 sweet or hot Italian sausage
   links, or a combination of
   both (about 1½ lbs.)
2 T. olive oil
2 onions, thinly sliced
1 T. crushed fennel seeds

1 T. chopped fresh or dried basil
1 T. finely chopped rosemary
½ t. hot Italian pepper
2 cloves garlic, minced
½ c. red wine vinegar
1 T. tomato paste
½ c. warm water

Cook the cauliflower in boiling, salted water for 1 minute. Drain and set aside. Cook sausage in a skillet, turning frequently until browned and cooked through. Remove sausage and cut in 1-inch lengths. Set aside. Pour off fat from skillet and add olive oil and cauliflower. Cook, shaking the skillet until cauliflower is lightly browned. Add more oil if necessary. Add onions and stir, cooking until onions are wilted. Add fennel seeds, basil, rosemary, pepper, garlic, and vinegar. Cook, stirring to blend, about 5 minutes over low heat. Dilute the tomato paste in warm water and add to skillet. Cover and simmer until cauliflower is barely tender, about 5-10 minutes. Return the sausages to skillet; mix well and serve hot. Serves 6.

MR. EDWARD GIOBBI

SAUSAGES WITH PEPPERS AND ONIONS

1½ lbs. sausage
2 large green peppers,
   sliced

2 large onions, sliced
1 T. oregano
1 glass white wine

Sauté sausage until browned. Drain off excess fat. Add peppers and cook for 5 minutes. Then add onions, oregano, and wine. Cook over medium heat until wine cooks down. Serves 6.

MR. EDWARD GIOBBI

ITALIAN SAUSAGES, BLACK AND GREEN

1 bunch broccoli
1½ lbs. sausage
1 glass dry white wine
4 T. olive oil
1 T. oregano

1 pinch dry hot pepper
3 cloves garlic, minced
1 can black Italian olives,
   drained

Wash broccoli, cut flowers apart, and skin and quarter stems. Cook in boiling salted water for 3 minutes. Drain and set aside. Sauté sausage in a skillet over medium heat. When cooked, drain off excess fat and add wine, olive oil, and seasonings. Then add cooked broccoli and olives. Simmer for 20 minutes. Add warm water when needed. Serves 6.

MR. EDWARD GIOBBI

ROAST LEG OF LAMB WITH ROSEMARY

6-7 lb. leg of lamb
2 garlic cloves
¼ t. salt
¼ c. finely chopped parsley

3 T. fresh or 3 t. dried rosemary
1 T. olive oil
2 t. anchovy paste

Remove most of fat from leg of lamb and lay leg on rack in roasting pan. With a small sharp knife, make 6 or 7 deep incisions in the heaviest section of the meat. Combine garlic cloves, finely chopped and mashed, with salt, parsley, rosemary and olive oil. Spread mixture over the surface of the meat and into cuts. Roast lamb in a 325° oven, basting frequently with water or light stock, for 3 hours, or until the meat is tender but still faintly pink inside. Remove roast to a heated platter. Add anchovy paste to pan juices and cook until it thickens slightly. Pour around roast. Serves 8-10.

MRS. WILLIAM K. STODDARD, RIVERDALE PLANTATION
HUGHES, ARK.

LAMB CHOP BÉARNAISE

6 double rib lamb chops
White wine

Béarnaise sauce

Marinate chops overnight in wine. Broil or grill. Serve with Béarnaise. Garnish with Green Minted Pears. (For recipes for Béarnaise and Green Minted Pears see Index.)

MRS. C. NILES GROSVENOR, III

SWEDISH LEG OF LAMB

5-5½ lb. leg of lamb
1 T. salt
1 t. dry mustard
1 clove garlic, sliced
1 c. strong coffee

2 t. sugar
2 t. whipping cream
¾ oz. brandy
3 T. flour
3 T. currant jelly

Preheat oven to 350°. Rinse lamb and dry well with paper towels. Rub with salt and dry mustard. Insert garlic into meat. Place on rack in roasting pan and put in oven. Total cooking time should be 2½-3 hours (or till meat thermometer registers 165°). When roast is half done, take out of oven and baste with mixture of coffee, sugar, cream, brandy and a little water. Turn roast and baste all over. At end of baking time, remove meat and let stand in a warm place at least 15 minutes. To make gravy: Stir flour into pan juices, then add currant jelly. If desired, omit the gravy and serve with mint sauce. Serves 8-10.

MRS. FRANK T. DONELSON, JR.

BARBECUED BUTTERFLY LEG OF LAMB

Leg of lamb   **Butter**
Salt and pepper to taste   **Hattie's Barbecue Sauce**

Have butcher bone leg of lamb. Season with salt and pepper, dot with butter.
Place in 300° oven for 45 minutes. Baste with Hattie's Barbecue Sauce (see
Index). Place on grill over smoldering charcoal. Continue basting with sauce
for approximately 45 minutes. Serves 8-10.

MRS. JOHN APPERSON, JR.

HAM TETRAZZINI

5 T. margarine   **2 t. salt**
½ lb. sliced mushrooms   **⅛ t. pepper**
¼ c. chopped onion   **1 t. lemon juice**
¼ c. flour   **8 oz. vermicelli**
2 c. chicken broth   **3 c. cooked ham, cubed**
1¼ c. coffee cream   **¼ c. grated Parmesan cheese**
1 c. grated yellow cheese

Melt margarine in skillet. Sauté mushrooms and onions. Blend in flour till
smooth. Add broth and cream, stirring till smooth and thickened. Add yellow
cheese, salt, pepper, and lemon juice. Stir till cheese melts. Lower heat and
simmer uncovered 10-15 minutes. While sauce is simmering, cook vermicelli.
Drain vermicelli and add to sauce along with ham. Spoon into a greased 2-
quart casserole and sprinkle with Parmesan cheese. This freezes well. Bake
at 400° 20-30 minutes. **Note:** Turkey or chicken may be substituted for the
ham. Serves 6.

MRS. GARY FALLS, CLARKSDALE, MISS.

COUNTRY HAM

Allow 25 minutes per pound for ham weighing 10-12 pounds; or 20 minutes
per pound for a larger one. Cover ham with cold water and soak 12 hours
in 2 different waters, to which has been added 1 cup vinegar for each gallon
of water. Remove and rinse in cold water. Place in large roaster on top of
stove. Pour over ham 1 gallon water, 1 cup black molasses and 1 cup vinegar.
Cover and allow to come to a rolling boil, then lower flame and let simmer
slowly until skin can be easily removed (about 2 hours). Remove ham from
solution, remove skin, puncture at intervals with ice pick and insert very small
slivers of garlic. Score, dot with whole cloves and place in preheated oven
300° for remaining cooking time, basting every 20 minutes with port wine.
Add water in bottom of pan as needed. Frequent basting is important. A good
companion for country ham is Mustard Sauce. (See Index.)

*Stuffed peaches make a marvelous garnish for country ham: Mix 4 tablespoons bour-
bon with 1 jar mincemeat and let stand a few hours. When ready to serve, spoon some
of mincemeat into the cavities of firm peach halves and bake at 400° till peaches are
tender.*

MRS. MILLARD HALL

VEAL CUTLET PARMIGIANA

Sauce:

6 T. olive oil	½ t. black pepper, freshly ground
¼ c. butter	6 c. (3 1-lb. cans) peeled
3 large mashed garlic cloves	plum tomatoes
16 fresh parsley sprigs	1 T. dried oregano
(leaves only)	1 T. anchovy paste
½ t. salt	2 T. tomato paste

Combine olive oil and butter in a saucepan and heat. Chop garlic and parsley together and add to the pan. Cook slowly for 5 minutes and then add salt and pepper. Drain the tomatoes and mash the solids. Add the tomatoes and oregano to the sauce and cook slowly for 30 minutes. Add anchovy paste and tomato paste; stir well and remove from the heat.

Veal:

4 lb. leg of veal	20 chives, chopped
3 c. Pepperidge Farm bread	4 c. sauce, hot
crumbs	8 thin slices Mozzarella
1 c. flour	Pinch of salt
5 large eggs, beaten	½ T. pepper
½ c. olive oil	8 heaping T. freshly grated
1 c. butter	Parmesan

Have butcher cut veal into 8 slices, 3 x 5 inches. Carefully pound them with a mallet. Put bread crumbs in a blender and blend until they are like sand. (Or to be painstakingly authentic, sift them.) Dip cutlets into flour, then into egg; then press into bread crumbs, coating both sides. Do this twice. Place olive oil and ½ the butter in a skillet and heat. Add the cutlets and sauté on each side for 5 minutes. Meanwhile, stir chives into remaining butter and keep soft. Preheat oven to 375°. Pour a thin layer of sauce in a large baking dish (or 2 medium ones). Place cutlets in sauce and spread chive butter on each cutlet. Place a slice of Mozzarella on each cutlet and sprinkle with salt and pepper. Spoon rest of sauce over the veal. Sprinkle grated Parmesan on top and bake for 20 minutes. Serve immediately. **Note:** It is better to buy less than 4 pounds meat than to try to work with more. Slices would be hard to work with and too thick to pound. This sauce may be served over spaghetti, either as is, or with mushrooms and shrimp added during the last 10 minutes of cooking time. Serves 8.

MISS ANNA MARIE HILL

CEN'S PORK CHOPS

8 1-in. thick pork chops,	2 oz. bourbon
boned	1 oz. soy sauce
1 small garlic clove, pressed	

Heat vegetable oil in a skillet until very hot and cook chops until golden. Add sauce made of garlic, bourbon and soy sauce. Simmer covered for 15-20 minutes. Pour some of drippings on each serving. Serves 8.

MRS. DAVID B. MARTIN

CROWN ROAST OF PORK

This is a very impressive, yet inexpensive main attraction . . .

9-10 lb. crown roast of	**1 T. salt**
pork (about 20 ribs)	**½ t. pepper**
3 T. lemon juice	**½ t. poultry seasoning**
3 T. salad oil	**1 t. grated lemon peel**
1 clove garlic, crushed	**3 T. flour**

Have butcher make crown roast at market. Preheat oven to 325°. Wipe meat with damp paper towels. At bottom of roast, cut slits between ribs, so roast will carve easily. Stand roast in shallow, open roasting pan without rack. Insert meat thermometer in center of meat, away from fat or bone. In small bowl, combine lemon juice, salad oil, garlic, salt, pepper, poultry seasoning, and lemon peel, mix well. Brush ½ of mixture over roast. Roast, uncovered, 2 hours. Brush roast with remaining lemon mixture and browned pan drippings. Roast 1 hour longer, or until thermometer registers 185°. Remove roast to heated platter. Cover loosely with sheet of foil, to keep warm while making gravy. To make gravy: Pour drippings and fat into a 2 cup measure. Skim off fat; discard. There should be about ⅓ cup drippings. Return drippings to roasting pan. Add 1 cup water; bring mixture to boil to dissolve any browned bits in pan. In small bowl, combine flour and 1 cup water, stirring until flour is dissolved. Pour into liquid in roasting pan and return to boil; reduce heat, and simmer, stirring until thickened and smooth. Season to taste. Pour into gravy boat.

To serve roast: Fill center with Cranberry-Apple Relish (see Index). Garnish ends of ribs with frills, if desired. (Center may also be filled with scalloped apples and every other rib garnished with a red crab apple.) Serve with gravy. Serves 10.

MRS. JAMES GUY ROBBINS

MARINATED ROAST PORK

Pork roast, loin end or	**¼ c. soy sauce**
shoulder	**1 T. fresh lemon juice**
¾ c. sherry	**3 garlic cloves, crushed**
½ c. chicken consommé	**¼ t. powdered ginger**
1 chicken bouillon cube	**1 t. salt**

Have butcher remove skin and bone from roast. Combine remaining ingredients to make marinade. Rub roast all over with salt and freshly ground pepper and place in bowl. Pour marinade over and let roast stand overnight, turning 3 or 4 times in the marinade. Remove roast from refrigerator several hours before cooking so that it will unchill. Roll and tie roast, place in roasting pan and pour marinade over. Bake at 325° for 45 minutes per pound or till meat thermometer registers 180°. Baste with pan juices every 20 minutes. Allow to cool 20 minutes before slicing. One pound of boned pork will serve 2 to 3; allow ¾ pound of bone-in pork for one person.

MRS. MILTON LYMAN KNOWLTON, JR.

SWEET AND SOUR PORK

3 lbs. pork, cut in 1-in. cubes ½ c. catsup
⅔ c. brown sugar ½ c. water
2 T. cornstarch 2 T. soy sauce
2 t. dry mustard Salt and pepper to taste
⅔ c. vinegar 2 green peppers, chopped
1 c. pineapple chunks, 2 onions, chopped
 undrained

Brown pork. Place in casserole. In a large pan, combine other ingredients except onion and pepper. Cook until thick and smooth. Pour over pork. Bake at 350° for 1½ hours. Put chopped peppers and onions over top and cook for 10 more minutes. Serves 6-8.

MRS. F. GUY ROBBINS, OSCEOLA, ARK.

VEAL BIRDS

6 medium veal cutlets Flour for coating
¼ c. chopped onion Shortening
2 T. butter 1 cube beef bouillon
¾ c. sliced, cooked 1 c. boiling water
 mushrooms (about 6 oz.) 1 c. red wine
½ c. cooked pork sausage, 8 oz. noodles
 only lightly drained 1 10-oz. pkg. frozen green
 (about ¼ lb.) peas, cooked and drained
¼ t. salt 3 large tomatoes, peeled and
½ t. sage cut into sixths
1½ c. coarse corn bread Additional bouillon for
 crumbs basting, if needed

Preheat oven to 350°. Pound each cutlet till ¼-inch in thickness. Dressing: Brown onions in melted butter. Combine with ½ cup mushrooms, sausage, salt, sage and corn bread. Toss lightly. Spread dressing on cutlets. Roll up tightly and secure with toothpicks. Dredge veal with flour; brown in hot shortening. **Cooking method I:** Place rolled veal in baking dish and pour bouillon (made by combining beef cube and boiling water) and ½ cup wine over meat. Bake in oven, basting frequently, 45 minutes to an hour, or till veal is tender. To make gravy: Remove meat from baking dish and thicken pan remains with a paste of flour and water. Add remaining ¼ cup mushrooms and wine to gravy. Stir over low heat till thickened. Place veal birds on a bed of noodles tossed with green peas or serve on a bed of rice. Garnish with tomato wedges. Ladle gravy over each serving of noodles and veal. **Cooking method II:** Place browned veal in large pot. Pour over veal the wine-bouillon mixture, cover, and cook on top of the range 45 minutes. Check occasionally for sticking. Thicken gravy as above. Veal birds can be made ready for cooking the day before. This is a beautiful and delicious main dish. The dressing would also be excellent with chicken or turkey. Serves 6.

MRS. SHERARD TATUM, JR.

PORK WITH CELERY

Have ½ lb. pork sliced thin and dredge with mixture of:

1 t. wine	**1 T. soy sauce**
2 T. cornstarch	

Heat 2 T. oil in pan and sauté pork till done. Set aside. Reheat pan and add:

2 T. oil	**2 c. celery, sliced diagonally**

Sauté celery for a few seconds; then add:

2 T. soy sauce	**½ c. soup stock**
1 t. wine	**The sautéed pork**

Serves 4.

MRS. JOHN HART TODD

VEAL IN MUSHROOM SAUCE

2 lbs. veal	**1 small can sliced mushrooms**
¼ c. oil	**½ c. sherry**
1 can mushroom soup	**Pinch of sage**

Cut veal in serving pieces and brown in hot oil. Place meat in a greased casserole and pour over a sauce made from soup, drained mushrooms, sherry and sage. Bake covered 1 hour at 325°. Serve over white or wild rice. Serves 6.

MRS. FRED TARKINGTON, JR.

SCALLOPINE ALLA MARSALA

6 veal cutlets	**3 T. butter**
1 c. grated Parmesan cheese	**Salt, cayenne to taste**
¼ c. butter	**1 t. meat extract**
1 c. thinly sliced fresh	**3 T. hot beef broth**
mushrooms	**¼ c. Marsala wine**

Have cutlets sliced ⅜ of an inch thick off a leg of veal. Have butcher pound veal between 2 pieces of wax or heavy paper until thin enough to see through. (When cooked, it will draw up to about the size and thickness it was before pounding.) Dip slices in Parmesan and sauté in ¼ cup butter until lightly browned on both sides. In separate pan, cook mushrooms in 2 tablespoons of the butter and season lightly with salt and cayenne. Put veal on heated platter with mushrooms on top. Dissolve meat extract in hot beef broth and add to butter in which mushrooms were cooked. Add remaining 1 tablespoon butter. Stir over very low flame until sauce is well mixed. Turn up heat and cook about a minute. When bubbling, add wine. Pour over veal and mushrooms. Serves 6.

MRS. JAMES W. WRAPE, COLLIERVILLE, TENN.

THIN VEAL IN WINE SAUCE

½ c. oil
3 lbs. very thin veal, cut
   in small serving pieces
Garlic salt

Seasoned bread crumbs
8 oz. mushrooms, sliced or whole
Salt and pepper to taste
¾-1 c. dry vermouth

Heat oil in skillet until hot. Brown veal slices which have been sprinkled on both sides with garlic salt and seasoned bread crumbs. Lower heat, cover veal slices with drained mushrooms, salt, pepper, and vermouth. Cover. Simmer slowly for 20 minutes. Add more vermouth and 2-4 tablespoons of water, if necessary, to keep moist and make gravy. When serving, sprinkle with lemon juice and chopped parsley. Serve over white and wild rice, combined half and half. Serves 8.

MRS. DENNIS COUGHLIN, KNOXVILLE, TENN.

ROAST VEAL WITH SOUR CREAM

4 lb. rolled rump of veal
1 t. dry tarragon
1 t. salt
1 t. pepper
1 t. mace
¼ lb. softened butter

2 carrots, sliced
5 small yellow onions
1 bay leaf
1 c. beef bouillon
1 c. sour cream, heated

Wipe roast carefully. Mix tarragon, salt, pepper and mace and rub into the meat. Place in a greased roasting pan, spread the meat with softened butter, and add vegetables and bay leaf. Place in preheated 450° oven and roast uncovered for ½ hour, turning once and basting. Reduce heat to 350° and continue cooking for 2 hours, basting occasionally. Remove meat and keep warm. On top of stove over low flame add bouillon to roasting pan and simmer, deglazing pan with spoon. Add a little hot gravy to sour cream; pour sour cream into gravy. Stir and beat, but **do not boil.** If sauce curdles add a little sweet cream and beat. Strain sauce, slice meat on platter and serve sauce separately. Serves 8.

MRS. CHARLES H. McGEE, BRUIN PLANTATION
HUGHES, ARK.

VEAL VERNON

8-10 lb. veal roast
4 T. shortening
2 c. bouillon
–1 bay leaf
6 whole peppercorns

1 lemon, sliced
Salt to taste
1 lb. small onions
½ c. sour cream

Brown roast in shortening and add bouillon, bay leaf, peppercorns and lemon. Simmer 3½ hours. Add salt and onions. Cook until onions are tender. Add sour cream. Let heat thoroughly and serve. Can be used for chops. Serves 10.

MRS. JOHN HART TODD

COUNTRY SMOTHERED VENISON

3 lbs. venison	**1 T. salt**
2 T. flour	**1 t. black pepper**
¾ c. chopped green pepper	**½ c. mushrooms**
½ c. chopped carrots	**½ c. red wine**
¾ c. sliced onions	**2½ c. stock, water or beer**

Cut venison steaks into ½-inch thick strips, 2 x 4-inches long. Tenderize by marinating or by pounding. Pounding with dull side of a butcher knife is quite effective and offers immediate cooking texture. Brown floured strips of venison until seared and remove from skillet. Add flour and brown. Reduce heat and add blend of peppers, carrots, onions, salt, pepper, mushrooms, wine and stock. Adjust with more flour or water to obtain desired thickness; then add steaks and simmer for 1-1½ hours in covered skillet. If you wish to lose the wild taste of venison, marinate 24 hours in Italian dressing. Serves 6.

MISS LIDA BLACK

Vegetables

ASPARAGUS, PETITS POIS AND MUSHROOM CASSEROLE

2 15-oz. cans green asparagus
2 1-lb. cans petits pois
1 can mushroom soup
1 small can mushrooms

¾ c. grated sharp cheese
1 c. soft white bread crumbs
2 T. melted butter

Chill the cans of asparagus 2-3 hours to prevent breaking on opening. About 40 minutes before serving time, open and drain. Arrange half the asparagus in a buttered 6 cup casserole. In a bowl, mix gently the peas, soup, mushrooms and cheese. Spoon ½ the mixture into casserole. Add asparagus; top with remaining mixture. Toss crumbs with butter and sprinkle on top casserole. Bake in 350° oven about 30 minutes or till crumbs are browned. Serves 8-10.

MRS. GARY FALLS
CLARKSDALE, MISSISSIPPI

SAUTÉED ASPARAGUS

2 T. oil
½ c. chicken stock
4 T. asparagus juice
1 T. wine

2 T. soy sauce
1 T. cornstarch
About 20 stalks cooked asparagus

Heat pan; add oil. Then add soup stock, asparagus juice, wine, soy sauce, and cornstarch. Stir until it boils. Add asparagus and continue cooking until hot. To increase, make twice; do not double. Serves 4-5.

MRS. JOHN HART TODD

CAMPFIRE BEANS

4 cans pork and beans
½ c. molasses
¼ c. catsup
2 T. minced onion

¼ t. celery salt
¼ t. black pepper
2 T. pickle relish
1 T. Worcestershire

Combine all ingredients and place in bean pot. Bake at 300° for 2½ hours. Serves 6.

MRS. EDWIN P. VOSS

CALIFORNIA BEANS

1 apple	1 1-lb. 12-oz. can tomatoes
½ c. onion	1 c. brown sugar
1 green pepper	1½ T. curry powder
Bacon drippings	Parmesan cheese
2 #303 cans kidney beans	

Chop apple, onion and pepper and sauté in bacon drippings. Drain beans and tomatoes well. Mix all ingredients, except cheese, and place in 2-quart casserole. Top with Parmesan cheese. Bake uncovered at 350° about 30 minutes. This freezes beautifully. Excellent served with ham, leg of lamb, roast beef. Serves 8.

MRS. ROBERT LOWRY

BLACK BEANS AND RICE

1 lb. dried black beans	Dash oregano
10 c. water	⅛ t. pepper
1 large green pepper, halved	1 bay leaf
⅔ c. oil	2 t. sugar
1 large onion, chopped	2 T. vinegar
4 small garlic pods, chopped	2 T. white wine
1 green pepper, chopped	2 T. olive oil
2 t. salt	2 c. raw rice

Clean beans well. Combine beans with water and green pepper. Bring to a boil, and then simmer for 45 minutes. Refrigerate overnight. Next day, sauté in oil the onion, garlic and chopped green pepper. While doing this, heat beans slowly over low heat until soft, about 1 hour. *When done, take a soup ladle of beans and purée it. Put puréed mixture into sautéed vegetables. Mix well and add to the bean pot while beans are still cooking. Add salt, oregano, pepper, bay leaf, sugar, vinegar and wine to bean pot. If beans seem too dry, add more water; however, beans taste better a little dry. When finished cooking, add olive oil and taste for seasoning. Flavor improves if made the day before serving. Serve over cooked rice. **Note:** If you are able to obtain canned black beans, start the recipe at the asterisk. This will save time. Serves 8-10.

This is not a pretty dish, but your guests will rave over its flavor.

MRS. DAVID B. MARTIN

GREEN BEANS AND WATER CHESTNUTS

3 cans whole green beans	Salt and pepper to taste
2 cans cream of mushroom soup	1 can French fried onion rings
2 cans water chestnuts	

Mix all ingredients except onion rings and put in a buttered 2-quart casserole. Bake 1½ hours at 300°. Sprinkle onion rings over top and bake 10 minutes longer. Serves 10.

MRS. DALE WOODALL

PAPA'S FARM BEANS

2 28-oz. cans pork and beans   10 dashes Worcestershire
⅓ c. light corn syrup   20 small spring onions or
⅓ c. maple syrup   4 medium onions, quartered
⅓ c. sorghum molasses   1 large green pepper, slivered
⅓ c. ketchup   Uncooked bacon

Mix first six ingredients and pour into a long, flat, 3-quart casserole. Trim
green stems from spring onions and peel the white part. Place the white onions
and the green pepper on top the beans. Do not stir. Bake 45 minutes at 350°.
Onions and peppers will brown. Cut bacon slices in half and cover casserole
top with the bacon. Return to oven and bake 1 hour at 350°. Serves 10.

MR. ROBERT R. PREST

LIMA BEANS IN SOUR CREAM

2 lbs. dried lima beans   1 lb. melted butter
1 pt. sour cream   4 t. dry mustard

Wash lima beans. Cover with cold water and let stand overnight. Next morning, simmer beans in water in which they have soaked, until tender but not
broken. Drain. Add sour cream, melted butter and mustard. Pour into a casserole and bake at 350° for 1½ hours. If desired, casserole may be rubbed
with garlic. Especially good with lamb or pork roasts. Serves 10.

MRS. FRED TARKINGTON, JR.

LIMA BEAN CASSEROLE

½ c. butter   1½ lbs. mushrooms, sliced
1 c. flour   2 pkgs. frozen lima beans, cooked
4 c. milk   4 hard-cooked eggs, chopped
Worcestershire to taste   Tabasco and salt to taste
½ c. Durkee's dressing   Buttered bread crumbs
1 c. grated sharp cheese

Melt butter in a saucepan, and stir in the flour. Then stir in the milk to make
a thick cream sauce. Season generously with Worcestershire and Durkee's.
Add cheese, mushrooms, lima beans, eggs, Tabasco and salt. Pour into a
casserole and cover with bread crumbs. Bake at 350° till crumbs brown. This
may be made ahead and reheated. Serves 18.

MRS. H. F. NORCROSS, FAIRVIEW FARMS, TYRONZA, ARK.

EDIE'S BEANS

2 cans French style green beans	1 c. grated sharp cheese
4 T. bacon drippings	½ c. sliced ripe olives
1 c. white sauce	Salt, pepper, garlic salt to taste

Drain ½ of liquid off beans. Cook beans in remaining liquid and bacon drippings for 30 minutes. Drain. Add sauce, ¾ cup cheese and the olives. Pour into a greased casserole. Sprinkle remaining cheese over top. Heat oven to 350° and cook about 30 minutes. Serves 8-10.

MRS. RAYMOND E. MANOGUE

GREEN BEANS WITH WATER CHESTNUTS

1 lb. fresh green beans	1 can water chestnuts, sliced
Bacon drippings	6 slices crisp bacon, crumbled

Cover beans with water, add bacon drippings and cook till done. Add water chestnuts during last 10 minutes of cooking. Drain and top with bacon. Serves 6-8.

MRS. RICHARD OWNBEY, NASHVILLE, TENN.

GREEN BEANS WITH WATER CHESTNUTS AND ALMONDS

4 pkgs. frozen string beans	1 pkg. slivered almonds, toasted
2 cans water chestnuts	

Cook beans according to package directions, adding sliced water chestnuts to beans. Drain, add some melted butter and sprinkle with toasted almonds. Serves 12.

MRS. CHARLES H. McGEE, BRUIN PLANTATION, HUGHES, ARK.

BROCCOLI SOUFFLÉ

3 10-oz. pkgs. frozen chopped broccoli	4 eggs, separated
¾ c. bouillon	2 t. chopped parsley
¾ c. whipping cream	4 T. finely chopped onion
½ c. butter	Salt and pepper to taste
½ c. flour	Cracked pepper to taste
	½ c. grated cheese

Cook and drain broccoli. Add bouillon to cream and scald. Melt butter and blend in flour. Gradually add cream mixture and stir until thick. Remove from stove and beat in egg yolks, parsley, onion, salt and pepper. Stir in broccoli and cheese. Can be made ahead to this point. When ready to serve, add stiffly beaten egg whites and turn into buttered casserole. Bake at 425° for 25-30 minutes. Serves 10.

MRS. ROBERT M. LEATHERMAN, COLUMBIA, MISS.

BRAISED CELERY

Hearts of celery   Melted butter
Stock

Cut whole celery stalks to desired length. Wash thoroughly and cook in boiling stock. When just tender, remove from stock and drain thoroughly. Serve with melted butter. Allow 1 bunch celery hearts, cooked in 1 cup stock, for every 2 people.

MRS. SNOWDEN BOYLE, JR.

FAR EAST CELERY

4 c. celery, cut in 4-in. lengths   ¼ c. diced pimiento
1 5-oz. can water chestnuts   ½ c. bread crumbs
1 can celery or cream of   ¼ c. toasted almonds
    chicken soup   2 T. melted butter

Cook celery in small amount of salted water for 8 minutes. Drain. Mix with water chestnuts, which have been drained and thinly sliced, soup and pimiento; then place in 2-quart casserole. Toast the bread crumbs and almonds in melted butter. Sprinkle over casserole. Bake at 350°, uncovered, for 30 minutes. Serves 6-8.

MRS. ALLEN COX, JR.

NED'S EGGPLANT STICKS

3 eggplants   1 t. pepper
1 c. breading mix   3 eggs
1 t. salt   ¼ c. milk

Peel eggplant and cut into finger-sized slices, ½ x 3 inches. Soak in ice water for 30 minutes. Drain well. Mix breading mix, salt and pepper. Beat milk and eggs. Dip eggplant in milk and eggs, then in breading mix. Place in refrigerator for ½ hour to allow coating to set. Deep fry in fat till golden brown. Serve as a vegetable as is, or serve as an hors d'oeuvre with a chili sauce dip.

MRS. RONALD BYRNES

EGGPLANT AND TOMATOES

1 large eggplant   Rosemary and basil
Salt and pepper   ½ c. bread crumbs
3 medium tomatoes

Peel eggplant and cut into ½-inch slices. Soak slices in salt water for a few minutes. Drain, then butter slices of eggplant on both sides. Season with salt and pepper. Cut tomatoes into ½-inch slices. Sprinkle slices with basil and rosemary, then salt and pepper. Sprinkle bread crumbs on each tomato slice. Place eggplant slices under broiler and broil 10 minutes or fry in skillet, turning slices from side to side. Place tomato slices on top of eggplant and run pan under broiler. Cook until tomatoes are tender. Serves 6-8.

MRS. WILLIAM W. DEUPREE

CREAMED MUSHROOMS

2 lbs. fresh mushrooms	1 c. grated Parmesan cheese
4 T. butter	(½ lb.)
4 T. dry sherry	1 t. salt
2 c. sour cream	½ t. freshly ground pepper
	1 t. Accent

Leave mushroom caps whole but chop the stems; sauté in butter for 2 minutes. Add sherry and cook 1 minute. Blend in sour cream, cheese, salt, pepper and Accent; cook over low heat until thickened. Serve on buttered toast. This can also be served from a chafing dish as an appetizer after thickening slightly with flour. A wonderful accompaniment for rare roast beef. Serves 8.

MRS. CHARLES H. McGEE, BRUIN PLANTATION, HUGHES, ARK.

MUSHROOMS STUFFED WITH SPINACH

12 large mushrooms	3 T. grated Parmesan cheese
3 T. butter	Dash Tabasco
1 garlic pod	Juice of 1 lemon
1 pkg. frozen chopped spinach	½ t. Worcestershire
3 T. Hellmann's mayonnaise	1 t. seasoned salt

Remove stems from mushrooms and discard. Wash mushroom caps and dry. Dip in melted butter in which garlic has been sautéed. Line a buttered flat casserole with the mushrooms. Cook spinach as directed on package. Drain liquid and add remaining ingredients to spinach, mixing thoroughly. Fill mushroom cavities with spinach mixture. Bake in 350° oven approximately 20 minutes till heated through. Serves 6.

MRS. C. NILES GROSVENOR, III

STUFFED MUSHROOMS

1½ lbs. mushrooms	2 t. salt
⅓ c. grated Parmesan cheese	¼ t. freshly ground
½ c. dry bread crumbs	black pepper
¼ c. grated onion	½ t. oregano
2 cloves garlic, minced	⅔ c. olive oil
2 T. minced parsley	

Buy large, even-sized mushrooms. Wash them in water with a little lemon juice, but do not peel them. Dry the mushrooms. Remove the stems and chop. Mix chopped stems with all ingredients except olive oil. Stuff the mushroom caps with this mixture. Pour a little oil into a baking pan. Arrange the mushrooms in it. Pour the remaining oil over them, being sure to get a little in each mushroom. Bake in a 350° oven for 25 minutes. Marvelous as a hot hors d'oeuvre or with meats as a vegetable. Serves 8-10.

MRS. HERBERT JORDAN, CAMBRIDGE, MASS.

MUSHROOM PIE

2 lbs. fresh mushrooms
6 T. butter
Salt and pepper
Lemon juice
Dash of soy sauce
3 T. flour

1½ c. chicken stock
½ c. Madeira wine
½ c. whipping cream, heated
1 stick pie crust mix
1 egg, beaten

Wash, dry, and remove stems from mushrooms. Heat 4 tablespoons butter, add mushrooms and sprinkle with seasonings. Cover and cook 10 minutes, stirring occasionally. Arrange mushrooms in buttered 1-quart casserole, piling them high in the center. To the juice in the pan, add remaining butter. Stir in flour and stock. Cook, stirring constantly, until thick. Add wine, cream, and salt and pepper to taste. Pour sauce over mushrooms. Roll out pie crust and cover mushrooms. Brush crust with beaten egg and make a few slits in the top. Bake for 15 minutes at 450º, then 15 minutes at 300º. Serves 8.

MRS. ROBERT M. LEATHERMAN, COLUMBIA, MISS.

MUSHROOM SOUFFLÉ

¾ lb. mushrooms
1 T. chopped onions
6 T. butter
6 T. flour
2 c. scalded milk

½ c. grated American cheese
Dash Tabasco
Salt and pepper to taste
6 egg yolks, well beaten
6 egg whites, beaten stiffly

Wash mushrooms. Chop caps and stems finely, and combine with onion. Sauté in 3 tablespoons of the butter until light brown. Put mushrooms aside. To the liquid and fat in the pan, add remaining 3 tablespoons butter. Blend in flour and add hot milk gradually. Cook, stirring constantly, until thick. Mix in cheese till melted. Add Tabasco, salt and pepper. Cool. Stir egg yolks into mixture. Then fold in egg whites. Pour into a greased 2-quart soufflé dish and place in a pan of warm water. Bake at 325º for about 1 hour or until firm. Serve at once. If you wish to hold back the soufflé, reduce heat to 275-300º during the last portion of baking. Serve with Shrimp and Almond Sauce (see Index). Serves 8-10.

FRESH ENGLISH PEAS

1 lb. English peas
1 T. sugar

Sprigs of mint

Unless it is the English pea season and they are very young and tender, use frozen peas. Cook peas with sugar and several sprigs of mint. Serves 6.

MRS. SNOWDEN BOYLE, JR.

PETITS POIS-FILLED PEPPERS

6 green bell peppers, cored
1 lb. fresh or canned mushrooms
2-3 T. butter
3 T. water

Lemon juice
Salt and pepper to taste
2 cans petits pois

Blanch peppers in boiling salted water for 5-10 minutes or until tender. Drain and put aside. Sauté chopped mushrooms (or whole caps if **very** small) in butter until browned on both sides. Add water and a few drops of lemon juice, salt and pepper and cook over low heat with lid on until done. Set aside, reserving any remaining pan juices. Heat peas. Drain and combine with mushrooms and mushroom juices. Fill peppers with mixture, dot each pepper with butter, and place in baking dish. Bake at 325° for 5-10 minutes until hot.

MRS. CHARLES BOONE

BUTTER-STEAMED NEW POTATOES

20-24 tiny new potatoes, about
1 inch in diameter
8 T. regular or unsalted butter

1 t. salt
⅛ t. white pepper
3 T. finely chopped dill

Scrub potatoes under cold running water. Pat thoroughly dry with paper towels. Melt butter in heavy 6-quart container equipped with a tight fitting cover. Add potatoes and sprinkle with salt and pepper. Coat thoroughly with butter by rolling the potatoes around in casserole. To insure success, cover must fit tightly. If you have doubts as to the tightness of your cover, first cover the casserole top with 2 thicknesses of foil (pinch edges down), then place cover on casserole. Cook over low heat 30-45 minutes. To insure not scorching potatoes, purchase an asbestos pad the size of your burner, and place pad under cooking pot. As potatoes cook, shake pot from time to time to prevent sticking. Potatoes are done when they can be easily pierced with tip of sharp knife. Sprinkle with dill and serve. These will stay warm (if covered securely) about ½ hour. Serves 6.

MRS. J. HAL PATTON, III

PATRICIAN POTATOES

4 large Idaho potatoes, baked
¾ c. butter
1 T. salt
1 c. whipping cream

1 t. black pepper
Chopped chives, optional
Grated Gruyere or cheddar cheese

Scoop hot potatoes from their shells and mix with all other ingredients except the cheese. Place in 2-quart casserole, dot with additional butter, and sprinkle with cheese. Bake at 375° for 15 to 20 minutes. Serves 6 to 8.

MRS. KEMPER DURAND

POTATOES ROMANOV

5-6 medium potatoes	¼ c. grated onion
1 c. sour cream	2 t. salt
2 c. creamed cottage cheese	½-1 c. grated sharp cheese

Cook potatoes in their jackets. Remove peel and cube potatoes to equal 6 cups. Combine with remaining ingredients, except sharp cheese. Place in a buttered casserole and top with cheese. Bake at 350° for 20-30 minutes. Serves 12.

MRS. WILLIAM PURDY

POTATO VOISETTES

24 small new potatoes	Parsley
Butter	

Boil peeled potatoes just till tender; dry potatoes and sauté in butter. Sprinkle with parsley after browned. **Variation:** Sprinkle potatoes cooked in this manner with Parmesan. Serves 6.

MRS. C. NILES GROSVENOR, III

STUFFED POTATOES

6 large Idaho potatoes	1 t. white pepper
10 strips bacon	Butter, melted
½ c. chopped shallots	Parmesan cheese
1½ c. sour cream	Paprika
1 t. salt	

Bake potatoes until well done. Fry bacon, drain and crumble. Sauté shallots in bacon grease. Scoop potatoes and place in skillet with fat and shallots, taking care to keep potato skin intact for stuffing. Mash potatoes. Add sour cream, bacon, salt and pepper. Mix well, stuff into shells and drizzle with melted butter. Sprinkle with Parmesan cheese and paprika. Bake in 350° oven for 15-20 minutes. Serves 6.

MRS. W. McDONALD THRASHER

SWEET POTATO BALLS

8 medium sweet potatoes or 4 cups mashed	Orange juice and sherry to taste 14 marshmallows
¼ lb. melted butter	1 c. corn flakes, crushed
⅔ c. packed lt. brown sugar	1 egg, beaten

Bake sweet potatoes. When done, remove from skins and cream with melted butter. Season with brown sugar, orange juice and sherry to taste. Cool. Roll ball of potato mixture around marshmallow. Place in refrigerator to set. Roll balls in beaten egg, then corn flake crumbs and deep fry. Serves 12.

MRS. WILLIAM NEELY MALLORY, MALLORY FARMS, CHATFIELD, ARK.

CONSOMMÉ RICE

½ medium onion, chopped
1 stick oleo
1 small can chopped mushrooms
1 c. rice
1 can beef consommé

Sauté onion in butter and add mushrooms. Add rice and consommé. Mix well and put in casserole. Bake covered at 350° for 45 minutes, or until broth is absorbed. Serves 6.

MRS. JEROME TURNER

GREEN RICE

4 c. cooked white rice
1⅓ c. chicken broth
⅔ c. sharp grated cheese
½ c. minced parsley
1 pkg. frozen chopped spinach, uncooked
½ c. melted butter
1½ t. Worcestershire
2 t. salt
2 t. grated onion
4 eggs

Instead of chicken broth, 2½ chicken bouillon cubes dissolved in 1¼ cups water can be used. Combine all ingredients. Place in a large buttered casserole. Bake at 325° for 1 hour. Serves 10.

MRS. THOMAS TODD

HERB RICE

1 c. uncooked rice
2 beef bouillon cubes
½ t. salt
½ t. rosemary
½ t. marjoram
½ t. thyme
1 t. chives
2 c. cold water
1 T. butter

Combine all ingredients in a heavy saucepan. When mixture boils, reduce heat. Stir once with fork and simmer covered for 14 minutes, or until liquid is absorbed. Serves 6.

MRS. VAUGHAN DOW

MUSHROOM-PECAN RICE

1 c. uncooked rice
½ t. nutmeg
1 can mushroom soup
Small can mushroom stems and pieces
3 oz. pecan or almond pieces
½ c. butter, melted

Cook rice, rinse, and season with nutmeg. In a well-greased casserole, layer rice, undiluted mushroom soup, mushrooms and nuts. Repeat layers, ending with nuts on top. Pour melted butter over all. Bake for 20 minutes at 350°. Serves 6-8.

MRS. GEORGE B. JETT

CHINESE FRIED RICE

½ lb. bacon
2 c. onions, coarsely chopped
2 c. cooked rice, cold

2 eggs, slightly beaten
2-3 T. soy sauce

Cut bacon in ½-inch pieces and cook till done. Push to one side of skillet and sauté onions over very low heat till done. DO NOT BROWN. Add cold rice and sauté. Add eggs, seasoned with soy sauce. Sauté till done. For variety add: 2 cups cooked meat or shrimp, chopped green pepper, or roasted peanuts. Serves 6.

MRS. JOHN HART TODD

SPINACH CASSEROLE

2 pkgs. frozen chopped spinach
3 small pkgs. cream cheese
  with chives
Juice of 1 lemon

1 lb. fresh mushrooms
Salt and pepper to taste
Buttered bread crumbs

Cook spinach until tender, drain, and put in 1-quart casserole. Blend in chive cheese, lemon juice, mushrooms, salt and pepper. Bake in 350° oven for 1 hour. Remove from oven and sprinkle with buttered bread crumbs. Run back in oven to brown. Serves 8.

MRS. BRADY BARTUSCH

SPINACH SUPREME

6 baby link sausages
2 pkgs. frozen chopped spinach

1 can mushroom soup

Cook sausage till brown. Drain and chop. Cook spinach and drain. Mix sausage, spinach, and mushroom soup and pour into a greased baking dish. Heat in 350° oven till bubbling. Serves 8.

SPEEDY SPINACH

2 boxes frozen, chopped spinach
1⅜-oz. pkg. onion soup mix

1 pt. sour cream
Salt and pepper to taste

Place the frozen spinach in a large saucepan over very low heat (add no water). Cover and watch carefully until spinach is thawed and cooked (about 10 to 15 minutes). Remove from heat, add the soup mix, sour cream and salt and pepper. Place the mixture in a 1½-quart casserole and bake at 300° for 30 minutes. This can be made ahead and baked at serving time. Serves 8.

MRS. ROBERT G. HEARD, JR.

TOMATOES STUFFED WITH SPEEDY SPINACH

12-15 ripe tomatoes   **Bacon Curls — one per tomato**
1 recipe for Speedy Spinach

Drop tomatoes in kettle of boiling water. Leave for about 5 seconds. Remove and place in cold water (this loosens the tomato skins). Peel the tomatoes. Scoop out a little of the pulp and discard. Drain tomatoes if need be. Sprinkle each tomato with a little salt and pepper. Mound some of the Speedy Spinach mixture in each tomato cavity. Bake at 325° for 25 minutes. Garnish top with a Bacon Curl (see Index). Tomatoes can be made about 6 hours before serving and refrigerated till time to cook. Spectacular results with very little effort! Serves 12-15.

MRS. ROBERT G. HEARD, JR.

MUSHROOM-STUFFED TOMATOES

6 medium tomatoes   **¼ c. fine dry bread crumbs**
1 pt. (1½ c.) fresh mushrooms,   **1 t. salt**
sliced   **Dash pepper and thyme**
2 T. butter   **1 T. melted butter**
½ c. sour cream   **2 T. fine dry bread crumbs**
2 egg yolks, beaten

Cut stem end from tomatoes and scoop out pulp. Turn shells upside down to drain. Chop pulp finely and measure 1 cup for use in stuffing tomatoes. Cook mushrooms in butter until tender. Combine sour cream and egg yolks. Add to mushrooms with the tomato pulp; mix well. Stir in the crumbs, salt, pepper, and thyme. Cook and stir until mixture thickens and boils. Place tomato shells in a 10 x 6 x 1½-inch baking dish. Spoon mushroom mixture into tomatoes. Combine 1 tablespoon melted butter and 2 tablespoons bread crumbs and sprinkle on top of tomatoes. Bake at 375° for 25 minutes. Serves 6.

MRS. BEN C. ADAMS, JR.

ROQUEFORT TOMATOES

3 tomatoes, halved   **½ t. onion powder**
3 T. Roquefort cheese   **⅓ c. dry bread crumbs**
1 t. Worcestershire   **Butter**
3 T. cream cheese   **Paprika**

Halve tomatoes. Mix together cheeses and seasonings. Blend well and smear on cut side of tomatoes. Sprinkle with bread crumbs, dot with a little butter and dust with paprika. Broil only 10 minutes. Serve with sprig of parsley on top. Serves 6.

MRS. ALLEN COX, JR.

TOMATOES WITH PEAS

6-8 large, firm tomatoes
Melted butter
Sugar

Salt and pepper
2 pkgs. frozen English peas,
cooked

Cut tomatoes in half. Brush cut sides with butter. Sprinkle with a little sugar, salt and pepper. Arrange on a baking sheet and broil for about 10 minutes or until tender. Place on a heated serving dish and smother with hot buttered peas. Serves 8.

MRS. CHARLES H. McGEE, BRUIN PLANTATION, HUGHES, ARK.

TOMATOES FILLED WITH SOUFFLÉ

12 small tomatoes
¼ c. prepared mustard
12 slices bacon, diced and
sautéed

2 12-oz. pkgs. frozen corn,
spinach or cheese soufflé,
thawed 1 hour
¼ c. grated Parmesan cheese
Parsley sprigs

Preheat oven to 375°. Cut a thin slice from top of each tomato. Carefully scoop out pulp to make a shell. Drain the shells upside down 15 minutes. Spread inside of each with 1 teaspoon mustard. Divide bacon evenly into tomatoes. Spoon soufflé into tomatoes. Sprinkle 1 teaspoon cheese over top of each. Arrange tomatoes in two 8-inch round baking dishes. Bake, uncovered, 20 to 30 minutes, or until golden brown on top. Garnish with parsley sprigs. Makes 12 servings.

MRS. JAMES GUY ROBBINS

STUFFED SQUASH

8 small yellow squash
1 pkg. frozen peas
4 T. melted butter
¼ c. coffee cream, warmed

Salt and pepper to taste
Bread crumbs
Butter
Parmesan cheese

Cut squash in half and cook about 7-10 minutes. The squash must be slightly firm. Do not let them get too soft. Remove inside of squash. Cook the peas according to package directions. Drain well and put in blender with butter, cream, salt and pepper. Blend thoroughly at low speed and then turn to high speed and blend to fine purée. Fill the squash cavity with purée of peas. Cover the purée with bread crumbs, dot with butter and sprinkle with Parmesan cheese. Bake at 350° until hot, about 15 minutes, and run under broiler to brown. These may be prepared ahead, then heated and browned. Other suggestions for filling: creamed mushrooms, cut-up tomatoes, creamed peas and carrots, or creamed spinach. Also, any of your favorite vegetables such as green beans, spinach or broccoli, may be used instead of peas in the above recipe. Serves 8.

MRS. CHARLES H. McGEE, BRUIN PLANTATION, HUGHES, ARK.

SQUASH CASSEROLE

2 lbs. squash	2 T. brown sugar
2 eggs	1 t. salt
¾ stick oleo	2½ c. small pieces of torn bread
Scant ½ c. milk	1 c. grated Cheddar cheese
½ medium onion, chopped finely or grated	

Cook the squash, drain well, and mash. In a separate bowl, beat eggs. Then mix together the squash, eggs, oleo, milk, onion, brown sugar, and salt. In a buttered casserole, put a layer of torn bread, a layer of squash mixture, a layer of cheese. Repeat the 3 layers and top with bread and dots of butter. Bake uncovered at 350° for 45 minutes. Zwieback crumbs may be substituted for the bread crumbs. Serves 8.

MRS. ALLEN HOLT HUGHES

ZUCCHINI

3 lbs. zucchini	⅛ t. Java cracked pepper
3 T. butter	Heaping T. chopped chives
3 whole green onions, chopped	Heaping T. minced parsley
1 t. Accent	⅓ c. water
½ t. sugar	Oregano
½ t. Beau Monde seasoning	

Wash zucchini; do not peel. Slice about ¼-inch thick. Into **heavy** pan, put butter, green onion, seasonings (except oregano) and water. Distribute sliced zucchini evenly around pan. Cover tightly and put on high heat until steaming. Then turn to lowest heat for 10 minutes or less. During last few minutes, sprinkle with oregano. Use yellow summer squash if zucchini is not available. Serves 6.

Zucchini is also marvelous boiled till just done in water to which a bay leaf has been added. Drain, discard bay leaf and toss zucchini with melted butter and grated Parmesan.

MRS. JAMES W. WRAPE, COLLIERVILLE, TENN.

GREEN GARLIC SPAGHETTI

6 T. melted butter	¼ t. salt
3 T. olive oil	½ t. freshly ground black pepper
6 T. minced parsley	2 dashes cayenne
6 T. minced green garlic or 5 garlic cloves, minced	¾ lb. spaghetti
3 T. basil	1½ c. freshly grated Parmesan cheese

Combine butter, oil, herbs and seasonings. Cook spaghetti just until done. Do not overcook. Add spaghetti and then cheese to butter mixture. Mix well to coat the spaghetti. Serves 6.

MRS. JAMES W. WRAPE, COLLIERVILLE, TENN.

GREEN VEGETABLES WITH SAUCE

1 pkg. frozen baby lima beans	1 can whole green beans
1 pkg. frozen English peas	

Cook vegetables separately, according to package directions. Mix together and heat. Drain and serve with the following sauce:

2 hard-boiled eggs	2½ t. Worcestershire
¼ t. mustard	½ t. chopped onion
1 c. mayonnaise	2 T. olive oil

Grate eggs finely and mix together with remaining ingredients. Serve at room temperature over the hot, green vegetables. Serves 8.

MRS. CHARLES G. SWINGLE, MARKED TREE, ARK.

VEGETABLES WITH MUSTARD SAUCE

6 T. butter, melted	2 T. lemon juice
3 T. sugar	3 pkgs. frozen broccoli (or)
2 T. prepared mustard	2 cans green beans
2 T. vinegar	Crumbled bacon

Prepare sauce from butter, sugar, mustard, vinegar, and lemon juice. Heat and pour over cooked vegetables. Sprinkle bacon over top. Serves 8.

Salads and Salad Dressings

CRISP CUCUMBER ASPIC

2 c. boiling water
6-oz. pkg. lemon-flavored gelatin
⅓ c. white wine vinegar
¼ t. salt
Green food coloring
2 medium cucumbers, pared and
    grated (2 c.)
½ c. finely chopped celery

1-2 T. horseradish
1 T. grated onion
2 t. snipped fresh dill
20 paper-thin slices cucumber
2 pts. cherry tomatoes
Crisp salad greens
½ pt. dairy sour cream

In medium bowl, pour boiling water over gelatin; stir until dissolved. Stir in vinegar, salt and few drops green food coloring. Set in bowl of ice, stirring occasionally, until mixture is consistency of unbeaten egg whites (about 35 minutes). Fold in grated cucumber, celery, horseradish, onion and dill until well blended. Turn into 5½ cup ring mold that has been rinsed in cold water and lined with the thin cucumber slices. Refrigerate until firm, at least 3 hours. To unmold, run a small spatula around the edge of mold, invert over platter, place a hot, damp cloth over inverted mold and shake gently to release. Fill center with tomatoes. Garnish edge with salad greens. Pass sour cream for topping. Serves 8-10.

CONGEALED GAZPACHO

2 pkgs. gelatin
3 c. tomato juice
¼ c. wine vinegar
1 clove garlic, crushed
2 t. salt
¼ t. pepper
Dash cayenne
2 large tomatoes, chopped
    and drained

½ c. finely chopped onion
¾ c. finely chopped green pepper
¾ c. chopped cucumber, drained
¼ c. finely chopped pimiento
Hot peppers and dilled okra
½ c. sour cream
½ t. salt
⅓ c. mayonnaise

Soften gelatin in 1 cup tomato juice. Heat until mixture simmers. Add remaining tomato juice, vinegar, garlic, 2 teaspoons salt, pepper and cayenne. Chill until mixture begins to set. Fold in tomatoes, onion, green pepper, cucumber, pimiento, and pour into a 6 cup mold. Unmold on salad greens. Surround with peppers and dilled okra. Spread top of salad with dressing made from sour cream, ½ teaspoon salt, and mayonnaise. Serves 8.

Helpful hint for serving molded salads: Pour into empty tin cans to mold. When ready to serve, unmold and slice off attractive rounds for individual servings.

MRS. RICHARD DIXON

TOMATO ASPIC

This is a mild aspic that may be used as you would fresh tomatoes.

4 c. tomato juice	2 T. unflavored gelatin
⅓ c. chopped onion	¼ c. cold water
¼ c. chopped celery leaves	3 T. lemon juice
2 T. brown sugar	1 c. finely cut celery
1 t. salt	Mayonnaise
2 small bay leaves	1 small jar black olives
4 whole cloves	Lemon wedges

Combine tomato juice, onion, celery leaves, sugar, salt, bay leaves, cloves. Simmer 5 minutes. Strain. Dissolve gelatin in cold water. Add gelatin and lemon juice to tomato mixture. Chill until partially set, then add celery. Pour mixture into individual molds (or into a single 2-quart mold) which have been greased with salad oil. **Variations:** Place a Stuffed Artichoke Heart, cheese side down, into partially congealed aspic. Press gently. Chill till set. Unmold on a bed of lettuce or spinach. Place a dollop of mayonnaise on top of aspic and top mayonnaise with black caviar. Garnish with a lemon wedge. If a single ring mold is used, center may be filled with pitted ripe olives, caper mayonnaise (mayonnaise into which drained capers have been folded), Shrimp Remoulade, or cottage cheese. If you choose, spread black caviar on top of caper mayonnaise or cottage cheese. Garnish filled aspic ring with wedges of lemons and/or limes, arranged spoke-fashioned. Serves 8.

Stuffed Artichoke Hearts:

1 3-oz. pkg. cream cheese	Lemon juice
Chives	Salt and pepper to taste
Worcestershire	8 artichoke hearts
Mayonnaise	

Let cream cheese come to room temperature. Cream and add seasonings, using enough mayonnaise to soften to a creamy paste. Gently spread hearts open and stuff centers.

MRS. MILTON LYMAN KNOWLTON, JR.

Tomato Aspic may also be served with Cucumber Sauce made by combining 1 c. mayonnaise, 1 c. chopped cucumber, 2 t. chopped chives, 1 t. chopped parsley, ½ t. salt, ½ t. dill seed. Chill.

MRS. CHARLES L. PIPLAR

CHINESE CABBAGE SALAD

1 head Chinese cabbage	¾ c. French dressing
1 red onion, chopped	Seasonings to taste
Crumbled bleu cheese	

Cut Chinese cabbage across into ¼-inch strips. Toss together with onion, bleu cheese, and French dressing. Season to taste. You will probably have to ask your grocer for the cabbage ahead of time. Serves 4.

MRS. EUGENE J. PIDGEON

COUNTRY COLE SLAW

½ head cabbage, shredded
1 onion, shredded
2 carrots, shredded
1 t. sugar

4 T. mayonnaise
3 T. vinegar
Salt and pepper to taste

Mix well and chill for several hours before serving. Serves 8.

MRS. WILLIAM J. BRITTON, III

RED CABBAGE SLAW

1 large head of red cabbage
2 or 3 onions, sliced

½ c. Kraft Coleslaw Dressing
½ c. Good Seasons Old Fashioned
French Dressing

Slice (do not grate) cabbage. Slice onions into thin rings. Combine dressings and toss with cabbage and onions. Serves 10.

MRS. ROBERT M. LEATHERMAN, COLUMBIA, MISS.

MOLDED BROCCOLI SALAD

2 pkgs. gelatin
1 can madrilène consommé
3 pkgs. chopped broccoli, cooked,
drained and mashed
4 hard-boiled eggs
1 c. mayonnaise

1 t. Tabasco
1 t. black pepper
3 T. Worcestershire
1½ t. salt
2 T. lemon juice

Dissolve gelatin in undiluted warm madrilène consommé. To broccoli, add finely mashed eggs. Add remaining ingredients to consommé; then fold in broccoli and eggs. Blend well. Put in mold which has been greased with mayonnaise—a sure way to unmold successfully! Chill. Serves 14-16.

MRS. HOWARD S. MISNER

MRS. DUDLEY'S SALMON MOUSSE

2 T. gelatin
½ c. cold water
1 lb. can red sockeye salmon
2 T. grated onion
1 c. finely diced cucumber
½ c. diced celery
¾ c. diced green pepper
1 T. Worcestershire

Dash Tabasco
Salt to taste
½ t. pepper
1 T. vinegar
3 T. lemon juice
1 c. thick mayonnaise
½ pt. whipping cream

Pour water over gelatin; then melt over hot water. Discard bones and skin from salmon. Mix salmon and its oil with vegetables. Add seasonings and set aside. Whip cream and mix with mayonnaise. Fold gelatin mixture into cream mixture. Pour all over salmon, blending well. Pour into oiled fish-shaped mold and refrigerate overnight. Turn into tray lined with lettuce and surrounded by sliced cucumbers or artichoke hearts. Serves 12.

MRS. CHARLES B. DUDLEY

SALMON MOUSSE

1 envelope unflavored gelatin	½ c. mayonnaise
½ c. boiling water	1 lb. can pink salmon
2 T. lemon juice	½ t. salt
1 medium onion, sliced	⅛ t. freshly ground black pepper
1-2 t. dill salt or ground dill seed	1 c. whipping cream
½ t. paprika	

Stir gelatin into boiling water until dissolved. In quart-sized blender put gelatin, lemon juice and onion. Blend at high speed 1 minute. Add dill salt or seed, paprika, mayonnaise, salmon, salt and pepper and blend at high speed for 2 minutes, or until smooth. Remove from blender and fold in the whipped cream. Pour into 4 cup fish mold that has been lightly greased with salad oil. Refrigerate until firm. Unmold on platter. Garnish top of mousse by overlapping thin slices of scored cucumber to simulate scales. Garnish edge with watercress and cherry tomatoes or wedges of hard-boiled eggs, small whole pickled beets, and Belgian endive. This may also be served on a bed of shredded lettuce. Serve with Avocado Dressing. Serves 6.

Avocado Dressing:

1 large overripe avocado	¼ t. onion salt
¼ t. garlic salt	¼ c. mayonnaise
Juice of 1 lemon	

Put all ingredients in blender at high speed until creamy smooth. Garnish top of dressing with paprika.

MRS. FLOYD HUMPHREYS DUNCAN

LOBSTER MOUSSE

1 3½-c. lobster mold	½ c. cream or evaporated milk
1 t. gelatin	1 T. lemon juice
⅓ c. catsup	9-oz. can shrimp or lobster
1 can tomato soup	1½ c. diced celery
1 T. gelatin	¼ c. chopped green pepper
1 3-oz. pkg. cream cheese	1 T. chopped pimiento
½ c. mayonnaise	

Lightly grease mold with oil or mayonnaise. Sprinkle the 1 teaspoon gelatin over catsup and heat, stirring constantly to dissolve the gelatin. Spoon the catsup into design in bottom of the lobster mold and place in refrigerator to congeal. Sprinkle the 1 tablespoon gelatin over tomato soup and heat soup to dissolve the gelatin. Cool. Soften cream cheese with mayonnaise and cream or evaporated milk. Add lemon juice to cream cheese mixture and stir into the tomato soup. Fold the shrimp or lobster, celery, green pepper and pimiento into the tomato soup mixture and pour over the congealed catsup to fill the mold. Refrigerate several hours. Unmold and garnish with watercress or endive. **Note:** Any fish-shaped mold will do, if you have no lobster mold. Serves 4-6.

MRS. MILTON LYMAN KNOWLTON, JR.

AVOCADO MOUSSE

1 3-oz. pkg. lime gelatin	1 scant t. salt
1 c. hot water	Dash Tabasco
2 c. avocado purée	¼ t. Worcestershire
Juice of 1 lemon	¾ c. sour cream
3 T. grated onion	1 T. finely chopped parsley
½ c. mayonnaise	

Dissolve gelatin in hot water; then cool. Add remaining ingredients to the avocado purée. Add avocado mixture to the gelatin. Pour into an oiled 1½-quart mold and refrigerate. Unmold on salad greens. This salad has many interesting possibilities: (1) Mold in a ring and fill center with Ceviche (See Index) or shrimp salad. (2) Garnish with clusters of fresh fruits, such as green grapes, plump strawberries, fresh pineapple sticks, and fill center of mold with mayonnaise combined with grated orange peel and chopped pecans. (3) Garnish with citrus fruits (grapefruit, orange, and mandarin orange sections) and serve with Piquant French Dressing (see Index). Serves 8-10.

MRS. JACK SHANNON

CRAB MEAT MOUSSE

2 lbs. crab meat	2 t. Worcestershire
2 c. finely chopped celery	2 t. vinegar
1 bottle capers, drained	4 envelopes gelatin
1 c. chopped olives	1 c. cold water
2 c. mayonnaise	1 c. heated milk
2 T. dry mustard	Lemon juice to taste

Mix crab meat, celery, capers and olives. Stir in mayonnaise. In a separate bowl, mix Worcestershire and mustard; then dissolve in vinegar. Soften gelatin in cold water and add to hot milk. Combine all ingredients, adding lemon juice to taste. Pour into 2-quart greased mold. If done in a ring mold, center of mold can be filled with mashed avocado seasoned with lime or lemon juice. Serves 12.

MRS. BEN C. ADAMS, JR.

HAM MOUSSE

1 envelope unflavored gelatin	½ c. chopped celery
¾ c. cold water	¼ c. chopped green pepper
1 c. mayonnaise	1 t. grated onion
2 c. chopped cooked ham	½ c. whipping cream

Sprinkle gelatin over cold water in saucepan. Place over low heat, stir until gelatin dissolves, 3-4 minutes. Gradually add to mayonnaise, stir until smooth. Chill until slightly thickened. Stir in ham, celery, pepper and onion. Fold in whipped cream. Pour into 1-quart mold and chill until firm. Surround with deviled eggs and watercress sprigs. Serves 4-6.

MRS. CHARLES L. PIPLAR

CHICKEN MOLD FITZMAURICE

1 large hen (4 lbs. or over)	⅛ t. cayenne
1 large onion, chopped	½ t. salt
2 celery ribs with leaves	1 pt. mayonnaise
2 t. salt	½ pt. whipping cream
Peppercorns	¾ c. chopped almonds
1 envelope unflavored gelatin	1½ c. minced celery
¼ c. cold water	3 minced pimientos
1 c. chicken broth	2 c. petits pois
1½ T. Worcestershire	Pimiento strips for garnish
½ T. scraped onion	

Cover hen with cold water. Add chopped onion, celery, salt and several peppercorns. Simmer 2 hours or until tender. Cool in broth. Remove chicken. Discard skin and bones; chop meat coarsely. Chill broth to remove grease; reserve 1 cup broth and heat. Sprinkle gelatin over cold water. Pour boiling broth over gelatin. Add Worcestershire, scraped onion, cayenne, and ½ teaspoon salt. Chill till slightly thickened. Add mayonnaise and whipped cream. Add chicken, almonds, minced celery, pimientos, and petits pois. Pour into 3-quart mold and chill. Unmold on greens and garnish top with pimiento strips. Serves 12.

MR. JOHN FITZMAURICE

EXOTIC CHICKEN SALAD

4½-5 lbs. chicken breasts, split	1 T. curry powder
Butter	2 T. soy sauce
Salt and pepper	2 c. celery, sliced
3 3¼-oz. pkgs. slivered almonds	3 6-oz. cans water chestnuts, sliced
2 c. mayonnaise, preferably homemade	2 lbs. seedless grapes
	Boston or Bibb lettuce

Brush chicken breasts with melted butter and sprinkle with salt and pepper. Wrap in heavy-duty aluminum foil and seal edges tightly. Place on shallow pan and bake in 350° oven for 1 hour. Cook, bone and cut in bite-sized pieces; there should be 2 quarts. Coat almond slivers with melted butter and spread on cookie sheet. Roast in 350° oven about 30 minutes or until they are a mellow brown. Spread on paper towels, sprinkle with salt, and set aside until just before serving. All this can be done the day before. A few hours before serving, mix mayonnaise with curry powder and soy sauce. If mayonnaise is not homemade with lemon juice, add 2 tablespoons lemon juice. Combine with chicken, celery, water chestnuts and grapes. Chill until time to serve. Arrange lettuce leaves around edge of large porcelain or silver platter. Mound chicken salad in center. Also interesting served in a dark wooden salad bowl. Sprinkle almonds over all. Serves 12.

VARIATION: One large can pineapple chunks, drained, may be added to this, along with additional mayonnaise. Place individual servings in half a hollowed pineapple (cut pineapple lengthwise, leave crown on).

MRS. NEWTON ALLEN
MRS. ALEXANDER DANN, JR.

CREAMED CHICKEN SALAD

4 whole chicken breasts, boned
Chicken broth or bouillon
3-oz. pkg. cream cheese
1 c. mayonnaise
½ c. sour cream

1 t. dill seed
Salt to taste
6-8 thick slices tomato
Holland Rusk
Toasted almonds

Bone chicken breasts and cook until tender in broth or bouillon. Cut chicken into cubes. Make a paste of cream cheese, mayonnaise, sour cream, dill seed and salt. Mix all together and chill. Place thick slice of tomato on Holland Rusk or lettuce leaf. Cover with salad. Sprinkle toasted almonds over top and garnish with parsley or sprig of dill. Serves 6-8.

MRS. ROBERT G. HEARD, JR.

CURRIED CHICKEN SALAD

Curry Mayonnaise:
   ½ c. mayonnaise
   1 T. chopped preserved ginger
     in syrup
Chicken Salad:
   3 c. cubed cooked chicken
     or turkey
   ¼ c. oil and vinegar dressing
   2 c. 1-in. chunks fresh pineapple
     or 1 lb. 4½-oz. can drained
     pineapple chunks

2 t. curry powder
1 t. grated onion
½ t. salt
½ c. whipping cream

1½ c. diced pared apple (1 large)
1½ c. seedless green grapes
¼ c. chutney
¼ c. chopped green pepper
Crisp lettuce

To make curry mayonnaise: Combine mayonnaise, ginger, curry powder, onion, salt and mix until well blended. Fold in cream, whipped. Refrigerate, covered, until needed. In a large bowl, combine chicken and oil and vinegar dressing, tossing until well coated. Refrigerate covered, at least 2 hours. Add pineapple, apple, grapes, chutney, and green pepper to chicken and mix well. Gently fold in curry mayonnaise until well blended. Refrigerate, covered, until chilled, about 2 hours. To serve, arrange lettuce on platter and mound salad in center. Garnish with watercress. Serves 6-8.

MRS. F. PEARSON ALLEN, JR.

EDITH'S STACKED SALAD SANDWICH

Holland Rusk
Tomato slices
Slices of chicken, ham or
   turkey
Sliced onion (optional)

Stuffed eggs
Slices of avocado
Mayonnaise, preferably homemade
Bottled chili sauce
Caviar

For each serving: On a Holland Rusk, stack a slice of tomato, then meat, onion, stuffed egg and avocado. Mix mayonnaise with chili sauce and pour over sandwich before serving. This dressing should be thick enough to cover it completely. Then top with a spoonful of caviar.

MRS. BURCH CAYWOOD

FRESH LOBSTER SALAD

6 1¼-lb. Maine lobsters

Drop lobsters into boiling, salted water. Return water to boiling and cook for 12 minutes. Remove lobsters and cool. Crack and remove all meat. Cut meat into 1½-inch chunks and place for several hours in the following marinade:

1 t. salt	Juice of 1½ limes
½ t. pepper	Juice of 1 lemon
1 T. frozen chives	Dash of wine vinegar
½ t. dry mustard	¾ c. corn oil
1 T. dried parsley	

Mix together dry ingredients. In a separate bowl, mix lime and lemon juices and vinegar. Add oil to dry ingredients, a small amount at a time, alternating with the juice mixture. Beat entire time with fork.

Before serving, add the following to the marinated lobsters:

½ c. chopped celery	½ c. homemade mayonnaise
2 hard-boiled eggs, coarsely grated	½ c. sour cream
	1 bottle capers, optional

Garnish salad with finely grated egg yolk, fresh or dried dill, fresh or dried minced parsley. Serves 12.

MRS. CHARLES TIFFANY BINGHAM

CAESAR SALAD

2 large heads romaine lettuce	6 anchovy fillets, diced and mashed
1 clove garlic	1 t. fresh black pepper
1 c. olive oil	½ t. salt
4 pieces stale bread	1 egg
Dash cayenne	3 T. lemon juice
Dash Tabasco	⅜ c. grated Parmesan cheese
½ t. sugar	

Tear off lettuce leaves. Wash well, drain and put in refrigerator to chill. Crush garlic clove and let it stand overnight in olive oil in the refrigerator. Trim crusts from stale bread, French if possible. Cut bread into cubes and brown these in about ¼ cup of the olive oil, which has been strained to remove garlic. Sauté over medium heat, being sure to brown on all sides. Drain croutons on paper towels. In a cup, add to the rest of the garlic-flavored oil a dash of cayenne, Tabasco, sugar and anchovy fillets. Break lettuce in pieces and put in a large bowl. Sprinkle with fresh black pepper and salt. Pour in the olive oil and mix thoroughly so that every leaf is coated. Boil egg for 1 minute; crack and drop into salad. Sprinkle egg with fresh lemon juice and toss salad. Sprinkle over top Parmesan cheese and the croutons. Serve immediately. Serves 6.

MRS. CHARLES H. McGEE, BRUIN PLANTATION, HUGHES, ARK.

BIBB SALAD

6 small heads Bibb lettuce
1 small can chopped ripe olives
1 can rolled anchovies

Oil and vinegar dressing
or
Bottled Italian dressing

Separate and wash lettuce. Drain well and dry with paper towels. Place in crisper of refrigerator to chill. Toss together all ingredients. Serve immediately. Serves 8-10.

MRS. EVERETT B. GIBSON

CEVICHE

This very spicy, cold Mexican fish salad is pronounced "se-vee-shee".

1 lb. raw white fish
Juice of 2 fresh limes
1 small onion, chopped
2 tomatoes, peeled and chopped
¼ c. olive oil
Chopped parsley

1-2 T. wine vinegar
To taste: Tabasco, oregano, salt
 and pepper
Chopped green pepper, optional
1 T. capers, optional

Clean fish of any skin or bone and dice. Place in a shallow glass or pottery dish. Pour lime juice over and marinate at least 3 hours, turning pieces with a wooden spoon, until it looks and flakes like cooked fish (don't be squeamish; the lime juice cooks the fish). Add rest of ingredients. Be heavy handed with the spices! Chill and serve as a first course over shredded lettuce (do eat the lettuce too), or as a luncheon entrée spooned into avocado halves, or serve with Avocado Mousse (see Index). This can be made the day before. Serves 5-6.

MRS. EPHRAIM B. WILKINSON, JR.

HEARTS OF PALM SALAD

Pinch each of tarragon, thyme,
 basil leaves
2 T. vinegar
½ t. salt
⅓ c. olive oil
1 T. Dijon-style prepared
 mustard

½ t. ground pepper
1 clove garlic, crushed
1 14-oz. can hearts of palm
3 c. watercress
2 c. torn romaine
1 c. torn iceberg lettuce

Soak tarragon, thyme and basil for 1 hour in vinegar. Dissolve salt in the seasoned vinegar. Add olive oil, mustard, pepper and garlic. Shake well. Drain hearts of palm and cut in serving pieces. Combine hearts of palm with watercress, romaine and lettuce. Place the greens in a large bowl. Toss with dressing. Serves 6-8.

NOTE: The purpose of tossing a salad is to coat each piece with just enough dressing. Just enough in this instance means very little. The test is that there should be no liquid in the bowl when the salad is gone. Add the dressing in small quantities, tossing till each leaf is glistening, but not dripping.

MRS. JAMES GUY ROBBINS

GREEK SALAD

2 medium cucumbers	1½ T. chopped celery
¼ c. sugar	3 tomatoes, cut in small wedges
1 c. vinegar	Crisp lettuce leaves
1½ T. chopped onion	½ t. black sesame seeds
	Greek or ripe olives

Remove ends from cucumbers. Scrape cucumbers but leave some green for color. Slice thinly. Dissolve sugar in vinegar. Place cucumbers, chopped onion and celery in bowl and marinate in the vinegar mixture for a couple of hours before serving. Chill. Season the tomatoes with salt and pepper. When ready to serve, drain liquid from cucumbers. Arrange cucumbers and tomatoes on lettuce leaves. Garnish with black sesame seeds, black salty Greek olives, or chopped ripe olives. Serves 6.

MRS. DENBY BRANDON, JR.

TOMATO AND ARTICHOKE SALAD

8 large tomatoes, thickly sliced and quartered	2 T. tiny pickled onions
1 large can artichoke hearts, halved	1 c. French dressing
	2 T. caviar
	Bibb lettuce

Combine first 3 ingredients and mix with French dressing (made with olive oil and lemon juice) to which caviar has been added. Mix just until thoroughly coated. Chill and serve in cups of Bibb lettuce. Serves 8.

MRS. JAMES W. WRAPE, COLLIERVILLE, TENN.

TOMATO WITH FROZEN CUCUMBER SALAD

4 cucumbers, peeled	1 envelope gelatin
3 stalks celery	¼ c. cold water
1 medium onion	½ c. Italian salad dressing
½ green pepper	8 tomatoes, hollowed slightly

Blend first 4 ingredients in blender. Dissolve gelatin in cold water. Heat Italian dressing. Mix all together and churn in ice cream freezer, or freeze in refrigerator freezer, whipping several times during freezing process. Scoop into hollowed tomatoes. Serves 8.

MRS. WILLIAM B. FONTAINE, JACKSON, MISS.

COLD ITALIAN TOMATOES

1 tomato per person	Grated Parmesan cheese
Salt	Tabasco
Pepper	Salad oil

Peel and slice tomatoes. Arrange in layers, seasoning each layer with salt, pepper, Parmesan cheese, and Tabasco. Drizzle a bit of salad oil over all. Cover and refrigerate overnight.

MRS. F. PEARSON ALLEN, JR.

SUPER SALAD BOWL

This salad has two secrets . . . crispy, cold greens and garlic croutons.

2 pkgs. Good Seasons Italian
   Dressing Mix
Mixed salad greens, to equal
   3 qts.
1 large can artichoke hearts
2-3 large tomatoes

2 large avocados
4 hard-boiled eggs
2 c. Garlic Croutons
Salt and freshly ground pepper
   to taste

Make salad dressing according to package directions. Two recipes of dressing may be more than is needed. Wash salad greens and dry thoroughly. Place in crisper of refrigerator for several hours. Drain artichoke hearts and cut in half. Marinate in some of dressing while greens are crisping. Peel tomatoes and cut into wedges. (Cocktail tomatoes may be substituted for large tomatoes.) When ready to serve, peel avocado and cut into slivers. Separate yolks from whites of eggs and chop yolks and whites separately. Tear greens (don't cut) into bite-sized pieces. Torn greens should equal 3 quarts. Place greens in a wooden salad bowl that has been rubbed with a cut clove of garlic. Place tomato wedges, drained artichoke hearts and Garlic Croutons (see Index) on greens. Pour some of dressing over, enough to coat ingredients, not drown them, and toss. On top center of tossed greens, place egg yolk. Circle yolk with chopped whites. Circle whites with avocado slices, arranged spoke-fashioned. Sprinkle with salt and freshly ground pepper and pour more dressing over the egg and avocado arrangment on the top. Do not toss again. Serve on chilled salad plates. A really special addition to this salad is cooked, crumbled bacon. **Note:** Never wash a wooden salad bowl. It should be wiped clean with paper towels instead. A salad bowl should mellow and season just the way a trusty old iron pot does. Serves 8-10.

MRS. MILTON LYMAN KNOWLTON, JR.

GREEN SALAD WITH VEGETABLES

Mixed salad greens to
   equal 2 qts.
1 can whole string beans,
   petite size

French dressing
1 can artichoke hearts
1 3-oz. pkg. cream cheese
Cream

Wash greens well and tear into bite-sized pieces. Shake off as much water as possible; then wrap in a tea towel and refrigerate. Heat beans in their own liquid. Drain well, and while still hot, place in a container with some French dressing. Repeat this same process with a can of artichoke hearts, after trimming and cutting hearts in half. Make small cream cheese balls by adding a little cream to cream cheese; roll the cheese in your palms to form balls. Refrigerate. To serve: Put greens in a large salad bowl, add marinated string beans and artichoke hearts, then the cream cheese balls. Add more French dressing and toss. Serves 8.

MRS. FRANK T. DONELSON, JR.

FRESH SPINACH SALAD

1 pkg. Good Seasons Cheese- Garlic Dressing Mix 2 lbs. fresh spinach	Yolks of 6 hard-boiled eggs 12 slices bacon, fried crisply

Make dressing according to package directions. Wash spinach thoroughly. Dry on paper towels. Refrigerate spinach till crisp. Before serving, tear spinach into bite-sized pieces; toss with dressing. Sprinkle crumbled egg yolk and crumbled bacon over top. Serves 8.

The bright yellow yolks on the dark green spinach make this salad beautiful as well as super-delicious!

MRS. RONALD BYRNES

ORIENTAL SPINACH SALAD

1 lb. raw spinach 1 can bean sprouts, drained	8 slices crisp bacon 1 c. oil and vinegar dressing

Toss cleaned spinach and bean sprouts. Add crumbled bacon. Toss with oil and vinegar (mixed one to one). Serves 8.

MRS. JOHN HART TODD

SPINACH AND MANDARIN ORANGE SALAD

1½ lbs. fresh spinach
1 can mandarin oranges
12 bacon strips, fried crisply
	Optional: artichoke hearts, hearts
	  of palm, pineapple chunks
	1 pkg. Good Seasons Bleu Cheese
	  or Garlic Dressing Mix

Wash and drain spinach. Mix spinach with mandarin oranges and bacon strips which are broken into small chips. Artichoke hearts, hearts of palm or pineapple chunks (cut into bite sizes) may be added to fill out the servings if necessary. Make dressing according to package directions, preferably using olive oil. Toss salad with dressing. This very beautiful salad serves as both a vegetable and a salad. Serves 6-8.

MRS. FRED TARKINGTON, JR.

MANDARIN ORANGES IN AVOCADO

3 small cans mandarin oranges 3 small avocados	3 small heads of Bibb lettuce

Dressing for salad:

⅓ c. olive oil ⅓ c. salad oil ⅓ c. wine vinegar ¼ t. salt	Pinch herb seasoning Pinch basil ⅛ t. ground pepper Pinch garlic powder

Combine dressing ingredients and shake well. Marinate oranges in dressing at least ½ hour. Peel avocado and cut in half. Place avocado half on bed of Bibb lettuce and fill with oranges. Spoon more dressing over. Serves 6.

MRS. ROBERT G. SNOWDEN

ORANGE SALAD MOLD

2 small cans mandarin oranges
1 large can crushed pineapple

2 pkgs. orange gelatin
1 small can frozen orange juice

Drain oranges and pineapple; saving juices. Add enough water to juices to make 3½ cups liquid. Heat 2 cups of this liquid and dissolve the gelatin in it. Then add remaining liquid. Chill until slightly thickened; then add fruit and undiluted orange juice. Chill until firm and unmold on lettuce or fresh spinach. This salad is light and refreshing besides being quick and sure! Serves 8.

MRS. VAN PRITCHARTT, JR.

SPICED PEACH SALAD

1 29-oz. jar spiced peaches
2 small pkgs. lemon gelatin
½ c. water

4 large, juicy oranges, peeled and chopped
1 c. chopped pecans
1 small jar maraschino cherries, drained and chopped

Drain spiced peaches and heat the juice. Pour hot juice over gelatin to dissolve and add water. Chop spiced peaches into small pieces. (This is easiest to do with kitchen scissors.) Add peaches, oranges and their juice, chopped pecans, and cherries to gelatin. Pour into molds and congeal. Makes 10 small molds.

A tart salad that is excellent with game or poultry.

MRS. EVERETT B. GIBSON

STUFFED PEAR SALAD

6 fresh pears
8 oz. cream cheese
4 oz. Roquefort or bleu cheese
Bibb lettuce

French dressing
Mayonnaise
Watercress, for garnish

Peel and core pears; then cut in half. Stuff center with mixture of cream cheese and Roquefort or bleu cheese. Place pear halves together again and stand upright on Bibb lettuce. At this time you may brush sides of pears with red food coloring for a pretty effect. Pour French dressing over pears and dollop a little mayonnaise on top. Garnish with a sprig of watercress. You may use canned pears if fresh are not available. Serves 6.

MRS. FRANK T. DONELSON, JR.

WATERCRESS SALAD

4 bunches watercress
4 hard-boiled eggs, chopped
8 strips crisp bacon, crumbled

4 T. finely chopped green onions
⅔ c. Good Seasons Old Fashioned Garlic or Bleu Cheese Dressing

Wash and pull watercress into small sprays. Dry on paper towels and crisp in refrigerator. Toss all ingredients to serve. Spinach may be substituted for watercress. Serves 8.

MRS. WILLIAM M. PREST

CONGEALED CRANBERRY SALAD

Begin preparing 2 days before serving.

1 c. ground cranberries	1 c. sugar
½ t. salt	

Combine above and allow to stand overnight in refrigerator.

2 envelopes gelatin	1 c. white grapes
¼ c. cold water	1 c. chopped pecans
¼ c. hot water	1 c. whipping cream

Moisten gelatin in cold water and then add the hot water. Dissolve. Stir in berry mixture. Add grapes and nuts. Fold in whipped cream and pour into mold; unmold on spinach leaves. Serves 8.

MRS. F. PEARSON ALLEN, JR.

CRANBERRY-APPLE MOLD

2 c. cranberries	1 c. boiling water
1 c. sugar	½ c. cold water
1 t. orange rind	2 c. diced apple
1 pkg. lemon gelatin	½ c. diced celery

Grind or chop cranberries finely. Add sugar and orange rind. Let stand 30 minutes. Dissolve gelatin in boiling water; add cold water. Refrigerate to congeal slightly. Add cranberries, apple, and celery. Pour into an oiled ring mold. Unmold on lettuce and garnish with mayonnaisé. Serves 8.

MRS. LAWRENCE L. CRANE, JR.

CRANBERRY MOLD

1 orange, unpeeled	1 pkg. cherry flavored gelatin
1 16-oz. can whole cranberries	1 T. unflavored gelatin
1 7-oz. can crushed pineapple	¼ c. walnuts, coarsely chopped
1¾ c. fruit liquid	Salad greens, orange slices

Grind orange and combine with cranberries and pineapple. Drain and measure juice, adding sufficient water to make 1¾ cups liquid. Bring 1 cup of this liquid to a boil, add gelatins and dissolve. Mix well and refrigerate until consistency of jelly. Remove from refrigerator and combine with strained fruits and nuts. Pour into oiled 4 cup mold and refrigerate until firm. Unmold on greens and garnish with orange slices. Serves 8.

MRS. ROBERT WALTERS

INSALATA

Iceberg or Boston lettuce   Salt
Olive oil

Quarter washed head of lettuce. Drain well and dry. Drench with olive oil and salt thickly. Allow 1 quarter head of lettuce per person.

MRS. JAMES W. WRAPE, COLLIERVILLE, TENN.

MIXED GREEN SALAD

Salad dressing   1 can artichoke hearts, drained
1 can whole green beans,   1 avocado, sliced
    drained   1 white or purple onion, thinly
2 lbs. fresh spinach   sliced

Using a salad dressing with an oil and vinegar base, marinate beans. Wash, tear, and crisp spinach. When ready to serve, toss all ingredients with dressing. Serves 8.

MRS. ROBERT M. LEATHERMAN, COLUMBIA, MISS.

DELICIOUS SUMMER SALAD

3 medium, fresh tomatoes   Italian dressing
Lettuce cups   Homemade mayonnaise
1 can whole green beans

Arrange sliced tomatoes or wedges of tomato on lettuce. Sprinkle with salt and pepper. Place green beans that have been marinated overnight in Italian dressing on the tomatoes, and top each with a dollop of mayonnaise. Easy and delicious! Can be made ahead. **Note:** To make perfect lettuce cups, pull away discolored leaves, core, and let stream of tap water run into hollowed cavity. Lettuce cups can then be gently pulled from head. When buying lettuce, purchase head that gives when squeezed, not one that feels rock hard. Serves 6-8.

MRS. E. JAMES HOUSE

ENDIVE-AVOCADO SALAD

8 stalks Belgian endive   Salt and pepper to taste
1 avocado, halved, peeled and   ¼ c. salad oil
    sliced   1 T. wine vinegar
4 scallions or green onions,   2 T. snipped parsley
    chopped

Chill endive in ice water until crisp. Dry gently with paper towels. Remove a few outer leaves and set aside. Cut endive stalks into large crosswise slices. In salad bowl, combine endive slices, avocado and scallions. Season with salt and pepper. Combine salad oil and vinegar; pour over salad and toss till vegetables are coated. Sprinkle with snipped parsley. Arrange reserved endive leaves around edge of bowl. Makes about 8 servings.

MRS. JAMES GUY ROBBINS

YELLOW SQUASH SALAD

2 lbs. yellow squash	½ c. sour cream
2-3 large heads Bibb lettuce	½ c. homemade mayonnaise
½ c. oil and vinegar dressing	Dill seed

Parboil small whole yellow squash in salted water until slightly tender. **Do not overcook.** Chill and slice. Season with salt. Lightly toss lettuce with dressing. Serve squash on bed of Bibb lettuce. Top squash with dressing made by combining sour cream and mayonnaise. Sprinkle dill seed generously over all. Serves 8.

MRS. C. NILES GROSVENOR, III

POTATO SALAD

6 medium sized potatoes, cooked and diced	2 chopped hard-boiled eggs
1 c. Italian or onion dressing	½ t. celery seed
1 onion, chopped finely	½ c. chopped celery
1 c. mayonnaise	Salt and pepper to taste
2 t. prepared mustard	Seasoned salt to taste

Marinate cooked, diced potatoes in Italian or onion dressing for several hours in refrigerator. Then combine with other ingredients and return to refrigerator until serving time. May garnish with lettuce, hard-cooked eggs and tomatoes. Marinating the potatoes gives them an extra-special taste! Serves 6-8.

MRS. WILLIAM M. PREST

CAULIFLOWER WITH GARDEN DRESSING

1 large head cauliflower	½ clove garlic
Sharp French dressing	2 T. vinegar
¼ c. sour cream	1½ t. lemon juice
½ c. mayonnaise	Salt and pepper
1½ t. anchovy paste	Chives
2 T. chopped parsley	Avocado, tomato

Wash and trim cauliflower (leave whole). Cook in boiling salted water till just tender. Drain and cool. Marinate in French dressing several hours. Mix sour cream, mayonnaise, anchovy paste, parsley, and crushed garlic. Thin with vinegar and lemon juice and season with salt and pepper. Chill. To serve: Drain cauliflower and place on bed of lettuce or watercress. Cover with dressing and sprinkle top with chives. Dust with paprika. Garnish with wedges of fresh avocado and tomato. Serves 6.

MRS. JOSEPH H. JOHNSON

BIBB LETTUCE WITH CAPER AND EGG DRESSING

1 hard-boiled egg	1 T. capers
¼ c. wine vinegar	¼ t. dry mustard
½ t. chopped chives	1 T. lemon juice
¾ c. oil (½ olive, ¼ corn oil)	¼ t. salt
Cracked pepper	6-8 heads Bibb lettuce

Chop egg finely. Combine all ingredients, except lettuce, in a jar and shake well. Wash and tear lettuce. Dry thoroughly and crisp in refrigerator. Pour dressing over lettuce. Serves 8-10.

MRS. JACK SHANNON

BASIC FRENCH DRESSING

The secret of this dressing is the-best-of-everything ingredients . . . good, rich, fruity olive oil or salad oil and fine cider or wine vinegar.

6 T. oil	**1 T. salt**
1½ T. vinegar or lemon juice	**½ t. freshly ground black pepper**

Combine and shake vigorously all ingredients. You may prefer a little more vinegar or lemon juice. This dressing should not be kept over a long period of time. **Variations:** (1) A clove of garlic crushed or rubbed into the salt (2) Dry or Dijon-style mustard (3) Tarragon, chervil, parsley, chives, or basil.

PIQUANT FRENCH DRESSING

⅓ c. sugar	1 t. grated onion
1 t. salt	4 T. vinegar
1 t. dry mustard	1 c. salad oil
1 t. celery seed	1 clove garlic, optional
1 t. paprika	

Mix the above ingredients. Let dressing stand for an hour; then remove garlic clove and refrigerate. Excellent over fruit . . . especially a salad of grapefruit and orange sections with slices of avocado.

MRS. WALLACE WITMER, JR.

POPPY SEED DRESSING

1½ c. sugar	3 T. onion juice
2 t. dry mustard	2 c. salad oil
⅔ c. vinegar	3 T. poppy seed
2 t. salt	

Mix sugar, mustard, salt and vinegar. Add onion juice and stir in thoroughly. Add oil slowly, beating constantly, and continue to beat until thick. Add poppy seeds and beat for a few minutes. Serve over fruit salad. Store in refrigerator. Do not freeze. Makes 3½ cups.

MRS. JOHN T. FISHER

COLD MARINATED VEGETABLES

2 large cans tiny whole beets	Zucchini
2 cans string beans	Cauliflower
Carrots	Minced parsley
Yellow squash	Freshly ground pepper

Drain beets and string beans, and put in separate containers. Add Dressing, shake well, and refrigerate. Cut the fresh vegetables into attractive bite-sized pieces. Cook each vegetable separately in rapidly boiling salted water for 4 to 5 minutes. They will not be tender. While hot, put in separate containers, add Dressing, and refrigerate. When ready to serve, drain well, arrange attractively on platter, and sprinkle with minced parsley and freshly ground pepper.

Dressing:

3 cloves garlic	¾ t. dry mustard
9 T. salad oil	Salt
6 T. olive oil	Fresh pepper
9 T. mixed vinegars	

Place garlic in combined salad oil and olive oil. Let stand several hours, then remove garlic. Add remaining ingredients. Blend well. Makes approximately 1¾ cups.

MRS. FRANK T. DONELSON, JR.

ASPARAGUS VINAIGRETTE

1 c. French dressing	1 t. parsley
1 t. finely chopped green olives	1 t. chopped gherkins
1 t. capers	2 pkgs. frozen all-green
1 t. chives	asparagus, cooked
	Chopped hard-cooked eggs

To French dressing, add olives, capers, chives, parsley and gherkins. Place well-drained, chilled asparagus on Bibb lettuce and pour sauce over all. Sprinkle with chopped eggs. Serves 6.

Sauces and Accompaniments

CURRIED FRUIT

3 jars fruit for salad	2 t. curry powder
or	¾ stick butter
1 can each: pears, apricots,	½ t. ground ginger
peaches, pineapple chunks	or nutmeg
1 can seedless Bing cherries	½ c. sherry
1 c. brown sugar	

All cans of fruit are approximately one pound cans. Drain fruit well and cut in large pieces. Grease a 3-quart baking dish with butter. Melt and cook together for several minutes the sugar, curry powder, butter and ginger. Put layer of fruit in greased dish and pour half the sauce over. Repeat with remaining fruit and sauce. Pour sherry over all. Cook in 325° oven for 1 hour. Serve hot, in bowls or ramekins, in place of a salad, or serve as a dessert topped with a dollop of sour cream. Serves 10-12.

MRS. HENRY W. JONES, JR.

HOT FRUIT COMPOTE

1 lb. 7-oz. can apricot halves	½ c. orange juice
1 lb. 14-oz. can purple plums	¼ c. brown sugar
1 lb. 13-oz. can peach halves	1 t. grated lemon peel
8 thinly sliced oranges	4 T. melted butter

Drain fruits and reserve syrup. In 2-quart buttered, rectangular baking dish, arrange a row of apricots in single file, next a row of purple plums, next a row of peach halves alternated with orange slices, then plums, and the last row apricots. Heat reserved juices, orange juice, brown sugar and lemon peel. Pour over fruit. Melt butter and pour over. Bake at 425° for 15-20 minutes. **Note:** The fruits in this compote form a pattern. Serve in individual dishes. Serves 8.

MOTHER'S CRANBERRY JELLY

4 c. cranberries	2 c. sugar
2 c. boiling water	

Wash cranberries. Pour boiling water over berries and cook 20 minutes, stirring to prevent sticking. Put through a sieve, and combine with sugar. Cook 5 minutes, or till jelly stage is reached. Serves 8.

MRS. WALK C. JONES, JR.

LEMON APPLES

Core, but do not peel, 4 firm York apples, and cut into ¼-inch slices. Put in skillet; add 3 tablespoons water, and paper thin slivers of 3 lemons. Smother apples with sugar; dot with butter and put lid on. When apples are tender, remove lid and simmer until juice is thick. Do not cook until apples fall to pieces. Serves 12.

MRS. CHARLES H. McGEE, BRUIN PLANTATION, HUGHES, ARK.

CHUTNEY PEACHES

Canned peach halves (½ peach per serving)
1 bottle mango chutney

Melted butter (for baked peaches only)
Parsley sprigs (for cold peaches)

These are meant to be a garnish for ham, pork, and especially lamb. Serve hot or cold. For hot peaches, drain peach halves and place cut side up on rack. Brush with melted butter. Spoon 1 tablespoon chutney into center of each peach. Place in baking dish and bake at 350° for 10-15 minutes, or till heated through. For cold peaches, drain peaches and fill cavity with chutney. Garnish with parsley sprigs.

MRS. MILTON LYMAN KNOWLTON, JR.

GREEN MINTED PEARS

Canned green minted pears   Mint jelly

Fill pear cavities with mint jelly. Serve as a garnish and complement for lamb.

MRS. C. NILES GROSVENOR, III

CREAM CHEESE-JAM SPREAD

Cream cheese or Neufchatel cheese

Strawberry jam

Break cheese with a fork. Pour jam over. Serve from a bowl as a spread for flavored rye crisps, toast, or warm muffins.

MRS. JAMES W. WRAPE, COLLIERVILLE, TENN.

CRANBERRY-APPLE RELISH

1 large orange
2 c. cranberries

1 c. sugar
1 lb. red apples (about 2 large)

Grate orange peel on coarse grater to make long shreds. Peel orange and cut into ½-inch cubes. Wash and drain cranberries; remove any stems. Chop cranberries very coarsely (or run through a food grinder). Combine the grated orange peel, cubed orange, cranberries, and sugar; mix well. Refrigerate until well chilled, several hours. Wash and core apples but do not pare. Refrigerate. Chop apples coarsely and toss lightly with cranberry mixture just to combine. This may be done a day or two ahead. Use to fill center of crown roast of pork or to accompany roast turkey. Serves 8-10.

MRS. JAMES GUY ROBBINS

GOURMET ICE-PICKLE STICKS

1 qt. dill pickles, drained   1 c. sugar
3 garlic buds   Liquid from dill pickles

Quarter drained dill pickles, reserving liquid. Place garlic buds in bottom of the jar and place pickles in jar. Pour sugar on top of the pickles. Let set, but turn jar upside down and then up, until the pickles are covered with sugar. Cover the pickles with the reserved liquid. Refrigerate and serve ice cold. Should be made several days ahead.

MISS MILDRED GATES

ENGLISH LEMON DESSERT

1 stick butter   1 egg, beaten
1 c. sugar   Ice cream, tart shells or Jacob's
1 lemon, juice and grated rind   Puff Biscuits

Melt butter and add sugar, lemon juice and rind. Stir over medium heat until smooth. Remove from fire and add egg. Return to fire and cook until mixture thickens slightly. Store in refrigerator. May be served over ice cream, in individual tart shells or on Jacob's Puff Biscuits. It is good and tart and men like it. Easy to keep on hand for a fancy dessert. As a sauce, it serves 10-12. Makes enough filling for 4-6 tart shells.

MRS. HARRY B. GUNTHER

HONG KONG SUNDAE

1 can mandarin oranges   1 can crushed pineapple
6-8 preserved kumquats, chopped   2 T. cornstarch
2 T. preserved ginger   Vanilla ice cream

Put oranges, chopped kumquats, ginger and pineapple into a double boiler. Heat. Thicken with cornstarch. Serve cold as a sauce over ice cream. May be made several days ahead.

MRS. JOHN HART TODD

DOT JONES' CHOCOLATE SAUCE

4 squares bitter chocolate   1½ c. sugar
1 stick butter or oleo   ½ pt. whipping cream
⅓ c. cocoa   2 t. vanilla

Melt chocolate in double boiler; add butter, cocoa and sugar. Cook 45 minutes, stirring often. Add cream and cook 10 minutes longer, stirring constantly, and slowly add vanilla. If it has the appearance of curdling when cream is added, do not be alarmed, as it will become smooth. Especially good served hot over peppermint ice cream. Can be kept several weeks in refrigerator Makes 3 cups.

MRS. HENRY W. JONES

BÉARNAISE SAUCE

The following ingredients should be at room temperature:

2 sticks margarine   Juice of two lemons
6 egg yolks

Combine with a silver spoon in top of double boiler. Stir over hot, not boiling, water continuously until sauce begins to thicken. It will thicken slightly after removal from heat. Remove top of pan from heat. The sauce may be served right away hot, or sit for several hours to be served at room temperature. This hollandaise cannot be reheated as it will curdle. 10 servings.

For Béarnaise add:

2 T. dry minced onion   2 T. dry tarragon flakes
2 T. dry parsley flakes

MRS. CHARLES TIFFANY BINGHAM

BLENDER HOLLANDAISE

½ c. butter   ¼ t. salt
3 egg yolks   Pinch cayenne
2 T. lemon juice

In a small saucepan, heat butter to bubbling, but do not let brown. Put rest of ingredients in blender. Cover container and turn on low speed. Immediately remove cover and pour in the hot butter in a slow, steady stream. When all butter is added, turn off motor. Makes ¾ cup.

MRS. WILLIAM M. PREST

CURRY MAYONNAISE

(For Crudités)

½ pt. mayonnaise   1 T. Worcestershire
1 t. onion juice   1 pinch ground cloves
3 T. catsup   1 bud garlic, minced
1 T. curry powder   Salt and pepper to taste

Mix all ingredients together and refrigerate. Makes 1¾ cups.

MRS. JAMES McCLURE, JR., SARDIS, MISS.

CRANBERRY-HORSERADISH SAUCE

(For Game, Ducks, Venison)

Cranberry sauce, homemade   Horseradish

Stir into cranberry sauce freshly grated horseradish, frozen horseradish or bottled red horseradish to taste. **Variation:** Horseradish may be combined to taste with applesauce. Good with roast pork.

MRS. J. TUNKIE SAUNDERS

SAUCE DUXELLES

2 T. butter
3 c. finely diced mushrooms
2 T. minced onion
½ c. dry Madeira or
   sherry wine

1 10½-oz. can beef broth or
   consommé
1 dash of pepper
2 T. flour
1 T. melted butter

Melt 2 tablespoons butter in skillet over medium heat. Add mushrooms and onion; cook, stirring frequently, 5 minutes. Add wine and cook 1 minute. Add beef broth and pepper. Simmer 5 minutes or until liquid is reduced to half. Make beurre manié by mixing flour with 1 tablespoon melted butter. Add to sauce, stirring until sauce thickens. Correct seasoning to taste. Especially good with beef. Makes about 3 cups.

MRS. JAMES GUY ROBBINS

MUSTARD SAUCE

1 T. prepared mustard
1 T. cider vinegar

Dash of pepper
1 c. mayonnaise or salad dressing

Combine mustard, vinegar and pepper in bowl. Add mayonnaise or salad dressing. Mix well. Easy to make; delicious with all meats. Makes about 1 cup.

MRS. JAMES GUY ROBBINS

HOT MUSTARD

1 10-oz. jar apple jelly
1 12-oz. jar orange marmalade

1 jar cream style horseradish
1 6-oz. jar prepared mustard

Combine all ingredients in electric blender or with electric mixer till smooth. Serve hot or cold. Store in jars in refrigerator.

MRS. NED MIMS·FRENCH

ONION SAUCE

2 T. butter
2 c. thinly sliced onions
   (2 medium)
¼ c. cider vinegar
1 10½-oz. can beef broth or
   consommé

1 T. flour
1 T. melted butter
Salt and pepper to taste

Melt 2 tablespoons butter in small saucepan over medium heat. Add onions; cook, stirring occasionally, until golden brown. Add vinegar; cook 1 minute, Add beef broth; bring to boiling. Simmer 5 minutes. Make beurre manié by mixing flour with remaining 1 tablespoon melted butter. Add to sauce, stirring until sauce thickens. Correct seasoning to taste with salt and pepper. This is especially tasty with calves' liver. Makes about 2 cups.

MRS. JAMES GUY ROBBINS

PUNGENT PEACH SAUCE

½ c. chutney, finely chopped	1 T. sugar
1 c. peach preserves	2 T. vinegar

Combine all ingredients in small saucepan. Cook over medium heat, stirring constantly, until bubbling. Chill. Excellent with chicken fondue. Makes about 1½ cups.

MRS. JAMES GUY ROBBINS

RAISIN SAUCE

½ c. brown sugar	Few grains of mace, nutmeg, and
½ T. dry mustard	cinnamon
½ T. flour	½ c. seedless raisins
½ T. salt	¼ c. vinegar
⅛ t. pepper	1½ c. water
¼ t. ground cloves	

Mix dry ingredients. Add raisins, vinegar and water. Cook to a syrup. Serve hot over ham. May be reheated. Serves 10-12.

MRS. RICHARD OWNBEY, NASHVILLE, TENN.

SHRIMP AND ALMOND SAUCE

1 can cream of shrimp soup	1 T. lemon juice
1 3-oz. pkg. cream cheese	½ pkg. sliced almonds

Heat all ingredients in saucepan until melted. Serve over broccoli, asparagus, or cheese or mushroom soufflé.

MRS. FRANK BARTON, JR.

SOUR CREAM-HORSERADISH SAUCE

½ pt. sour cream	Horseradish to taste
1 pkg. dry garlic dressing mix	

Combine ingredients and serve with tongue or roast beef. Best made 24 hours ahead.

MRS. JOHN C. BARTON

STEAK IN SPANISH MARINADE

¼ c. orange juice	1 t. ground cumin
¼ c. tomato juice	1 t. oregano
2 T. lime juice	½ t. crushed red pepper
2 T. olive oil	2 t. minced garlic
1 t. paprika	

Mix all ingredients together well. Marinate either steak or broilers overnight. The flavor is **delicious** and much enhanced by charcoal broiling. Enough marinade for 3 pounds of meat.

MRS. RICHARD DIXON

HATTIE'S BARBECUE SAUCE

1 c. tomato catsup	1 T. olive oil
1 c. vinegar	1 t. dry mustard
1 c. water	⅛ t. celery salt
1 pod garlic, minced	2 T. butter
1 t. salt	1 t. sugar
1 t. crushed red pepper	1 t. Worcestershire

Simmer all together for 20 minutes. Especially good for barbecuing lamb.

MRS. JOHN APPERSON, JR.

BARBECUE SAUCE

2 26-oz. bottles catsup	1 T. parsley flakes
1½ c. water	1 T. thyme
1 stick butter	1 T. sage
1 c. coarsely chopped celery,	1 T. oregano
plus leaves	1 c. vinegar
1 coarsely chopped large onion	½ c. Worcestershire
4 whole lemons, quartered	½ c. brown sugar
1 T. rosemary leaves	Salt and pepper to taste
2 T. prepared mustard	

Boil all ingredients for 10 minutes; then simmer for 1 hour, stirring occasionally. Keep in refrigerator. Makes 3 quarts.

When barbecuing ribs or chicken, cook meat in oven till nearly done. Then place meat on grill over hot coals and baste with barbecue sauce till done.

MRS. W. G. LOGAN, JR.

SAUSAGE-PECAN DRESSING

¼ lb. butter	1 T. salt or to taste
1¼ c. finely chopped onion	1½ t. ground pepper
1 c. finely diced celery	6-8 c. coarse corn bread crumbs
½ c. chopped celery tops	¾ c. Madeira or chicken broth
1½ t. thyme	1 c. pecans
½ lb. sausage	

Melt butter and add onion, celery, celery tops and thyme; sauté gently. Sauté sausage in separate skillet. Add salt and pepper to the corn bread crumbs, then add crumbs to skillet with sautéed vegetables. Drain sausage. Add sausage and Madeira to sautéed vegetables. Put in more melted butter and some of rendered sausage fat if needed. Taste for seasoning. Add pecans. Makes enough stuffing for a 10 pound bird.

MRS. JAMES GUY ROBBINS

BACON CURLS

Fry strips of bacon till brown, but not crisp. Remove skillet from heat. Removing 1 strip at a time, place the bacon strip on a paper towel. Run the tines of a fork under one end of the strip and quickly roll up (jelly-roll fashion). Secure the bacon curl with a toothpick. It is best to cook not more than 4 or 5 strips of bacon at a time, as the curls are impossible to make if bacon becomes too crisp or cold. Simple to make, delicious to eat, and pretty to see! These can be made ahead and refrigerated till time to use. Use as a garnish or as an hors d'oeuvre.

MRS. ROBERT G. HEARD, JR.

CROUTONS
(For Salads or Cooked Vegetables)

CHEESE CROUTONS: Combine 1 tablespoon melted butter with 1 tablespoon grated Parmesan cheese. Add 1 cup bread cubes, cut in ½-inch squares, and toss lightly. Spread on baking sheet and toast in 350° oven about 5 minutes or till golden.

GARLIC CROUTONS: Leave crusts on slices of bread and cut into tiny cubes. Toast in slow oven, stirring frequently, till dry and golden brown. Melt butter in skillet and add a peeled garlic clove. Remove garlic when browned. Add croutons; toss till butter-coated. Store in a covered jar in refrigerator. Heat before serving, if desired.

Breads

BRIOCHE A TÊTE

2 pkgs. yeast	4½ c. sifted flour
¼ c. lukewarm water	1 c. softened butter
½ c. plus 1 T. milk	5 eggs
1 T. sugar	1 egg yolk
2 t. salt	1 T. milk

In a large bowl, blend yeast with warm water until dissolved. Stir in milk (previously heated to scalding, then cooled), sugar and salt. Beat 2 cups flour into yeast mixture using mixer or sturdy spoon. Add softened butter and continue beating until blended. Add remaining flour and eggs, one at a time, beating thoroughly with each addition. Dough now will be soft and sticky. Continue beating until dough is shiny and elastic, about 10 minutes on medium speed of mixer, or 20 minutes by hand. Lift dough into 2 equal parts. Chill dough thoroughly before shaping, a minimum of 4 hours. Shape both pieces into smooth, round balls. Place each into large buttered 9-inch brioche molds or a 2-quart round baking pan. Cover with waxed paper and let rise in warm place until doubled in size, about 2 hours. Brush with glaze made of 1 egg yolk and 1 tablespoon milk. Bake in 350° oven for 1 hour, until well browned and a wooden skewer comes out clean when inserted. Cool in pan on wire rack, or serve warm. Each brioche yields 16 1-inch slices.

To stuff a brioche: Cut a round from the bottom of the brioche and reserve it. Scoop crumbs out of the center of the brioche, leaving a shell about ½ to ¾-inch thick. Pack the shell evenly with duck liver pâté, or with a whole block of chilled imported foie gras. Slice off the pâté or foie gras evenly with the bottom of the brioche and put the reserved round back in place, securing it with a little butter. Chill the pâté en brioche and cut into wedges.

MR. AND MRS. JOHN LARY

BUTTER STICKS

6 T. butter	1 T. sugar
2 c. biscuit mix	½ c. milk

In oven, melt butter in 13 x 9 x 2-inch baking dish. In mixing bowl, combine biscuit mix, sugar, and milk. Stir with fork till a soft dough is formed. Beat vigorously 20 strokes. Turn out on board lightly floured with biscuit mix. Knead 10 times and roll to an 8 x 12-inch rectangle. Cut dough in half lengthwise; then cut each half crosswise into 16 strips. Dip each strip in melted butter, coating both sides. Arrange in two rows in dish used to melt butter. Bake till golden, about 12 minutes. Granulated sugar and/or cinnamon may be sprinkled on top, if desired. Serve warm. Makes 32.

MRS. BEN C. ADAMS, JR.

ROLLS

1 yeast cake	4 c. sifted flour
1 c. lukewarm water	1 egg
¼ c. sugar	1 t. salt
½ c. melted butter	½ c. melted butter

Dissolve yeast in water. Add sugar, ½ cup melted butter, 2 cups flour and egg. Then add remaining flour and salt, mixing well after each addition. Place dough in bowl and cover with damp cloth. Cool in refrigerator at least 2 hours; overnight is best. Roll out ⅓ to ½-inch thick and cut into 2-inch diameter circles. Dip in ½ cup melted butter until completely covered. Fold over. Place snugly together in pan. Let rise in warm place 2 hours, until doubled in size. Bake at 400° for 12 minutes or until brown on top. To freeze: After cutting, place on pan covered with waxed paper. Freeze, then store in plastic bags. When ready to bake, remove from freezer and let rise 3 hours. Makes 4-5 dozen.

MRS. WILLIAM GALBREATH

IRISH SCONES

3½ c. flour	2 t. baking powder
1 stick butter	1 egg
½ t. salt	⅔ c. milk
¼ c. sugar	

Mix 3 cups flour and butter, cutting butter into flour. Add salt, sugar, baking powder; mix well. Beat egg and add milk to egg. Add this mixture with a few quick strokes. Dough will be tough if handled too much. If this is not a manageable dough (it will probably be too runny), add more flour for a not-too-stiff dough. On a floured board, roll with a few light strokes till about ¾-inch thick. Cut into squares and then into triangles. They will be a little lumpy and not as neat looking as biscuits. Bake on floured baking sheet at 425° for 10 minutes or till lightly browned. Makes 24.

MRS. R. HENRY LAKE, HOUSTON, TEX.
MRS. C. L. KENNEDY, HOUSTON, TEX.

SESAME CHEESE LOAF

2 T. sesame seeds	1 T. dried parsley flakes
½ c. softened butter	1 loaf Italian bread,
1 envelope cheese sauce mix	about 13-in. long

Heat oven to 400°. Pour sesame seeds into a small dish and bake about 5 minutes or until golden brown. Blend butter, sauce mix and parsley together. Cut bread in half lengthwise. Spread cheese mixture over cut surfaces; sprinkle with sesame seeds. Cut bread in diagonal slices about 1½-inches apart, being careful not to cut all the way through. Bake 5-10 minutes, or until lightly browned. Serves 6-8.

MRS. JAMES GUY ROBBINS

CINNAMON-NUT COFFEE CAKE

Cake:

2 sticks butter	¼ t. salt
1½ c. sugar	1 t. baking soda
4 eggs, separated	1 c. buttermilk
3 c. flour	2 t. baking powder

Cream butter and sugar. Add egg yolks one at a time. Sift flour with salt and soda 6 times. Add flour to batter, alternating with buttermilk, adding baking powder to flour before the last addition. Beat egg whites stiffly and fold into batter.

Cinnamon Mixture:

½ c. sugar	¼ c. minced raisins
1 c. chopped pecans	1 T. cinnamon
1 t. cocoa	

Mix all the above ingredients to form the cinnamon mixture. Then, pour a little of the batter into a greased and floured tube or bundt cake pan. Sprinkle some cinnamon mixture over batter. Alternate batter and cinnamon mixture, ending with cinnamon mixture. Dot generously with butter. Bake at 375° for 1 hour. (This may be made ahead of time and frozen. However, it is better made the day before serving.) When well sealed, this cake keeps very satisfactorily over a period of several days. Serves 12.

MRS. MILTON LYMAN KNOWLTON, JR.

SPOON BREAD

1 c. water	1 c. corn meal (water-ground best)
2 c. milk	3 eggs, well beaten
1 t. salt	¼ c. melted oleo or butter

Scald water and milk together. Add salt and meal. Cook and stir until thick. Fold in beaten eggs and butter and pour into greased 2-quart casserole. Bake at 350° for 1 hour. Serve immediately. Serves 6.

MEXICAN CORN BREAD

1 c. yellow corn meal	1 #303 can cream style corn
1 c. milk	½ lb. rat cheese, grated
¾ t. salt	1 large onion, finely chopped
½ c. bacon drippings	4 canned Jalapeño peppers,
2 eggs, slightly beaten	chopped
½ t. soda	

Combine corn meal, milk, salt, bacon drippings, eggs, soda, corn and mix well. Grease a #9 black iron skillet and heat. Sprinkle a very thin layer of corn meal and let brown lightly. Pour ½ of batter in skillet; sprinkle cheese evenly, then onion, then peppers. Pour on remaining batter. Bake 45-50 minutes at 350°. Serves 6-8.

MRS. F. GUY ROBBINS, OSCEOLA, ARK.

WHOLE KERNEL CORN BREAD

1 c. flour	2 eggs
1 c. yellow corn meal	1 c. milk
4 t. baking powder	3 T. melted butter
1 t. salt	1 can (8¾-oz.) cream
¼ c. sugar	style corn

Beat ingredients together. Bake 30 minutes in greased 9 x 13-inch dish at 400°. Cut into squares and serve hot. Serves 8.

MRS. RICHARD DIXON

MONKEY BREAD

⅔ c. sugar	⅔ c. margarine
1 t. salt	⅔ c. butter
1 c. mashed potatoes	1 c. milk
1 pkg. yeast	6 c. sifted flour
½ c. lukewarm water	2 eggs

Mix sugar, salt and potatoes in bowl. Dissolve yeast in water. Melt butter and margarine in milk over low heat and add to sugar mixture. Cool to lukewarm. Add yeast and half of flour. Beat eggs; add to remaining flour. Combine the 2 mixtures and mix well. Let rise about 1 hour. Stir down and place in refrigerator. When ready to bake, melt more butter and dip small elongated rolls of dough in it. Place rolls of dough in well-buttered ring mold, making only 2 layers. Bake at 350° for 30-40 minutes. When serving, tear bread off with fingers instead of cutting with a knife. Serves 8-10.

MRS. EDWARD W. NEWTON

PUMPKIN BREAD

2 c. white sugar	1 t. salt
2 c. brown sugar	4 t. soda
1 c. vegetable oil	1 t. ground cloves
1 c. dates, chopped	1 t. ground cinnamon
4 c. pumpkin	1 t. ground nutmeg
5 c. flour	Chopped nuts, if desired

Mix sugars, oil, dates and pumpkin together. Sift dry ingredients together and combine with pumpkin mixture. Grease bottoms of 4 one-pound coffee cans; divide mixture among them. Bake 1 hour or longer at 350°. When cool, cover cans with plastic lids and store in refrigerator. This will keep for several weeks. **Do not freeze.** Makes 40 large slices.

This bread makes a grand winter dessert served with a hard sauce or soaked with bourbon and topped with whipped cream.

MRS. VAUGHN MARSHALL, LITTLE ROCK, ARK.

LEMON MUFFINS

1 c. butter or shortening	2 c. flour
1 c. sugar	2 t. baking powder
4 eggs, separated	1 t. salt
½ c. lemon juice	2 t. grated lemon peel

Cream butter and sugar until smooth. Add well-beaten egg yolks and beat until light. Add the lemon juice alternately with the flour which has been sifted with baking powder and salt, mixing thoroughly after each addition (do not over-mix). Fold in stiffly beaten egg whites and grated lemon peel. Fill buttered muffin pans ¾ full and bake at 375° for about 20 minutes. These freeze well and are nice split and toasted for breakfast. Makes 24.

MRS. SNOWDEN BOYLE, JR.

MUFFIN CAKES

2 sticks butter, softened	3½ c. sifted flour
2 c. sugar	2 t. baking powder
3 eggs	1 c. milk

Beat butter and sugar till fluffy. Beat in eggs. Sift together the flour and baking powder. Stir in the flour mixture by thirds, alternating with the milk. Last addition should be flour. Beat only enough to blend well. Fill greased muffin tins ⅔ full. Bake in 350° oven 20-25 minutes. Makes 30 large muffins, 100 miniature tea muffins. Confectioners' sugar may be sifted over these cakes for an added touch, or they may be glazed while warm with Citrus Glaze.

MRS. JAMES W. WRAPE, COLLIERVILLE, TENN.

Citrus Glaze: Heat ¼ c. lemon juice, ¼ c. orange juice, ¼ c. pineapple juice, and 2 T. butter. Add 2¼ c. unsifted confectioners' sugar to the juices. Stir till blended. Pour over muffin cakes, unsliced sponge cake, pound cake, or white cake while it is still warm.

MRS. J. TUNKIE SAUNDERS

MUSH MUFFINS

A recipe for the men in your life . . .

1½ c. corn meal, sifted	2 eggs
6 c. water	2 T. shortening
1 t. salt	

Combine meal, water and salt and put in double boiler. Cook until "floppy" (consistency of grits) and turn off. Grease muffin **irons** thoroughly and heat in 450° oven until smoky, about 10 minutes. **This is very important and the secret.** Beat eggs and shortening into the corn meal mixture. Fill muffin irons ½ full. Bake 30 minutes in 450° oven. These muffins should be crisp on the outside and mushy on the inside. Use only the old-fashioned iron muffin tins, no substitutes. Makes 30 muffins.

MRS. H. DOUGLAS CHISM

BANANA MUFFINS

1 egg	¾ t. salt
⅓ c. salad oil	2 t. baking powder
½ c. sugar	¼ t. soda
½ c. mashed banana	Tart jelly (red currant,
1¾ c. sifted flour	quince, guava, cranberry)

Beat egg slightly; stir in oil and sugar. Add banana and mix well. Sift flour with remaining dry ingredients; add to first mixture and stir just till liquid and dry ingredients are combined. Grease muffin tins and fill ⅔ full with batter. Place 1 teaspoon jelly in center of each filled cup. Bake at 375° for 15 minutes. Makes about 12.

MRS. MILTON LYMAN KNOWLTON, JR.

BLUEBERRY-ORANGE MUFFINS

3 c. sifted flour	2 eggs, slightly beaten
4 t. baking powder	¾ c. milk
¼ t. soda	½ c. melted butter
¾ c. sugar	1 T. grated orange peel
1½ t. salt	½ c. plus 1⅓ T. orange juice
2 c. blueberries	

Sift together flour, baking powder, soda, sugar and salt. Stir in blueberries, tossing lightly till coated. Beat together remaining ingredients; pour into dry ingredients and stir just till dry ingredients are moistened. Fill greased muffin tins ⅔ full (or pour into a greased loaf pan to make blueberry bread). Bake muffins 20 minutes at 425°; bake loaf 1 hour and 10 minutes at 350°. If desired, remove muffins from tins while hot and dip tops in melted butter; then dip into a sugar mixture made by combining 1 cup sugar with 2 teaspoons cinnamon. **Muffin variation:** Reduce blueberries to 1 cup and add 1 cup chopped pecans. Makes 24 muffins.

MRS. MILTON LYMAN KNOWLTON, JR.

PANCAKE CRÊPES

½ c. flour	1 c. milk
½ t. salt	1 T. butter
¼ c. sugar	3 eggs, separated

Combine dry ingredients and sift into a bowl. Add milk, butter, egg yolks and stir. Beat till smooth with an egg beater. Wash and dry beater thoroughly. Beat whites till stiff and fold into mixture. Cook small pancakes on a well buttered griddle. Batter is easiest to pour from a small pitcher. Batter can be made the night before, but do not fold in egg whites till the last minute. Serve for breakfast topped with fruit or syrup. Makes 24 3-inch crêpes.

This is a very light, "eggy" pancake.

MRS. J. LESTER CRAIN, JR.

TURN-BUT-ONCE PANCAKES

2 c. buttermilk
3 eggs, separated
1 c. sour cream
4 T. melted butter
2½ c. sifted flour

1 T. baking powder
1 t. salt
1 T. sugar
2 t. soda

Beat together buttermilk and egg yolks. Stir sour cream and melted butter into buttermilk mixture and blend well. Sift dry ingredients together. Add to buttermilk mixture, stirring by hand, until **just** blended. Do not stir until smooth. Beat egg whites stiff and fold into batter mixture. Heat your griddle. Pour on pancake batter and cook until bubbles appear on top of each pancake. Turn only once and cook until done. If batter appears too thick, add more buttermilk. Makes 24 3-inch pancakes.

MRS. JOHN M. MAURY

BLUEBERRY BREAKFAST ROLL

2 c. flour
2½ t. baking powder
½ t. salt
¼ c. sugar
¼ c. butter

1 egg
Milk
1 c. or more fresh or frozen
   blueberries
2 T. sugar

Sift flour, baking powder, salt and sugar together. Cut butter into mixture. Break egg into a cup and add milk to make ¾ cup. With fork stir liquid into first mixture. Roll on floured board to 12 x 8-inches. Spread with well-drained blueberries and sprinkle with 2 tablespoons sugar. Roll tightly and place on greased cookie sheet. Bake at 375° for 25 minutes. Spread with melted butter and sprinkle with additional sugar. Makes 10 thin slices.

MRS. RICHARD DIXON

ANGEL BISCUITS
(Refrigerator Yeast Rolls)

5 c. sifted flour
3 t. baking powder
1 t. soda
1 t. salt
¼ c. sugar

1 c. shortening
1 pkg. dry yeast
2 T. warm water
2 c. buttermilk

Sift together dry ingredients. Cut in shortening. Dissolve yeast in warm water (water that is too hot will kill yeast) and add to buttermilk. Add liquid to dry mixture and stir until all flour is moistened. Cover and place in refrigerator. When ready to use, pinch off amount needed, roll out about ¼-inch thick, and cut out rolls in any desired shape. Place, sides touching, on baking sheet and cook at 450° until brown. If desired, you may allow rolls to rise before baking. Makes about 4 dozen.

MRS. H. K. BARWICK, WYNNE, ARK.

PERRE'S WAFFLES

2 c. flour
½ t. salt
4 t. baking powder

2 eggs, separated
1½ c. milk
1 stick butter, melted

Mix dry ingredients. Beat together egg yolks and milk, and mix with dry ingredients. Pour in melted butter; then fold in stiffly beaten egg whites. Makes about 7 waffles.

MRS. B. PERCY MAGNESS, JR.

Desserts

COCONUT CHARLOTTE RUSSE

1½ T. gelatin	2 egg whites
¼ c. water	2 c. grated fresh coconut
1 c. coffee cream	1½ c. whipping cream
1 c. sugar	1 t. almond extract

Sprinkle gelatin over water and let soften for 5 minutes. Scald coffee cream, then remove from heat. Stir in ½ cup sugar and the gelatin until both are dissolved. Cool mixture and chill, stirring frequently, until it begins to thicken. Beat egg whites with ½ cup sugar until they hold a shape. Fold egg whites, grated fresh coconut, whipped cream and almond extract into mixture. Pour the mixture into a charlotte mold or a bowl and chill until it is firm. Unmold the charlotte russe on a cold platter and pour over some of the caramel sauce. Serve remaining sauce over individual servings. This is also attractive served in sterling sherbets.

Caramel sauce:

1 c. plus 2 T. brown sugar	2 T. butter
½ c. coffee cream	1 t. vanilla
2 egg yolks, beaten	Pinch salt

In the top of a double boiler, stir together all ingredients. Cook mixture over gently boiling water, stirring constantly, until thickened. Cool the sauce before serving. An unusual, delicious dessert. Serves 10-12.

MRS. RICHARD OWNBEY, NASHVILLE, TENN.

LEMON CHARLOTTE RUSSE

1 T. unflavored gelatin	Grated lemon rind
½ c. cold water	1 pt. whipping cream
4 large eggs, separated	2 doz. ladyfingers
1 c. sugar	½ c. toasted almonds
½ c. fresh lemon juice	

Soften gelatin in cold water and dissolve over hot water. Set aside. Beat egg yolks until thick and lemon colored. Add sugar slowly while continuing to beat until stiff. Add lemon juice and grated rind. Continue beating. Add gelatin to egg mixture. Beat egg whites until light and fluffy. Fold into lemon mixture. Whip cream and fold into lemon mixture. Pour into a bowl that is lined on the sides and bottom with ladyfingers. Fill bowl half full of custard, add another layer of ladyfingers and fill rest of way with custard. Sprinkle top with toasted almonds. Refrigerate 24 hours. This is pretty done in a crystal container. Serves 10.

MRS. THOMAS KEESEE, JR.

COFFEE BAVARIAN

1 envelope gelatin
½ c. sugar
⅛ t. salt
2 T. instant coffee
2 eggs, separated

1¼ c. milk
½ t. vanilla
1 c. whipping cream
Additional whipped cream and
   chocolate curls, to garnish

Mix together gelatin, ¼ cup of the sugar, salt and instant coffee in a saucepan. Beat together egg yolks and milk; add to gelatin mixture. Place over very low heat, stirring constantly, until gelatin is dissolved and mixture is slightly thickened, about 6 minutes. Remove from heat and add vanilla. Chill until mixture mounds slightly when dropped from a spoon. Beat egg whites until stiff, but not dry. Gradually add remaining ¼ cup sugar and beat until very stiff. Fold into gelatin mixture. Fold in whipped cream. Turn into a 5-cup mold. Chill until firm. Unmold and serve with additional whipped cream and chocolate curls. Can be made day before serving. Serves 8.

MRS. EVERETT R. COOK

ICE CREAM CAKE

15 ladyfingers, split
1 can frozen orange juice,
   undiluted
2 qts. vanilla ice cream, softened
2 pkgs. frozen raspberries
2 9-oz. cans crushed pineapple
1 T. frozen lemonade concentrate
1 t. almond flavoring
1 t. rum flavoring

6 maraschino cherries, chopped
3 T. chopped nuts
1 c. whipping cream
4 T. powdered sugar
1 t. vanilla
Fresh strawberries, optional
Mint leaves, optional

This is performed in 3 parts. The dessert freezes well and can be prepared, except for garnishes, a week ahead. The whole recipe can be made up and the left-over portion, including that covered with whipped cream, can be served at a later date. **First:** Line the bottom and sides of a spring-form pan with the ladyfingers. Mix the undiluted can of orange juice with 1 quart of the softened ice cream. Spread this over the ladyfingers as the bottom layer. Freeze. **Second:** Crush the raspberries and strain to remove the seeds. Add the pineapple, drained, and the lemonade concentrate. Freeze this mixture until partially frozen and then beat. Spoon this over the orange-ice cream mixture and re-freeze entire thing. **Third:** Add to 1 quart of softened ice cream the almond flavoring, the rum flavoring, the cherries and the nuts. Pour over the raspberry layer and freeze overnight. **To serve:** Take the dessert out of the freezer and remove from the spring-form pan about 2 hours before serving. Put on a serving dish. Cover the dessert with sweetened whipped cream. To sweeten, add the powdered sugar and vanilla flavoring to the cream and then whip. Decorate with fresh strawberries and mint leaves. Place in the refrigerator until serving time. Serves 12.

MRS. FRANK T. DONELSON, JR.

CHOCOLATE ICE BOX CAKE

2 8-oz. pkgs. semi-sweet	4 eggs, separated
chocolate chips	1½ t. vanilla
½ c. sugar	2 c. whipping cream
¼ t. salt	3 doz. large ladyfingers
½ c. hot water	

Melt chocolate in top of double boiler. Add 4 tablespoons sugar, the salt and water. Cook, stirring constantly, over boiling water until slightly thickened. Add beaten egg yolks, beat well. Cook for 2 minutes longer. Stir in vanilla. Remove from heat. Beat egg whites until foamy. Add remaining sugar gradually and continue beating until stiff. Fold into chocolate mixture. Chill. When thoroughly chilled, fold in 1 cup cream, whipped. Pour ½ into spring-form pan which has been lined on bottom and sides with ladyfingers. Add another layer of ladyfingers, and pour on remaining chocolate mixture. Chill for 24 hours. Serve topped with remaining whipped cream. Serves 12.

MRS. S. SHEPHERD TATE

EGGNOG FROSTED CAKE

1 angel food cake	¼ t. nutmeg
½ c. butter	2 T. sherry and 2 T. whiskey
2 c. powdered sugar	or 4 T. Scotch
2 egg yolks	5 T. coffee cream
1 t. vanilla	1½ c. whipping cream

Cut cake into 4 layers with serrated knife. Cream butter with sifted sugar till fluffy. Blend in 1 egg yolk at a time. Stir in vanilla, nutmeg, liquor and coffee cream. Spread on cake layers and reassemble cake. Whip heavy cream and ice cake. Sprinkle with nutmeg. Refrigerate at least 6 hours. Serves 12.

MRS. J. HAY BROWN

MOCHA CAKE KAHLÚA

2 T. unflavored gelatin	⅛ t. salt
¼ c. cocoa, unsweetened	½ c. Kahlua
¾ c. cold water	1 qt. whipping cream
1 T. instant coffee powder	½ marbled pound cake
4 eggs	Chocolate shavings
½ c. sugar	

Combine gelatin, cocoa, water and coffee. Let stand for 5 minutes, then dissolve over hot water. Cool. Beat eggs well. Add sugar and salt and continue beating until fluffy. Combine egg mixture with gelatin mixture and Kahlúa. Beat ¾ quart whipping cream and fold into other mixture. Line bottom and sides of spring-form pan with ½-inch cake slices. Pour mixture into pan. Refrigerate until congealed. Whip remaining cream. Top with whipped cream and shaved chocolate. **Note:** Plain pound cake may be substituted for marbled cake. See Index for recipe to make Homemade Kahlúa. Serves 10-12.

MRS. RONALD BYRNES

MOCHA CAKE

Make this light-as-air cake 24 hours before serving time:

1 pkg. angel food cake mix, to which you add (when adding water to mix):

1 T. instant coffee	**1 t. vanilla**

When cake is cool, ice with:

1½ c. whipping cream	**¾ t. vanilla**
3 T. sugar	**1 T. instant coffee**
2 T. dry cocoa	

Whip cream. Fold in remaining ingredients. Ice cake and refrigerate until serving time. Serves 12.

MRS. RICHARD W. HUSSEY, TUNICA, MISS.

FANNIE JONES' LEMON CAKE PUDDING

1 c. sugar	**Grated rind of 1 lemon**
4 T. flour	**3 eggs, separated**
2 T. melted butter	**1½ c. milk**
⅛ t. salt	**Whipping cream**
Juice of 1½ lemons	

Mix together first 6 ingredients. Beat yolks well and add to lemon mixture. Then add milk. Beat egg whites till stiff and fold into batter. Pour into buttered ramekins. Set ramekins in baking pan containing boiling water. Bake at 350° for 45 minutes or till lightly browned on top. Serve topped with whipped cream. May be made a day ahead. Serves 8.

MRS. J. TUNKIE SAUNDERS

TIPSY PUDDING

Especially suited for Christmastime . . . .

2 small pkgs. vanilla pudding	**½ c. red cherries, chopped**
1 slightly stale yellow sponge cake, baked in sheet form	**½ c. coconut flakes**
	½ c. pecans, chopped
Brandy or brandy flavoring to taste	**1½ pts. whipping cream**
1 small can crushed pineapple	
½ c. pitted dates, chopped	

Make pudding according to package directions and cool until thick. Make day before so that it will be very thick. Cut cake into 2 layers. Sprinkle lower layer with brandy. Mix drained pineapple, dates, cherries and coconut. Sprinkle with more brandy; then let mixture drain completely. Combine fruit mixture with pudding. Add nuts and mix well. Spread mixture as filling for cake. Replace top and ice with whipped cream flavored with brandy. Cut into 2-inch square pieces. **Note:** Cake can be made as a regular sponge cake, cut in half and filled. Fruit filling also fills the center hole. Serves 20.

MISS MARGARET HYDE

MARSHMALLOW PUDDING

2 10-oz. bags marshmallows
2 10-oz. bottles maraschino
  cherries
2 c. broken pecans
1 c. bourbon

1 pt. whipping cream
1 large angel food cake
½ pt. whipping cream, optional
Additional cherries, optional

Cut marshmallows into bite-sized pieces (a pair of kitchen scissors helps). Drain cherries and chop coarsely, saving juice. Combine marshmallows, cherries, and pecans in a large bowl. Pour juice and bourbon over mixture. Cover and let stand overnight in refrigerator, stirring several times. Whip 1 pint whipping cream and fold into mixture just before serving. Angel food cake may be sliced in individual servings, putting the pudding on top, or the whole cake may be cut into 2 layers and filled with the pudding. Pudding will fill cake layer, hole and top generously. Ice with additional ½ pint cream, whipped, and decorate with the additional cherries. Serves 16.

This cake is pink and white and very tall when iced—a spectacular sight that smacks of Christmas!

MRS. ROBERT BONNER

RASPBERRY MOUSSE

1 pkg. frozen red raspberries
1 T. unflavored gelatin
½ c. cold water
4 egg yolks, slightly beaten
½ c. sugar

Pinch of salt
4 egg whites
¼ c. sugar
1 c. whipping cream
Pralines

Fold a 6-inch-wide piece of wax paper in half, lengthwise. Brush 1 side with oil and wrap around top of a 1-quart soufflé dish, oiled side in, forming a 3 or 4-inch standing collar. Secure with tape. Thaw berries and sieve, or purée in blender. Sprinkle gelatin over cold water to soften. Place yolks in top of double boiler and gradually beat in ½ cup sugar and salt. Cook over simmering water, stirring constantly, till thickened. Remove from heat, stir in gelatin till dissolved. Let mixture stand till cool, **but not set.** Stir in purée. Beat whites till they hold a shape, and gradually add ¼ cup sugar to make a shiny meringue. Gently fold meringue into purée mixture. Whip cream till stiff. Fold into mousse. Pour into mold and chill till firm. Remove collar before serving and sprinkle with crushed pralines. Serves 10.

MR. AND MRS. H. DOUGLAS CHISM

ANGEL FOOD CAKE WITH SOUR CREAM

1 angel food cake
2 pts. sour cream

Berries in season (strawberries,
  raspberries, etc.)
Brown sugar

Cut cake in ½ horizontally. Ice inside and out with sour cream. Garnish with berries. **Immediately** before serving, sprinkle cake generously with brown sugar. Serves 12.

MRS. EUGENE J. PIDGEON

COFFEE MOUSSE

1½ c. strong coffee
1 T. gelatin
⅔ c. granulated sugar
½ c. milk

3 eggs, separated
¼ t. salt
½ t. vanilla

Mix coffee, gelatin, ⅓ cup of the sugar and milk. Heat in top of double boiler until gelatin dissolves. Beat egg yolks slightly and mix with remaining sugar and salt. Add to mixture in double boiler. Cook until mixture thickens. Fold in stiffly beaten egg whites and vanilla. Pour into mold and chill until firm. Serve with whipped cream. **Note:** The mousse may be used to fill Filled Chocolate Cups (see Index). Serves 6.

MRS. E. BRADY BARTUSCH

EGGNOG MOUSSE

Sponge cake:
2 c. sifted flour
1½ c. sugar
3 t. baking powder
1 t. salt
¾ c. cold water

7 eggs, separated
½ c. salad oil
2 t. vanilla
2 t. lemon rind, grated
½ t. cream of tartar

Sift flour, sugar, baking powder and salt into mixing bowl. Add water, egg yolks, oil, vanilla and lemon rind. Beat with spoon until well mixed. In large bowl, beat egg whites, adding cream of tartar, until very stiff. With a rubber spatula, fold flour mixture into egg whites a little at a time. Pour into a 9-inch ungreased tube pan. Bake 55 minutes to 1 hour in preheated 325° oven. Remove from oven and invert over neck of a bottle. Remove from pan when completely cooled. Cut out center of cake, making center hole 2 inches greater in diameter. Fill center with mousse:

1 T. unflavored gelatin
½ c. cold milk
3 eggs, separated

¼ c. bourbon
½ c. sugar
½ pt. whipping cream

Dissolve gelatin in milk. Heat over hot water to melt. Beat egg yolks until thick. Add dissolved gelatin slowly. Add whiskey and sugar. Beat cream until thick and fold into egg mixture. Beat egg whites until stiff. Fold into eggnog mixture with a rubber spatula. Refrigerate until mixture begins to set. Pour eggnog in cavity and place part on top of cake. Refrigerate overnight. Ice cake with:

½ pt. whipping cream
2 T. sugar

1 t. vanilla

Whip cream; add sugar and vanilla. Ice cake and garnish with candied fruit, nutmeg, or chopped pecans. Surround with holly and holly berries. This cake is famous at Grace St. Luke's annual church bazaar. Serves 12.

MRS. ALLEN APPLEGATE

MANDARIN MOUSSE

2 11-oz. cans mandarin oranges
Water or sherry
1 c. cold milk

2 3¾-oz. pkgs. whipped-type
orange dessert mix

Drain oranges and reserve syrup. Add water or sherry to juice to make 1 cup. Empty packages of dessert mix into deep bowl and add milk. Beat at low speed 1 minute. Add juice and beat at high speed 2 minutes. In lightly oiled mold, arrange ½ of 1 can of orange sections. Pour 1 cup of mixture over orange sections. Fold remaining oranges into remaining mixture, and pour into mold. Cover with plastic wrap. Refrigerate 4 hours or overnight. Unmold on platter. Garnish with whipped cream, fresh fruit or serve plain. Very tart . . . especially good after fish. Serves 8.

MRS. C. WHITNEY BROWN

MISS HILL'S APRICOT SOUFFLÉ

7 oz. dried apricots
1¼ c. sugar
6 egg whites

Whipped cream
Sliced almonds, toasted

Barely cover dried apricots with water and 1 cup of the sugar. Cook till apricots are soft. Purée mixture and measure 1 cup for use. Purée should be very thick, not runny. Beat egg whites stiff, gradually adding ¼ cup sugar. Fold in purée, stirring with a flat wire whisk. Turn mixture into top of 2 or 2½-quart double boiler which has been buttered and sprinkled with sugar, including the lid. Cover and cook over boiling water 1 hour. Turn out on a serving platter, garnish with ring of whipped cream and almonds. Serves 8.

This light, tart soufflé may be kept waiting over hot water 40 minutes after it is cooked, thus making it a very successful company dessert. During cooking and waiting, be certain that water neither touches the upper pan nor completely boils away. Excellent after game.

MISS ANNA MARIE HILL

HOT APRICOT SOUFFLÉ

1 7-oz. pkg. dried apricots
¼ c. sugar
1 T. lemon juice

½ t. grated lemon rind
Pinch salt
5 egg whites

Cover dried apricots with hot water and let stand for about 2 hours. Put apricots and liquid in sauce pan; bring liquid to a boil and simmer gently, covered, for about 25 minutes, or until they are tender. Drain apricots and force through a fine sieve, or purée them in a blender with a little of the juice. There should be approximately 1 cup thick purée. While purée is still warm, stir in sugar, lemon juice, rind and salt. Fold mixture into stiffly beaten egg whites. Pour into a buttered and sugared 6-cup soufflé dish and bake in 350° oven 30-35 minutes. Serve at once with whipped cream. Serves 6.

MRS. SNOWDEN BOYLE, JR.

CHOCOLATE SOUFFLÉ

2 c. milk
2 oz. bitter chocolate
4 T. butter
2 T. flour

⅔ c. sugar
6 eggs, separated
2 t. vanilla
Dash of salt

Heat milk in top of double boiler. Add chocolate cut in pieces. Stir until chocolate melts. In another saucepan melt butter. Stir in flour; then stir roux into hot milk. When smooth, add sugar. Beat egg yolks until light. Add a little of the hot milk to the eggs to warm; then add yolks to milk mixture. Stir over heat until thickened. Cool and add vanilla. This much can be done several hours ahead. Beat egg whites stiff, adding a dash of salt. Fold into chocolate mixture. Put in an ungreased 1-quart soufflé dish. Set dish in pan of water and bake in a preheated 350° oven for about 50 minutes. This soufflé can be held about 15 minutes by turning down oven temperature after it has finished baking. Serve hot with sweetened whipped cream. Serves 6.

MRS. FRANK T. DONELSON, JR.

CHOCOLATE MOUSSE

1 lb. German sweet cooking
  chocolate
10 eggs, separated
2 T. Grand Marnier

1 T. instant coffee
½ c. boiling water
1 c. whipping cream

Melt chocolate in double boiler; cool. Separate eggs while cold, then let yolks and whites come to room temperature. Beat yolks till thick and lemon colored. Add Grand Marnier. Combine boiling water and coffee and add to yolk mixture. Combine with chocolate and blend till smooth. Beat egg whites till frothy and add 10 dashes cream of tartar. Continue beating till whites are very stiff. Fold carefully into chocolate mixture and pour into an 8-cup greased mold. Refrigerate 24 hours. Unmold, if desired, and garnish with whipped cream and chocolate curls. This may also be garnished with candied red cherries. This very rich dessert serves 10 to 12.

CRÈME BRÛLÉE

A dessert that can be made even two days ahead of time.

1 pt. whipping cream	3 T. cognac
3 T. brown sugar	4 egg yolks, beaten

Step one:
Scald cream in top of double boiler; do not let it boil. Add brown sugar and cognac and stir until sugar is melted and blended. Fold mixture into bowl containing beaten egg yolks; then put mixture into a round glass ovenproof dish (about 8-inches in diameter). Place dish in pan of hot water in center of pre-heated 250° oven for 1½ hours to set the custard. Remove, cool, cover and refrigerate.
Step two:
Cover mixture evenly with ½-inch coating dark brown sugar. Place it under HOT broiler and watch it constantly, turning it if sugar starts to burn in spots. A brown crust will form, but you must watch it constantly. (This may be placed in a pan of ice cubes while sugar is being melted.)
Step three:
At least 1 hour before serving, splash a thin coating of cognac on top of the dessert. Serves 4 (or 6 with normal appetites).

LETITIA BALDRIGE HOLLENSTEINER, NEW YORK, N.Y.

SPANISH FLAN

4 eggs	14 oz. homogenized milk
1 14-oz. can sweetened condensed milk	4 T. sugar

Beat eggs thoroughly; strain into mixing bowl. Add sweetened condensed milk and homogenized milk. Mix thoroughly. Place sugar in the bottom of a 1½-quart ring mold and caramelize. Pour custard mixture over caramelized sugar. Set mold in a shallow pan of water and bake at 325° for 1 hour or until set. Unmold and chill. Serves 8.

MRS. DAVID B. MARTIN

SYLLABUB

A medieval dish . . . it's pretty, easy and historic.

1 pkg. frozen raspberries	1½ pt. whipping cream
4 oz. Madeira	Sugar to taste
1 doz. ladyfingers, split	

Put raspberries in strainer to thaw. Extract all juice and reserve. Add Madeira to juice. Refrigerate pulp and juice separately. Line individual soufflé dishes or sherbets with ladyfingers. Pour juice over until they are well soaked. Whip cream with sugar till stiff. Fold pulp of raspberries into whipped cream and spoon over ladyfingers. Serves 6.

MRS. B. PERCY MAGNESS, JR.

COLD LEMON SOUFFLE WITH WINE SAUCE

1 envelope unflavored gelatin	2 t. grated lemon rind
¼ c. cold water	1½ c. sugar
5 eggs, separated	1 c. whipping cream
¾ c. fresh lemon juice	

Sprinkle gelatin over cold water to soften. Mix egg yolks with lemon juice, rind, and ¾ cup of the sugar. Place in double boiler over boiling water and cook, stirring constantly, until lemon mixture is slightly thickened (about 8 minutes). Remove from heat and stir in gelatin until dissolved. Chill 30-40 minutes or until mixture mounds slightly when dropped from spoon. Beat egg whites until they begin to hold their shape; then gradually add ¾ cup sugar until all has been added and whites are stiff. Beat cream until stiff. Fold whites and cream into yolk mixture until no white streaks remain. Pour into a 2-quart soufflé dish and chill 4 hours or more. Serve with Wine Sauce.

Wine Sauce:

½ c. sugar	1 t. grated lemon rind
3 t. cornstarch	2 T. butter
½ c. water	½ c. dry white wine
3 T. fresh lemon juice	

In a small saucepan, mix together sugar and cornstarch. Stir in water, lemon juice and rind until smooth. Add butter. Bring to a boil, lower heat and cook until thickened (about 3 minutes). Remove from heat and stir in wine. Chill, stirring occasionally. Serve this rich soufflé sparingly. Serves 8-10.

MRS. RALPH GORE

FROZEN SOUFFLE WITH HOT STRAWBERRY SAUCE

1 qt. vanilla ice cream	1 c. whipping cream
24 macaroons, crumbled	4 t. powdered sugar
4 T. orange juice or Grand Marnier	4 T. chopped toasted almonds

Soften ice cream slightly; stir in crumbled macaroons and orange juice or Grand Marnier. Fold in whipped cream. Spoon into 6-cup mold or metal dish. Sprinkle surface with powdered sugar and almonds. Cover with plastic wrap. Freeze until firm, 4-5 hours, preferably overnight. Loosen edges and wrap with warm towel 4-5 seconds. Turn out on chilled platter and serve with Hot Strawberry Sauce. Serves 8.

Hot Strawberry Sauce:

1 qt. fresh strawberries or 2 10-oz. pkgs. frozen sliced strawberries	Sugar to taste 4 T. orange juice or Grand Marnier liqueur

Hull fresh berries and cut in half. Mix sauce just before serving. Put berries in a saucepan with sugar (about 1 cup for fresh berries). Simmer until soft but not mushy. Remove from heat and add orange juice or Grand Marnier. Serve warm over frozen soufflé.

MRS. ROBERT E. NORCROSS, FAIRVIEW FARMS, TYRONZA, ARK.

STRAWBERRY SOUFFLÉ

2 pts. strawberries (2½ c.
　purée), or 4 10-oz. boxes
　frozen
2 envelopes gelatin
¼ c. water
⅔ c. sugar

4 egg yolks, well beaten
⅛ t. salt
1 T. lemon juice
4 egg whites
½ c. sugar
1 c. whipping cream

Cut 3-inch band of wax paper long enough to go around top of 1½-quart soufflé dish. Fasten to dish with tape. Purée strawberries well in blender. Soften gelatin in water in top of double boiler. Add ⅔ cup sugar, egg yolks, salt and 1 cup mashed berries. Stir well. Cook over boiling water about 5 minutes or until gelatin is dissolved. Remove from heat and cool slightly. Add lemon juice and remaining berries. Chill until the consistency of unbeaten egg white. Meanwhile, beat egg whites until frothy. Gradually add ½ cup sugar, beating until whites form soft peaks. Whip cream and fold into egg whites. Fold in chilled berry mixture and pour into soufflé dish. Chill overnight. To serve: Remove paper collar and serve from soufflé dish garnished with additional strawberries and whipped cream. Serves 8-10.

MRS. JAMES GUY ROBBINS

MINTED PINEAPPLE SOUFFLÉ

½ c. sugar
½ c. water
1 8½-oz. can crushed pineapple
½ c. pineapple juice (from
　canned pineapple)
½ c. milk
1 3¾-oz. pkg. vanilla-flavored
　whipped dessert mix

2 T. green crème de menthe (or
　1 t. peppermint extract and 2
　drops green food coloring)
2 egg whites
¼ c. sugar
Mint leaves
6-8 chocolate cookies or
　fudge cakes

Bring to a boil the ½ cup sugar and water. Cook over low heat for about 5 minutes. Remove from heat. Cool. Drain crushed pineapple, reserving ½ cup juice. Add the crushed pineapple to the sugar syrup. In another bowl, combine milk and vanilla-flavored whipped dessert mix. Whip at high speed with an electric beater 1 minute. Add the reserved pineapple juice and green crème de menthe. Whip 2 minutes more. Add pineapple mixture. Set in freezer to cool about 5 minutes. Meanwhile, beat 2 egg whites until stiff. Gradually add ¼ cup sugar and continue beating until the mixture forms peaks. Fold into the cooled pineapple-dessert mixture; stir thoroughly. Spoon into a 1-quart soufflé dish or attractive serving bowl. Freeze at least 2 hours, stirring occasionally. Garnish with mint leaves. Serve from its own dish accompanied by chocolate cookies or fudge cakes. Serves 6.

MRS. JAMES GUY ROBBINS

POTS de CRÈME

3 c. whipping cream
½ c. sugar
1 T. vanilla

5 egg yolks
Chocolate curls
Whipped cream

In saucepan combine cream and sugar; cook over medium heat, stirring occasionally, until sugar is dissolved and mixture is hot. Remove from heat, stir in vanilla. With a wire whisk or rotary beater, beat egg yolks until blended, but not frothy. Gradually add hot cream to mixture, beating constantly. Strain into 8 ungreased 5-ounce ramekins or custard cups. Place in shallow pan filled with ½ inch water. Place in preheated 325° oven. Bake 30 minutes, or until mixture begins to set around edges. Remove from water. Let cool 30 minutes on wire racks; then refrigerate, covering each well. Chill at least 4 hours or overnight. To serve, garnish each well with sweetened whipped cream topped with chocolate curls. Serve with macaroons, if desired. Serves 8.

MRS. MILTON LYMAN KNOWLTON, JR.

MAZIE'S MIRACLE

1 lb. sweet butter
2 c. sugar
1 doz. eggs, separated
4 doz. (10 oz.) amaretti
   (Italian macaroons)
1 c. bourbon

4 squares unsweetened
   chocolate, melted
1 t. vanilla
1 c. chopped pecans
2 doz. double ladyfingers
1½ c. whipping cream

Cream butter and sugar together until light and fluffy. Beat yolks until light and beat into creamed mixture. Soak macaroons in bourbon. Beat chocolate into the butter mixture. Add vanilla and pecans. Beat egg whites until stiff but not dry and fold into chocolate mixture. Line a 10-inch spring-form pan around the sides and on the bottom with split ladyfingers. Alternate layers of soaked macaroons and chocolate mixture in the lined pan. Chill overnight. Remove sides of pan and decorate top with whipped cream. Serves 20.

MRS. ROSS LYNN

LEMON ANGEL

Juice of 6 lemons (or more)
1 T. gelatin
3 lemon rinds, grated

6 eggs, separated
1½ c. sugar
1 angel food cake

Heat lemon juice until hot, but not boiling. Dissolve gelatin in the hot juice and cool. Beat lemon juice mixture, grated rind, egg yolks and ¾ cup sugar. In a separate bowl, beat whites and ¾ cup sugar. Fold the 2 mixtures together. Saw off brown edges of cake. Break into bite-sized pieces. Fold cake into lemon mixture. Pour into a 3-quart dish or mold and refrigerate until set. Garnish with whipped cream and maraschino cherries. Serves 8.

MRS. GARY FALLS, CLARKSDALE, MISS.

VACHÉBÉ

1½ c. vanilla wafer crumbs
½ stick margarine, melted
8 oz. cream cheese
1⅓ c. plus 1 T. confectioners' sugar
1 T. water
⅓ c. chopped pecans
1 T. cornstarch
4 T. cold water
1 pt. fresh or canned blueberries
½ pt. whipping cream

Mix vanilla wafer crumbs with margarine. Place in 8-inch square pan and press down to form bottom crust. Heat in 300° oven for 10 minutes. Cool. Mix cream cheese with powdered sugar and 1 tablespoon water. Spread this with a fork over the crust layer. Sprinkle pecans on top of this. Dissolve cornstarch in 4 tablespoons cold water. Heat blueberries with a small amount of water and sweeten to taste. Add cornstarch and bring to a boil. Simmer just long enough to dissolve sugar and cornstarch. Cool. Spread over cream cheese and nut layer. Cover with whipped cream and place in freezer just long enough to "set" whipped-cream topping. Cut into squares and serve. (The name Vachébé comes from vanilla, cheese, and berries.) Serves 8.

MISS ELIZABETH LYNN, TALLAHASSEE, FLA.

Cakes

STRAWBERRY JAM CAKE

1 c. butter
2 c. sugar
3 eggs
1 c. strawberry jam
3 c. flour
½ t. salt
1 t. soda
3 T. cocoa
1 t. cinnamon
1 c. buttermilk
½ c. pecans, broken

Cream butter and sugar until light and fluffy. Add eggs, 1 at a time, beating well after each addition. Add strawberry jam and beat 2 minutes at medium speed. Sift all dry ingredients together and add alternately with buttermilk. Add nuts and mix well. Line 2 9-inch pans with wax paper and bake at 350° for 45 minutes. Frost with caramel icing. Serves 16.

Caramel icing:

2 c. dark brown sugar
1½ c. granulated sugar
2 T. white corn syrup
1 c. plus 2 T. whipping cream
¼ c. butter

Cook all ingredients together, **except** butter, until it forms a very soft ball when tested in cold water. Remove from heat, add butter, and cool until lukewarm. Beat until creamy and spread between layers, on sides, and on top of cake.

MEMPHIS DAIRY COUNCIL

BIG TOP BIRTHDAY CAKE

1 can (1 lb. 5-oz.) vanilla frosting	Animal crackers
½ c. chunk-style peanut butter	Yellow frosting from pressurized
3 T. milk	can or plastic tube
2 9-in. yellow cake layers	Ring-shaped candies
½ c. cinnamon-apple jelly	

Blend ¼ cup vanilla frosting with peanut butter and milk in small bowl; spread over 1 cake layer; top with second layer. Spread remaining frosting around side and ice a 1-inch rim on top of cake. Spread jelly on un-iced portion of cake top. Press animal crackers in groups of 2 into frosting around side of cake. Using a writing tip, press out yellow frosting in lines over and around animals to resemble cages. Press candy rings into frosting for wheels on cages and candle holders around top edges. Serves 10.

MRS. EDWIN P. VOSS

TEEPEE CAKE

1 box caramel or spice cake mix	1 bag twisted type licorice sticks
1 box caramel, burnt sugar or	1 16-oz. funnel
butter brickle frosting mix	1 wooden board to use for platter
1 small bag M & M's	

Follow directions for cake mix and bake in 13 x 9-inch baking dish. When cool, cut flat cake into triangles as shown:

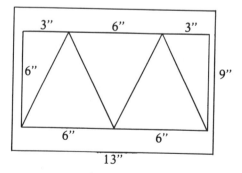

Invert funnel on wooden board and tape securely. Pad around neck of funnel with plastic wrap for a smoother shaped cone. Ice 1 triangle at a time and lean against funnel. Smooth cracks with remaining icing. Decorate base of teepee with thin 1-inch strips of licorice and dot with M & M's. Cut longer strips for the sticks "bracing" the teepee (insert in top of cake).

BOAT CAKE

1 9-inch square cake	Lifesavers
White icing	Paper flag
2 T. cocoa	

Bake and cool a 9-inch square cake. Cut cake diagonally in ½ to make 2 triangles. From 1 triangle cut off a strip 2¼-inches wide. Arrange pieces on tray, using triangles as sails and strip as hull. Prepare white icing; blend cocoa into ½ of it. Spread white frosting on sails; brown frosting on hull. Put a line of brown frosting between sails as mast. Add lifesaver portholes and a paper flag. Serves 12 adults.

MRS. EDWIN VOSS

HERSHEY BAR CAKE

2 sticks butter	8 melted small plain Hershey bars
2 c. sugar	2½ c. sifted cake flour
4 eggs	1 c. buttermilk
2 t. vanilla	Pinch of soda
Pinch of salt	1 c. chopped pecans

Cream butter and sugar. Add eggs, 1 at a time. Add vanilla, salt, melted Hershey bars, flour, buttermilk mixed with soda, and nuts. Pour into greased bundt pan. Bake at 300° for 1 hour and 40 minutes. Sift powdered sugar over cake or fill center with sweetened whipped cream. Slices can be served with a scoop of ice cream. Serves 10-12.

MRS. WILLIAM A. COOLIDGE, JR.

KENTUCKY BOURBON CAKE

¾ lb. butter	1 c. chopped candied pineapples
2 c. sugar	1 c. chopped candied cherries
6 eggs	1 c. orange marmalade
½ c. molasses	2 lbs. chopped pecans
4 c. flour	1 c. bourbon
1 heaping t. baking powder	Apple slices
2 t. ground nutmeg	
1 lb. raisins	

Cream butter and sugar; add eggs, 1 at a time. Beat well. Add molasses and mix well. Sift flour, baking powder, nutmeg. Put fruits, marmalade and nuts in large bowl. Add 1 cup flour mixture and coat fruit. Add remainder of flour to creamed mixture alternating with bourbon. Stir in nuts and fruits. Grease 1 large mold or 2 large loaf pans which have been lined with greased brown paper. Spoon batter into pans and cover with greased brown paper. Bake at 250° until toothpick inserted in center comes out clean, about 2½ to 3 hours. Wrap cake in cloth which has been dampened in whiskey; place in tin container. Add apple slices and cover container. Let sit until cake has ripened, 3-4 weeks, or longer. Cake will keep indefinitely. Serves 16-20.

MRS. BEN C. ADAMS, JR.

CHOCOLATE CHEESE CAKE

18 chocolate wafers	1 c. sugar
¼ c. melted butter	3 eggs
¼ t. cinnamon	2 t. cocoa
1 8-oz. pkg. semi-sweet chocolate	1 t. vanilla
1½ lbs. cream cheese, softened	2 c. sour cream

Preheat oven to 350°. Crush enough wafers with a rolling pin to make 1 cup of crumbs. Melt butter in saucepan; mix in crumbs and cinnamon. Press the crumb mixture on bottom of an 8-inch spring-form pan, then buckle sides on. Chill. Melt chocolate in top of double boiler. In large bowl, beat the softened cheese until fluffy and smooth; then beat in sugar. Add eggs, 1 at a time, beating after each addition. Beat in melted chocolate, cocoa and vanilla, blending thoroughly. Beat in sour cream. Pour into pan and bake 1 hour and 10 minutes. Cake will still be runny, but becomes firm as it chills. Cool at room temperature. Then chill in refrigerator at least 5 hours before serving. Remove sides to serve. Garnish with whipped cream, if desired. This dessert cannot fail! Serves 12.

MRS. DONALD G. AUSTIN, JR.

CHOCOLATE-RUM CAKE

1 pkg. (1 lb. 3-oz.) yellow cake mix	1 T. grated orange peel

Preheat oven to 350°. Lightly grease and flour two 9-inch cake pans. Make cake according to package directions, adding grated orange peel. Bake about 30 minutes, or until surface springs back when gently pressed with fingertip. Let cool in pans 10 minutes. Turn out onto wire racks; let cool completely.

Frosting:

4 squares unsweetened chocolate	1 T. white rum
1 c. sifted confectioners' sugar	1 T. orange juice
2 eggs	

Melt chocolate over hot, not boiling, water. With a wooden spoon, beat in confectioners' sugar alternately with eggs. Beat in rum and orange juice; continue beating until smooth. Set aside.

Rum-Cream Filling:

2 t. unflavored gelatin	½ c. sifted confectioners' sugar
2 T. water	⅓ c. white rum
2 c. whipping cream	1 c. coarsely chopped walnuts

Sprinkle gelatin over water; let stand 5 minutes to soften. Set in pan of hot water; heat, stirring until gelatin is dissolved. With rotary beater, beat cream with sugar just until slightly stiff. Gradually beat in rum and gelatin until mixture is stiff. To assemble cake: Halve each layer crosswise. On cake plate, put layers together with Rum-Cream Filling. Ice top and sides with frosting. Press walnuts around edge of cake, covering completely. Refrigerate until serving, overnight if desired, or at least several hours. Makes 10 servings.

MRS. HARRY SCHMEISSER, JR.

CHOCOLATE SHEET CAKE

2 c. sugar	3 T. cocoa
2 c. sifted flour	2 eggs, slightly beaten
½ t. salt	½ c. buttermilk
1 stick butter	1 t. vanilla
½ c. shortening	1 t. soda
1 c. water	

Sift sugar, flour and salt in a bowl. Set aside. In a saucepan, bring the butter, shortening, water and cocoa to a boil. Remove from heat and pour over the dry ingredients. Mix well. Beat in eggs and other ingredients, mixing well. Pour into a greased and floured 10 x 15 x 1-inch pan and bake for 30 minutes at 325°.

Icing:

3 T. cocoa	1 box powdered sugar
6 T. milk	1 t. vanilla
1 stick butter	1 c. broken pecans

While the cake is baking, make the icing. Bring just to boiling the cocoa, milk and butter. Remove from heat and add the sifted powdered sugar and vanilla. Stir in the nuts. Pour over the cake while the cake is hot. This is the secret of this scrumptious dessert! Serves 15.

Variations: The addition to the cake batter of 1 teaspoon cinnamon is very nice. Also, for a richer chocolate flavor, add more cocoa to the batter and icing.

MRS. FRANK T. DONELSON, JR.

PEACH CRISP

Large peach halves, canned (½ peach per serving)	3 T. bourbon per peach half
Almond macaroons	½ inch brown sugar per peach half

Place peach halves in shallow dish that can be placed under the broiler. Crumble fresh macaroons into each half and pour bourbon over the macaroons. Allow to soak a few minutes. Cover each half with about ½-inch brown sugar. Run under the broiler until the sugar almost burns or until it reaches a dark brown crisp stage. May be served with whipped cream.

MRS. RALPH GORE

STRAWBERRY SHORTCAKE

2 c. flour	½ c. butter
4 t. baking powder	¾ c. milk
½ t. salt	1 qt. fresh strawberries
2 T. sugar	½ pt. whipping cream

Mix dry ingredients. Cut in butter, and quickly stir in milk. Toss on floured board and roll out. Cut out with biscuit cutter or roll large enough for 2 round pans. Bake in 425° oven 12-15 minutes. Split biscuits. Fill and top with sweetened strawberries and whipped cream. Serves 6-8.

MRS. CHARLES L. PIPLAR

EASY RUM CAKE

Prepare cake day before planning to serve:

1 small pkg. instant vanilla pudding	½ c. water
1 box yellow cake mix	½ c. salad oil
½ c. light rum	4 whole eggs

Combine pudding mix and cake mix. Add rum, water and oil. Next add eggs, 1 at a time, beating after each addition. Bake in a greased bundt cake pan for about 1 hour at 350°. Remove from oven and let cool while you prepare the following sauce:

1 c. sugar	1 stick butter
¼ c. water	2 oz. rum

Mix sugar, water, and butter together in a saucepan. Bring to boiling and cook for 1 minute. Cool and add rum. Turn cake out on a sheet of aluminum foil. Crimp edges of foil so that they make a "bowl" for the cake. Punch cake with toothpick. Pour rum sauce over cake very slowly so that sauce can soak in. Some sauce will not soak in, so spread it over cake with knife when ready to serve. Just before serving, sift confectioners' sugar over top. **Note:** For Christmas, this cake can be decorated with little plastic angels set around top like candles. Serves 16.

MRS. WILLIAM A. COOLIDGE, JR.

PRUNE CAKE

Dried prunes (about 18 large)	1 t. cloves
1 t. soda	1 t. allspice
1 c. butter or margarine	1 t. nutmeg
1 c. sugar	3 eggs, beaten
3 c. sifted flour	1 c. buttermilk
1 t. cinnamon	½ c. chopped pecans

Soak dried prunes in boiling water to cover until softened. Drain. Remove seeds and chop. Seeded, chopped prunes should equal 1 cup. Add soda to prunes. While soda is dissolving, cream butter and sugar. Sift together flour and spices. Stir beaten eggs into buttermilk. Add flour-spice mixture to creamed butter-sugar mixture alternating with buttermilk and eggs, beating well after each addition. Add prunes and pecans. Pour into 2 well greased and floured cake pans. Bake in 350° oven 30-45 minutes. Cake is done when top browns and cake pulls away from sides of pan. Cool and remove from pans. Ice with Butter Icing. Serves 12-15.

Butter Icing:

½ c. butter, softened	Juice of 1 large lemon
1 box confectioners' sugar, sifted	Grated rind of 1 orange

Cream butter, add sugar gradually. Add lemon juice and rind. Stir until of spreading consistency.

MRS. DANIEL FISHER

KIRSCH ON POUND CAKE

Slice pound cake; saturate with chilled Kirsch. Top with whipped cream.

MRS. HYDE BOONE

APPLE CAKE

2 eggs	1 t. baking powder
2 c. sugar	1 t. cinnamon
1¼ c. salad oil	2 t. vanilla
3 c. flour, sifted	3 c. diced apples
1 t. salt	2 c. chopped nuts

Add eggs, 1 at a time, to sugar and mix well. Gradually pour in salad oil and mix. Mix together sifted flour, salt, baking powder, and cinnamon and add to sugar mixture. Mix well. Add vanilla; fold in apples and nuts and pour into two 11 x 7-inch pans. Bake in 350° oven for 30 minutes or until browned. Can serve with whipped cream. Serves 16.

MRS. JOHN H. SHUTE, JR.

BANANA CAKE

½ c. butter	2½ t. cloves
½ c. oil	5 t. cinnamon
2 c. sugar	1 t. soda
4 eggs	1 box raisins
3 c. flour	2 c. broken pecans
½ t. salt	8 large ripe bananas

Cream butter, oil and sugar. Add well beaten eggs. Mix flour with salt, spices, soda and sift. Add raisins and nuts to flour, then add to egg mixture. Stir in well mashed bananas. Bake at 300° for 3 hours in a loaf pan or 1½-2 hours in a tube pan. Serves 18-20.

MRS. C. C. McGEE

MRS. M. A. RICHARDSON'S PRUNE CAKE

4 eggs	1 t. ground cloves
1 c. oil	1 c. buttermilk
2 c. sugar	1 t. soda, dissolved in milk
2 c. sifted self-rising flour	1 c. pitted, chopped prunes
1 t. cinnamon	(about 18)
1 t. nutmeg	1 c. pecans (optional)

Beat eggs until foamy, and add oil and sugar. Blend in flour, spices, buttermilk and soda. Add prunes and pecans. Pour into tube or bundt cake pan, which has been greased and floured, and bake 1 hour at 350°. Serves 12-15.

MRS. SNOWDEN BOYLE, JR.

Pies

LEMON CHEESE PIE

1 c. vanilla wafer crumbs	2 eggs, beaten
2 T. melted butter	½ c. sugar
1 T. sugar	1 c. sour cream
4 3-oz. pkgs. cream cheese	1 T. sugar
¼ c. lemon juice	1 T. grated lemon rind

Make the crust by mixing vanilla wafer crumbs, melted butter and 1 tablespoon of sugar. Press firmly on bottom and sides of buttered 8-inch pie plate. For filling, blend cream cheese and lemon juice thoroughly. Add eggs and sugar and beat until smooth. Pour into crust. Bake at 350° for 15-20 minutes or until firm. Cool 5 minutes. Mix sour cream, 1 tablespoon sugar and grated lemon rind. Spread over pie filling and bake 10 minutes longer. Chill in refrigerator 5 hours before serving. Makes 6-8 servings.

MRS. WILLIAM M. PREST

CHOCOLATE CREAM MINT PIE

3 squares unsweetened chocolate	¼-½ t. peppermint extract
¾ c. butter	8-inch baked pie shell
1 c. sugar	½ pt. whipping cream
3 eggs	

Melt chocolate and let cool. Cream butter and sugar. Beat the eggs. Add chocolate and beaten eggs to creamed butter. Beat mixture until smooth on "high" with an electric mixer. Add peppermint extract and pour into baked and cooled pie shell. Chill and serve with whipped cream. To increase, make twice. Serves 5.

MRS. MAURY WADE, JR.

MRS. McGEE'S DERBY PIE

1 c. sugar	1 stick butter, no substitutes
4 eggs	1 c. pecans or English walnuts,
1 c. white Karo	chopped
1 t. vanilla	1 6-oz. pkg. chocolate chips

Mix first four ingredients and blend well. Melt butter and add to first mixture along with the remaining ingredients. Pour into a 10-inch unbaked pie shell. Bake at 350° for 50 minutes or till set. This very rich dessert will serve 8.

MRS. BRUCE E. CAMPBELL, JR.

BLACK BOTTOM PIE

For crust:

14 crisp ginger snaps, crushed	5 T. melted butter

Line 10-inch pie pan, sides and bottom pressed flat and firm, with combined ginger snaps and butter. Bake 10 minutes in 300° oven.

Basic filling:

1 T. unflavored gelatin	1 T. corn starch
1¾ c. milk	Pinch of salt
½ c. sugar	4 egg yolks

Soak gelatin in a little cold water. Scald milk and add sugar mixed with corn starch and salt. Then add beaten egg yolks. Cook in double boiler, stirring constantly until custard thickens and coats spoon. Stir in gelatin. Divide custard in half.

Chocolate layer:

2 squares melted unsweetened chocolate	1 t. vanilla

To half the custard, add melted chocolate and vanilla. Pour into crust.

Rum layer:

4 egg whites	½ c. sugar
⅛ t. cream of tartar	1 T. rum

Cool other half of custard. Beat egg whites and cream of tartar, adding sugar slowly. Fold into cooled custard and add rum. Spread over chocolate layer which should be cool; chill in refrigerator. **Note:** More rum may be added.

Whipped cream layer:

2 T. sugar	Grated unsweetened chocolate
½ pt. whipping cream	

Whip together sugar and cream and spread on pie. Grate bitter chocolate coarsely on top. Refrigerate overnight. Serves 6.

MRS. JAMES W. WRAPE, COLLIERVILLE, TENN.

RUM PIE

Pie shell:

1¼ c. graham cracker crumbs	¼ c. melted butter
¼ c. sugar	

Mix crumbs and sugar; then add butter. Press into 9-inch pie pan and chill.

Filling:

3 egg yolks	½ pt. whipping cream
½ c. sugar	¼ c. light rum
½ envelope gelatin	Bittersweet chocolate shavings
¼ c. cold water	

Beat egg yolks until thick and add sugar. Dissolve gelatin in cold water and heat until almost boiling. Gradually add to egg mixture. Whip cream until stiff and fold gently into egg-gelatin mixture. Add rum. Top with chocolate shavings and chill. Serves 6.

MISS ANNA MARIE HILL

MINCEMEAT PIE

1 recipe for 10-in. double-crust
  pastry
3 c. prepared mincemeat with
  brandy and rum
1 c. applesauce

1 c. pared, diced tart apple
1 can (4-oz.) walnuts, coarsely
  chopped
1 egg yolk
Rum Sauce

Prepare piecrust. Roll out two-thirds of pastry to ⅛-inch thickness. Fit into a 10-inch pie plate; trim overhang to 1 inch. Roll out remaining pastry to a 12-inch circle. Cut with pastry wheel or knife, into ½-inch wide strips. Preheat oven to 400°.

Filling: In large bowl, combine mincemeat, applesauce, diced apple, walnuts. Turn into pie shell. Moisten edge of shell slightly with cold water. Arrange 5 pastry strips, 1 inch apart, across filling; press ends to rim of shell. Place 5 strips diagonally across first ones, to make lattice; press ends to rim of shell. Fold overhang of lower crust over ends of strips, to make a rim. Flute rim. Beat egg yolk with 1 tablespoon water. Brush over lattice top, but not on edge of pastry. Sprinkle lattice with sugar. Bake 30-35 minutes, or until crust is nicely browned. Let pie cool slightly on wire rack. Serve pie warm, with flaming Rum Sauce, whipped cream, vanilla ice cream, or hard sauce. This extremely rich pie will serve 10.

Rum Sauce:

⅓ c. granulated sugar
⅓ c. light brown sugar,
  firmly packed
1 c. water

1 lemon wedge
1 orange wedge
½ c. dark rum

Combine sugars with water; cook over medium heat, stirring until sugars are dissolved. Add lemon and orange wedges; bring to boil. Boil, uncovered, 20 minutes. Discard fruit. Just before serving add rum. Heat over very low heat just until vapor rises. Remove from heat. Ignite with match, and take flaming sauce to table. Spoon over each piece of warm mincemeat pie.

MRS. JAMES GUY ROBBINS

APPLE PIE EN PAPILLOTE

5-6 large baking apples
½ c. sugar
2 T. flour

½ t. nutmeg
2 T. lemon juice
9-inch unbaked pie shell

Pare and core apples; cut in large chunks. Mix sugar, flour and nutmeg and sprinkle over apples, coating evenly. Put apples in 9-inch unbaked pie shell and drizzle lemon juice over them.

Topping:

½ c. sugar
½ c. flour

2 t. cinnamon
½ c. butter

Mix sugar, flour and cinnamon and cut in butter. Sprinkle topping over apples. Slide pie pan in paper bag. Tie securely. Place on cookie sheet and bake at 425° for 1 hour. Split bag open. Remove pie and set on wire rack to cool. Let cool about an hour before serving. Serve with ice cream or whipped cream. Serves 6.

MRS. WILLIAM K. STODDARD, RIVERDALE PLANTATION, HUGHES, ARK.

RUTH'S BOURBON PIE

Crumb crust:

1½ c. vanilla wafer crumbs	1 T. sugar
½ c. melted butter	½ c. crushed pecans

Combine all ingredients and press into 10-inch pie plate. Bake 5 minutes at 400°. Cool completely.

Filling:

½ lb. butter, no substitutes	6 eggs
1 box confectioners' sugar	⅓ c. bourbon

Cream butter and sugar with large size mixer. Add eggs, one at a time, and mix very well after each addition. If using a small portable hand mixer, use only 5 eggs. Add bourbon in a very slow stream. Bourbon cooks egg mixture. The filling will look curdled at first, but will become smooth and creamy. Turn into crumb crust and chill or freeze overnight. Improves and mellows with age. If made more than a day ahead, freeze and thaw before serving. This is a very rich pie. Serves 8-10.

To make this Bourbon Pie really elegant, bake it in a quiche pan, so that the pie can be removed from the baking pan and taken to the table, looking for all the world like something from a French pastry shop!

MRS. DENNIS COUGHLIN, KNOXVILLE, TENN.

PUMPKIN CHIFFON PIE

1½ c. canned pumpkin	1 envelope gelatin
¾ c. packed brown sugar	¼ c. cold water
½ t. salt	3 egg whites
½ t. ginger	¼ t. cream of tartar
½ t. allspice	6 T. sugar
3 t. cinnamon	1 10-inch or 2 8-inch baked
3 large egg yolks	pie shells
½ c. milk	Whipped cream

Mix together pumpkin, brown sugar, salt, ginger, allspice and cinnamon. Beat egg yolks slightly and mix with milk. Combine the two mixtures and place over low heat, stirring constantly until boiling. Boil 1 minute and remove from stove. Add gelatin which has been dissolved in cold water. Chill in bowl until partially set. Beat egg whites with cream of tartar and gradually add sugar. Beat until stiff. Fold whites into pumpkin mixture and pour into pie shell(s). Chill 3 hours. Serve topped with whipped cream. Makes one 10-inch or two 8-inch pies.

MRS. ROBERT LOWRY

Tarts and Tortes

PETITS CHOUX
(Tiny Cream Puffs)

1 c. water	¼ t. salt
½ c. butter	4 eggs
1 c. sifted flour	

Heat water and butter in a deep pan. Add flour and salt to water and stir rapidly over heat until batter follows spoon around pan. Remove from heat and add eggs one at a time, beating well with a wooden spoon after each addition, until batter is shiny, smooth, thick and holds its shape. Spoon batter by teaspoonfuls on an ungreased cookie sheet about 1 inch apart. Swirl each mound so it will burst into puffs as it bakes. Bake in 400° oven about 45 minutes or until puffed and golden brown. When puffs are done, remove from oven and pierce the side of each with a fork. These freeze beautifully, but frozen puffs must be crisped in 425° oven for 3-4 minutes before filling. Split and fill puffs with seafood or chicken salad; sweetened whipped cream, ice cream or French Custard. Makes 55-60.

French Custard:

⅓ c. sugar	1½ c. milk
1 T. flour	1 slightly beaten egg yolk
1 T. cornstarch	1 t. vanilla
¼ t. salt	½ c. whipping cream

Mix first four ingredients. Gradually stir in milk. Cook and stir until mixture thickens and slightly boils. Cook, stirring constantly, 2-3 minutes longer. Add some of the hot mixture to the egg yolk, then return egg mixture to custard. Return custard to heat, stirring constantly, until mixture comes just to a boil. Remove from heat, add vanilla, and cool. Beat smooth. Before serving, fold in whipped cream and fill puffs. Keep custard refrigerated if made ahead.

If you wish to "gild the lily", custard-filled puffs can be frosted with your favorite chocolate frosting, white frosting, or white frosting tinted a pastel with food coloring. Canned frosting works very well. Sprinkle nonpareils over the frosting or perch a candied violet atop.

MRS. MILTON LYMAN KNOWLTON, JR.

FRENCH CREAM TARTS

1 8-oz. pkg. cream cheese	6 pastry shells
1 c. confectioners' sugar	Fruit
½ pt. whipping cream	Additional whipped cream
1 t. vanilla flavoring	

Soften cream cheese, add sugar and whip. Fold in whipped cream and flavoring. Pour into cooked pastry shells and place fruit on top. Suggested fruits: strawberries, blueberries, pineapple chunks, raspberries, cherries. Garnish with whipped cream. Cherries or strawberries are especially good. Serves 6.

MRS. GEORGE R. DAY, JACKSON, MISS.

PLUM PUDDING TARTS

¾ c. chopped raisins
¾ c. chopped dates
¼ c. chopped nuts
1 c. light brown sugar

1 T. flour
1 egg
Juice and rind of 1 lemon
6-8 uncooked tart shells

Mix together all ingredients and spoon into uncooked tart shells. Bake in 400° oven about 20 minutes. Cool and top with whipped cream or hard sauce. Fills 6-8 tarts.

MRS. LEON JONES

BLUEBERRY TARTS AU COINTREAU

12 tart shells
1 3¼-oz. pkg. instant vanilla
  pudding
1 c. milk
1 c. whipping cream

⅛ t. salt
1 T. cointreau
3 c. blueberries, well drained
  and dusted with powdered sugar

Make the pudding according to package directions, using the milk and cream for the liquid. Add salt, then cointreau. Fill tarts with pudding and heap with blueberries. Sprinkle with more powdered sugar. Serve with whipped cream. Serves 12.

MRS. ROBERT WALTERS

PECAN APPLE TARTLETS

1 pkg. pie crust mix
1 1-lb. 9-oz. can apple pie
  filling

1 4-oz. pkg. shredded Cheddar
  cheese
36 small pecan halves

Prepare pie crust mix, following label directions, or make pastry from your favorite double-crust recipe. Roll out, half at a time, on a lightly floured pastry cloth or board, to a 14 x 10-inch rectangle. Cut out 12 rounds with a 3-inch plain or scalloped cutter. Fit each round into a tiny muffin-pan cup, pressing firmly against bottom and side. Reroll all trimmings and cut out to make 36 shells in all. Spoon apple pie filling into shells, dicing any large pieces of apple, if needed, to fit. Bake in 400° oven for 30 minutes, or until filling bubbles up and pastry is golden; remove from oven. Sprinkle cheese over apple filling. Bake 3 minutes longer, or just until cheese melts; remove from oven. Press a pecan half into top of each tart. Remove carefully from pans at once; cool on wire racks. Serve slightly warm or cold.

Note: Make pastry shells ahead, if you wish; cover tightly and chill. Fill and bake no more than two hours ahead so shells will be crisp. Makes 36.

PECAN TASSIES

Pastry:
    ½ c. butter   1¼ c. flour
    1 3-oz. pkg. cream cheese

Filling I:
    1 beaten egg   ½ t. vanilla
    ¾ c. brown sugar   ½ c. chopped pecans
    1 T. melted butter

Filling II:
    1 egg   ⅔ c. sugar
    3½-oz. can flaked coconut

Mix ingredients for pastry as for pie crust. Chill for 1 hour. Pinch off balls of dough and press into miniature muffin tins. Combine ingredients of either filling. Fill unbaked shells half full. Coconut and pecan fillings fill about 35 pastry shells each. Bake pecan filled shells 20 minutes and coconut shells 12 minutes at 350°. Cool and serve. Powdered sugar may be sifted over the pecan pastries, if desired. These may be made ahead and frozen. Pastry recipe makes 60-70 small pastries.

MRS. WILLIAM A. COOLIDGE, JR.

MERINGUE TART

    3 egg whites   1 t. vanilla
    ½ t. baking powder   1 t. vinegar
    ⅛ t. salt   1 t. water
    1 c. sugar, sifted

Place in a bowl egg whites, baking powder and salt. Beat egg whites until they are stiff. Add sifted sugar slowly, ½ teaspoon at a time, alternating with a few drops of the combined liquids (vanilla, vinegar, and water). Beat constantly. When all the ingredients have been added, continue to beat the meringue for several minutes. Heap it up on the lightly greased platter or dish from which it is to be served or in a spring-form pan. Shape the meringue like a pie or tart with a heavy edge, using a spatula or knife. Bake in a 275° oven for 1 hour, or longer. When ready to serve, fill center with vanilla ice cream, top with fresh raspberries, peaches, strawberries or any fresh fruit. Top this with toasted shredded coconut. If fresh fruit is out of season, use frozen, but put it on dessert while still frosty so fruit won't be mushy. This is also delicious filled with orange or pineapple ice topped with whipped cream, or with scoops of coffee ice cream and served with hot fudge sauce. Too good to be true! Serves 8.

MRS. ALLEN COX, JR.

FILLED CHOCOLATE CUPS

3 squares semi-sweet chocolate   Whipped cream
1½ t. shortening   Shaved chocolate
6 paper cupcake liners   Chopped nuts
Ice cream, sherbet or
    coffee mousse

Melt chocolate and shortening over hot water. Stir until smooth. Remove from
hot water and allow chocolate to cool until thick enough to spread. Watch
closely. Spread chocolate onto bottom and around sides of fluted or plain
paper cupcake liners. Place in muffin pans or on flat pan. Chill or freeze firm.
Carefully remove liners from chocolate cups. Fill with ice cream, sherbet,
or mousse. Enclose in aluminum foil or plastic and keep in freezer. At serving
time top with whipped cream. Garnish top with shaved chocolate and chopped
nuts. Serves 6.

MRS. WILLIAM M. PREST

CRUSHED TOFFEE MERINGUE

1 recipe Meringue Tart   6 Heath Bars
½ pt. whipping cream   1 qt. coffee ice cream
Rum to taste

Using the recipe for Meringue Tart (see Index), shape it into a large ring or
small individual meringues on a cookie sheet. This can be baked ahead and
frozen. Shortly before serving, ice meringue with whipped cream flavored
with rum and mixed with 5 chopped Heath Bars. Fill center of meringue with
ice cream. Put a small amount of the flavored whipped cream on top. Sprinkle
with remaining Heath Bar crumbs for garnish. This dessert never fails to
please the men. Serves 6.

MRS. B. PERCY MAGNESS, JR.

CREAM CHEESE TARTS

1½ c. graham cracker crumbs   ¼ c. sour cream
¼ c. sugar   2 eggs
¼ t. cinnamon   1 t. vanilla
¼ c. melted butter   ½ c. sugar
12 paper muffin cups   Sour cream and berries, as
1 lb. cream cheese   garnish

Mix crumbs, sugar, cinnamon in a large bowl; add butter. Press mixture in
12 paper muffin cups that have been put inside a muffin tin. In a small bowl,
beat rest of ingredients until smooth. Pour mixture into muffin cups. Bake
in a 350° oven for 16 minutes. Chill and peel off paper; garnish with a dash
of sour cream and fresh berries or 1 teaspoon of berry preserves. You can
freeze these in the paper cups. Defrost at room temperature 1½ hours before
serving. Makes 12 tarts.

MRS. FLOYD HUMPHREYS DUNCAN

GLAZED FRUIT TARTLETS

A simplified version of the classic French cream tart, these tartlets are fit for royalty . . . they're scrumptious, as well as beautiful.

Tartlets: Recipe makes 6 4-inch dessert tarts or 30 2-inch bite-sized coffee or tea tartlets. All parts may be made ahead **but** cannot be assembled more than 3 hours before serving. They become soggy if left standing too long.

Pastry: 1 recipe for 2 crust 10-inch pie or 1 10-oz. package piecrust mix. Make pastry. Using miniature muffin tins or Swedish tartlet tins, press pastry into tin cavities, forming 30 bite-sized tartlet shells; or make 6 4-inch tart shells. Prick with fork; refrigerate 30 minutes. Bake at 450° till golden brown, about 10 minutes. Cool; remove from pans. Make several weeks ahead of party and freeze, if desired.

Crème Pâtissière:

1 3⅝-oz. pkg. instant vanilla	1½ c. coffee cream
pudding and pie filling mix	¼ t. almond extract

Make mix as label directs, substituting cream for milk and adding almond extract. Make the day before serving, cover and refrigerate.

Fruit: Any of the following, alone or in combination, may be used:

Pineapple tidbits	**Blueberries**
Maraschino cherries	**Raspberries**
Whole strawberries	**Green grapes**
Bananas	

Glaze:

½ c. currant jelly	1 T. Kirsch (optional)

Over moderate heat, stir jelly till melted. Remove from heat. Stir in Kirsch. Add a little water if jelly seems too thick. Make just before tartlet assemblage.

Assemblage: Fill tartlet shells with crème; top each with fruit; spoon warm glaze over each. Refrigerate until ready to serve. **Note:** The beautiful jewel colors of these tartlets make a lovely sight when served on a large silver tray, especially if several varieties of fruit are used.

Variations:

(1) Fill tartlet shells with crème. Dip drained, stemmed maraschino cherries into melted chocolate. Place 1 cherry atop each tartlet. Sprinkle edges with multicolored nonpareils. Let tartlets dry on racks for 1 hour.

(2) Fill shells with chocolate pudding, top with whipped cream (flavored with instant coffee or rum and confectioners' sugar, if desired).

MRS. MILTON LYMAN KNOWLTON, JR.

TINY CHARLOTTES

Ladyfingers	**Whipping cream**
Vanilla flavored "Whip and	**Cherries**
Chill"	

Separate ladyfingers and cut in half. Spread thickly with vanilla flavored "Whip and Chill" made according to directions. Top with a bit of whipped cream and a half cherry.

MRS. ERIC BABENDREER

KOLACKY
(Open-Faced Tarts)

½ lb. butter
8-oz. pkg. cream cheese
2 c. flour

1 c. powdered sugar
2 t. baking powder

Cream together butter and cream cheese. Sift together flour, sugar and baking powder. Blend well the butter mixture with flour mixture. Roll into 3-inch diameter roll, wrap and refrigerate for several hours. Slice ¼-inch thick and shape into 3-inch circles. Press down center and fill with choice of fruit centers. **Fillings:** chopped apricots, pineapples, or prunes. Baby food desserts are good and very easy to use. Bake 15 minutes at 350°. Makes 30 tarts.

MRS. JAMES R. BROOKS

BLACK FOREST TORTE

Cake:

4 1-oz. squares unsweetened
    chocolate
1¾ c. flour
1¾ c. sugar
1¼ t. soda
1 t. salt

¼ t. baking powder
⅔ c. soft-type margarine
1¼ c. water
1 t. vanilla
3 eggs

Heat oven to 350°. Melt chocolate and cool. Brush sides and bottom of four 9-inch round layer pans with soft-type margarine. Bake only 2 layers at a time if desired. Measure into large mixer bowl all ingredients except eggs. Beat at low speed to blend; then beat 2 minutes at medium speed, scraping sides and bottom of bowl frequently. Add eggs and beat 2 minutes more. Pour ¼ of batter (about 1 cup) into each pan. Layers will be thin. Bake 15-18 minutes, or until done. Cool slightly and remove from pans. Cool thoroughly.

Chocolate filling:

1½ 4-oz. bars German's sweet
    chocolate
¾ c. soft-type margarine

½ c. chopped toasted almonds

Melt chocolate over hot water. Cool. Blend in margarine and stir in nuts.

Cream filling:

2 c. whipping cream
1 T. sugar

1 t. vanilla

Beat cream with sugar and vanilla until stiff. Do not overbeat.

To assemble:
Place bottom layer on serving plate. Spread with ½ the chocolate filling, next layer with ½ the cream filling. Repeat, ending with cream filling. Decorate with chocolate curls. Refrigerate. Will freeze nicely. Serves 14.

MRS. C. WHITNEY BROWN

MAZARINE TORTE

1⅓ c. flour	½ c. softened butter
1 t. baking powder	1 egg
⅓ c. sugar	½ c. raspberry jam

Heat oven to 350°. Grease round layer pan or spring-form pan. Blend dry ingredients. Mix in butter and egg until all the flour is moistened. Press dough evenly on bottom and sides of pan. Spread ¼ cup of the jam over the dough. Chill, covered, while preparing filling and frosting.

Filling and frosting:

½ c. butter	2 eggs
⅔ c. sugar	½ c. sifted confectioners'
1 c. blanched almonds, chopped	sugar
or ground	2 t. lemon juice
½ t. almond extract	

Cream butter and sugar and stir in almonds and almond extract. Add eggs one at a time, beating well after each addition. Spoon filling over jam. Bake about 50 minutes. Cool torte in pan and carefully remove. Spread remaining ¼ cup jam over the top. Drizzle with frosting made by mixing until smooth, confectioners' sugar and lemon juice. Serves 10.

MRS. DONALD G. AUSTIN, JR.

SACHER TORTE

This dessert is a specialty of the famed Sacher Hotel in Vienna . . . .

¾ c. butter	1 c. sifted flour
¾ c. sugar	¼ c. apricot jam
6 eggs, separated	Chocolate icing
6 oz. unsweetened chocolate,	1 pt. whipping cream
melted	

Preheat oven to 325°. Cream butter with ¼ cup of the sugar and beat until fluffy. Add egg yolks, one at a time, beating well after each addition. Stir in chocolate. Beat egg whites until foamy. Gradually add the remaining ½ cup of sugar and continue beating to make a stiff meringue. Fold the meringue gently into the chocolate batter until no white shows. Then fold in the flour. Pour into a greased and floured 8-inch spring-form pan. Bake for 1 hour. Let stand 10 minutes, then remove rim. Cool on pan's base. Spread jam over top of cake. If jam doesn't spread easily, thin it with water. Frost with chocolate icing. Slice the torte and serve with a spoonful of whipped cream. Garnish with grated orange peel. This will not double. Serves 12.

Chocolate icing:

¾ c. sugar	½ c. semi-sweet chocolate bits
6 T. water	2 T. butter

Combine sugar and water in a small saucepan and cook, stirring until sugar has dissolved. Continue cooking, without stirring, to 234° on a candy thermometer or until the syrup spins a short thread when dripped from a spoon. Meanwhile, melt chocolate and butter in a pan over hot water. Remove from heat and stir until smooth. Pour syrup slowly over the melted chocolate, stirring gently, until smooth, cool and slightly thickened. Pour the icing over the cake, spreading it down onto the sides. This will make a very thin coating.

MR. JOHN J. FITZMAURICE

Frozen Desserts

ICE CREAM BALLS

This is simply ice cream for dessert. However, it is a different touch, delicious and beautiful . . . .

Any flavor ice cream may be used. The following are particularly good:

Peppermint	**Almond**
Coffee	**Vanilla**
Vanilla with chocolate bits	**Strawberry**

Using a scoop, make balls of ice cream about the size of tennis balls. Place on wax paper lined tray in freezer to harden, making certain they are covered after freezing. When ready to serve, remove from freezer and serve one to each guest, passing hot fudge sauce to ladle over. These are even better if rolled in coconut or chopped pecans before putting in freezer to harden. **Note:** This method of making ice cream balls ahead is a grand idea for children's birthday parties.

MRS. MILTON LYMAN KNOWLTON, JR.

BOZO BALLS

Ice cream balls are decorated as clowns' heads.

Ice cream balls	**Red-hot candies**
Doilies	**1 pressurized can colored**
Ice cream cones	**frosting or whipped cream**
Chocolate drops	

Make balls of ice cream and put each on a small doily. Place cone on each ball for clown's pointed hat. Use chocolate drops on ice cream for the eyes and red-hot candies for the mouth. Using frosting or whipped cream, make a scalloped clown's collar around base of ice cream ball. These may be made ahead and frozen.

MRS. ALEXANDER WELLFORD

BING CHERRY PARFAIT

1 can Bing cherries	**2 doz. almond macaroons**
½ c. bourbon	**1 c. chopped pecans**
½ gal. vanilla ice cream	**Whipped cream topping**

Soak drained cherries in bourbon for 24 hours. Soften ice cream and add cherries, which have been cut in half, and liquid in which cherries have soaked. Fold in crumbled macaroons and chopped pecans. Mix thoroughly. Fill parfait glasses and place in freezer. Whip cream and add after the mixture has frozen. Serves 8.

MRS. ANDREW JACKSON HAYS, JR.

FROZEN LEMON CREAM

10 large lemon shells	2 c. sugar
2 c. milk	Juice of 4 lemons
2 c. whipping cream	Grated rind of 4 lemons

Slice tops off 10 lemons and remove all pulp. Cut a thin slice from bottom of each lemon shell so it will stand upright. Stir milk, cream and sugar together until sugar is thoroughly dissolved. Pour mixture into refrigerator tray and freeze until it is mushy. Add grated rind and juice of 4 lemons; beat mixture well with a rotary beater and freeze again for 2 hours. Beat cream again thoroughly; return to freezer again until solid. Fill each lemon shell with frozen lemon cream, piling it high. Serve on individual plates garnished with a leaf (ivy, mint, etc.). If you wish, a few drops of yellow food coloring will give this a more "lemony" color. Serves 10.

MRS. ROBERT M. LEATHERMAN, COLUMBIA, MISS.

Variation: Omit grated rind. Do not spoon Lemon Cream into lemon shells. Instead, scoop it into sherbets and pour over each serving 1 tablespoon sherry.

MRS. CHARLES E. KOSSMANN

RASPBERRY SHERBET WITH FRESH FRUIT CASSIS

3 pts. raspberry sherbet	¼ c. creme de cassis
2 grapefruit	1 lb. frozen whole strawberries
2 pears	(thawed slightly, undrained)
2 c. green grapes	

Use your prettiest tiered 6-cup mold for this elegant dessert. Press softened sherbet firmly and evenly into mold. Freeze until firm (overnight). Peel grapefruit; section into large bowl. Pare, quarter, and core pears. Cut each quarter into 2 or 3 slices. Halve grapes, remove seeds. Combine fruit, cassis and strawberries. Refrigerate, covered. Toss several times to blend. **To serve:** With spatula, loosen around edge of mold, then dip mold quickly in warm water; invert in chilled shallow bowl. Spoon fruit mixture around sherbet mold. Serves 10.

MRS. CHARLES H. McGEE, BRUIN PLANTATION, HUGHES, ARK.

CARAMEL ICE CREAM PIE

1 roll butterscotch cookies	1 12-oz. jar of caramel sauce
(from dairy case)	
½ gal. ice cream	

Slice and bake cookies according to directions on package. Line bottom and sides of a 10-inch pie plate with cookies and crumble rest of cookies to use as topping. Put ice cream in a bowl to soften. Stir caramel sauce into ice cream. Spoon mixture into pie plate. Sprinkle rest of crumbled cookies on top of pie. Refreeze. Ice cream pie is better if it is made several days ahead and left in freezer until party or serving time. Serves 10-12.

MRS. RANDOLPH TURNER

ICE CREAM PUMPKIN

3 qts. vanilla ice cream	1 t. vanilla extract
2 t. pumpkin-pie spice	6 drops red food coloring
3 pts. whipping cream	5 drops yellow food coloring
1 c. confectioners' sugar	Candied citron (1½ by ¼ by ¼ in.)

Should be done a day ahead. Line 2 identical 1½-quart bowls with foil. Chill. Let ice cream soften slightly. Spoon 1½ quarts into each bowl, sprinkling with spice. Smooth tops and freeze, covered, overnight. To assemble pumpkin: In large chilled bowl, combine cream, sugar, vanilla, and food coloring. Beat mixture till stiff. Refrigerate. Turn ice cream out of bowls; remove foil. Place the 2 flat surfaces together, to form a ball. Place on a cookie sheet. With small spatula, spread whipped cream evenly over ice cream ball; make grooves with spatula, to give a pumpkin-like appearance. Insert piece of citron in top, for a stem. Place pumpkin in freezer till needed. Set pumpkin on serving tray. Decorate with autumn leaves. Serve with chocolate sauce, if desired. Makes 16 servings.

FAKE WATERMELON

1 medium dark green watermelon	Chocolate chips
3½ gal. ice cream or sherbet	

Split melon in half lengthwise and remove all pink flesh from one half. You may make melon balls and freeze for later use. Only the hollowed half is used for this dessert. Slice a little off the outside bottom to keep melon from rocking. Chill the melon shell. Soften ice cream, fill melon with any combination of three kinds of ice cream or sherbets. Make certain you end up with a rosy color on top. Place in freezer. When ready to serve, sprinkle top with chocolate chips. Suggested combinations are: (1) chocolate chip, pistachio, and raspberry sherbet; (2) lime, pineapple, and raspberry sherbets. Serves 25-30.

MRS. CHARLES LOWRANCE, DRIVER, ARK.

FLAMING POLYNESIAN ICE CREAM

1½ qts. vanilla ice cream	1 T. cornstarch
2 4-oz. cans flaked coconut	¾ c. orange curaçao or cointreau
2 11-oz. cans mandarin oranges	

Day before party: Shape ice cream into balls and make sauce. Divide ice cream into 12 portions (this allows for some seconds). Spread coconut on large piece of wax paper. Roll ice cream quickly in coconut, forming each into a ball. Place on cookie sheet; place in freezer. Drain oranges; reserve syrup. Blend small amount of orange syrup with cornstarch. Stir in remaining syrup and ¼ cup liqueur. Cook over medium heat, stirring constantly, until thickened and bubbly. Remove from heat; add oranges. Cool; chill. Just before serving, arrange ice cream balls in serving dish or in coconut shells. Heat orange sauce until bubbly. Heat remaining ½ cup liqueur in small saucepan. Ignite. Pour carefully over hot orange sauce. Stir with large serving spoon; spoon flaming sauce over ice cream. Serve at once. Makes 8 servings.

MRS. JAMES GUY ROBBINS

FLOWERPOT ICE CREAM

1 qt. chocolate ice cream
6 marshmallows
48 small spice gumdrops
12 spearmint candy leaves

½ square baking chocolate, melted
48 round toothpicks
6 green plastic straws
6 small flowerpots

If clay pots are used, line with aluminum foil. If ceramic or paper cups are used, this is not necessary. Spoon ⅔ cup chocolate ice cream into each pot, packing it down well. Cut straws into 4-inch lengths. Stick a toothpick into ice cream and slide straw over it, making "stem" for flower. Cover with plastic wrap or tie in plastic bag, tying securely. Freeze at least 4 hours; or do several days ahead. To make each daisy you'll need 8 gumdrops, 4 toothpicks, 2 candy leaves and 1 marshmallow. (Slightly stale marshmallows work better.) Put 4 toothpicks through the side of each marshmallow so that ends stick out like 8 petals. Cut the sharp tips off to protect small children. Put gumdrop on each toothpick end. Paint faces on marshmallows with melted chocolate, or food coloring, using tiny brush or end of toothpick. Ten minutes before serving time take pots out of the freezer and let stand for 5 minutes. Attach marshmallow daisy to straw. Put toothpicks in leaves and stick into ice cream. Serves 6.

MRS. RANDOLPH TURNER

LEMON FLOWER POTS

1 recipe Frozen Lemon Cream
  (See Index)
½ doz. almond macaroons

Soda straws
1 bottle green sugar crystals

Line bottom of tiny flower pots with macaroons. Mound the firm lemon mixture in each pot and stand a straw in each. Return to freezer. When ready to serve, sprinkle green crystals on top and put a flower (fresh, paper, etc.) in each straw. Serves 10.

MRS. ANDREW JACKSON HAYS, JR.

CRÈME DE MENTHE BOMBE

1 gal. pineapple sherbet
1 c. green crème de menthe

1 pkg. frozen grated coconut
Fresh fruits to garnish

Allow sherbet to soften. Thoroughly mix sherbet with crème de menthe in electric mixer. Pour into 3-quart ring mold and refreeze. Day of party unmold on chilled silver tray allowing room for side decorations. Sprinkle coconut on top of sherbet ring. Refreeze on tray. At serving time garnish with fresh fruits such as strawberries, sliced peaches, blueberries, grapes, etc. Sprinkle confectioners' sugar on fruit and add sprigs of ivy or mint for greenery on tray. Serves 8-10.

MRS. J. R. HYDE, JR.

CHOCOLATE ALMOND DESSERT

1 pt. whipping cream
⅔ c. sweetened condensed milk
1 c. chocolate syrup

1 t. vanilla
¼ t. almond extract
½ c. toasted slivered almonds

Mix all but almonds in bowl and chill overnight. Whip until it stands in peaks. Add nuts, stir, then freeze. May be put in individual bowls or in one large bowl. Serves 6-8.

MRS. WILLIAM B. FONTAINE, JACKSON, MISS.

BUTTER CRUNCH CRUST
(For Ice Cream)

1 stick butter
¼ c. light brown sugar, packed

1 c. sifted flour
½ c. chopped pecans

Heat oven to 400°. Mix above ingredients with hands or pastry cutter. Spread flat in 9 x 11 x 2½-inch pan. Bake 15 minutes. Take from oven and stir with spoon. Save ¾ cup for topping. Immediately press rest of mixture on sides and bottom of pan. Cool and fill with ice cream. Then put remaining crumbs on top and freeze. Serves 8.

MRS. MARION BROWN

FROZEN LIME PIE

1 can sweetened condensed milk
¼ c. fresh lime juice
¼ c. fresh lemon juice
Grated lime and lemon rind
Few drops green food coloring
3 eggs, separated

¼ t. cream of tartar
9-in. graham cracker crust, chilled
½ pt. whipping cream
Shredded coconut
Maraschino cherries, optional

Combine milk, fruit juices, rind, food coloring. Beat egg yolks slightly and add to first mixture. Set aside. Beat egg whites until they peak and add cream of tartar. Fold gently into lemon-lime mixture. Pour into chilled crust. Freeze pie. Before serving, spread top with whipped cream, sprinkle outside edge with coconut, and dot "coconutted" edge with red cherries. Beautiful and delicious! Serves 6-7.

Graham Cracker Crust:
   1⅓ c. graham cracker crumbs
   ⅓ c. melted butter

⅓ c. dark brown sugar
½ t. cinnamon

Grease 9-inch pie pan well. Mix crumbs, brown sugar, cinnamon, and butter until crumbly. Press into pie pan with spoon. Chill until ready to use. Any crumb crust pie cuts more evenly (and you will have less breakage of crust) if you wrap a hot, steaming towel around bottom of pie pan just before slicing.

MRS. FRANK Z. JEMISON

MOCHA DESSERT

3 pkgs. ladyfingers
1 c. boiling water
2 T. instant coffee
1 lb. pkg. marshmallows

2 T. sherry
1½ pts. whipping cream
Grated chocolate to garnish

In top of double boiler, mix boiling water and coffee. Slowly add marshmallows, stirring constantly until they are dissolved. Cool. Add sherry. Whip cream and fold gradually into coffee mixture. Pour into spring-form pan that has been lined on sides and bottom with ladyfingers. Freeze. When serving, turn out of mold and top with grated chocolate. Serves 8.

MRS. THOMAS KEESEE. JR.

PEACH WHISKEY MOLD

9 whole macaroons (or 18 halves)
½ c. bourbon

½ gal. peach or vanilla ice cream

Crumble macaroons in bourbon (reserve a few whole macaroons) and let stand for a few minutes. Let ice cream soften. Mix ice cream and macaroons. Pour into a mold. Line the top of mold with reserved macaroons. Place in freezer. To serve, turn out of mold onto a dish. Serves 6-8.

MRS. KEITH LANE WATSON

RASPBERRY BOMBE

This gorgeous dessert should definitely be taken to the table to be admired before being sliced and served . . . .

1 4-5-qt. metal mold, chilled
½ gal. red raspberry sherbet
2-3 pts. pink peppermint or strawberry ice cream

1 c. whipping cream
½ c. chopped candied fruits or chopped maraschino cherries
Frosted green grapes

To mold: Line chilled mold with softened sherbet and freeze hard. Soften ice cream and add as a layer over sherbet. Freeze hard. Whip cream and fold in candied fruit. Fill center of mold with the whipped cream-fruit mixture and freeze hard. To serve: Invert mold and wrap with hot towel to loosen contents on chilled silver tray. Cover unmolded sherbet loosely with metal mold and return to freezer to harden (takes just a few minutes). Garnish with frosted green grapes (or holly leaves at Christmas). Slice like cake. Serves 12.
To frost grapes: Dip small bunches in slightly beaten egg whites, then into granulated sugar. Place on rack to dry.
Variation: The following may be added to the whipped cream in place of the ½ cup candied fruits: ¼ c. chopped candied fruits or maraschino cherries, ¼ c. chopped almonds, 3 T. powdered sugar, dash of salt, rum flavoring to taste. Fold preceding into whipped cream and fill center of mold as above.
Note: This may be made several days ahead of serving.

MRS. B. PERCY MAGNESS, JR.

HOMEMADE PEPPERMINT ICE CREAM

1 qt. milk	½ t. salt
1 lb. crushed peppermint candy	2 eggs, beaten
2 T. flour	2 qts. coffee cream
½ c. sugar	Chocolate sauce

Heat milk and peppermint candy to scalding. Mix the dry ingredients and then add the beaten eggs. Add this to the milk and cook slowly until thickened. Cool and add coffee cream and freeze in an ice cream freezer. Serve with Dot Jones' Chocolate Sauce (see Index).

MRS. ROBERT M. LEATHERMAN, COLUMBIA, MISS.

QUICK PEPPERMINT ICE CREAM

½ gal. vanilla ice cream   10-12 sticks peppermint candy

Soften ice cream. Crush candy with a rolling pin between sheets of waxed paper..Add candy to the ice cream and refreeze. Unbelievingly easy and delicious! Serve with hot or cold chocolate sauce. Serves 12.

A very passable coffee ice cream can be made in the above fashion by substituting instant coffee crystals for the peppermint candy. Add the coffee to taste. Stir ice cream till coffee crystals seem to dissolve. Refreeze.

MRS. FRANK T. DONELSON, JR.

MACAROON TORTONI

1 c. whipping cream	½ c. crumbled and sieved almond
¼ c. sifted confectioners' sugar	macaroons
1 egg white, stiffly beaten	2 t. sherry or dark rum

Whip cream and gradually fold in sugar. Fold in egg whites alternately with the macaroon crumbs and the sherry. Pack mixture into individual ramekins or paper muffin cups. Sprinkle tops with more macaroon crumbs, and freeze the tortonis. Garnish with half a maraschino cherry, if desired. Makes 6.

MEADE'S DELIGHT

3 chocolate squares	Coffee chip ice cream
2 c. sugar	½ pt. whipping cream
1 can evaporated milk	Crème de cacao to taste
1 pkg. chocolate wafers	Pecans

Melt chocolate squares in double boiler. Add sugar and milk, and cook until thickened. Cover the bottom of a dish with the chocolate wafers and pour the cooled chocolate sauce over the wafers. Cover sauce with ice cream and top with whipped cream flavored with crème de cacao. Sprinkle pecans on top. Place dessert in freezer. Remove shortly before serving time and cut into squares.

MRS. TROY R. DOUTHIT

FROZEN ORANGE CUPS

6 oranges
1 qt. French vanilla ice cream
1 can mandarin orange sections

Mint
Candied or maraschino cherries

Cut tops from oranges and reserve. Scoop out oranges with a spoon, being very careful not to go through the skin. Set ice cream in a bowl and allow to soften. With fork mash mandarin sections into ice cream. Refill oranges with mandarin cream and replace tops. Garnish with mint leaves. Wrap in foil and freeze for at least 4 hours. When ready to serve, remove foil and allow frost to form (takes about 5 minutes). Serve surrounded with mint and a few cherries. Serves 6.

MRS. CHESTER GELPI, NEW ORLEANS, LA.

TOFFEE ICE CREAM PIE

1¼ c. chocolate wafer crumbs
¼ c. melted butter
12 small Heath Bars
½ gal. vanilla ice cream
1 stick butter

1 large pkg. chocolate chips
2 c. powdered sugar
1 large can evaporated milk
2 t. vanilla

Mix chocolate wafer crumbs and melted butter and line a 13 x 8-inch pan. Pat down and put in refrigerator to harden. Refrigerate Heath Bars to harden. Crush. Soften vanilla ice cream and mix with Heath Bars. Put in crust and let stand in freezer overnight. **Sauce:** Melt butter and chocolate chips. Add powdered sugar and evaporated milk. Cook about 8 minutes or until thickened. Add vanilla. Serve warm over dessert. Serves 8-10.

MRS. RALPH HON

Cookies and Candies

LEMON SQUARES

2 c. flour
1 c. butter, no substitutes

½ c. powdered sugar

Let butter come to room temperature and blend with the flour and sugar. Press into a 9 x 13-inch pan and bake at 325° for 20 minutes or till brown around the edges. While crust is baking, mix together the following:

2 c. sugar
4 eggs, slightly beaten
4 T. fresh lemon juice
2 T. grated lemon rind

4 T. flour
2 t. baking powder
¼ t. salt

Pour above over baked crust and bake at 350° for 25 to 30 minutes. Cool and sift powdered sugar over top. Cut into small squares. Makes about 3 dozen.

MRS. JOHN W. BARRINGER

FUDGE CAKES

1 stick butter	4 eggs
2 1-oz. squares unsweetened chocolate	1 c. broken pecans
1 c. flour	Optional: 1 9-oz. chocolate bar
2 c. sugar	

Melt butter and chocolate in top of a double boiler. Sift together the flour and sugar. Add melted mixture and eggs to dry ingredients and mix well. Stir in nuts. Pour into a well-greased 2-quart rectangular baking dish. Bake at 325° for 45 minutes. After cake has cooled, confectioners' sugar may be sifted over all or cake can be iced.

Optional icing: Remove cake from oven 10 minutes before end of baking time. Break the chocolate bar into squares and place evenly over the hot cake. Return to oven for last 10 minutes of baking. Chocolate bar should soften sufficiently so that it can be spread over the cake with spatula. Allow cake to cool. This recipe is as easy as a mix, inexpensive and delicious. Freezes beautifully.

To serve: Cut into 12 squares and top with ice cream, or cut into 1-inch squares and serve as "nibbles". Makes 40 small squares.

MRS. GROOM LEFTWICH

VERNON'S SPICED NUTS

1 c. sugar	6 T. milk
1 t. cinnamon	1 t. vanilla
¼ t. salt	2 c. pecan halves

Mix sugar, cinnamon, salt and milk together in a saucepan. Boil to a soft ball stage (240° on candy thermometer). Remove from heat. Add vanilla and nuts. Stir until mixture is grainy and turn out on waxed paper. Separate nuts when cool and store in tight container.

BUTTER TOFFEE

1 c. butter	4 4½-oz. chocolate bars
1⅓ c. sugar	1 c. toasted, blanched almond bits
1 T. light corn syrup	1 c. finely chopped pecans
3 T. water	

Melt butter in large pan; add sugar, corn syrup and water. Cook to hard crack stage (300° on a candy thermometer), stirring occasionally. Add almonds. Spread in a greased 13 x 9 x 2-inch pan. Cool. Melt chocolate bars. Turn candy out on waxed paper and spread with ½ the chocolate. Sprinkle with ½ cup pecans. Cover iced side and invert. Spread remaining chocolate on the other side and sprinkle with remaining nuts. Break into pieces.

MRS. WILLIAM M. PREST

MY GRANDMOTHER'S BROWNIES

2 c. sugar	2 t. vanilla
½ c. cocoa	½ t. baking powder
½ lb. butter or margarine	2 c. pecans (optional)
4 eggs	Confectioners' sugar
1 c. sifted flour	

Mix cocoa and sugar. Cream cocoa mixture with butter. Beat in eggs one at a time. Beat in flour and then vanilla. Stir in baking powder last. Bake in 10 x 14-inch greased pan at 350° for about 40 minutes. When cool, sprinkle with confectioners' sugar and cut into squares. Makes about 35 brownies.

MRS. FRED BEESON

BUTTERFUDGE FINGERS

2 squares unsweetened chocolate	¾ c. flour
⅓ c. butter	½ t. salt
1 c. sugar	½ t. baking powder
2 eggs	½ c. chopped pecans

Preheat oven to 350°. Melt chocolate and butter in double boiler. Pour into a mixing bowl and beat in sugar and eggs. Sift dry ingredients together and add to chocolate mixture. Add nuts. Spread in greased 8-inch square pan and bake for 25 minutes. Cool before icing.

Topping:

¼ c. butter	1 t. vanilla
2 c. confectioners' sugar	1 sq. unsweetened chocolate
3 T. milk or cream	1 T. butter

Brown butter over medium heat, and blend in sugar, milk, and vanilla. Spread over brownies. Then melt chocolate square and 1 tablespoon butter. Cool and spread over first topping. Cut in 2 x 1-inch fingers. Makes 32.

MRS. WILLIAM M. PREST

RUSSIAN ROCKS

1 c. butter	1 t. cinnamon
1½ c. sugar	1 box raisins
3 eggs	1 box sugar-coated dates
3 c. flour	¾ lb. broken pecans
1 t. allspice	1 t. soda in 1 T. hot water

Cream butter and sugar; add beaten eggs. Mix flour, allspice and cinnamon. Add raisins, cut-up dates and broken pecans to flour mixture. Gradually add flour mixture to creamed mixture. Mix well. Thin occasionally with soda water. Bake small cookies on greased cookie sheets at 425°. When brown on bottom, run under broiler to get tops brown. Remove from cookie sheet and let cool. They become crisp when cool. Makes about 6 dozen.

MRS. FRANK G. BARTON

SCOTCH SHORTBREAD

1 c. softened butter, no substitutes   2½ c. sifted flour
½ c. plus 2 T. sugar

Cream butter. Add sugar while creaming. Stir in flour. Mix thoroughly with hands. Chill. Roll out between two pieces of waxed paper until about ¼-inch thick. Cut with small, fancy cutters. Make designs with the tines of a fork on the top. Place on ungreased baking sheet and bake in a 375° oven for 20 to 25 minutes. They are **not** supposed to be brown. Makes about 2 dozen.

MRS. HERBERT JORDAN, JR.

JAM TEA DAINTIES

1 c. flour, sifted   1 stick butter
2 T. confectioners' sugar

Filling:
    6-7 T. jelly, jam, preserves or
    baby food fruit desserts

Mix flour and sugar. Cut in butter with a pastry cutter until mixture is crumbly. Work dough into a ball in hands and knead until smooth. Pinch off about ½ tablespoon of dough at a time; work into a ball and mash into a circle in palm of hand. With lightly floured fingers, press circle of dough into a miniature muffin tin to make a tartlet shell ¼-inch thick. Fill each tart with a scant teaspoon of filling. Bake until golden around edges, about 12 minutes at 425°. Cool tarts at least 30 minutes on wire rack while still in pan. When cool, loosen very carefully around edges with knife and lift gently. Cool completely on wire racks. **Note:** If any openings are left in pastry the filling will leak through, the tarts will stick and they will be impossible to remove. An easier version of the above is to triple the recipe, drop by teaspoonfuls on a cookie sheet; make indenture on top of each and fill with jelly. Makes 16.

Fillings for the Jam Tea Dainties can be geared to your color scheme or the season of the year. For example, fill with mint and red currant jelly for serving at Christmas.

MRS. MILTON LYMAN KNOWLTON, JR.

ORIENTAL CHEWS

1½ c. sugar   1½ c. pecans
1⅛ t. baking powder   4½ T. candied ginger, finely
1⅛ c. flour   chopped
½ t. salt   3 eggs, separated
1½ c. chopped dates   Confectioners' sugar

Mix and sift dry ingredients. Add chopped dates, nuts and ginger. Beat egg whites and yolks separately. Stir beaten yolks into first mixture. Fold in egg whites. Put into 12 x 14-inch cookie sheet and bake at 275° for 20 minutes. Cut, while hot, into 1-inch squares and roll into balls at once. Then roll in powdered sugar. These freeze well. Makes 4 dozen.

MRS. J. G. GORDON, III

EGGNOG CAKES

¾ c. butter	3 t. baking powder
1¼ c. sugar	¼ t. salt
8 egg yolks	¾ c. milk
2½ c. sifted flour	1 t. vanilla

Cream butter and sugar until light and fluffy. Add yolks and blend well. Sift dry ingredients three times; then add to the sugar mixture, alternating with the milk and vanilla. Beat until smooth. Pour into 3 square pans lined with waxed paper. Bake 20 minutes at 350°. After cake cools, cut into small squares.

Whiskey sauce mix:

1 stick butter	½ c. chopped nuts
1 lb. sifted confectioners' sugar	½ box vanilla wafers, crushed
1 c. bourbon	

Cream butter and powdered sugar. Mix well and add whiskey and nuts. Dip squares of cake on all sides in bourbon mix and roll in crumb mix. Store in airtight containers. Improves with age. Do not taste for 3 days. Freezes well.

Angel food cake squares may be substituted for made-from-scratch cake. Brandy or sherry may be substituted for the bourbon.

MRS. ANNIE F. BROUGHER, SARDIS, MISS.

MISS RUTH'S PASTRY

1 c. butter	2 c. flour
1 c. sugar	1 c. broken nuts
2 egg yolks	¾ c. strawberry jam

Cream butter and sugar; fold in egg yolks, add flour and nuts. Divide mixture in half. Spread ½ in bottom of 10 x 6-inch pan. Top with jam and spread remaining pastry over this. Bake about 1 hour in a 325° oven. Cool and cut into squares. Sprinkle with powdered sugar, if desired. These freeze well. One stick butter and 1 stick margarine may be substituted for butter. Bake for first 30 minutes on second rack and raise to third oven rack for last 30 minutes. Makes 15 2-inch squares.

MRS. FRED TARKINGTON, JR.

POPCORN BALLS

5 qts. popped popcorn	½ c. light corn syrup
2 c. sugar	1 t. vinegar
1½ c. water	1 t. vanilla
½ t. salt	

Keep popped corn hot and crisp in slow oven (300-325°). Butter sides of saucepan. In it combine sugar, water, salt, corn syrup and vinegar. Cook to hard ball stage (250°). Add vanilla. Pour slowly over popped corn, stirring just enough to mix thoroughly. Lightly butter hands before shaping into balls. Wrap in clear plastic wrap and tie with gay ribbon. Makes 20 balls.

MRS. EDWIN P. VOSS

GINGERBREAD MEN

1 c. shortening
1 c. sugar
½ t. salt
1 egg
1 c. molasses
2 T. vinegar
5 c. sifted flour

1 T. ginger
1 t. ground cloves
1½ t. soda
1 t. cinnamon
Half and half cream
2 c. confectioners' sugar

Thoroughly cream shortening, sugar and salt. Stir in egg, molasses and vinegar. Beat well. Sift dry ingredients; stir into molasses mixture. Chill about 3 hours. On lightly floured surface roll to ⅛-inch thickness. Cut with gingerbread man cutter. Place 1-inch apart on greased cookie sheet. Bake at 375° about 6 minutes. Cool and remove to rack. When completely cool decorate with red hots and confectioners' icing. **Icing:** Add a little half and half cream to confectioners' sugar to make a paste that will go easily through a pastry tube. Makes 4 dozen 6-inch gingerbread men.

MRS. EDWIN P. VOSS

CHOCOLATE COOKIE BRITTLE

1 c. margarine
1½ t. vanilla
1 t. salt
1 c. sugar

2 c. sifted flour
1 6-oz. pkg. semi-sweet chocolate
  morsels
1 c. finely chopped walnuts

Preheat oven to 375°. Combine margarine, vanilla, and salt in bowl, and blend well. Gradually beat in sugar. Add flour, chocolate morsels, and ¾ cup walnuts; mix well. Press evenly into ungreased 15 x 10 x 1-inch pan. Sprinkle remaining ¼ cup walnuts over top and press lightly. Bake at 375°, for 25 minutes or until golden brown. Cool, then break into irregular pieces. Makes about 1¾ pounds.

MRS. GRIMES SNOWDEN

COCOONS

2 sticks butter
4 T. sugar
Pinch of salt

1 T. sherry
2½ c. sifted flour
1 c. chopped pecans

Cream butter and sugar until light and fluffy. Add salt and sherry. Continue to work until sherry disappears. Add flour gradually. Add nuts. Roll marble-sized pieces in hands and place on ungreased cookie sheet. Bake in preheated 275° oven for about 45 minutes. **Variation:** These may be rolled into log shapes or crescent shapes. Roll in powdered sugar. Makes 85 cocoons.

MRS. W. H. WILLEY, JR.

PEPPERMINT MERINGUES

2 egg whites	1 small pkg. chocolate chips
Dash of salt	Peppermint flavoring to taste
¼ t. cream of tartar	Few drops green food coloring
¾ c. sugar	

Preheat oven to 350° for ½ hour. Beat egg whites, salt and cream of tartar until frothy. Gradually add sugar and continue to beat for 15 minutes. Fold in chocolate chips, peppermint flavoring and green food coloring. Turn off oven. Put mixture on ungreased cookie sheet by spoonfuls and place in oven for 1½ hours. Do not open oven door during cooking time. **Variation:** Omit peppermint flavoring and food coloring and add 1 t. vanilla and ¼ c. chopped nuts to remaining ingredients. Makes about 36 meringues.

MRS. JAMES R. BROOKS

VIENNESE BROWNIES

1 4-oz. pkg. German's Sweet Chocolate	½ c. plus 1 T. unsifted flour
5 T. butter	1½ t. vanilla
1 3-oz. pkg. cream cheese	½ t. baking powder
1 c. sugar	¼ t. salt
3 eggs	½ c. chopped nuts
	¼ t. almond extract

Melt chocolate and 3 tablespoons butter over very low heat. Stir; then cool. Cream 2 tablespoons butter with cream cheese. Gradually add ¼ cup sugar, creaming till fluffy. Blend in 1 egg, 1 tablespoon flour, and ½ teaspoon vanilla. Set aside. Beat 2 eggs till lemon colored. Slowly beat in remaining ¾ cup sugar till mixture thickens. Add baking powder, salt, and ½ cup flour. Blend in chocolate mixture, 1 teaspoon vanilla, nuts, and almond extract. Spread half the chocolate batter in a greased 8- or 9-inch square pan. Top with cream cheese mixture. Spoon remaining chocolate batter over top. Then zigzag knife through batter to obtain marble effect. Bake at 350° about 35 to 40 minutes. Let cool and cut into 20 bars or 16 squares.

LAYER COOKIES

1 stick butter	1 12-oz. pkg. chocolate pieces
1 c. graham cracker crumbs	1 14-oz. can condensed milk
1 c. shredded coconut	1 c. chopped nuts

Melt butter in pan and sprinkle cracker crumbs over the butter. Next add a layer of coconut and a layer of chocolate pieces. Pour milk over all this and top with nuts. Do not stir. Bake for 30 minutes at 350° in 13 x 9 x 2-inch pan. **Note:** Butterscotch pieces may be substituted for the chocolate pieces. Let cool completely before cutting into 30 pieces.

MRS. WILLIAM M. PREST

MELTING MOMENTS

1 c. shortening or butter
1 c. brown sugar
1 egg, slightly beaten
1¾ c. sifted flour
½ t. salt

1 t. baking soda
½ t. baking powder
1 t. vanilla
½ c. chopped pecans

Melt shortening and let cool for about 15 minutes. Add brown sugar and egg, mixing well. Add flour, salt, soda and baking powder which have been sifted together. Mix well. Add vanilla and chopped pecans, folding all together. Drop by teaspoonfuls on ungreased cookie sheet and flatten with a fork. Cook at 350° for 8-10 minutes. Let cool before removing from pan. Makes about 5 dozen 2-inch cookies.

MRS. GUY E. JOYNER, JR.

STUFFED DATE DROPS

1 lb. (70) pitted dates
1 3-oz. pkg. pecans or walnuts
¼ c. shortening
¾ c. brown sugar
1 egg

1¼ c. flour
½ t. baking powder
½ t. soda
¼ t. salt
½ c. sour cream

Stuff dates with nut halves and set aside. Cream shortening and sugar until light. Beat in egg. Sift dry ingredients; add alternately with sour cream to creamed mixture. Stir in dates; drop on a greased cookie sheet, one date per cookie. Bake at 400° for 8-10 minutes. Cool and top with frosting.

Frosting:
Lightly brown ½ c. butter. Remove from heat. Gradually beat in 3 c. sifted confectioners' sugar, ¾ t. vanilla. Slowly add water until of spreading consistency (about 3 T.). Preparation time for these is long; advisable to make ahead and freeze. Makes 5½ dozen cookies.

MRS. JAMES R. BROOKS

SOUR CREAM FUDGE

2 c. brown sugar
1 c. white sugar
1 c. sour cream
3 squares unsweetened chocolate
¼ c. white corn syrup

¼ c. butter
Pinch of salt
1 c. chopped nuts
1 t. vanilla

Place sugars, sour cream, chocolate, and syrup in large pan and cook very slowly until soft ball stage, or 234° on candy thermometer. Remove from heat; stir in butter and let cool. Beat until it begins to harden. Add salt, nuts and vanilla. Pour into a buttered 8-inch square pan and allow to harden. Makes about 25 pieces.

MRS. HERRICK NORCROSS, FAIRVIEW FARMS, TYRONZA, ARK.

APRICOT ALMOND CAKES

½ c. butter	1½ c. flour
½ c. sugar	1 t. baking powder
1 t. almond extract	½ c. ground almonds
1 egg	Apricot jam

Cream together butter and sugar. Add almond extract and egg. Beat well; then fold in mixture of flour, baking powder and ground almonds. Work to stiff paste. Press ½ of mixture into greased 8-inch layer pan and spread thinly with apricot jam. Spread remainder of mixture over jam. Bake 30 minutes in 350° oven. Cool and cut into 16 2-inch squares.

MRS. J. DAVID HEUER

SAND TARTS

½ c. butter	2 t. baking powder
1 c. sugar	White of 1 egg
1 egg	1 T. sugar
1¾ c. flour	¼ t. cinnamon

Cream butter and add sugar slowly. Mix in well-beaten egg. Add flour that has been sifted with baking powder. Chill overnight. Roll ½ of dough at a time on floured board until ⅛-inch thick. Using cookie cutter, cut into desired shapes. Brush with white of egg and sprinkle with sugar and cinnamon. Put on buttered sheet and bake for 8 minutes at 350°. Makes about 30 cookies.

MRS. SYDNEY RIDDLE

CREAMY PRALINES

2 c. sugar	2 T. butter
1 t. soda	1 c. pecan halves
1 c. buttermilk	1 t. vanilla
¼ t. salt	

Mix sugar, soda, buttermilk and salt in saucepan and cook for 5 minutes over medium heat. Add butter and pecans and cook until mixture reaches soft ball stage. Remove from fire, cool and beat until creamy. Add vanilla, and drop by spoonfuls on waxed paper.

MRS. S. D. WOOTEN, III

ICEBOX COOKIES

1 lb. butter	6 c. sifted flour
1 lb. brown sugar	1 lb. pecans
1 egg	

Cream butter, add sugar, and mix well. Beat in egg, then sift in flour. Add pecans and mix all ingredients thoroughly. Divide into 4 parts, roll into logs in waxed paper and place in icebox overnight. Slice thin and place on cookie sheet. Bake for 10-15 minutes in 350° oven. Yield: 2-3 dozen cookies.

MRS. CHARLES D. RICHARDSON

FRUITED PECANS

2 c. sugar	Juice of ½ lemon (about 1½ T.)
1 T. flour	Juice of 1 orange (about ½ c.)
½ c. plus 2 T. milk	Grated peel of 1 orange
1 T. butter	4 c. pecan halves

Combine sugar and flour in saucepan. Add milk and butter and bring to a boil over moderate heat. Stir in juices and orange peel. Continue cooking until candy thermometer registers 236°, or until soft ball forms when a little of the mixture is dropped in cold water. Place pecans in 10-inch skillet; pour hot syrup mixture over nuts. Cook over moderate heat, stirring constantly, until syrup is creamy and nuts tend to separate (about 20-25 minutes). Pour nut mixture onto brown paper and separate nuts with two forks. Cool and store in tightly covered container. Yield: 6½ cups or 1¾ pounds.

Fruit Desserts

MELON BALLS IN WINE

1 watermelon	Pineapple chunks, fresh or canned
1 honeydew melon	1 12-oz. can frozen orange juice
2 cantaloupes	concentrate
Bing cherries (fresh or	1 c. dry white wine
canned, pits removed)	3 limes, for garnish

Cutting lengthwise, remove top ⅓ of watermelon. Scallop edge using a teacup as a guide, notch edges, or cut in the shape of a basket. Cut melon balls from pulp; then remove remaining pulp from shell, leaving shell intact. Cut melon balls from cantaloupe and honeydew. Combine all fruits with undiluted orange juice and wine. Toss lightly and refrigerate for at least 4 hours. Put fruit into watermelon basket and place on tray. Garnish "handle" of basket with wedges of lime (attach by spearing lime with toothpicks which have a maraschino cherry atop one end). Squeeze lime over serving of fruit. Melon basket may also be garnished with garlands of fresh ivy and fresh flowers (daisies, day lilies, etc.). For additional ways to shape a melon, see Garnishes.

MRS. T. RALPH PRICHARD

STRAWBERRIES PUCCINI

Fresh strawberries	Sugar
Fresh pineapple chunks	Grand Marnier
Freshly grated coconut (optional)	

Sprinkle fruit with sugar and marinate in Grand Marnier at least 4 hours. Allow ½ cup per serving.

MRS. CHARLES TIFFANY BINGHAM

FRESH FRUIT AND CHEESE PLATTER

On a large platter, arrange the following:

Block of soft yellow cheese with cheese knife, surrounded by various types of crackers.

Grapefruit half, scooped out and cut with a sawtoothed edge, overflowing with mandarin orange sections.

½ honeydew melon scooped out and filled to overflowing with balls of honeydew, cantaloupe and watermelon.

Bunches and bunches of green, black, and red grapes.

1 pineapple, cut lengthwise, filled with pineapple spears and unpeeled apple wedges.

Strawberries with stems left on.

Small container for toothpicks, for spearing fruit.

FRESH FRUIT IN WHITE WINE

4 peaches	**1 pt. strawberries**
3 pears	**Sugar**
2 apples	**¾ c. white wine**
2 bananas	

Arrange layers of fresh fruits, peeled and sliced rather thinly, sprinkling each layer with sugar before adding the next. Use peaches, pears, apples, bananas, strawberries, or any combination in season. Pour white wine over fruit and chill for 2 hours. In place of sugar and wine, you may use ¾ cup cold sugar syrup and 1 tablespoon kirsch. Serves 8.

MR. AND MRS. JOHN LARY

FRESH PEACHES IN CHAMPAGNE

Tulip champagne glasses	**Champagne**
Fresh peaches	

Prick whole peaches with fork. Place one peach in bottom of each champagne glass and fill with iced champagne. Guests sip their champagne, then eat the juicy peach.

MRS. WILLIAM NEELY MALLORY, MALLORY FARMS, CHATFIELD, ARK.

MARINATED MELON BALLS

Melon balls, preferably honeydew	**Lemon juice**
Crème de menthe	

Place bowl of melon balls over crushed ice and pour a bit of chilled crème de menthe over all. Sprinkle with lemon juice. Beautiful served in a hollow stem champagne glass . . . eat melon balls and sip remaining liqueur.

Variation: (1) Marinate honeydew in port for 1 hour. To serve: Garnish with sprigs of mint. (2) Soak variety of melon balls in rum and lime juice. Dust with powdered sugar.

GRAPES WITH BROWN SUGAR CRUST

Remove green **seedless** grapes from stem, wash and roll in paper towel to absorb excess water. Stir in sour cream until each grape is coated. Pack in a flat dish with sides. Chill for 4 hours. Serve topped with brown sugar crust and curaçao. This recipe is relative—it can be made to serve as many as you wish—you only need more grapes and sour cream.

Brown Sugar Crust:

Butter a cookie sheet well. With fingertips, pat medium brown sugar on sheet to make a thin lacy layer. You will be able to see the tin in some places through sugar. Make a paper pattern the size of top of dish to be used for grapes and lay this pattern on the brown sugar. Remove extra sugar with spatula and discard pattern. Put cookie sheet under broiler until sugar is slightly burned and glazed. You must watch this every second. Take out and when slightly cool, begin loosening edges with a spatula. Crust will appear similar to a large praline. It is very brittle, so care must be used when removing. To serve: The crust is placed on top dish containing any fresh fruit mixed with sour cream, or on top crème brûlée, applesauce or ice cream. Pour a little curaçao over each serving. Crust can be frozen and reheated slightly before serving.

MRS. CHARLES H. McGEE, BRUIN PLANTATION, HUGHES, ARK.

WINE-FROSTED GRAPES

4 bunches large, white seedless
  grapes
8 egg whites
4 T. white wine

Sifted, powdered sugar
Mint leaves and flowers to
  garnish

Blend wine and egg whites with a wire whisk until almost frothy. Pinch off small bunches of grapes, no more than 5-6 per bunch. Dip and coat with wine mixture. Roll in powdered sugar. Place on waxed paper in the refrigerator to harden. Mound on platter and garnish.

MRS. CHARLES TIFFANY BINGHAM

BANANAS FLAMBÉ

2 T. brown sugar
1 T. butter
1 ripe banana, peeled and
  sliced lengthwise

Dash cinnamon
½ oz. banana liqueur
1 oz. white rum

Melt brown sugar and butter in flat chafing dish. Add banana and sauté until tender. Sprinkle with cinnamon. Pour banana liqueur and rum over all and flambé. Baste with warm liquid until flame burns out. Serve immediately over vanilla ice cream. Serves 1.

This dessert is a good one to make at the table but be sure to have all your ingredients together before you start.

MRS. WILLIAM K. STODDARD, RIVERDALE PLANTATION, HUGHES, ARK.

FRUITS WITH MOLDED CONFECTIONERS' SUGAR

To serve with fresh fruits . . . Any size mold can be used, from a jigger glass (for an individual serving) to a 3-4 cup decorative mold (for centering a luscious tray of assorted fresh fruits). Sift confectioners' sugar into mold. Level off top of sugar even with top of mold. Drop mold several times, ever so gently, on counter top to settle sugar. Add additional sugar to again fill mold to top. Place serving plate or tray on top of mold. Holding mold securely, invert mold onto tray. Do not remove mold from sugar yet. Surround mold with fruit for dipping. Gently tap mold with spoon or knife handle. Remove mold from sugar. Voilà! Gorgeous. This is so easy to do. Mold can be filled the day before and unmolded at serving time. One thought: The mold is very fragile and will begin to crumble when the first piece of fruit is dipped into it. Nevertheless, its initial beauty and ease of preparation make it well worth doing.
Variation: Press sifted dark brown sugar into bottom of mold, enough to cover bottom of mold about ½-inch deep. Press firmly into place with fingers. Proceed as above. You'll get your molded confectioners' sugar with a lovely brown crown.

MRS. MILTON LYMAN KNOWLTON, JR.

BANANAS au RHUM

1 stick butter	1 T. lemon juice
1 c. sugar	Grated rind of 1 lemon
¼ c. water	1 t. vanilla
¼ c. rum	6 small bananas

In a heavy skillet, melt butter; then add sugar and water. Cook till reduced to a heavy syrup. Add rum, lemon juice, rind, and vanilla. Peel and halve bananas lengthwise. Place in hot syrup and cover. May be warmed whenever ready to serve. Serves 6.

MRS. CHESTER GELPI, NEW ORLEANS, LA.

BAKED PEARS

10-12 firm pears	1 T. cinnamon
4 T. vinegar	1 c. water
1 T. salt	4 T. lemon juice
2 c. sugar	1 t. vanilla
2 T. flour	Butter

Peel, core and quarter pears. Cover with water containing vinegar and salt; drain. Do not rinse. Place in boiler, cover with fresh water and cook until fork goes in fairly easily. Drain. Arrange pears in a buttered flat baking dish. Sprinkle over pears a mixture of sugar, flour and cinnamon. Combine water, lemon juice, and vanilla and pour over pears. Dot with butter. Cook 45 minutes in 400° oven until syrup thickens. Brown in broiler at last minute. Serves 8.

MRS. WILLIAM K. STODDARD, RIVERDALE PLANTATION, HUGHES, ARK.

CHERRIES JUBILEE

1 lb. can pitted dark sweet cherries	¼ c. brandy, Kirsch or cherry brandy
¼ c. sugar	Vanilla ice cream
2 T. cornstarch	

Drain cherries, reserving syrup. Cherries should measure 2 cups. In saucepan, blend sugar and cornstarch; gradually stir in reserved cherry syrup, mixing well. Cook and stir over medium heat until the mixture thickens and bubbles. Remove from heat; stir in cherries. Place mixture in top of double boiler or chafing dish. Keep hot over water heated just to boiling. Heat liqueur in small metal pan with long handle. (If desired, pour heated brandy into large ladle.) Carefully ignite heated brandy and pour over hot cherry mixture. Stir to blend liqueur into sauce and serve immediately over ice cream. Makes 2 cups of sauce. (For a dramatic effect at your dinner table, dim the lights just before flaming the sauce.) Serves 6-8.

MRS. DENBY BRANDON, JR.

FRUIT THAÏS

1 lb. fresh or canned peaches	½ cup sherry
1 lb. fresh or canned apricots	1 c. brown sugar
1 lb. fresh or canned pineapple chunks	1 c. slivered almonds
1 lb. fresh or canned pears	1 doz. or more dry macaroons, crumbled
1 lb. fresh or canned cherries	1 stick butter or oleo
1 lb. bananas	Brandy (optional)

Drain and dice fruit. Marinate in sherry at least 2 hours. Drain fruit and arrange in baking dish in layers, sprinkling each layer with sugar, almonds, macaroons, and pats of butter. Cover top with crumbs and bake 20 minutes at 350°. If desired, warm some brandy, pour over dish and ignite. Serves 16.

MRS. ROBERT DONNEL WARREN

RUBY FRUIT

½ qt. ginger ale	2 #2½ cans pears or peaches or pineapple chunks or mixed
Juice of 1 orange and 1 lemon	
1 stick cinnamon	1½ c. currant jelly
2-3 whole cloves	Red food coloring

Simmer ginger ale, juices, cinnamon and cloves for 4-6 minutes and pour over fruit in baking dish. Let stand for 2 hours, then bake for 30 minutes in preheated 300° oven. Cool and drain. Remove fruit to serving bowl. Beat currant jelly and add enough red coloring to give ruby color. Blend with 2 tablespoons of the hot juice. Spoon over fruit so each piece is coated. Chill. Serves 8.

Mock Devonshire cream:

1 c. whipping cream	½ c. sour cream
2 T. powdered sugar	1 T. vanilla

Whip cream and fold in other ingredients. Serve fruit topped with Devonshire cream.

MR. JOHN FITZMAURICE

PEACH FRITTERS WITH ORANGE SAUCE

1 c. sifted flour
1 t. salt
1 t. baking powder
2 eggs
1 c. milk

2 T. melted butter or margarine
6 firm, ripe, unblemished peaches
¼ c. sugar
Oil or shortening for frying

Sift flour, salt and baking powder into mixing bowl. Beat eggs well; beat in milk and butter. Stir into dry ingredients gradually, until batter is smooth. Let stand at room temperature for 1 hour. Plunge peaches into boiling water; remove and plunge them into cold water. Slip skins off peaches; then halve and remove stones. Cut each half into 4 equal-sized wedges. Place peaches in bowl; sprinkle with sugar. Let stand until batter is ready to use. Put enough oil or shortening into skillet or deep, heavy saucepan to measure 1½ inches deep when heated. Dry peach wedges on paper towels. Dip in batter with fork or tongs; let excess batter drip off into bowl. Fry a few at a time, in hot fat (375°) for 3-5 minutes or until golden brown. Drain on paper towels. Serve hot with Orange Sauce. These must be served immediately. Makes 8 servings.

Orange Sauce:

½ c. sugar
1 T. cornstarch
1 c. sweet wine

1 c. orange juice
1 T. grated orange rind

Combine sugar and cornstarch in small saucepan. Stir in ¼ cup wine gradually until mixture is smooth. Stir in remaining wine and orange juice. Bring to a boil over low heat, stirring occasionally. Cook 1 minute. Remove from heat. Stir in orange rind. Serve warm. **Note:** Can be made the day before and reheated. Makes about 2 cups.

MRS. JAMES GUY ROBBINS

BAKED ALASKA SERVED IN PINEAPPLES

4 small ripe pineapples
Rum

4 pts. pineapple or vanilla
ice cream

Cut pineapples lengthwise. Hollow out, discarding hard core. Cut remaining pineapple into bite-sized chunks and soak in rum to cover for 2 hours. Mix pineapple with softened ice cream and put in freezer to harden. Do not allow pineapple ice cream to freeze hard. When ready to serve, mound into pineapple shells, cover with meringue and bake in 425° oven until meringue is brown. Serve at once.

Meringue:

4 egg whites
Pinch of salt

½ t. lemon juice
1 c. confectioners' sugar

Beat egg whites and salt until frothy. Add lemon juice and continue to beat until whites are stiff. Gradually beat in sugar and continue beating until meringue is thick and glossy. Spread thickly over the ice cream and swirl into peaks. **Note:** Depending on size of pineapples, this might not be enough meringue. Cover the green spikes of the pineapple with foil when baking to prevent their burning. Serves 8.

MRS. CHARLES H. McGEE, BRUIN PLANTATION, HUGHES, ARK.

Beverages

CITRUS PUNCH WITH FROZEN FLOWERS OR FRUIT

12 c. water
9 c. grapefruit juice
3 c. lemon juice

6 c. orange juice
4 c. sugar

Pour water into sectioned ice trays and add one of the following fruits to each section: red or green maraschino cherries, mandarin orange sections, pineapple chunks, lemon or lime slices, mint sprigs. Use one fruit or any combination. Combine remaining ingredients for punch, making certain sugar is thoroughly dissolved. Chill. Place frozen cubes in bottom of punch bowl and pour punch over. A frozen flower ring may also be made for your punch bowl. Place flowers such as open roses and azuratum in a ring mold with the blooms down. To secure, fasten tape from outside rim to inside rim, wrapping around stem. Cut excess stem. Fill ¾ of ring with water and freeze. Before serving, dip mold into warm water and turn out into punch bowl for a floating bouquet. Punch serves 35.

MULLED CITRUS PUNCH

Excellent for breakfast or brunch or in the evening with vodka or rum.

¼ c. sugar
¼ c. water
6 whole cloves

2 2-in. sticks cinnamon
1 qt. orange juice
2 c. cider

Make a syrup of the first 4 ingredients by simmering 10 minutes. Remove spices. Add orange juice and cider. Serve from a tureen. Float clove-spiked oranges in punch for decoration and additional flavor. Makes 12 4-ounce servings.

MRS. RICHARD DIXON

COFFEE PUNCH

1 pt. milk
2 qts. strong coffee, cooled
2 t. vanilla
½ c. sugar

½ pt. whipping cream
1 qt. vanilla ice cream
Freshly grated nutmeg

In a large pitcher, combine milk, coffee, vanilla and sugar. Stir and chill until party time. Place ice cream in punch bowl. Pour coffee mixture over ice cream. Cover ice cream with whipped cream and top with nutmeg. Serve in punch cups. **Variation:** Whipped cream may be flavored with brandy or sherry. Chocolate ice cream may be substituted for the vanilla. Makes 10 5-ounce servings.

MRS. THOMAS KEESEE, JR.

ORANGE PUNCH

6 c. fresh orange juice	2 qts. orange sherbet
1 c. fresh lemon juice	4 c. ginger ale, chilled
½ c. maraschino cherry juice	Garnish: orange slices centered
½ c. sugar	with maraschino cherries

Combine juices with the sugar. Chill. To serve: Place sherbet in punch bowl and pour ginger ale and fruit juices over sherbet. Float orange slices in the punch. Serves 25.

SHERBET PUNCH

2 32-oz. cans frozen orange juice	4 6-oz. cans frozen pineapple juice
4 18-oz. cans frozen lemonade	1 gallon pineapple sherbet

Add water to juice concentrates according to directions on cans. Chill and pour over sherbet just before serving. Recipe may be cut in half. Serves 50.

MRS. J. HAL PATTON

FRUIT PUNCH

1 qt. tea	1 pt. lemonade
1 qt. cranberry juice	2 qts. ginger ale
1 qt. orange juice	

Mix together well. Inexpensive and tasty for a large group. Serves 30.

MRS. BARCLAY McFADDEN

REAL FRENCH CHOCOLATE

½ c. semi-sweet chocolate pieces	1 t. vanilla
½ c. corn syrup	1 pt. whipping cream
¼ c. water	2 qts. milk

Over low heat, melt chocolate with corn syrup and water and place in bowl in refrigerator until cool; then add vanilla. This can be done early in the day. About an hour before serving, begin to whip cream, adding the chocolate mixture **as you whip.** You will achieve mounds of heavy chocolate, which you can put in a crystal or silver bowl in the refrigerator. Before serving, heat milk to scalding, and place in a silver coffee pot or urn. Place bowl of chocolate and hot milk on serving tray on table, and fill each person's cup ¾ full of chocolate. Then add enough milk to dissolve the chocolate. Each guest will then stir her own. Serves 20.

MRS. CECIL HUMPHREYS

PEPPERMINT EGGNOG PUNCH

1 pt. soft peppermint ice
   cream
2 c. dairy eggnog
1 pt. 12-oz. bottle club soda
1 c. whipping cream

⅓ c. crushed peppermint
   candy
Few drops red food coloring
16 peppermint sticks

Spoon ice cream into punch bowl. Add eggnog and chilled club soda, mixing well. Stir in food coloring. Spoon whipped cream over surface. Put stick of peppermint in each cup to be used as a stirrer. Top each serving with a little crushed peppermint. Makes 16 4-ounce servings.

MRS. ROSS LYNN

EGGNOG

1 qt. milk
2 c. sugar
1 qt. whipping cream
6 eggs, separated

½ pt. brandy
¾ pt. rum
1½ pts. bourbon
Freshly grated nutmeg

This eggnog should be made at least the day before serving. Combine milk and sugar and stir till sugar dissolves. Whip cream. Separate eggs and beat yolks well. Using low speed on electric mixer, add brandy very, very slowly to yolks. In the same manner add the rum, then the bourbon. Add sugar-milk solution to the yolk mixture. Beat egg whites till they hold soft peaks. Fold whipped cream into liquor mixture; then lightly fold in egg whites. Sprinkle with nutmeg. Chill and serve. Makes 1 gallon.

MRS. JAMES W. WRAPE, COLLIERVILLE, TENN.

MINT ICED TEA

3 c. boiling water
12 large sprigs mint

4 tea bags

Combine above ingredients and let cool. Remove tea bags and mint.

1 c. orange juice
¼ c. lemon juice

1 c. sugar
6 c. water

Combine juices with sugar and water. Stir to dissolve sugar. Strain mint-tea and combine both mixtures. Pour over ice and garnish with an orange slice or a sprig of mint. Serves 6-8.

MRS. THOMAS KIMBROUGH

INSTANT SPICED TEA

1 large jar Tang
¾ c. instant tea with lemon
1½ c. sugar

1½ t. ground cloves
1½ t. ground cinnamon

Combine all ingredients. To serve, use 2 teaspoons of mixture for each cup of boiling water. Mixture will keep in jar for use at any time.

MRS. WADE CREEKMORE, JR., MEADVILLE, MISS.

WITCHES' BREW

8 c. sweet cider
4 sticks cinnamon

16 cloves
Sugar to taste

Boil mixture in half gallon pot for 10 minutes. Strain and serve while hot in orange mugs or store-bought Halloween cups. Makes 8 cups.

MRS. TED LEWIS

CAESAR'S BOWL

2 c. diced pineapple
½ c. simple syrup
½ c. lemon juice
½ c. orange juice
1½ c. unsweetened pineapple
  juice

1⅓ c. peach brandy
2 fifths rum, one light and
  one dark
Block of ice
2 qts. soda or 2 bottles champagne
1 pt. sliced strawberries

Place pineapple, sugar syrup, fruit juices, peach brandy and rum in punch bowl. Add block of ice. Pour in soda or champagne and strawberries. Makes 40 servings.

For an added touch, freeze an upright fresh pineapple in the block of ice, leaving crown exposed. Float ice block in Caesar's Bowl. Decorate exposed crown with tiny gold ball ornaments.

MRS. GILES COORS, JR.

MRS. PHILLIPS' CHRISTMAS PUNCH

1 large can cranberry juice
1 qt. ginger ale

1 qt. light rum

Combine all ingredients. Makes 25 glasses.

MRS. JOHN S. PHILLIPS

ICED COFFEE PUNCH

1 gal. strong coffee
¼ c. Jamaican rum
½ gal. coffee cream

1 c. sugar
1 qt. fudge ripple ice cream

Make coffee in advance, add sugar and allow to cool in refrigerator. Just prior to serving, add coffee cream and rum and pour over ice cream. Serves 20-24.

MRS. CHARLES P. OATES, JR.

MILK PUNCH

1½-oz. brandy, bourbon,
  or rum
1 c. milk (or half and half)

1 t. sugar
Crushed ice

Combine ingredients in shaker. Shake well. Pour into glass; sprinkle with nutmeg. One serving.

MRS. JAMES GUY ROBBINS

PLANTERS PUNCH

Crushed ice
1 jigger orange juice
2 jiggers pineapple juice

1 jigger water with 1 T. sugar
1 jigger light rum
1 jigger dark rum

Mix first 5 ingredients together. Pour dark rum on top. Garnish with cherry or orange slice. One serving.

MR. WILLIAM METCALF PREST

ROMAN PUNCH

1½ fifths gin
1½ fifths white label rum
36 oz. fresh lemon juice

36 oz. fresh orange juice
18 oz. simple syrup

Mix, stir well and pour over cracked ice. Approximately 40 servings.

MRS. GILES COORS, JR.

RUM PUNCH I

2 large cans frozen orange juice
3 small cans frozen limeade
2 small cans frozen lemon juice
1 8-oz. bottle pure lime juice
1 qt. water

½ lb. confectioners' sugar
1½ fifths light rum
1 small block ice
1 box strawberries
1½ qts. sparkling water

Mix all the fruit juices with the water. Add sugar to taste. Add rum and taste again. Place block of ice in a punch bowl and pour punch over ice. Add strawberries. Just before serving, add sparkling water. Serves 50.

Guaranteed to make the conversation sparkle!

MRS. JOHN S. KING, JR.

RUM PUNCH II

1⅛ c. water
1⅛ c. sugar
1½ c. lemon juice
1½ c. grapefruit juice
5 c. orange juice

6 c. pineapple juice
2 qt. water
1 fifth dark rum
1 fifth light rum

Mix water and sugar for simple syrup. Boil for at least 5 minutes. Chill. Mix simple syrup and all remaining ingredients. Refrigerate for at least one hour to blend. Pour into punch bowl over a block of ice or ice ring (in which colorful fruit pieces or non-toxic fresh flowers have been frozen). Makes 75 servings.

GLEU VEIN
(Hot Wine)

1 qt. Burgundy
4 oranges, sliced and
    studded with 6 cloves

4 lemons, sliced
3 cinnamon sticks, in pieces
1 c. sugar

Simmer wine, add fruit, spices, and sugar. Stir to dissolve sugar. Let stand 10 minutes over low heat. Remove fruit pieces and cloves. Serve in heavy mugs. Best served when weather is chilly or cold. Serves 4-6.

MRS. BYRON WINSETT

For many years Mr. Clarence Moody has at Christmas brewed a punch that through
time has come to be known as Clarence Moody's Holiday Punch. He has mailed the
recipe over the years to every state in the Union and many foreign countries. Here are
his two versions . . . one for consumption, the other is simply for a pleasant Christmas-
time odor.

CLARENCE MOODY'S HOLIDAY PUNCH
(For Consumption)

3 pieces ginger	6 small oranges
1 3-in. stick cinnamon	1 gal. apple cider
8 whole cloves	1 qt. pineapple juice
3-4 cardamon seeds	½ t. salt
6 lemons	

Tie spices in a bag of fine cheesecloth. Peel and cut the lemons and oranges
into thin slices and add to the combined cider and pineapple juice. To this
mixture add the spice bag and bring to a very low simmering boil. Stir as it
simmers for 15 minutes; then add the salt and stir vigorously. Serve hot. Just
prior to serving add as much rum as desired. This is similar to the old English
Wassail-type punch. Makes 40-50 servings.

CLARENCE MOODY'S HOLIDAY ODOR PUNCH
(Not For Consumption)

1 qt. pineapple juice	3 3-in. sticks cinnamon
1 qt. water	16 whole cloves
1 qt. apple cider	1 t. allspice
4 pieces ginger	1-2 t. pickling spice

Combine all ingredients in a large cooking kettle and bring to boiling. Boil
for several minutes. Reduce heat and simmer, allowing house to be filled with
a wonderful Christmastime odor.

CHAMPAGNE PUNCH

1 lemon, sliced thin	4 jiggers brandy
1 orange, sliced thin	4 jiggers apricot liqueur
1 qt. fresh strawberries	4 bottles champagne
4 pieces cucumber rind	1 pt. bottle soda water

Pour all ingredients over a block of ice in a punch bowl. Stir and ladle into
glasses. Has a flavor very much like French 75. (Fresh raspberries or frozen
strawberries or raspberries may be substituted for the fresh strawberries.)
Makes 32 servings.

MISS JO ANN CULLUM, FORT WORTH, TEX.

LA FONDA SANGRIA

4 lemons	3 c. cracked ice
4 navel oranges	2 c. red or white table wine,
6 T. water	chilled
1 c. plus 2 T. sugar	2 c. carbonated water, chilled

Slice lemons into round slices. Cut oranges into thin slices, then cut slices in half. Put half the fruit in the bottom of each of two 2-quart pitchers. In a small saucepan, combine water and sugar. Cook over moderate heat until mixture comes to a boil and sugar is dissolved, stirring constantly. Cool. Pour half the sugar syrup, 1½ cups cracked ice and 1 cup wine into each pitcher. Add 1 cup carbonated water to each. Stir with a wooden spoon to blend mixture. Serve in 14 to 16-ounce glasses with a slice of lemon and orange in each glass. Very good with fondue. Serves 6.

MRS. JAMES GUY ROBBINS

MAY WINE

1 gal. Vino Rosso	2 qts. fresh strawberries
2 qts. ginger ale	

Any jug-type red wine may be substituted for the Vino Rosso. Wash berries but do not cut or remove stems. Chill all ingredients; then combine. Fifty servings.

MRS. BARCLAY McFADDEN

MIMOSA

1 part champagne	1 part orange juice

Combine and fill chilled champagne glasses.

MRS. RICHARD RANSON

MARTINI OR MANHATTAN BOWL

Hollow out a shallow cavity in center of a block of ice. Float block of ice in punch bowl. Fill the hollow with olives and fill the punch bowl with Martinis; or fill the hollow with cherries and the punch bowl with Whiskey Sours or Manhattans.

MRS. WILLIAM NEELY MALLORY, MALLORY FARMS
CHATFIELD, ARK.

BLOODY MARY

1 32-oz. can tomato juice	1 t. sugar
8 oz. vodka	1 T. salt
2 T. Pickapeppa Sauce	Juice of 4 limes
4 T. Worcestershire	6 dashes Tabasco

Mix together and serve over ice. Serves 8.

MR. WILLIAM METCALF PREST

BULL SHOT

1 oz. beef consommé
1 oz. Snap-E-Tom Tomato
   Cocktail
Dash bitters

Dash Worcestershire
Dash seasoned salt
Dash seasoned pepper
Dash Fines Herbes

Combine all ingredients and chill thoroughly. To serve, add jigger of vodka and twist of lemon. One serving.

MRS. C. NILES GROSVENOR, III

FROZEN DAIQUIRI

1 can frozen limeade
1 limeade can of light rum

1 tray ice, shaved or crushed
Cherries

Place limeade concentrate, rum, and ice in blender and blend until consistency of snow. Serve topped with a cherry. Serves 4.

Peach daiquiri: Add 4 fresh or canned peach halves to blender for 4 servings.
Banana daiquiri: Add 1⅓ ripe bananas to blender for 4 servings.
Strawberry daiquiri: Add to blender package frozen or ½ pint fresh strawberries per 4 servings.

MRS. ROBERT NORCROSS, FAIRVIEW FARMS
TYRONZA, ARK.

DEPRESSION COCKTAIL

9 jiggers gin
3 jiggers sweet Italian
   vermouth
2 jiggers grenadine

3 lemons, or 2 lemons and
   2 limes, juiced
White of 1 egg

Shake all ingredients together with cracked ice. Serves 8.

My uncle gave me this recipe many years ago, saying he had used it during the early 30's when a bottle needed to be stretched. It is surprisingly potent.

MRS. CARRUTHERS LOVE

BLUEGRASS MINT JULEP

For one serving:
   3-4 mint leaves
   1 t. sugar
   1 t. water

Shaved ice
2 jiggers bourbon whiskey

Chill silver julep cups or 12-ounce glasses in refrigerator. When cup is chilled, mix mint leaves with sugar and water in julep cups. Fill cup with finely shaved ice. Pour in one jigger of whiskey and energetically stir until ice has dropped one or two inches and frost begins to appear. Fill remainder of julep cup with crushed ice and pour in another jigger of whiskey. Decorate with sprigs of mint and serve with short straws.

MRS. JOHN FINLEY, JR.

IRISH COFFEE

1 jigger Irish whiskey
Black coffee
3 cubes sugar

1 heaping t. pure or
whipped cream

Into a large, warm whiskey glass, pour Irish whiskey and fill ¾ full with strong, black coffee. Add sugar. Top with cream, poured gently over a teaspoon. Do not stir. Delicious! One serving.

MRS. BEN C. ADAMS, JR.

HOMEMADE KAHLUA

1½ c. instant coffee
3 c. boiling water
6 c. sugar

1 vanilla bean
Fifth of vodka

Dissolve coffee in boiling water, add sugar and vanilla bean. Let cool and add vodka. Pour in gallon jug, seal and let stand for 30 days. Serve as a dessert sauce or as a liqueur.

MRS. MARY J. RYLEY, LA JOLLA, CAL.

MARGARITA

A quick way to warm up a party . . .

1 part tequila
1 part triple sec liqueur

1 part fresh lime juice

Rub edge of glass with fresh lemon and dip edge in salt. Mix the above ingredients and serve in salt-rimmed glass over cracked ice. One serving.

MRS. RICHARD DIXON

SHERRY SOUR

1 bottle California
dry sherry

1 6-oz. can pink or regular
lemonade concentrate

Combine ingredients in pitcher and mix well. Store in refrigerator at least overnight. Serve over ice cubes. Makes 9 to 10 3-ounce servings.

MRS. JACK DALY

24 HOUR COCKTAIL

12 lemons
Fifth of whiskey
Equal amount of water

1½ c. sugar
Dash of salt

Squeeze lemons and save rind. Boil water, add sugar and let it dissolve. Add lemon rinds and boil 5 minutes. Add whiskey, lemon juice and pinch of salt. Cover and let stand till cool. Strain and keep in refrigerator. Serve over ice.

MRS. T. GRIMES SNOWDEN

Setting the Scene

Table Settings

One of the main ingredients for any party is your table. Beautifully and ingeniously set, the scene and your food will seem all the more delicious. Always plan ahead in order to have time to assemble what you need. Set the table the day before, or, better yet, two days ahead. Dress your table as painstakingly as you do yourself, and **don't be afraid to improvise.** Every party is an opportunity for adding a new twist, and the prettiest tables are those that follow no rules but mix formal with informal, pattern with pattern, and color with color.

Of course, there are certain basics, such as your china, crystal, and silver, that never change from party to party; but many are the ways to use them over and over, with new variations. All you need is a little inspiration and a pinch of imagination. Take your cue from the season . . . a certain color, what is growing in your garden, a picture in a magazine, or from the food being served, as they do in some European countries. For example, if a seafood is the main course, feature seashells and salmon pink snapdragons or carnations on a blue tablecloth . . . a fitting background for the "fruits-de-la-mer" menu. Then think! Think fruit, vegetables, trailing ivy, porcelain figures, or a big china soup tureen. If your table becomes a bit crowded, move your centerpiece off center or, instead of a centerpiece, entwine your chandelier with greenery to resemble a hanging basket. Did you ever use individual bouquets at each place instead of one big one? Did you ever consider hanging a bouquet **over** a crowded sideboard rather than setting it on the sideboard itself? Where colors are concerned, almost anything goes. Make the table setting a fantasy of colors or make it a soothing monochromatic scene.

Go on a new-ways-to-use-old-things kick. Forage through the attic and storage closets . . . but make certain you carry your imagination with you. Tucked away and almost forgotten might be a random cache of demitasse cups, salt cellars, quilts, or pressed glass mugs. Matched sets are totally unimportant. Fill the cups with flowers and use as individual bouquets at each place setting. Quilts make different and interesting tablecloths. Mugs may be used for cold soups or cocktails. A set of miniature mugs can be used for after-dinner cordials. A tarnished brass urn can be cleaned and used for punch or gazpacho.

Your table linens need attention and will serve to unify your entire setting. If your dining table is very old and beautiful, you need no covering at all . . . only its highly polished surface. Tablecloths, centerpieces, can come from anywhere. The lovely floral sheets on the market today are grand. Should you find yourself limited to only one cloth, don't despair. Change its look by using a runner down the middle; a floral print in spring, a tweed or plaid in autumn, even odd rolls of wallpaper can be used. When choosing your cloth or place mats, remember to look for a relationship in scale, color, or motif to your china. Blue willow china looks marvelous on a bold bandana print cloth or on gingham checks which play up its country look. Complement your plain white gold-bordered china with a sheer overcloth of white organdy and a pastel pink undercloth. Very lovely and formal!

Go creative, and you will have a table that is truly memorable and the highlight of your party.

"Gather Ye Rosebuds..."

How to preserve cut flowers and foliage gathered from your garden

The wise hostess, the one who is always thinking ahead, will plant her garden with flowers which can conveniently be brought inside when she is ready to entertain. By growing her own bouquets, she provides herself with an immediate and ready supply of flowers; she saves herself frantic, last-minute trips to the local farmers' market, and she eliminates extra florist bills.

When planting flowers for cutting, consider the following:
(1) The season during which the flowers will bloom: Plant so that you have a continuance of blossoms . . . from early spring, through late fall.
(2) The color schemes of the areas in which you wish to use the flowers: What a shame to grow beautiful flowers only to find that a different hue of the same variety would have looked so much lovelier in that Imari bowl on the entry hall table.
(3) Your china and table linens: You most assuredly want flowers for the dining table itself . . . ones that will enhance and complement a table setting. If salmon pink looks glorious with your patterned china, plant a Camelot rosebush.

When your garden is in full bloom and you are ready to impress guests with stately bouquets, put on a pair of garden gloves, grab up a pair of shears and go forth to harvest!

Now the problem is keeping the freshness of the flowers you cut. Nothing is more frustr ·ting than to cut a beautiful bouquet, spend precious time arranging it, only to l ve the flowers wilt and die.

The first thing to remember is that flowers, once they are cut, must have an immediate and continuing supply of water. That is why, even if your flowers come readily arranged from the florist, you must always add more water or spray them with water. This first water should be fresh and warm, never cold, as this shocks the flower. Carry along a bucket of water when you go into the garden to cut. Plunge the flowers into the water immediately. Be sure, too, that your flower shears are sharp. Dull shears crush soft stems and make it impossible for them to absorb adequate water. Whenever possible, condition your flowers by keeping them in deep water for an hour or two, out of a draft and the sun, before arranging.

Try to cut your flowers early in the morning, before the day gets warm, or late in the afternoon. Condition them overnight. This procedure does not work, however, on woody stemmed plants such as holly or flowering branches. In order for these to absorb water their stems must be crushed on the ends.

The following are some helpful pick-me-ups for certain flowers:
Anemones— Add ½ cup vinegar to 2 cups water.
Chrysanthemums— 10 drops oil of cloves to 2 quarts water.
Clematis (large)— 3 tablespoons grain alcohol and a pinch of soda to 1 pint water.
Cosmos— 1 teaspoon sugar to 1 pint water.

Daisy—3 drops oil of peppermint to 1 quart water.

Dianthus (pinks, carnations)—Cool water up to the flower heads.

Evergreens—Submerge in water several hours; then add 1 tablespoon glycerine to 1 quart water.

Gardenia, Camellia—Wrap in wet tissue overnight. These flowers never drink after being cut and absorb water only through their petals.

Gladiolus—5 tablespoons vinegar to 1 quart water.

Iris—3 drops oil of peppermint to 1 quart water.

Lilies—1 cup vinegar to 2 quarts water.

Marigolds—2 tablespoons sugar and 1 tablespoon salt to 1 quart water.

Peonies—3 tablespoons sugar to 1 quart water.

Petunias—1 teaspoon sugar to 1 pint water.

Roses—2 tablespoons powdered alum or 2 tablespoons table salt to 1 quart water.

Snapdragons—2 tablespoons salt to 2 quarts water.

Tulips—Roll in wet newspaper to keep stems straight, then place in cold water up to flower heads. Then arrange in copper bowl or place copper penny in container.

Violets—Tie in bunches, submerge in water for two hours after picking, then put in a container of ice water.

When "gathering rosebuds" from the garden, don't overlook anything useable. For example, the interesting variegated leaves of a bush, the long flower spikes which are sent up by certain ground covers, wild flowers (such as red and white clover), and on and on. The limits of your imagination are your only boundaries!

Gilding the Lily

Food decorations and garnishes

Food tastes better, and is, of course, more festive, when it is beautifully decorated. Just as champagne should not be drunk from a paper cup, good food should not be merely served. Bring it on with some fanfare and let it be showcased to appear at its best.

In order for the hostess to decorate her creations with ease, the following tools and kitchen utensils are helpful:

Assortment of baking pans—Bundt, spring-form, brioche, quiche pan (which has a removable bottom), Swedish tartlet tins, muffin pan (the miniature muffin tins are invaluable).

Assortment of molds—Used for baking, frozen desserts, or gelatin molds. These include metal molds, ramekins, soufflé dishes and custard cups.

Gadgets—Melon ball scoop, ice cream scoop, lemon stripper, decorative cutters (these range from the large cookie cutter size to the tiny truffle cutters), butter curler, butter boards (for making butter balls).

Cake decorator and pastry bags—These can be used for piping frostings, whipped cream, vegetable purées, potatoes, softened cream cheese.

Knives—A convenient assortment . . . all kept very sharp.

GARNISHES

Roses—Roses of lemon, lime, turnip, tomato or cucumber: Cut a thin slice from the bottom of the vegetable or fruit to form a base; then cut a continuous spiral strip 1-inch wide around the fruit or vegetable, being careful not to break the strip. Curl peel around to resemble rose and attach to reserved base.

Carrot Flowers—(1) For flat pansy-like flowers: Cut wafer-thin slices and attach in overlapping patterns. (2) For a lily shape: Cut elongated, diagonal slices. Curl one slice around a thin strip of carrot or cucumber, like a cone; wrap another slice with the petal curled out and spear together with a toothpick at the base. (3) For a fringed flower: Peel a large carrot. Using a long flexible blade, make rapid, up and down sawing motions, slicing a thin continuous spiral similar to pencil sharpener shavings. Curl strip into a wide cone and secure at base with a toothpick.

Daisies—Cut turnip, rutabaga, apple, cucumber, or carrot into thin slices. Cut circles with a small round cutter, or, for a decorative shape, use canapé cutters. Some of these may be dyed with food coloring to make different colored "daisies"; center with a slice of olive (black or green), radish or carrot.

Radishes—For rosettes, cut stem and end from large radish, make gashes on sides to resemble half slices. Chill in ice water until serving time. For a "spiked flower" use radish with root intact.

Butter Balls—Scald a pair of wooden butter paddles in boiling water for 30 seconds; chill in ice water. Cut ¼-pound bar of firm butter in 1-inch squares. Cut each square in half; stand each half upright on paddle. Smack butter between paddles. Holding bottom paddle still, rotate top paddle to form ball. If butter clings to paddles, dip them again into hot water; then into ice water. Drop finished balls into ice water and refrigerate. Dip paddle into ice water before making each ball.

Butter Curls—Let butter curler stand in hot water at least 10 minutes. Pull curler firmly across surface of ¼-pound bar of firm butter (butter should not be too cold or curls will break). Drop curls into ice water and refrigerate. Curler should be dipped into hot water before making each curl.

Butter in Molds—Soften butter to room temperature. Line mold with aluminum foil or plastic wrap. Press softened butter into lined mold. Chill till hard. Unmold and remove liner. Any shape mold may be used.

To make decorative balls—Using a melon ball cutter, cut balls from apple, cantaloupe, avocado, canned jellied cranberry sauce, melons, beets, turnips.

DRINKS

There are many new and different twists for serving all kinds of drinks.

Confetti Ice Cubes—(1) In compartments of an ice tray, place fresh berries, mint leaves, and lemon or orange wedges. Fill with colored water or fruit juice and freeze. (2) Make different colored ice cubes by freezing liquid in miniature geometric-shaped molds.

Lemon or Lime Twirls—Slice fruit, trim peel away, curl peel and secure with a toothpick. Drop in ice water till ready to serve. Remove pick and tuck a sprig of mint in center.

Orange Blossom—Take a slice of fruit and fashion into a pinwheel. Make four equal triangles by partially slicing toward core. Take alternate corners of triangle and secure at center with a toothpick. Top with a posy.

To keep drinks cold in punch bowl—For daiquiris, make a ring mold of frozen daiquiri mix, layered with sliced limes and pineapple chunks. When the ring melts in the bowl, the drinks do not become watery. In the same way, any icy block of clam or tomato juices spiced with pepper sauce and trimmed with radish circles cools a punch bowl of Bloody Marys . These ice blocks may be made up well in advance and stored in the freezer. Fresh fruits can also be frozen and used as you would a block of ice. Nectarines, peaches, whole pineapples, cherries, and grapes all freeze well.

Ice Rings—Fill a large ring mold with boiled water and let stand till cool, stirring occasionally to remove air bubbles which would make the ice cloudy. Then freeze. To center mold with decorations such as mint leaves, berries, etc., first freeze the ring a third full of water, add garnish, then add water to fill two-thirds full. Freeze again. Then fill to top and freeze again.

Iced Bottle—Empty a bottle of aquavit or vodka. Place bottle in center of half-gallon waxed milk carton. Pour water up to the bottom of the neck of the bottle and freeze. Peel off carton and fill bottle with ice cold high-proof liquor. Return to freezer if you wish (liquor will not freeze). To serve: Put bottle in shallow bowl and wrap small towel around its neck.

Unusual Punch Bowls—Tureens, colorful enameled mixing bowls, brandy snifters, animal shaped cookie jars and copper fish cookers make good punch bowls.

Icy Glasses—(1) Fill a scooped-out watermelon with crushed ice, then put glasses upside down in the ice. They will be frosted and ready for any cooling drink. (2) For special drinks, coat the rim of a glass with lemon juice, twirl in sugar or salt.

Flower-Lei Straws—Thread one end of a soda straw or thin bamboo skewer through the centers of several fragrant flowers. Insert other end in drink.

SALADS

To perk up drooping lettuce leaves or cups—Spread out in a single layer on a platter lined with damp paper toweling. Put a sheet of dry paper toweling on top. The lettuce will crisp in refrigerator after a few hours.

Special serving suggestions for chicken salad—Fill scooped-out pineapple halves, cooked and chilled artichokes (choke removed), or halved and cored cucumbers.

Decorate with cooked vegetables—Add color and taste treats to your salad platters. Choose such things as lengthwise slices of yellow squash, green beans, baby carrots, tender asparagus, slivered beets, or cauliflower buds. Improve the flavor of these cooked vegetables by marinating in salad dressing for several days.

Dress up a cold trout or molded seafood mousse—Use a large rhinestone as the fish's eye. Make a small garland of flowers to place around fish's neck. Place on a bed of chopped or cubed jellied consommé.

MAIN COURSE

Eye-appealing borders for seafood and meat:
(1) Lemon cups filled with tartar sauce.
(2) Cranberry sauce or chutney in peach halves.
(3) Mincemeat baked in orange cups.
(4) Small pickled beets stuffed with seasoned cream cheese.
(5) Scored mushroom caps.
(6) Top orange slices or pineapple slices with interesting shapes of cranberry jelly. (Slice canned jelly ¼-inch thick and cut with cookie cutters.)
(7) Fruit Brochettes—Thread small fruits or pieces of fruit on slender bamboo skewers. Coat fruits with lime juice and maple syrup. Place around roasted meat or spear into top of roast. Particularly beautiful on ham.

To Top a Crown Roast:
(1) For the glittering effect of a crown, perch preserved kumquats or crab-apples onto the bone ends.
(2) Back silver foil with an 8 x 6-inch strip of red contact paper. Make a 3-inch cut every ¼-inch, then cut whole strip in half. Curl edges with scissors and form individual tubes to place on bone ends. Use as frills for turkey legs also.

Leg Frills for Turkey Drumsticks:
Fringe two pieces of white or pink tissue paper or aluminum foil and wrap unfringed part around end of bird's legs. Foil will remain in place. Paper frills can be taped on.

Garnishes for egg dishes:
(1) **Browned Apple Rings**—Slice firm unpeeled apples ¼-inch thick, and dust them with flour. Heat enough butter in a skillet to cover the bottom, add the apple rings and cook them, turning frequently, until they are golden brown and just tender. To serve, top the rings with cooked sausage patties.

(2) **Sautéed Cocktail Tomatoes**—Sauté gently one box of cherry tomatoes in one half stick of melted butter, shaking the skillet vigorously, until the skins are slightly wrinkled. Season the tomatoes to taste with salt. Use as a garnish for a platter of scrambled eggs.

HORS D'OEUVRES

Try scooped-out vegetables, such as acorn squash, cabbage, lettuce, pumpkins, and fresh green peppers for containers. Good for dips, spreads. They may be lined with foil, if necessary, to make a sturdier holder.

The following "trees" would also make lovely centerpieces:

Shrimp Tree—Make a stately shrimp tree the day before the party by studding a tall Styrofoam cone with parsley. Each shrimp is secured to the cone with a toothpick and attached in a spiral design.

Crudités Tree—Attach fresh, crisp celery, radishes, carrots, cucumbers, cocktail tomatoes and cauliflower pyramid-fashion on a cone.

Olive Tree—Make a topiary tree by studding a Styrofoam ball with pitted or stuffed black and green olives. For pebbles at the base, use a handful of almonds.

Tricks with Picks—(1) Use straight pretzels in cheese squares instead of toothpicks. (2) Colorful picks make bright skewers for fruit. (3) Wooden Oriental picks make fine skewers for meat and cheese kabobs or fruit kabobs.

Decorative Cold Platters—(1) Make an ice mold in any fancy container to use for the center of your platter. (2) For a cool feeling, use round mirrors for hors d'oeuvre platters.

On the Hibachi—(1) Grill tiny hot dogs and hamburgers on the hibachi and place on miniature buns. (Order the buns from your favorite bakery.) (2) With the hibachi on the hearth, have the makings for shish kabobs on a buffet table. Let each guest combine his own and cook it to his taste.

CENTERPIECES

(1) Hollow a head of cabbage or lettuce and fill with a proportionately sized container to hold flowers or contrasting greenery.

(2) Make a blooming pineapple by covering a water-soaked oasis base with fresh flowers and topping it with curling ostrich plumes.

(3) Make a Rose en Gelée by mixing ⅔ cup sugar and 2 envelopes gelatin. Add 2 cups boiling water to dissolve, then add 1 cup cold water. Pour over an inverted flower in bowl, which should be slightly larger than the flower, and refrigerate. Use cellophane tape from one side of bowl to other to hold stem in place. Chrysanthemums (shaggy), spider lilies, bunches of violets and pansies or a poinsettia may be used, depending on the season and occasion. Turn out in center of platter as you would a molded salad.

(4) Stud a cone-shaped Styrofoam form with fresh strawberries (do not remove stems).

DESSERTS

Cakes, Toppings and Fillings:
(1) For a lacy design, place a paper doily on the top of a one-layer cake and sift confectioners' sugar over doily. Carefully remove the doily.
(2) Make a pinwheel design on the top of a frosted cake with chopped walnuts. Press more walnuts against sides of cake.
(3) Make an icicle pattern by letting chocolate mixture drizzle down the sides of a white frosted cake. (To make chocolate mixture, melt a 1 ounce square of unsweetened chocolate with ½ teaspoon shortening.)
(4) For beautiful cakes, bake in bundt pan, spring-form pan, or use cake decorators. Bake cake in tube pan, frost with pretty pastel icing. Place flowers in small vase in the center of the cake.

Fancy Finishes with Pastry:
(1) Distinguish fruit pies by cutting out the shape of an apple, cherry, leaves, etc. from pastry dough. Bake separately and top pie with designs.
(2) Make pastry twists by taking flat lattice strips and twisting. Then lay across pie. Cross these with similar twists and make a diamond pattern.

Orange and Lemon Cups:
Wash and dry fruit, slice top off each piece, and carefully remove fruit with a small, curved grapefruit knife. Trim edge in scallops, zigzag, or leave straight. Trim bottom so fruit cup will sit steady on the plate. Fill as desired. (Good for ices, sherbets, or fresh fruits drizzled with a liqueur.) Orange cups filled with a bunch of frosted grapes make a lovely garnish for game. For a quick job of hollowing out fruit, use an electric orange juicer.

Frosted Grapes:
Wash and dry grapes well. Separate grapes into small clusters and brush grapes with slightly beaten egg whites. Roll in granulated sugar and place on wire rack for one hour to dry.

Ways with Melons:
Carved melons may be used in many novel ways . . . as containers for fruit balls, punch, flowers, ice cream balls, or layers of sherbet. The ways to carve them are almost unlimited.
Punchmelon—Stand the melon on one end and cut off the top half. You may need to level the bottom to make it sit firmly. Scoop out meat and fill with favorite cold punch.
Cannon—Lay long watermelon on one side. Cut off ⅓ of melon. From the smaller cut-off portion, slice two round "wheels". From the remaining ⅔ melon, scoop melon balls. Attach wheel slices to lower end of melon (wheels of cannon) and attach a "wick" (piece of string) to tail end of melon. Refill hollowed portion with melon balls (cannon balls), and let them spill out one end.

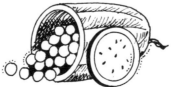

Whale Melon—From a well-shaped striped or dark green watermelon, draw the design of whale on the rind with a grease pencil. Cut along the lines with a sharp knife, removing the rind in small pieces. Cut eyes from leftover rind and pin in place. Scoop out flesh.

Basket—Cut watermelon in the shape of a basket, leaving a handle over the top. Edges may be notched, left plain, or scalloped.

Edges of Melons—Notch, making edge jagged; scallop, using a teacup as a guide, or leave level and plain.

Perhaps one of the best ways to enhance the beauty of the food you serve is to arrange it to emphasize its natural beauty: crisp salad greens in clear plastic bowls, popovers in wicker baskets, butter in tubs, sliced fruits in clear containers . . . fill a brandy snifter with red cocktail tomatoes to serve before dinner, serve Screwdrivers in a clear crystal pitcher, or shellfish in coquilles imbedded in ice.

To increase a recipe— Most recipes can be increased. Very often, however, you must taste carefully for seasonings. For recipes that involve baking, it is best to make the recipe twice, rather than doubling the quantity. Caution should also be used when baking two batches of anything in the same oven at the same time.

Purchasing Food

How to figure amounts needed when cooking for company

Beef—¼-½ pound of boneless meat per person, depending upon guests (male or female, old or young, etc.) and rest of menu. If you plan a number of side dishes, you'll need less meat.

Ham—About 3 ounces of boneless, cooked meat per person.

Fish (fillets)—About 4 ounces per person.

Oysters and Shrimp—From 6-12 per person. Less if used as an appetizer, more if served as the main course.

Poultry—4 ounces baked, boneless meat, ¼-½ chicken, fried.

Vegetable Salads—⅔-1 cup per serving.

Vegetables—½ cup per serving (figure 3-4 servings from every package of frozen vegetables).

Ice Cream—Approximately ½ cup per serving. There are 4 cups in 1 quart of ice cream (about 8 servings), 16 cups in 1 gallon (about 32 servings).

Coffee—1 pound of coffee plus 2 gallons of water makes 40 cups.

Tea—To make hot or cold tea in quantity, make tea concentrate ahead of time. Tea concentrate: Bring to boiling 1½ quarts fresh, cold water. Remove from heat and add ¼ pound loose tea leaves. Stir, then cover and brew for 4 minutes. Strain into a teapot or jar and cover tightly. Can be stored at room temperature for several hours. Makes enough concentrate for 40-45 cups of hot tea or 30-35 glasses iced tea.
For hot tea: Combine 2 tablespoons tea concentrate with 5 ounces boiling water for one serving; or combine 1 cup concentrate with 1½ quarts boiling water to make 10 servings.
For iced tea: Strain concentrate into 5 quarts cold water. Pour over ice to serve. If tea becomes cloudy, add just enough boiling water to restore its clarity.

Hot Chocolate—For 25 servings, gradually stir 3 cups chocolate syrup into 4½ quarts hot milk. Keep hot by placing over hot water. To make chocolate syrup: Combine 6 squares unsweetened chocolate and 1¾ cups hot water in a saucepan over low heat, stirring till thick and blended. Add 1½ cups sugar and ¼ teaspoon salt and bring to boiling. Boil 2 minutes, stirring constantly. Remove from heat and add ¾ teaspoon vanilla. Cool. Keep covered in refrigerator till ready to serve. Makes 3 cups.

Bar Measurements—1 bottle wine — 24 ounces
1 wine glass — 4 ounces
1 fifth — 16 1½-ounce jiggers

Food for a cocktail party, tea, reception, sherry party—Allow 10 bites per person. Figure up the number of canapés, sandwiches, and hors d'oeuvres that each recipe makes and divide by 10. This will tell you how many people you can gracefully serve.

Making tea sandwiches—There are approximately 23 ½-inch slices in a 12½-inch loaf of bread, and 32 ½-inch slices in a 15½-inch loaf. Six ½-inch lengthwise slices can be cut from an unsliced loaf of bread. **Fillings:** Figure 2 tablespoons for each crosswise slice of bread; figure ⅓ cup filling per lengthwise slice of a 12½-inch loaf and ½ cup per lengthwise slice of a 15½-inch loaf.

𝒥ndex

Party Potpourri

Name

Street Address

City   State   Zip

Telephone

Your Order	Qty	Total
Party Potpourri at $14.95 per book		$
A Sterling Collection at $22.95 per book		$
Heart & Soul at $21.95 per book		$
The Memphis Cookbook at $10.95 per book		$
Tennessee residents add 8.25% sales tax on total book purchase		$
Postage and handling at $6.00 per book		$
Total		$

Method of Payment: [   ] Check payable to Junior League of Memphis

[   ] American Express   [   ] MasterCard   [   ] VISA

Account Number   Expiration Date

Signature

To order, mail or fax:
Junior League of Memphis
3475 Central Avenue • Memphis, Tennessee 38111
Telephone: (901) 452-2151 • Fax: (901) 452-1470
Website: www.jlmemphis.org

Profits from the sale of these books will be returned to the
community through JLM projects.

Photocopies will be accepted.